Spies and Intrigues

The Wrath to Come
The Great Impersonation

E. Phillips Oppenheim

Leete's Island Books
New Haven, Connecticut

Published by arrangement with the Oppenheim John Downes Memorial Trust by Leete's Island Books, Inc., Box 1131, New Haven, CT 06505

Library of Congress No. 84-80143.
ISBN: 0-918721-13-6

The Wrath to Come

The Great Impersonation

THE WRATH TO COME

BOOK ONE

CHAPTER I

It is a passage which might well be haunted with memories of the famous courtesans, dignitaries, criminals "de luxe" and aristocrats of the world,—the long straight stretch of passage leading from the Hotel de Paris to the International Sporting Club of Monte Carlo. Nevertheless it seemed to Grant Slattery a strange place for this meeting which, during his last two years' wandering about Europe, he had dreaded more than anything else on earth. Complete recognition came slowly. Each slackened speed as the distance between them diminished. When they came to a standstill there was a moment's silence.

"Gertrude!" he exclaimed.

"Grant!" she murmured.

The purely automatic exercise of this conventional exchange of greetings helped him at first through what must always have been a bitter and terrible moment. For though Grant Slattery had every quality which goes to the making of a man, he had also, about some things, a woman's sensitiveness.

"It is a long time," she said softly.

"Time is entirely relative," he remarked didactically.

She seemed a little helpless. It was an embarrassing situation for her and a painful one for him, this encounter with the girl who had jilted him publicly in the face of all Washington society and eloped with his rival. This meeting in the curved archway passage with a flunkey at either end was the first since he had taken leave of her at her house one night three years ago, after an evening at the opera. She had lain in his arms for a moment, her lips had met his willingly—even as he had often remembered since—with a touch of somewhat rare passion. And on the morrow she had become the Princess von Diss and had sailed for Berlin.

"This was bound to happen some day," she said, regaining her self-possession almost to the point of calmness. "I hope that you are going to be nice to me."

"I was prepared even to be grateful," he answered, with a little bow. "Alas! now that I see you I find it impossible."

"Very nice indeed," she approved. "I don't think I have changed much, have I?"

"You're looking more beautiful than ever," he assured her.

She smiled. His eyes told her that he spoke the truth.

"And you," she went on, "you're just the same—a little more dignified perhaps. They tell me that you have left the diplomatic service. Is that so?"

"Yes."

"Why?"

"No work left," he replied. "We move on towards the millennium."

Their eyes met for a moment. There was a silent question in hers which he ignored.

"Where were you going?" she enquired.

"I've been lunching at the Club," he answered. "I was just going to stroll across to the tennis courts for an hour."

"You can come to the Rooms with me instead," she suggested. "We will find two chairs and talk for a little time. We can't part like this."

He hesitated.

"Am I likely to meet your husband?"

"My husband is not in Monte Carlo at present. I hope you're not going to be horrid about him, Grant—you won't want to fight a duel or anything of that sort?"

"If I had felt that way about it," he answered, "it would have been at an earlier stage of the proceedings. A woman has a right to change her mind. I have harboured no grievance against any one."

He turned with her and they made their way to the Bar, almost deserted at that early hour, for it was barely four o'clock, and the Rooms were only just opened. They found two comfortable chairs and sat for a few moments in silence. Each was taking stock of the other. He had spoken the truth when he had declared that she was more beautiful than ever. She was very fair, her complexion exquisitely creamy, with scarcely a tinge of colour. Her eyes were so deep a blue that they seemed at times almost to attain to that rare and wonderful shade commonly termed violet. Her hair was yellow, the colour of the faint gold in the morning sky. Her lips were a little fuller than the delicacy of her features required, but beautifully shaped. Her figure he thought improved. She still possessed the grace of long limbs and a slender body, but she had passed from a threatened thinness to a gracious but still delicate shapeliness. He looked admiringly at her beautiful fingers as she withdrew her gloves.

"You always liked my hands," she murmured, studying them for a moment.

His eyes were fixed upon a ring she wore, — a thin platinum guard with a single beautifully set pearl. She smiled at him.

"Terribly wrong of me to keep it, I know," she admitted. "But I have. Do you want it back, Grant?"

"No," he answered, a little brusquely. "But —— "

"But what?"

"I am not going to flirt with you," he declared.

She threw her head back and laughed.

"The same familiar Grant, honest to the point of pugnacity. Why, my dear man, how do you ever expect to shine as a diplomatist?"

"I have given up the idea," he reminded her.

"So you are not going to flirt with me," she sighed.

He avoided the challenge of her eyes, secretly delighted that he found it so easy.

"Since we are here, we must order something," he insisted, summoning the waiter. "The fellow has been watching us reproachfully for the last five minutes."

"It's very early, but I'll have some tea," she acquiesced resignedly.

Grant gave the order and turned back to his companion. He was forced to make conversation in order to avoid drifting too rapidly into the intimacies of the past.

"You find life amusing in Berlin?" he asked politely.

"Not at all. Berlin bores me. That is why I'm here. And I

can see perfectly well that you are going to do your best to bore me too. I am disappointed in you."

"That" he complained, "is a little hard. Now that I am a free man, I am full of intelligent interest in Berlin. I hoped that you might gratify my curiosity."

"You were there yourself for two years," she reminded him drily.

"But that was five years ago. The evidences of what I suppose must be called the Royalist movement had only just then begun to appear. Prince Frederick, for instance, was still at school—he had scarcely shown himself in public. Now they tell me that he is almost a popular idol."

Gertrude von Diss gazed thoughtfully into her little gold mirror and used her powder puff with discretion.

"My husband being a member of the Government," she said, "I never discuss politics. I wonder if I shall find a place at one of the baccarat tables. I have lost so much in my small way at roulette that I think I shall give it up for a time. It is not amusing to lose always."

"I'll go and see, if you like," he offered politely.

"Presently. Tell me about yourself. Why did you give up the Diplomatic Service?"

"Because there are no diplomatic activities left nowadays for the citizens of the United States," he replied. "The whole world has become a gigantic mart for tradespeople to buy, sell, and exchange wares. Consuls can do our business. And then I came into the Van Roorden money and turned lazy, I suppose."

"I don't follow you at all," she declared. "Even if commercial achievement has become the guiding lamp of the world, I don't in the least know what you mean by saying that there is no diplomacy left for the United States. Commerce is one of the chief reasons for diplomatic exchanges, isn't it? I know my adopted country people think so."

He shrugged his shoulders.

"Very likely," he confessed. "Don't take me too seriously. I was only inventing a justification for my laziness."

She indulged in a little grimace.

"You are distressingly uncommunicative," she observed. "I begin to suspect that we are both very clever people. All the same," she went on reflectively, "I don't see why we shouldn't exchange confidences. It might be amusing."

"It wouldn't be a fair bargain," he assured her. "Your husband holds a high official position in Berlin. He must be brought into touch with people who are intimately acquainted with the trend of political thought in every country. I am nobody and I know nobody."

A smile played for a moment at the corners of her lips.

"You have developed a new and most becoming trait," she declared. "You're the first modest man I've met for years. We don't raise them in Berlin."

"The conceit passed out of my system three years and two months ago," he answered a little bitterly.

She laid her hand upon his. Her voice was almost caressing.

"There is something I shall tell you about that, some day," she promised, "something which will help you to understand. Meanwhile try and believe that I too have suffered. I was not so callous as I seemed."

The old spell was upon him for a moment but he told himself that it was only his senses which were enchained; the rest of him was free.

"I am glad to hear that," he told her with well-simulated indifference.

The room was invaded by a crowd of young people, mostly in flannels, who had evidently come down from the tennis courts. The young woman who seemed to be the ringleader of their gaiety — a very attractive looking young person indeed in her white tennis clothes and smart hat — flashed a smile of welcome at Grant as she entered the room. The smile was modified as she glanced a little curiously at his companion. When they had settled down for tea at an adjacent table, however, she looked over her shoulder.

"We are having a riotous party to-night," she announced, "dining first at the Villa, coming down here and going on to dance somewhere afterwards. Will you be my escort?"

"With the utmost pleasure," he assented promptly. "But sha'n't I be getting into trouble? What about Bobby?"

She shook her head dolefully and dropped her voice.

"Misbehaved," she confided. "Seen at Nice when he ought to have been playing tennis, yesterday afternoon — terrible! Something Russian, covered with jewels! Bobby can't afford that sort of thing, you know. We're sending him to Coventry for at least two days."

"Poor fellow!" Grant murmured sympathetically.

"Don't be a hypocrite," the girl laughed. "You know you're glad. I don't think I shall ever look at him again. And I'm all rebound! Not later than eight-thirty dinner, please. Dad told me that he wanted to see you, but we're not going to leave you at home to study bridge problems."

"I shall be punctual," Grant assured her.

"Can't talk any more," she concluded, turning away. "These greedy people are eating up all the chocolate éclairs. As it is, every one's had more than his share. You are a pig, Arthur!"

"Who is she?" Gertrude enquired under her breath. "I dislike her anyhow. I wanted you to dine with me."

"I don't know whether I ought to apologize," he observed, "for having lost the American habit of introducing. Her name is Susan Yeovil. She's very charming and very popular. Her little set keep things moving down here."

"Is she by any chance the daughter of the English Prime Minister?" Gertrude asked eagerly.

Grant nodded.

"Lord Yeovil is down here for the International Congress," he replied. "They have a villa at Cap Martin."

"What does he want to see you for?"

"I thought that you might have learnt our secret from what Lady Susan said," he confided. "We solve the 'Field' bridge problems together. Very interesting, some of them."

"You're simply horrid," she declared impatiently.

It was the old pout which he remembered so well and a momentary tenderness beset him. He crushed it back.

"What are you in Monte Carlo for alone, just now, Gertrude?" he demanded, turning the tables upon her.

She drew a newspaper cutting from a thin gold card-case and handed it to him. It contained a list of visitors at the various

Riviera hotels, his own name amongst them — underlined. He took the slip of paper from her fingers and looked at it long and earnestly. Then he handed it back without remark.

"That is why I came," she confessed. "It is perhaps just as foolish an impulse as the impulse which swept me off my feet and made a horrible woman of me three years and two months ago. But it came and I yielded to it. And now, the first night that I am here, you are dining out. You actually accept an invitation from that forward young woman whilst you are sitting by my side."

He smiled imperturbably. His impulse of tenderness had passed. He knew now why she had come, and the knowledge gave him an advantage. She had no idea that she had betrayed herself.

"I told you that I had lost my conceit," he said, "and I am not going to take you literally. There is no hardship, you see, in exchanging Berlin for Monte Carlo in February."

"There are other places on the Riviera," she reminded him. "We have a villa at Cannes and quite a number of friends there. Let me know the worst, Grant. What about to-morrow?"

"To-morrow I am entirely at your service," he replied, "except for the matter of some tennis in the afternoon. We must lunch together."

She sighed contentedly.

"You aren't going to be absolutely horrid, then?"

"I couldn't be for long," he assured her. "All the same, I am afraid that I'm running a terrible risk."

Again the smile — and with it the little stab at his heart. He was a man with instincts of faithfulness.

"I may be running that risk myself," she whispered.

CHAPTER II

PRESENTLY Grant and his companion rose and moved to the Rooms, crowded now with a strange medley of people, men and women of every nationality, and speaking every tongue, differing racially but brought into a curious affinity,—the women by the great dress-makers of the world, the men by the unwritten laws of Saville Row. The corner in which they found themselves was an auspicious one and they stood for a moment or two looking on. They themselves were the objects of some attention. Gertrude, after her last season divided between London and Paris, had become recognised as a beauty of almost European fame. Her companion—Mr. Grant P. Slattery was the name upon his visiting card—had also acquaintances in most of the capitals of the world. In a way he was a good foil to the woman by whose side he stood,—a tall, good-looking young American, a little slimmer than the usual type, looking somewhat older than his thirty years, perhaps because of a certain travelled air, a quiet assurance born of his brief but successful diplomatic career in three of the great capitals.

"My adopted country people are back again in force," Gertrude remarked.

"They interest me more than any other people here," Grant confessed. "It is as though the nation had changed its type."

"Explain yourself, please," she invited.

"I must speak frankly if I do," he warned her.

"As frankly as you please. I hold no brief for my husband's country people. I like some of them and hate others."

"Well, then," he continued, "it seems to me that the women are no longer blowsy and florid and over-dressed, the men no longer push their way and swagger. Somehow or other the women have learnt how to dress and the men have acquired manners. They are not in the least like the travelling Germans of say thirty years ago — just before the war."

"They are feeling their way," she remarked cynically.

He looked down at her with the air of one who has listened to wise words. In reality, it was he who was feeling his way.

"I am not so sure," he reflected. "I wonder sometimes whether the whole nation has not changed, whether the war did not purge them of their boastfulness and conceit, whether this present generation has not acquired a different and a less offensive outlook."

"Do you really believe that?" she asked.

"I am simply speculating," he answered. "To begin with there is a great change in your aristocracy. Young Prince Frederick, for instance. Every one says that he has modelled himself exactly upon what the present King Edward VIII of England was like when he was a lad of twenty. All the older statesmen tell us that he was the most popular young man in the civilised world, modest, democratic, charming. These are not Teutonic qualities, you know, but your Prince Frederick is certainly developing them."

"I wonder," she murmured.

"Tell me, what is your own attitude towards your husband's country people?" he went on, almost bluntly. "Do you like them or don't you? And, more important still, do you believe in them or don't you?"

She looked around her a little nervously. The Rooms were thronged with people but the corner in which they were standing was still almost isolated.

"My friend," she confided, "I am a simple woman and not a psychologist. I live amongst the German people. I do not dislike them as I am sure I should have disliked the Germans of thirty years ago, but I do not understand them. You must remember that of the Germans who made their country the most hated in the world before the war of nineteen-fourteen, I naturally knew nothing. I wasn't even born when the Peace of Versailles was signed. The German of those days is, so far as I am concerned, as extinct as the dodo!"

"If he is not extinct," Grant said, "he is at least not in the limelight."

"He has perhaps learnt to wear the sheep's clothing," she suggested. "You will not be able to induce me to say one word either for or against these people whom I confess that I do not understand. If you would really like to know all about them," she went on, "shall we ask the one man who ought to know? Have you ever met Prince Lutrecht?"

"Never," Grant replied. "I know of him, of course, and I have heard Lord Yeovil speak of him several times lately. They meet most days, of course, at Nice."

"I shall present you," she promised. "You will find him a most interesting and delightful man, and, if my husband is to be believed, it is he who, for the next generation, will decide the destinies of his country."

"It will give me great pleasure to meet him," Grant assured her. "He was not in office when I was in Berlin but I remember being told he had a great dislike to America and Americans."

She shrugged her shoulders.

"His father was of the Hohenzollern régime," she remarked, "and the Republican Government of to-day is a bitter pill for the aristocracy of a score of generations. He seems to be alone just now. Wait until I call you."

She crossed the room and was welcomed cordially by a tall, exceedingly aristocratic-looking man, apparently about sixty years of age, dressed with the utmost care, handsome and with a charming smile. A moment or two later he made his way with Gertrude by his side to where Grant was standing. He brushed aside Gertrude's formal introduction.

"I had interests in the Foreign Office at Berlin when Mr. Slattery was at the American Embassy," he said. "I remember him quite well. I regret very much to hear that you have left the Service, Mr. Slattery. We need all the help we can get nowadays from Americans of your status and culture."

"Germany has shown lately that she needs no help from any one, sir," Grant replied.

The Prince smiled gravely.

"You are very kind. There is no power on earth which could

hinder the German people from attaining to their destiny. But we need understanding and we need sympathy. We are not always represented to our friends as we would wish. I hope that I shall see more of you in Monte Carlo, Mr. Slattery. I am staying at the Villa Monaco and shall be glad to receive your visit. I am usually to be found at home, at any time when the Congress at Nice is not sitting."

He passed on, with a low bow and a whispered farewell to Gertrude, leaving in Grant's mind a curious impression of unfriendliness, for which he could not in the least account. Even his civility had seemed unnatural.

"They say that he is to be our next President," Gertrude confided.

Her companion watched the Prince thoughtfully as the latter paused to accept the greetings of a friend.

"I don't think I ever met a man who looked so ill-fitted to be the President of a great democracy," he remarked drily.

"Could you think of a more suitable post for him?"

He nodded.

"I could more easily imagine him the Mephistophelian chancellor of an autocrat."

"Back in the Hohenzollern days?"

"Or in the days which may be in store for us," he replied.

She looked into the baccarat room.

"An empty place at my favorite table!" she exclaimed. "Call on me early to-morrow, Grant, and we'll plan something. Forgive my hurrying. I can't afford to miss this."

He watched her pass into the outer room and seat herself contentedly in the vacant place. Then he strolled from table to table, risking a louis now and then, but scarcely waiting to see the result. A spirit of restlessness pursued him. He stood aloof for some minutes, watching Gertrude immersed in the baccarat. Then he wandered into the Bar, where Susan Yeovil presently found him. She sank into a chair by his side.

"Broke!" she announced ruefully, turning her little handbag inside out. "Not a louis left, and the others won't be ready to go home for an hour yet."

"Can I be of any assistance?" he ventured.

She shook her head.

"I've been too nicely brought up. I couldn't possibly borrow money from you. Tell me about the beautiful lady."

"She was very well known three or four years ago in Washington as Gertrude Butler," Grant confided. "She is the woman to whom I was engaged and who married Prince Otto von Diss."

She was instantly grave.

"You poor thing!" she exclaimed. "How horrid for you meeting her like that. Did you mind much?"

"I don't know," he replied. "I was asking myself that question as you came up. I have never been able to analyse exactly my feeling for her, either during those days of our engagement or since. I was very much in love with her, if that counts for anything."

"It doesn't," she assured him. "Being in love is just a spring disease. I fancied myself in love with Bobby before I heard of him advertising himself with that Russian lady in Nice. Six sets of tennis this afternoon, three éclairs and the cocktail you are going to give me presently have completely cured me."

"Fancy intruding your own experiences in such a serious matter! You are only a child," he reminded her with a smile.

"I'm nineteen," she retorted. "Surely that is old enough for anything. I am of age for the great passion itself, if only it would arrive, and arrive quickly. I believe I heard that croupier call out number fourteen. I know I shall end by besmirching my good name and borrowing a louis from you."

He laid a handful of notes upon the table beside them. She shook her head again.

"Don't tempt me," she begged. "Besides, I think I would rather talk. I am interested in the Princess. Tell me just how you are feeling about her."

"I couldn't," he confessed.

"Is she here without her husband?"

"Yes."

"Cat! Of course she's come to flirt with you."

"I don't think so. I think she has come here with an altogether different purpose."

"What purpose?"

He smiled at her with affected tolerance.

"After all, you know," he said, "young people shouldn't be too curious."

She drew away from him petulantly.

"I wonder," she complained, "why you always persist in treating me as though I were a child."

"Well, aren't you?" he rejoined. "Nineteen isn't very old, you know."

"Anyway, if father can tell me things," she argued, "I don't see why you should be so secretive."

"What does your father tell you?"

"Nothing that I am going to repeat to you, Mr. Inquisitor. I will tell you this, though," she went on, dropping her voice a little. "He isn't at all happy about the way things are going over at Nice. Did you know that it was he who insisted upon sittings being suspended for a day, and that he and Arthur sent no less than twenty cables away last night."

"Yes, I knew," he admitted, "but I had no idea that you did."

She permitted herself a friendly little grimace.

"I only mentioned it just to show that every one doesn't ignore me as you do," she observed. "Here's Arthur. He's having a day off, isn't he?"

The young man came up and displayed a handful of plaques. He was good-looking in a pale, rather tired way.

"Why do I slave for your father, Lady Susan," he demanded, "for a vulgar pittance, when there are thousands to be picked up here without the slightest effort?"

"Vulgar pittance!" she scoffed. "I'm sure Dad, or rather the country, pays you quite as much as you're worth. Besides, look at the number of free meals you get!"

"This to the private secretary of a Prime Minister!" the young man groaned. "Why, my dear child——"

"I'm nobody's 'dear child'!" she interrupted. "I am 'Lady Susan' to you two men, except perhaps after a dance, or in the moonlight, or on the river, when I feel yielding and let either of you call me 'Susan.' Please, get it into your heads that I am nobody's 'child.' In this age of flappers, nineteen is almost passé. I could be married to-morrow if I chose."

"Heaven forbid!" Arthur exclaimed. "At any rate unless it were to me."

"You'd have to change considerably before I'd marry either of you," she declared. "If you've won all those plaques, you can lend me one. You can get it out of Father to-night."

"And you refused to borrow from me," Grant said reproachfully.

"Well, you see Arthur is one of the household," she explained, "and I don't feel the same way about him. Besides, I shall probably repay him in ten minutes. I feel that my luck is in."

She strolled off. The Honourable Arthur Lymane sank into her vacant place.

"You're coming up to-night, Slattery?"

"I'm dining."

"The Chief wants to see you particularly," Lymane confided, dropping his voice. "He's already cabled to Washington. There's a damned funny atmosphere about the proceedings at Nice this time. Nothing that amounts to anything without doubt, but every one seems to be so jolly mysterious."

"Is that so?" Grant murmured.

"The Chief took the bull by the horns yesterday when he suspended sittings for twenty-four hours. It gives us a breathing spell, anyway."

"Have you any idea what's at the bottom of it all?" Grant asked.

His companion shook his head.

"The Chief will talk to you to-night. He may be more communicative with you than he has been with me. By Jove! Grant, old fellow!" he exclaimed, his tone suddenly changing to one of wondering admiration. "There's the most beautiful woman I've ever seen in my life. Coming straight at us, too."

The young man had already risen to his feet as though about to take his departure, but, as Gertrude crossed the room towards them, he remained transfixed, watching her. His look was no ordinary stare. The admiration it expressed was, in its way, too subtle and too involuntary.

"She's coming straight at us," he repeated, in an agitated whisper. "For heaven's sake, if you know her, Slattery, present me."

Gertrude, smiling, came towards them. She seemed already to appreciate the situation. Grant rose to his feet.

"Congratulate me!" she exclaimed. "I've won thirty thousand francs."

"Come and celebrate with us," Grant invited, drawing up a chair for her. "Let me present my friend, Mr. Arthur Lymane — the Princess von Diss."

CHAPTER III

THE uproarious little dinner party at the Villa Miranda drew to a close. Lord Yeovil rose to his feet and laid his hand on Grant's shoulder.

"My young friend," he said, "let us leave this scene of debauchery for a few minutes. You and I will take our coffee together in my den. Thank heavens, none of my colleagues or any members of our new Yellow Press were present here to-night. You were the only silent person, Arthur," he added, pausing on his way to the door. "You look as though you had seen a vision."

The young man, whose silence had indeed been noticeable, looked up.

"I have," he admitted.

"Arthur has fallen in love with a beautiful stranger," Susan called out. "Something must be done about it. Now that we've sent Bobby to Coventry we can't really spare Arthur. Dad, isn't it one of the duties of a Prime Minister's private secretary to flirt with his daughter when she feels so disposed?"

"Certainly," Lord Yeovil agreed.

"It is also," Grant reminded her, with a slight smile, "part of the duties of a Prime Minister's daughter to see that his secretary doesn't fall under the influence of fascinating but mysterious strangers."

"That settles your hash, young man," Susan declared, across the table. "You stick to me to-night."

"I think I'll resign," Arthur announced. "These conferences are a great strain on my nervous system as it is."

"Wouldn't you be scared if Dad took you at your word!" Susan observed, reaching over the table for the cigarettes. "You'd never get another job."

"You're all very rude to me," Arthur complained, with a show of dignity. "I am considered in political circles to be a young man of much promise. The *Daily Sun* said so last week."

There was a chorus of derision, in the midst of which Grant and his host made their way to a small sitting room at the back of the house. Coffee and *liqueurs* were upon the sideboard, and upon the table was a copy of the *Field* and two packs of cards.

"Now, my young friend," Lord Yeovil invited, "help yourself to anything you fancy, and there upon the table you will find a highly interesting bridge problem — by way of bluff. Only, whatever we may have to say to one another, let us get it over quickly. The great thing is not to keep Susan waiting. She doesn't understand the interference of international history with her amusements! First of all, have you anything fresh to report?"

"Nothing very definite, sir," Grant acknowledged. "But, in a sense, my cruise to Archangel was a success."

"You mean that you were right in your suspicions?"

"I obtained a good deal of evidence in support of it, evidence which is now in the hands of the British Admiralty. I was at Archangel for a fortnight and I had letters of introduction to two of the Russian admirals. I spent a lot of time on their ships. They were almost as hospitable as the sailors of the old régime."

"Tried to drink you under the table and that sort of thing, I suppose."

Grant smiled.

"I survived the ordeal, but I am afraid that my liver is temporarily deranged," he admitted. "I obtained a lot of quite useful information. Personally I am absolutely convinced now that the Russian fleet has never been trained or adjusted to form a separate unit. It is intended to act in conjunction with the German fleet in some unknown enterprise. A number of the engineers and gunners are Germans and there is a distinct atmosphere of German discipline about the whole outfit. In addition, as I dare say you've heard, they're all armed with German guns. Of course, even a non-expert can easily understand," he went on, after a brief pause, during which he accepted and lit a cigar which his host had silently passed him, "that two nations like Germany and Russia might easily keep within the tonnage allowed them by the Washington Conference, and yet, if each concentrated upon a particular sort of armament, they would, when brought together, be a more formidable fighting unit than the united forces of any two countries who had each spread out their tonnage to make an individual unit."

"You think that is the basis of this understanding between Germany and Russia?" Lord Yeovil asked.

"I am convinced of it," Grant replied. "Internal evidence was more difficult to get than external, but I have obtained a certain amount of proof that, contrary to the provisions of the Pact, there exists a secret naval understanding between Germany and Russia. Fortunately for us and for every one it is Great Britain's turn this year to police the seas, so I have made an exhaustive report to your Admiralty. I'm pretty certain that there'll be British warships in the Baltic before many weeks are past."

"You didn't come back in the yacht?"

Grant shook his head.

"I came back overland, sir. I spent four days in Berlin,—my second visit as a traveller from the Bethlehem Steel Company."

"Pick up anything?"

"Not much," was the grim acknowledgement. "They're pretty close-lipped in Berlin just now, and I had to be careful. I came away, however, with the absolute conviction that there is something in the air. There is what we used to call 'cyclonic disturbance' about, and the trail led here. You probably know more about it than I do."

"That 'cyclonic disturbance' is brewing, all right," the other assented. "We're in the thick of it at Nice. The day before yesterday we came almost to a deadlock over a question which Lutrecht persisted in raising and which we discussed for hours. I am going to treat you with a great deal of confidence, as I always have done, Grant. Years ago, when you were First Secretary at your Embassy in London, and I was Foreign Minister, I discovered that you shared one conviction which has been at the root of the whole of my policy from the moment I entered the Cabinet. That conviction is that the interests of Great Britain and the United States of America are inextricably and inevitably identical. I sha'n't dilate. There it is in plain words, the text of my political life, and because I know that you share it, I have treated you with a confidence I have not extended even to one of my own countrymen. I am now going beyond the limits of official propriety. I am going to tell you what the trouble has been at the last two meetings of the Pact. It has been this: Lutrecht, apparently out of a clear sky, has enunciated this principle and claims the confirmation of the Pact; that, whereas every nation of the Pact stands together against aggression by any member of it against another member, there is nothing in its constitution to prevent two members of the Pact arriving at a separate and individual understanding as regards proceedings directed against any nation not a member of the Pact. Do you follow me, Grant?"

"To the bitter end," was Grant's reply. "The thing's as plain as a pikestaff. I have felt this coming for years. We are close on the trouble now."

"Well," Lord Yeovil continued, "I suspended proceedings for twenty-four hours to obtain the opinion of some international jurists. I shall delay them for another twenty-four hours until after to-morrow's meeting."

Grant leaned a little forward in his chair. It was obvious that he was deeply moved.

"I can't tell you, sir, how much I appreciate your confidence," he said, "and honestly I think the fact that you have been willing to give it to me has been and will be helpful to the peace of the world. And now I am going to ask you something else. You are postponing the consideration of Prince Lutrecht's arguments until after to-morrow, as you admit, with a purpose. Is that purpose your intention to propose to the Conference that the United States be once more invited to join the Pact?"

The Prime Minister eyed his vis-à-vis, for a moment, with inscrutable countenance. He was no longer the indulgent father of a tomboy daughter or the genial host of a young people's party. He looked every inch of him the great statesman he really was.

"Where did you get that from, Grant?" he demanded.

"You know my position, sir," the young man replied earnestly.

"I am the one foreign Secret Service agent my country can claim. Even then, I'm not official. I have money to spend and I spend it. I have sources of information and I use them. I have friends in Washington, too, with whom I am in touch hour by hour. This is not a question of betrayal; it is more divination. They expect that invitation on the other side, sir. And the best of them hope for it. Will it be forthcoming?"

Lord Yeovil considered for a full minute. Then he knocked the ash from his cigar.

"Well," he admitted, "you've seen your way to the truth, Grant. I'm going to risk it. It's a big thing so far as I am concerned. If, by any chance, the Conference opposes me, my resignation will be inevitable. If, by any chance, I get the thing through, and Washington refuses, I shall be the most discredited politician who ever placed his country in a humiliating position."

"I don't think the United States will refuse," Grant declared. "It is most unfortunate that the matter will have to go to the Senate and be publicly discussed because, of course, as you know, there are always malignant influences in a polyglot country like ours. But I know the feeling of the people who count. They want to come in like hell."

"I expect you've been supplying them with a little information," Lord Yeovil observed.

Grant nodded.

"I never leave them alone," he admitted. "To a certain extent I'm afraid they look upon me as an alarmist for the simple reason that there is scarcely a single citizen of the United States who doesn't believe absolutely in the impregnability of his country. However, I think I've stirred them up a little in Washington, and there's more to be done in that way, yet. Do you feel inclined to tell me, sir, what would be the prospect of the voting if you bring forward your motion to-morrow?"

"They appear to me to be in our favour," was the deliberate reply. "When the Pact was first formed any invitation to join it had to be unanimous. Lately, however, that has been modified. Unless there are four dissentients now, any nation proposed, becomes, if willing to join, 'ipso facto' a member of the Pact. I can conceive two; it might be possible to conceive three dissentients. I can put my finger upon no possible fourth."

"I see," Grant murmured. "By the bye was Baron Naga at Nice yesterday?"

"He was."

"Do you know if he has received any dispatches from home since the last sitting?"

Lord Yeovil considered for a moment.

"He must have," he acknowledged, "because he was able to give us a very crude description of these flying boats of theirs, which the Italians are so curious about. He had no information at all two days ago when the matter came up."

"I'd give in the neighbourhood of a million dollars to see that dispatch," Grant declared.

There was still a great deal of noise in the dining room and in the passage. Lord Yeovil walked to the door and locked it. Then he came back to his place. He spoke slowly and with the air of one choosing his words.

"Slattery," he said, "it has been in my mind for two years to propose a further invitation to your country to join the Pact, because, in my opinion, conditions during the last decade have entirely altered, and the position of your country outside the Pact, even though she may be considered the greatest power in the world, has become anomalous and dangerous. She has subscribed to the Limitation of Armaments, which she herself inaugurated, and has scrupulously carried out her obligations. With all her power and wealth she is unable to launch a single battleship or put under arms a single regiment of soldiers beyond the proportion allotted to her by the other subscribing powers. Yet, although she is in this position, she is not a member of the Pact. That is to say, that, legally speaking, any two or three nations who do belong to the Pact might attack America with superior forces and the other members of the Pact would be powerless."

"You have placed the matter in a nutshell, sir," Grant agreed. "It was the consideration of these things which brought me to Europe and keeps me employed here. America, when the great call came, rose magnificently to her opportunities. She stretched across to Europe, and though, indeed, others bore the brunt of the burden, she ended the war of nineteen-fourteen. Since then, without a doubt, she has had a political relapse. Her statesmen have lost a certain measure of insight and vision. She has sunk back into the parochial. Politics have become more than ever a game and a profession. Her statesmen are so busy fighting over their own national problems that they have never envisaged the danger upon the horizon. That has been my view. It is my view to-day."

"Go on," Lord Yeovil invited. "You have not been in Europe during these last twelve months for nothing."

"I am convinced," Grant declared, "that Germany and Japan have arrived at an understanding to strike at America. I am convinced for that reason that they will oppose your invitation to America to-morrow. If they do not and I have wasted my time, then God be thanked for it. I shall go back to polo and golf, hunt the hounds at Pau, and never take myself seriously again."

The older man helped himself to a cigarette and tapped it thoughtfully upon the table without lighting it.

"There is just one thing, Slattery," he said. "I have the greatest respect and liking for Naga. I cannot somehow believe that he would oppose me to-morrow unless he first gave me some intimation of his intention. Besides, he isn't in the least bellicose. I believe him to be an honourable man, and I can't imagine his being mixed up in any Teutonic plot."

Grant nodded.

"I, too," he agreed, "have a great respect for Naga. At the same time, with these Orientals, one has to remember it is their country first, their country second, their country all the time."

There were warning sounds from outside—the exodus of all the young people into the hall. Insistent voices called for Grant. He slipped across and unlocked the door.

"You had better go," his host advised. "We understand one another and there is nothing more to be done at present. To-morrow, after the meeting of the Conference, we shall know where we stand."

"It's a private meeting, isn't it?"

"Yes. Thank God, we've managed to keep the Press out. Between you and me, Grant, if there were no newspapers, all the nations of the world would be sitting round in a family party. There would be no wars and very few quarrels. It is the enlightened Press of this generation which provides the fuel for tragedy."

The door was thrown open.

"'X to lead the ace of hearts and make the grand slam!'" Lady Susan cried. "Do come along, Grant. Whatever do grand slams in print matter? I have *liqueurs* on with Arthur that we're in the Club in twelve minutes. Do you think your Rolls-Royce is equal to it?"

"Nine-and-a-half is my time," Grant replied. "Nine, if you run up the stairs. Come on!"

The little party hurried off, their automobile lights flashing through the darkness of the curving drive, their voices disturbing the owls and waking many echoes in the violet stillness. Then the last car glided off down the hill and the Villa was left in silence.

Towards it, from the other side of Nice, came thundering through the darkness a great limousine, with its four lights flaring and siren whistle blowing. Outside, the driver sat with a face like a graven mask, with one thought in his brain. Inside, a man lay back amongst the cushions, upon whose forehead the sign of death seemed to already rest.

CHAPTER IV

Lord Yeovil, after the departure of the young people of the house, settled down to spend an evening after his own heart. He rang for his servant, ordered the wood fire to be replenished, exchanged his dinner coat for a smoking jacket, and lit a battered-looking briar pipe, which was the delight of his life. He was beginning to feel the need for a period of cool and impartial deliberation. For the last ten days he had been presiding over the meetings at Nice of the Pact of Nations, an organisation established in Paris in nineteen-thirty, and now, twenty years later, the guiding force of the world. Its bitterest critics — and, at its inauguration, there had been many — were forced now to admit that the Pact had become one of the brilliant successes of the century. Its conception had first been mooted at a Trade Conference at Genoa in nineteen-twenty-two, and its provisions, subsequently drawn up with the utmost care by a committee of European law makers, practically made war amongst its members impossible. France had been able to abandon herself at last to a sense of complete and luxurious security. Germany, admitted after some hesitation, had apparently been amongst its most law-abiding members. The Limitation of Armaments, the great pacific scheme initiated by the President of the United States early in nineteen-twenty-one, was still carried on as a separate institution but with numerous affiliations. There was only one great drawback to the Pact, one flaw alone which prevented its being the greatest association ever formed during the world's history, and that drawback was the fact which, at the present moment, was giving both Grant Slattery and Lord Yeovil cause for the greatest apprehension. The United States, after a period of profound deliberation, during which great dissensions had arisen, had decided to be the one great power outside its influence. For the same reasons which had kept her for so long out of the war of nineteen-fourteen, she had reiterated her policy of self-determination and had once more declared Europe outside the sphere of her political interests. Her position had been the principal subject of discussion amongst statesmen and thinkers for many years. No administration, however, had been strong enough to change it, and it was universally accepted now as an unassailable attitude. She had ample justification for believing herself strong enough to fight her own battles and defend her own honour. Her position was in its way magnificent and evoked the florid and rhetorical praise of many of her own writers, especially those who were in any way Teutonic in their origin. Those who, like Grant Slattery, saw the sinister side of the situation, were few and their voices unheard in the great glad pæan of thanksgiving in which her Press, day by day, and month by month, glorified and exaggerated her unexampled and amazing prosperity. Without a doubt America had become the richest country in the world.

It was of America that Lord Yeovil, who had once been an exceedingly popular Ambassador at Washington, was thinking as he smoked his disreputable pipe, lounging in an easy-chair, his feet upon the fender. He had a profound respect for Grant Slattery, whose handling of various intricate matters, whilst First Secretary in London, had won his unqualified approval. The young man had seemed at that time assured of an ambassadorship, and his complete withdrawal from the Diplomatic Service had been a mystery even to his intimates. Lord Yeovil knew the reason for that withdrawal and was day by day growing more thoroughly to appreciate it. He was thinking of it now as he smoked his meditative pipe, wondering exactly how much real information Grant had picked up in Berlin, wondering, too, whether that small cloud which had already appeared on the political horizon was destined to seriously disturb the thirty years of peace.

The sound of wheels in the drive and the pealing of the bell broke into his reflections. He glanced at the clock. It was a few minutes past eleven,—an impossible hour for an ordinary caller. Presently Andrews, a young typist employed by his private secretary, knocked at the door and entered.

"I'm sorry to disturb you, sir," he said, "but Baron Naga is here and asks if you will receive him."

"Baron Naga!" the Prime Minister repeated in amazement. "At this hour of the night!"

"He seems to have come straight from Nice," the young man confided.

"I will see him, unofficially, of course,—delighted. But what on earth is the urgency?"

"His Excellency gave me no intimation, sir."

"You can show him in," Lord Yeovil directed. "Explain that I'm out of harness and spending a quiet evening."

Baron Naga himself was obviously paying no visit of ceremony. He had not changed his clothes for the evening and was wearing the frock coat and dark trousers in which he usually appeared at meetings of the Conference. His complexion was always rather more waxen than sallow, but to-night it seemed positively ghastly. His little formal bow before he advanced to shake hands was unsteady. A man of another race and different manner of life might have been suspected of drunkenness.

"My dear Baron!" Lord Yeovil said hospitably. "This is very friendly of you. I hope you do not bring me bad news. Sit down, please," he invited.

The Ambassador sank into an easy-chair. He was most undoubtedly ill.

"I am much obliged to you, sir, for receiving me at this late hour," he said. "My errand is of some importance. I have come to announce to you, in the first place, that my Imperial Master has accepted my resignation from the highly honourable post of Ambassador to Great Britain, and also, from the representation of Japan at the Pact of the Nations. I shall not, therefore, be attending the Meeting to-morrow."

"God bless my soul!" Lord Yeovil exclaimed. "I regret very much to hear this."

"Your lordship is very kind," was the agitated reply. "Baron Katina is on his way from Berlin to take my place at the Pact of Nations, and Count Itash is already on the spot if anything of urgency should occur. My Imperial Master has not, I believe, as yet signified his wishes so far as regards my successor at St. James's."

"But, my dear Baron, this is most terrible news!" the other declared. "Most unexpected, too. It you will allow me to say so, there is no one with whom it has been a greater pleasure to work or whose loyal support during the past sessions of the Pact I have more appreciated."

"You are very kind, Lord Yeovil, most gracious," his visitor repeated, a little wistfully. "It has come to pass, however, that on a very vital matter I have found myself unable to conform to the desires and policy of those in whose hands the destiny of my country rests. It is a great grief to me."

"I am sure it must be," the Prime Minister assented, watching his visitor closely. "You have made me very curious. I was not aware that there was any subject of policy at present under consideration which could give scope for a difference of opinion of such drastic moment."

"The greatest tragedy of this matter is now to come," Baron Naga continued solemnly. "For my country's sake I am here to betray her confidence. I shall place you, sir, in possession of certain information which, as President of the Pact of Nations, should be disclosed to you. After I have spoken, you will hear of me no more. It is for the ultimate good of Japan and my people —but for the moment the words I must speak are treason and for speaking them I must pay the price."

Lord Yeovil was seriously disturbed. There was something in his visitor's attitude and demeanour which were beyond his comprehension.

"But, my dear Baron," he began——

The Ambassador moved uneasily in his chair. There were blue lines under his eyes. It was more than ever obvious that he was very ill.

"A thousand pardons," he interrupted weakly, "but I have perhaps underestimated the action—I am weaker than some of my years—listen, I implore you!"

Lord Yeovil hastened to the little sideboard and poured out a glass of brandy.

"Don't distress yourself, Baron," he begged. "You can tell me anything you wish to presently. I am always at your service. Drink this, please."

Baron Naga clutched at the glass, clutched at his throat. He made a passionate attempt to speak. The words, however, were almost incomprehensible.

"Katina and — Lutrecht — America — the beginning — the great scheme — Itash knows — God of my parents!"

The glass rolled from his fingers. His head dropped forward. Lord Yeovil rushed to the bell.

"Telephone for a doctor," he directed the butler, who answered it. "Baron Naga is ill."

But Baron Naga was no longer ill. Both master and servant knew the truth as they stood and looked at the crumpled-up figure in the chair.

CHAPTER V

THERE is an inner annex to the Bar at the Sporting Club, at either end of which a discreet flirtation is entirely in order. Grant, wandering in for a whiskey and soda towards midnight, was suddenly transfixed by the sight of Gertrude and Arthur, their heads very close together, the young man's air of devotion unmistakable. He watched them with a deepening frown. Suddenly he felt a touch upon his arm. Susan stood by his side. Her voice was as gay as usual, but she was pale and a little tired.

"Disgraceful, isn't it?" she exclaimed. "We're absolutely deserted. I'm afraid Arthur's lost his head altogether."

"He's a fool!" Grant declared.

She looked at him a little wistfully.

"Do you mind so much?"

"I mind because——"

He broke off in his sentence. After all, his peculiar knowledge of Gertrude was better kept to himself for the present.

"Well, I don't like to see him make a fool of himself," he concluded a little awkwardly. "The Princess is a married woman and has a jealous husband. She is also a hardened flirt."

"We thought of going on directly," she announced. "What ought we to do about Arthur?"

"I'll go and tell him as soon as you're ready," Grant offered.

"We're all here now. Rose and Tommy are outside, and Bobby's gone for his coat. We've had to forgive him. He's so terribly penitent. We've four without him if you like. I suppose you could look after me with an effort," she added, looking up at him.

"Of course I could, but we ought to let him know we're going," Grant decided. "I'll step across and tell him."

Susan turned towards the cloak room, and Grant made his way towards the two people whom they had been discussing. Gertrude welcomed him with a smile, half challenging, half provocative. Her companion was inclined to be querulous.

"Lady Susan wants to know whether you're coming along with us, Lymane?" Grant said. "We're all quite ready."

The young man glanced at the clock.

"Much too early," he grumbled. "There'll be no one there before one o'clock."

"The others seem to wish to go."

"Well, there are four of you," Lymane pointed out. "I'll come along presently."

"I think you'd better come with us," Grant persisted. "That is, if the Princess will spare you."

"But I will not spare him," she laughed. "I like him very much. He says much nicer things to me than you do and I do not see why you should hurry him away, just as we are getting on so nicely."

"Neither do I," Lymane agreed. "Make my excuses, there's a good chap. I'll come along within half an hour or so. Lady Susan is in your charge, anyway, not mine. I'm the odd man out."

Grant turned away with the slightest of bows. He found the little party waiting for him downstairs, reinforced by the advent of another young man, a friend of the Lancasters.

"Arthur is hopelessly enslaved," Grant announced. "The beautiful Princess has him in her clutches. He says he'll come along presently. I should doubt whether we see him again this evening."

"It doesn't really matter whether we do or not," Susan remarked, as she stepped into the car, by Grant's side. "That nice Wheeler boy who plays tennis so well is coming along, so we shall get all the dancing we want. Are you going to dance with me, Grant? And why do you look so cross?"

"I'm not really cross," he assured her, "but Arthur, when he likes, can be such a hopeless young ass. Anyway, I'll get the first dance with you."

They glided across the square, past the gardens and into the quiet street on the right-hand side. They entered the restaurant to the strains of modified jazz music, ordered champagne and sandwiches and sat down at a round table.

"You do dance well, you know, Grant," Susan told him after their second turn.

"You're rather wonderful yourself after eight sets of tennis," he observed. "Is it my fancy or are you a little pale?"

"I did feel tired a little time ago," she admitted. "It's passed off now, though. What a shame one of you have to sit out."

"Bobby isn't going to sit out long," he pointed out. "Young rascal!"

They watched the young man lead away one of the professional danseuses. Susan laughed heartily.

"Just like Bobby," she declared. "He can't dance for nuts. If he wanted to dance with a professional though, I wonder why on earth he didn't choose the little one at the next table to us."

Grant glanced at the girl whom his companion had indicated, at first carelessly, but afterwards with genuine interest. She was seated at a small round table close to their own,—dark, pale, almost sallow, with rather narrow eyes of a deep brown shade, silky eyebrows and eyelashes, and black hair in which, as she moved her head to the music, there seemed to be a gleam of wine colour. She was plainly dressed in a black taffeta gown and she wore no jewellery of any sort. There was something about her expression peculiarly inscrutable and yet Grant fancied that as his eyes met hers she intended in some mysterious way to let him know that she had observed his interest.

"What a quaint creature," he observed. "I wonder who she is?"

"She's one of the professional dancers," Susan told him. "She was here on Monday, and when we were here the week before. She was dancing all the time with the Japanese Count then, the young man who does the interpreting at Nice. Look at Bobby being taught new steps; isn't he priceless?"

The evening wore on in the usual way. The little party danced incessantly, drank a moderate quantity of champagne and a great many orangeades, and watched the throng of people with a certain amount of interest. Suddenly Susan touched Grant on the arm.

"A tragedy!" she whispered. "Look at the dark young woman's face. Her Japanese Count has just come in with another woman."

Grant turned around and was just in time to catch an expression on the girl's face which, for a moment, almost shocked him. The slightly scornful air of inscrutability was gone, the lips had parted, there was a gleam of white teeth, her eyes had narrowed almost into slits, and her eyebrows had drawn closer together. It was all over in a moment, so quickly indeed that Grant wondered whether it had really been murder that he had seen there. She even glanced across the room and nodded carelessly at the young man and the girl, a danseuse from a neighbouring café. Grant exchanged a questioning glance with Susan.

"Do you know," he said, "it seemed to me, for a moment, that she was going to play the virago."

"She looked like a little fiend," Susan replied. "Bother, here comes Arthur. I suppose I shall have to dance this with him."

Lymane came in, full of apologies. He was a little absorbed in manner and he took the chaff to which he was subjected in a somewhat spiritless fashion.

"Don't see what any one's got against me," he remarked, as he helped himself to a glass of wine. "You're a man over, already. What about this dance, Lady Susan?"

"The next," she answered, waving him away. "After that, you, please, Grant."

Grant and Arthur Lymane were left alone. At the adjoining table the dark girl with the inscrutable face was smoking cigarettes and drinking tea, glancing occasionally towards them.

"Lymane," his companion said. "May I take a liberty with you?"

"Go ahead."

"I don't think you're altogether wise to cultivate your acquaintance with the Princess von Diss."

"Why the devil not?" the young man demanded.

"If you're going to take it like that, there's no more to be said about it. Sorry I interfered."

"You'd better tell me what you mean, anyway."

"Mine is simply the obvious point of view," Grant explained. "You are the private secretary of the Prime Minister of your country, who is also President of the Pact of Nations. I do not think that I would become too intimate or be seen too much in public with the wife of a German statesman of Von Diss's known proclivities."

Lymane lit a cigarette with trembling fingers.

"You're out of your mind, Slattery," he declared.

"Perhaps," was the quiet rejoinder. "The advice I have offered you is for your own good."

"The usual cant," the young man sneered. "Why you might have been born thirty years ago. What's the difference between Germany and the other nations? What's the Pact done, I should like to know, if it hasn't brought them all into a group? You seem to be harking back to the primeval days when German spies and adventurous princesses were the stock in trade of the sensational novelist."

"Such people may still exist," Grant persisted.

"Rubbish! What is there to spy about? They're all making a fuss over at Nice, but I've come to the conclusion that it doesn't amount to anything. You're a bit of an alarmist, I know, Slattery, but I'm not. In any case, to take exception to my friendship with the Princess simply because you yourself have had a misunderstanding with her is neither more nor less than ridiculous."

Grant looked at his companion curiously.

"I am sorry you take it like that," he said. "I will admit that I hold a somewhat gloomy view of the international situation just now, but you are wrong when you suggest that I have had any sort of a misunderstanding with the Princess."

"At any rate, Von Diss is not a particular friend of yours, is he?" the young man asked meaningly.

Grant rose to his feet.

"Look here, Lymane," he protested, "there are limits to the disagreeable things you may say to me. I think——"

It was one of those happenings which Grant could never explain, even to himself. He rose to his feet simply with the intention of leaving his companion for a moment or two. As he did so, unseen to him, the girl at the next table rose also. She held up her arms quite naturally, without saying a word, without even looking directly towards him. No word of invitation passed from either one to the other. When, afterwards, Grant asked himself how that dance had come about, he could only surmise that the girl had willed it.

CHAPTER VI

"I SUPPOSE," Grant remarked, after their first turn of the room, "that I must be psychic."

"Why?" the girl asked.

"Because, although you have never addressed a word to me, not even since we commenced to dance, I believe that you have something to say."

"It is not you who are psychic," she replied. "It was I who conveyed that impression to you. We will stop now. Come this way, please."

She led the way to two chairs set in a retired corner of the Bar, which was just then almost deserted.

"That was a very short dance," he complained.

"You dance very well," she answered, "but to talk is sometimes more important."

He looked at her with quickening curiosity. In her strange, quiet way she was, without a doubt, attractive, but in an absolutely unanalysable manner. Not only was she without ornaments, but her dress itself was made in the plainest possible fashion. There was no colour upon her cheeks or carmine upon her lips. She seemed even to have disdained the powder puff.

"What will you have?" he asked, as a waiter drew near. "Some champagne?"

"Thank you," she replied. "I never drink wine. I will have some tea and some cigarettes."

"Aren't you a little unusual for a place like this?" he asked.

"Very," she admitted. "At first they did not wish to take me. Now they know better. I can bring them custom when I choose."

"You speak very good English," he said, "but you are not English, are you?"

"My mother," she told him, "was Japanese. My father was a Levantine. I was born in Alexandria. There are only two things

I can do in the world—dance and speak many languages. But no, there is a third. I can hate."

"Well, I hope you won't hate me?" he remarked, smiling.

She studied him for a moment and it seemed to him that it was the first time that their eyes had met.

"No," she assured him. "I shall never hate you, nor shall I ever love you. Perhaps that is as well or the young lady at your table would be jealous."

"There is no one at my table who is particularly interested in me," he declared.

"That is not true," she replied. "Lady Susan Yeovil is very much interested in you."

He was half amused, half inclined to be irritated at what seemed like presumption.

"The young lady and I are very good friends," he observed.

"That may be your feeling but it is not hers," she said composedly. "You look as though you thought that it was not my affair. It is not. I will speak to you of another matter."

"As soon as you please. I must be getting back to my friends before long."

She stirred her tea lazily.

"I shall not keep you from them," she promised. "Do you know the man who came in with Yvonne Cortot from the Café de Paris?"

"I have never seen him before," Grant replied.

"His name is Itash," she confided, "Count Itash. Some of the girls call him Sammy—I do not know why. You are an American, are you not?"

"I am," he admitted.

"You are a patriot?"

"I think I may call myself one," he assented, a little bewildered.

"Then you should beware of Count Itash," the girl said slowly, "Count Itash, whom Yvonne christened Sammy. Count Itash does not love your country. He would hurt you if he could."

Grant felt that she was watching him out of the corners of her eyes. He laughed with pretended scorn.

"My dear young lady," he protested, "all that sort of thing died a natural death many years ago. I don't suppose there is any great friendliness between our nations but we get on all right nowadays."

"Do you? I am not so sure. Count Itash does not think so either. I have heard him speak of disputes in Washington."

"Count Itash seems to be a very indiscreet young man," Grant observed. "There may have been a little trouble lately but all these things are settled now in a friendly way."

"There is something coming soon," she warned him, "which will not be settled in a friendly way. There is a demand soon to be made in Washington which may end in a threat."

"A threat of what? The days of wars are over."

She turned her head slightly.

"Only for those," she reminded him, "who belong to the Pact of Nations."

"What on earth do you know about the Pact of Nations?" he asked curiously.

"I know everything there is to be known. I have a capable instructor."

"I am more than ever convinced," he said drily, "that Count Itash is a very indiscreet young man."

She knocked the ash from her cigarette onto a plate.

"Count Itash has never addressed a word to me on the subject in his life," she assured him.

"Who is your informant, then?"

"Count Itash."

"You indulge in conundrums," he remarked.

"Why waste time on the unimportant?" she queried scornfully. "I can tell you great truths. What does it matter how I came by them? You would scarcely believe me if you knew, and it really does not matter. The truth is all that matters."

"Who is it that you imagine to be plotting against my country?" he asked.

"Japan and Germany. Possibly China also. You know what Germany lives for? Revenge. As the years go by, her schemes mature. She is nearer the end now than at any time. Shall I tell you of two things which will happen before many years have passed?"

"I fancy that you're a prophet of woe. Let's hear, anyway."

"Prince Frederick will have been proclaimed Emperor of Germany, and Germany and Russia will have declared war against the world."

"Has your informant also vouchsafed the information as to where the money is to come from?"

"From the conquest of America."

"God bless my soul!" Grant gasped.

The orchestra was playing a waltz now. The music seemed to reach them in little ripples of melody. The sound of voices grew louder, and even the popping of corks more insistent. A young man came round towards the Bar and paused to glance meditatively at the two occupants of the almost empty room. Afterwards he ignored them and seated himself on one of the stools in front of the Bar.

"Itash is uneasy," she whispered. "He does not wish very much that I talk to you. He has no idea that I know what I know, but you see how restless he is. Something tells him that there is danger about. Sammy!"

The young man swung round on his stool and came towards them at once.

"Let me introduce to you my new friend, Mr. Grant Slattery," she said coolly. "Count Itash."

"I am very glad to meet you, sir," Itash declared, speaking English with a somewhat guttural accent for one of his race.

"And how is it that you have left Yvonne?" the girl enquired. "You had better hurry back, or she may make you jealous. There are many here who like to dance with her."

"Yvonne! That is nothing!" he answered. "An affair of the moment. Will you dance with me, Cleo? That is if you, sir, will permit," he added, turning to Grant.

"By all means," the latter assented, "but Mademoiselle will return?"

"I shall most certainly return," the girl promised. "There is a great deal more that I have to say to you, Mr. Slattery. I like very much to talk to you. You understand so well the things that interest me."

"The prodigal returned!" Rose Lancaster exclaimed, as Grant rejoined the little party. "I think that we ought to send him to Coventry just as we did Bobby."

"Nonsense!" Susan expostulated. "Every one dances with these professionals. The only point is whether Grant was quite justified in taking her to such a very secluded corner. Votes on the subject, please!"

"She is a most attractive-looking young woman," Lymane declared. "Something about her quite different. I thought at first she was a little shopgirl out for a holiday."

"I didn't," Susan remarked drily. "I've seen her dance. Her name is Mademoiselle Cleo, and she used to be at the Palais Royal. What did you talk to her about, Grant?"

"To tell you the truth," he replied, "we were in the midst of a most interesting conversation when her young Japanese admirer came and dragged her away. We're going to finish it later."

"You're engaged to dance this with me, anyhow," Susan reminded him, rising to her feet.

They moved off, danced, and waited for the encore.

"I wish you hadn't been so attentive to that young woman," Susan said abruptly.

"Why?"

She waited for a moment until they were out of the crowd. "There's some trouble between them already," she whispered. "Was he jealous of you, do you suppose?"

Grant looked across the room. Itash and the girl were seated at a table together, Itash leaning towards his companion, his face dark and even threatening. The girl smiled back at him with a look of obvious disdain. Close at hand, Yvonne, the little danseuse from the Café de Paris, whom Itash had brought with him, watched them both with growing anger.

"I'm afraid there's going to be trouble there," Susan observed. "This is just the sort of thing which makes one realise, after all, that these places are rather sordid."

"I don't think you need feel like that," Grant assured her. "As a matter of fact, a very interesting situation has developed.

Itash, unlike most of his race, seems to have been a little communicative to the girl. Now he has made her wildly jealous and she threatens to talk. I believe that he is terrified."

"Talk? What about?"

"Lady Susan," he said, dropping his voice a little and drawing his chair nearer to hers, "you have been your father's confidante to some small extent, and I dare say you can understand that, while these Congressional Meetings are going on at Nice, we are in the centre of a very hotbed of intrigue. The threads sometimes show themselves in the most unlikely places. I rather fancy that there is one of them to be caught hold of here."

"How exciting!" she murmured. "I felt sure, from something Dad said, that there was trouble brewing. Who's misbehaving, Grant?"

"The two from whom trouble was always to be apprehended," he answered. "It's all tremendously interesting, only what I can't understand is how a close-mouthed fellow like Itash could ever have let a word escape him. As a matter of fact, the girl herself said that he hadn't. And yet she knows. She has given me plenty to think about already."

They danced again once or twice. Afterwards Susan was claimed by Lymane, and Grant strolled across towards the Bar. As soon as she saw him alone, Mademoiselle Cleo rose to her feet with the obvious intention of joining him. Itash laid his hand upon her wrist, leaned forward and spoke to her fiercely. She only laughed. Grant, however, who had caught the young man's expression, was suddenly anxious. He had a feeling that the field of action had broadened, that they were no longer in the little night restaurant, but on the arena of a prospective and far-reaching battleground. Itash, his face dark with anger, had risen to his feet. Yvonne came up and touched him on the arm. He only pushed her away. She went off, laughing, with some one else. Cleo, ignoring Itash's attempts to detain her, came smiling towards Grant.

"I am afraid," he said politely, "that you are in trouble."

"Yes," she assented. "I am in trouble with my friend, Count Itash. If he knew what I had told you—what I am going to tell you—he would certainly kill me. The most amusing part of it is that, as he sits there, biting his nails and cudgelling his brains, he cannot imagine how it is that I know."

"How *do* you know?" Grant asked curiously. "Have you spied upon him, listened to private conversations, stolen his papers?"

"Not one of these," she answered. "Yet I know. I know of the great plot, started six years ago and now rapidly drawing near to fruition."

"Are you going to tell me about it?"

"As I learn the details, yes," she promised. "Day by day and week by week, you shall know everything. In the meantime, alas! I must make friends with him again. Unless we are friends there are some things which I shall never know. But when I do know them, you shall be told. It is my will to wreck his schemes."

"Who is working with him?" Grant enquired.

She looked across the room to where the young man's vengeful eyes seemed to be glaring at them from behind his spectacles.

"Your intelligence should tell you that," she replied. "Germany, of course. Well, I like Germany well enough. They are a great people. I am not so fond of England. But Itash is to be destroyed."

"Is it my fancy," Grant asked, as she rose to her feet, "or are you just a little unforgiving?"

She looked back at him over her shoulder.

"I despise all people," she said, "who forgive. I never change, I never forgive, I never forget, I never break a promise. I go back to Itash now because there are things I do not know, but he will have little joy of me. I promise you that."

She swung across the room, laughed down at the young man who awaited her, and sat by his side. He began talking in a low, fierce tone. She leaned back, fanning herself. Grant returned to his own table.

"A very amusing place, this," he observed. "What about another bottle of wine?"

"Certainly not," Susan declared. "Arthur has paid the bill, and we've made up our minds to go. Bobby has danced five times with that girl with the ginger hair. You have absented yourself twice with the nondescript young woman. And I have come to the conclusion that this is no place for a nice girl to spend a happy evening."

"Believe me," Grant began——

"Not a word," she interrupted. "We're all going home. Three o'clock, and tennis to-morrow before lunch. Of course," she concluded, "you needn't come, unless you want to. As a matter of fact, though, I should think you've made quite enough mischief for one night. The Japanese youth looked as though he were trying to think out some complicated form of murder for you, when you disappeared with the young woman."

"I shouldn't be surprised if his thoughts were turning that way," Grant admitted. "He's a sulky brute. Hullo! Here's Andrews! I wonder what's up."

The young man who had just entered approached Lymane and whispered in his ear. They talked for a few moments in agitated monosyllables. Then Lymane turned towards the others.

"Andrews has just brought some extraordinary news," he announced. "Baron Naga motored over from Nice to the Villa to-night, was taken ill and died there an hour or so ago."

Grant looked across the room. Itash was still talking volubly. Cleo was still listening with the same inscrutable look.

CHAPTER VII

GERTRUDE was more than content with her luncheon companion on the following morning. In some subtle but unmistakable way Grant's attitude seemed to have changed. He looked at her with undisguised admiration and the table which he had selected was in the most secluded corner of the famous restaurant at the end of the Arcade. She gave a little cry of delight as she leaned over the great bowl of pink roses which were awaiting her.

"How wonderful!" she exclaimed.

"How wonderful to have you here," he murmured gallantly.

She looked at him with a faint air of surprise. Yesterday he had seemed all reserve, sometimes even a little cold. To-day his deportment was almost that of a lover.

"Why are you so much nicer than yesterday?" she asked, as she took her place.

"My resistance is weakening," he confessed.

She gave a little sigh of content.

"I think," she confided, "that I am going to enjoy my luncheon. But before we say another word—tell me some more about this horrible tragedy. What was it? Heart disease?"

Grant nodded.

"The doctor thought so. I believe that he is making a further examination."

"Why did Naga motor all the way from the other side of Nice to see Lord Yeovil so late last night?" she enquired.

"Something to do with the meeting at Nice," he replied indifferently. "Let's talk about ourselves, Gertrude."

She allowed her hand to rest for a moment on his. Again she looked at him, half curiously, half with gratification.

"You are really much nicer than the Lymane boy," she declared, "and I thought that I should have to rely upon him for a flirtation."

"You'll do nothing of the sort," he announced brusquely.

"Mayn't I dine with him?"

"No," was the firm reply. "He has his work to attend to and you have me to look after."

She gave her undivided attention for a few moments to the *hors d' œuvres* and made a selection.

"Well," she decided, "we will postpone the discussion."

"If a flirtation is necessary to your peace of mind and contentment of spirit," he continued, "I must dig into the memories of my own sombre past."

"Dear me," she sighed, "I am afraid poor Otto is going to be very jealous."

"I was very jealous of him once," Grant reminded her. "It's my turn now."

"How much are you in earnest?" she asked curiously.

"I shall endeavour to show you."

"The life of an attractive woman," she murmured, "is full of complications."

"So are the lives of her victims," he commented. "Besides, there happens to be a little owing to this particular victim."

"Owing?" she repeated.

"I mean it. If you have any thoughts to spare from your husband, any kindness to give, any affection to bestow, these gifts belong to me."

Again she looked at him searchingly.

"Why are you so changed since yesterday?"

"Yesterday the old soreness had come back," he explained. "I loved you and hated you. To-day things seem to have fallen into a clearer perspective. I don't hate you any more."

"And do you — love me a little?"

He looked into her eyes which, before his earnest gaze, became faintly troubled.

"Grant," she whispered, "I don't know whether I want you to talk to me like this. I have a horrible feeling somehow that you're not serious. And besides — supposing I were to lose my head."

"Even then," he said, "you might look upon it as atonement."

She became silent for a time, obviously disturbed. The subjects which had filled her mind had been forcibly ejected.

"I can't think—really I can't think, Grant, what possessed me in those days," she murmured reminiscently. "Otto was so furiously in love with me, and he was so violent. I hesitated and then he seemed to have it all his own way. And I rather wanted to be a Princess."

"Don't let's talk about the past," he begged, his mouth hardening a little. "The only correct philosophy is to live from day to day. Let us talk about to-day, and then to-morrow."

She was almost embarrassed.

"Grant dear," she expostulated, "you mustn't make love to me like this before everybody. Prince Lutrecht always comes here to lunch and Cornelius Blunn arrived early this morning."

"Cornelius Blunn," Grant repeated. "One of the most interesting men in Europe, I should think."

"He is an intimate friend of my husband's," she remarked drily, "and for a widower, he's rather great on the domestic virtues. If we meet him I'll present you."

"How much of the rest of your day am I permitted to claim?" he enquired. "I should think we could dodge this virtue-loving millionaire somehow or other."

"But what about poor Mr. Lymane?" she demanded. "He has sent me a roomful of roses already this morning."

"Life," Grant declared, "is going to be full of disappointments for that young man."

"Meanwhile," she suggested, smiling, "supposing we leave off talking nonsense for a little time. I should like to hear some more about Baron Naga. Have you been up to the Villa this morning?"

"Yes, I went up to see if there was anything I could do. They are terribly upset, of course."

"Why did he come all the way from Nice at that time of night?" she asked for the second time.

"There was no particular reason that I know of, except that things are not going quite so smoothly as they should at the Conference," he confided. "Baron Naga, I think, wanted to explain his position."

"In Berlin they say that the Pact is breaking up," she told

him, dropping her voice a little. "I never thought that it would last so long. America did well to keep out of it."

He nodded with assumed self-satisfaction.

"Yes, I think we did the right thing," he agreed. "America doesn't need allies, and she certainly doesn't want to be dragged in to pull the chestnuts out of any one else's fire. She is great enough to stand alone. No one can hurt her. Thank God no one wants to."

"I wonder," Gertrude reflected. "America has enemies, you know."

"Pooh! None that really count," he assured her. "Japan, of course — furious because we won't let her little yellow men come in and become citizens. And I suppose a portion of Germany's historic hatred descends upon us, too. Apart from that, we are all right."

"Supposing America were asked to join the Pact to-day; do you think she would consent?"

"I'm sure she wouldn't," he replied confidently. "Not the ghost of a chance of it. She's been out for all these years, making her own commercial treaties, and to-day is easily the richest country in the world. Why should she change?"

"Why, indeed," Gertrude murmured. "I was just interested to know how you felt about it."

"I feel as our President feels," he continued, "and most of our thinking men. We are satisfied. We shouldn't get into a state of nerves even if Japan got leave to start building a couple more cruisers a year. By the way, I wonder whom they will send to take Naga's place at the Pact?"

"Katina is coming from Berlin," she told him. "I believe he is on his way already. I don't suppose I should have told you that," she added, with a little laugh, "but you see I'm beginning to have confidence in you — or rather in your indifference to these things."

"Why did you ever doubt me?" he asked. "I told you yesterday that I had finished with politics."

"Well," she explained, "you know how careful Germans are. You used to be in the Diplomatic Service, and I've heard you spoken of once or twice as a person who ought to be watched

I think I can clear your suspicious character now, though."

"I'm afraid I'm too lazy," he answered, "to be seriously interested in anything. The Van Roorden millions wrecked my ambitions. You'd have been a very rich woman if you'd waited, Gertrude."

"If I'd waited," she sighed, looking at him for a moment, and then dropping her eyes.

The restaurant, which had been almost empty at their first coming, had now filled up. Gertrude looked about her in surprise.

"Why, I never saw these people come in," she declared. "There's Prince Lutrecht over there. And a whole party of your friends. I don't think Lady Susan likes me."

Susan nodded and smiled across the room. Her eyes, however, had a shade of reproach in them as they met Grant's.

"Like you? Of course she likes you," he protested. "If there's an unpopular one in the party, it isn't you. Look how Lymane is glaring at me. Gertrude, you won't dine with him, will you?"

"My dear Grant, how on earth am I going to get out of it?" she asked.

"I'll get you out of it all right," he promised. "Tell me, who is the corpulent gentleman of pleasant appearance, with the hat too small for his head, who is standing upon the threshold, beaming at you?"

"That is Cornelius Blunn," she whispered. "He's a dear thing. Do be civil to him for my sake. He could make mischief with Otto if he wanted to, and I'm afraid he's coming to speak to me."

The newcomer — stout, genial and jovial — was crossing the room, smiling as though the whole of Monte Carlo was some tremendous joke and the fact of meeting the Princess its supreme consummation. He lumbèred up like a great elephant, moving clumsily on his rather short legs. But the air with which he raised Gertrude's fingers to his lips was the air of a courtier.

"Why, Princess," he exclaimed. "How delightful to find you, and how good for one's national self-respect to discover that no one in this wonderful place can even hold a candle to a compatriot."

"Always a flatterer," she smiled. "Let me introduce Mr. Grant Slattery. Mr. Cornelius Blunn."

Mr. Blunn shook hands pleasantly, but without enthusiasm. His manner suggested that Grant's presence as Gertrude's sole companion needed some further explanation.

"Mr. Slattery is one of my oldest friends," she continued. "We were children together in Washington."

Mr. Blunn beamed. A great smile seemed to rise from the depths of his nature. He was a man of sentiment and he recognised the claim of old friendships. He took the affair under his protection.

"Delightful!" he exclaimed. "Mr Slattery, you must not doubt my sincerity when I say that it is always a pleasure to meet an American. I am no stranger in New York. I was one of the first who dared show himself there after the terrible days of the War. I was a youngster then—but it hurt. Still, I said to myself, I will go there. It is the home of many of my race. If there is still bad feeling between us, it must perish. And it has perished. Of that I am assured. It has indeed."

"Do you travel in England, too?" Grant asked.

Mr. Blunn was no longer a completely happy man. He sighed.

"In England—no," he answered. "That is another matter. Princess, I kiss your fingers. My luncheon will be a happier meal for the pleasure you have brought into the room. Mr. Slattery, I envy you, sir. So does every man, but I bear you no grudge."

He departed, ponderous yet light-footed, elephantine yet dignified. Grant gazed after him with genuine curiosity.

"If I were up against that man in a business deal or a political imbroglio," he murmured, "I should feel that I needed all my wits about me. A person of that type is more dangerous than all the Lutrechts in the world."

"Dangerous? But how, dangerous?" she queried. "Mr. Blunn is a great philanthropist and an enthusiastic patron of the arts. In what respect could he be dangerous?"

"Only if he chose to be," Grant answered carelessly.

"Could I be dangerous, if I chose to be?" she demanded.

"You are dangerous," he assured her. "You are the most dangerous woman in the world, to my peace of mind. And the terrible part of it all is that you are a German. You belong to a race with whom the domestic virtues are a positive fetish."

"Just because I married Otto?"

"Just because you married Otto," he acknowledged. "Germans have the knack of making Germans of their wives."

"Absurd!" she laughed. "What is there Teutonic about me? German women haven't my figure, and they certainly couldn't wear my clothes."

"Externally you have advantages," he admitted. "All the same you have married a German and you are a governed woman."

"How you hate my adopted country," she exclaimed.

"I do not," he objected. "I hate neither the country nor the people. My feeling is entirely different. I don't mind admitting that if I were a seriously minded politician I should be afraid of them."

"But why?" she asked. "What is there to fear? Industrially the world is open to every one since war was done away with."

"Perhaps so."

"But isn't it, Grant, really? The Pact includes every European nation, as well as Japan. Then there's the Limitation of Armaments as well. Every nation is more or less on an equal footing, and they are all pledged not to fight one another. You must admit that Germany has kept the conditions of the Pact faithfully. Where can fear lie?"

"Where, indeed? You mustn't take me too seriously, Gertrude. I only meant that, so far as I can see, Germany is well on the way to becoming the second most powerful nation in the world. But honestly, I don't know why we're talking politics. I lost all interest in them years ago. Do you know what I did yesterday?"

"Tell me," she begged.

"I wired to Cannes for my yacht. It should be here to-morrow."

She looked at him for a moment steadily. Then a tinge of colour stole into her cheek. She seemed suddenly a little nervous.

"I wish I knew which was the real Grant," she murmured.

"What do you mean?"

"The Grant of yesterday — or the Grant of to-day."

CHAPTER VIII

"One needs to be long-suffering to cope with one's friends," Susan remarked, when an hour later she found herself seated side by side with Grant on a bench at the tennis courts. "Last night you showed marked attentions to a danseuse; this morning you have been flirting disgracefully with that beautiful princess, thereby reducing poor Arthur to despair, and now you propose to devote a few minutes to me for the first time to-day. I am beginning to fear, Mr. Grant Slattery, that you are going to be a disappointment to me."

"Not at tennis, anyhow," he assured her. "You and I are going to wipe the ground with the Lancasters."

"Our thoughts are on different planes," she declared. "I speak of life and you of tennis. I think we shall beat them, if you stand up to the net and don't poach."

"How's your father to-day?" he asked a little abruptly.

"Quite all right, considering. It must have been a terrible shock to him to see that poor old man collapse with scarcely a moment's warning."

"Naga was a great statesman," Grant remarked. "One of the last of the old school. Come on, it's our court."

On the way across, an acquaintance hailed Grant. By his side stood Count Itash — sometimes called Sammy.

"Slattery, Count Itash says that he has only an informal acquaintance with you and would like an introduction," the former said. "Count Itash — Mr. Grant Slattery."

Grant held out his hand. The other, after a little bow, accepted it. He was an insignificant-looking person amongst the athletic young men by whom he was surrounded, but his eyes, behind his horn-rimmed spectacles, were exceptionally hard and piercing.

"I am glad to meet you, Mr. Slattery," he said. "Could you, before you leave the courts, spare me a minute or two?"

"With pleasure," Grant assented. "We are going to play the best of three sets here. I'll look for you afterwards."

"You are very kind, sir."

"Who's your little friend, Grant?" young Lancaster enquired curiously. "He's the fellow we saw at the Carlton last night, isn't he?"

"That's the chap," Grant replied. "He rejoices in the name of Itash. I believe I have heard that he is attached to thc Japanese Embassy in Berlin and is doing secretarial work for their section here. Queer-looking card, isn't he?"

"I couldn't make out where I'd seen him before," Lancaster observed. "I remember now; I used to see him driving about with Baron Naga. Dismal-looking beggar, isn't he?"

"I expect the poor young man is upset about his Chief," Susan remarked. "What did he want, Grant?"

"Wanted to speak to me," was the indifferent reply. "He's going to wait until after we've finished our three sets."

"You're going to get some part of what's coming to you," Susan laughed. "You took his dancing companion away last night and you spoiled Arthur's luncheon to-day. Why don't you get a girl of your own?"

"I try," Grant confessed humbly. "I'm afraid I'm not popular with the sex."

"That's your fault," Susan insisted. "A nicely brought-up girl always likes a well-behaved man. Now get up to the net and remember we've money on this set. Serve!"

The tennis courts presented a gay scene as the afternoon wore on. There was the usual crowd of English and French people, the women nearly all in white, the men, especially the foreigners, showing a little more variety in their costumes. The sun was shining and every one seemed inspired by the soft exhilaration of the air, the beauty of the glittering blue sea below, and the mountains behind. There was a crowd too of more elaborately dressed spectators, a fluttering of many-coloured parasols, and all the time the cheerful hum of light-hearted conversation in many tongues. With characteristic patience, Count Itash — sometimes called Sammy — sat on his solitary bench and waited — a solemn, almost ghoul-like figure, on the outskirts of the gaiety. At the conclusion of their sets, Grant, after he had received the congratulations of his partner, went over and seated himself by his side.

"What do you wish to say to me, Count Itash?" he enquired.

"I offer apologies, but I am in some trouble," the young man explained earnestly. "It concerns the lady with whom you talked last night."

"Mademoiselle Cleo?"

"The young lady who is so called," Itash assented. "She has been my companion for some time here in Monte Carlo. I will now be very truthful. I have taken a fancy to another girl. Such things happen."

"Quite so," Grant agreed. "But I can't exactly see how this concerns me."

"It is in this way. Cleo is very, very angry. She knows that I am in the Diplomatic Service, — that I am, in fact, occupying a very confidential and important position down here. She makes a pretence of having obtained possession of secret information concerning the affairs over which I watch, and she threatens to make use of it."

"Well?"

"But I have never confided in her, not one word," the young man declared. "We Japanese are not like that. We do not talk. We carry our secrets in our brain."

"Then if you have told her nothing, what are you afraid of?" Grant asked.

"I have told her nothing," Itash repeated vehemently, "nor can I think of a single written line of a compromising nature which could possibly have come into her possession. Yet I am disturbed in my mind. Cleo is a strange being. She has the gift of speaking the truth. Not all people have it. When she speaks a thing, one's heart feels that it is true. So when she tells me that there are secrets of mine which have come within her knowledge, I am afraid. She came to you last night, and she talked to you earnestly. I ask you, sir, did she tell you anything of those affairs confided to me, the disclosure of which could amount in any way to a breach of faith?"

"Not a word," Grant assured him. "To be quite frank, I don't know what you're talking about."

The young man passed his hand across his forehead.

"Mr. Slattery, sir," he confessed, "I am in great distress of mind and body. The death of my Chief last night was terrible, and all the time I cannot escape from this load of anxiety which weighs upon me."

"I should use a little common sense," Grant advised. "If you know that you have told her nothing, if you know that you have committed none of your secrets, whatever they may be, to paper, can't you realise that she is only trading upon your fears?"

"That must be so," Itash muttered.

"Furthermore," Grant continued, "if she had secrets to tell, why on earth should she bring them to me? I am the last person in the world likely to be interested in them."

The young man shot a sudden quick glance at his companion. Then he blinked a great many times behind his spectacles.

"I see that," he acknowledged. "You are not in the Diplomatic Service, Mr. Slattery?"

"In my younger days I was Secretary at Berlin and London for a short time," Grant told him. "When I came into my money, however, I chucked it. The young lady's choice of me as a confidant would have been ridiculous."

"Just so," Itash agreed. "Then she told you nothing?"

"Nothing at all."

"Nor did she give you the impression that she had anything to tell?"

"She gave me no impression at all, except that she was rather a mysterious young person, suffering from an acute fit of jealousy."

Itash rose slowly to his feet. He held out his hand.

"I apologise humbly, Mr. Slattery," he said. "I see that I have been very foolish. Thank you for listening to me. I will go now."

"You are not going to play?"

Itash shook his head sorrowfully.

"It would not be reverent. In a week or two, perhaps, if I am still here."

He made his way towards the gate,—an odd figure, in his ceremonious black apparel. Susan looked after him curiously.

"Well, have you promised to let him have his girl back again?" she asked Grant, as he returned to her side.

"I have assured him that I am not a serious rival for her favours," he rejoined. "The young man seems comforted."

"Got your hands pretty full as it is, haven't you?"

"Look here," Grant said severely. "Kindly remember that I have just steered you to victory on the tennis courts, and in a day or two, if you behave yourself, I will be able to take you for a cruise in the *Grey Lady*. Incidentally I should be glad if you would further bear in mind the fact that I am a great many years your senior. A little more respect, please. Now, come along, and I'll give you a lift down to the club for tea."

"Thank you. I thought of going with Bobby."

"You may have thought of it, but you are coming with me," he insisted.

"Rather a bully, aren't you?" she observed coolly. "However, perhaps I'd better. Bobby gets so affectionate in those little *voitures,*—thinks one needs steadying all the time. You're above that sort of thing, aren't you?"

"The springs of my Rolls-Royce," he began——

"Oh, bother the springs of your Rolls-Royce," she interrupted. "I'm coming with you because I want to get to the club quickly and because I like your car."

"The worst of being a millionaire!" Grant complained gloomily, as he took his place at the wheel. "One is tolerated only for one's possessions."

"They're generally the best thing about a millionaire," Susan declared. "All the same, if there were an unattached English one in the market, I think that I should like to marry him."

"What's the matter with a perfectly good American one?" he suggested.

"Entrancing idea, but illusionary," she rejoined drily. "I hate syndicates, or *réchauffés*. I'm going in to tidy up, Grant. Try and get the round table in the corner."

She jumped out and ran lightly up the steps. Grant backed his car to the pavement and was in the act of following her when the blue-liveried commissionaire, hat in hand, accosted him mysteriously.

"A young lady asked me to give you this as soon as you arrived, sir," he announced, presenting a twisted-up half sheet of paper.

"Sure it's for me?" Grant asked a little doubtfully.

"Mr. Grant Slattery," the man declared. "The young person knew your name, sir."

Grant thrust the note into his waistcoat pocket. He felt a curious conviction as to its source. To add a touch of coincidence to the affair, on the opposite side of the way, Itash was leaning over the wall, apparently watching the shipping in the harbour.

CHAPTER IX

As a yachtsman Mr. Cornelius Blunn did not shine sartorially. As a guest and conversationalist at Grant's improvised cruise on the following day he was easily the most popular man on board. Susan, who had been his neighbour at lunch, watched him pacing the deck, with a look almost of affection in her face.

"Princess," she confided to Gertrude, "I think your friend, Mr. Blunn, is the most amusing man I've ever met."

Gertrude smiled.

"He is one of those impossible persons who never grow up," she declared. "A picnic like this is the joy of his life. He was simply delighted when I gave him Mr. Slattery's message. The strange part of it is that he can scarcely cross the gangway of a steamer without being violently ill. Yet a cruise like this he simply revels in."

"Make his fortune as a raconteur on the music-hall stage," Bobby Lancaster chuckled. "Some of the stories he told after you girls had come up on deck! — there was one about a little Dutch girl. I really must——"

"Bobby," Susan interrupted severely, "I am ashamed of you. The story will reach us all in due course through the proper channels. You will tell your sister, of course. She will tell me. And so on."

"Then there was another about an Italian maid."

His sister rose to her feet and thrust her arm through his.

"Bobby," she said, "you and I will take a little walk. You have brought this upon yourself. I can't see you chuckling there and leaving me to wonder what it's about all the time. We'll stroll down to the bows."

"This roundabout business is trying but decent," Susan observed. "I suppose I shall have to wait at least another quarter of an hour. In the meantime, Mr. Slattery, I adore your yacht."

"She really is wonderful, Grant," Gertrude intervened. "You hadn't anything like this in the old days, had you?"

"Perhaps it was as well," Susan murmured, with a rare impulse of ill humour.

Gertrude smiled across at her rival. Grant had scarcely left her side all day and she was beginning to feel a little sorry for this very charming young English girl to whom her coming was likely to prove so disastrous. Even the picnic had been arranged at her suggestion.

"Well, the yacht has arrived, and other things," she remarked. "It is never too late in this world, so long as one has the will. Grant, I want to go to the Dutch East Indies."

"I'd better tell him to put in at Naples and coal, then," he suggested.

"You will kindly remember," Susan observed, "that you have the Prime Minister of the greatest empire in the world on board, who will be required at Nice at a quarter to eleven to-morrow morning to preside over the little tea party there."

"That is unfortunate," Gertrude sighed. "Such a quarrelsome little tea party too, isn't it?"

Lymane, who was seated in the little circle, moved in his chair uneasily. Grant turned slightly towards her.

"Quarrelsome, is it?" he repeated. "How do you know that?"

"Oh, the air is full of rumours," she answered carelessly. "Yesterday, for instance, everybody was saying that that poor dear Baron Naga had committed suicide because America was to be invited once more to come into the Pact."

"I thought it was because he found he had one funnel too many on his latest cruiser," Bobby Lancaster remarked.

"Idiot!" his sister exclaimed. "That's the business of the Limitation of Armaments Congress, not the Pact."

"Naga, as a matter of fact, represented his country on both Boards," Lymane pointed out. "Too much for one man. I know that he dreaded that journey to Washington every year."

The stewards appeared with tea. Lord Yeovil and Cornelius Blunn joined the little group. The latter removed his hat, dragged his chair out to where he could get the full benefit of the sunlight and the breeze, and smiled on every one beatifically.

"Mr. Slattery," he said, "you are, without exception, the most fortunate man in the world. You own the most perfect yacht I have ever seen, you have no business or other cares, you have the friends who make a man happy. It is a wonderful existence."

Grant smiled.

"Rather a lazy one, I am afraid," he admitted.

"Laziness is the only sound philosophy of life," Blunn insisted. "If you have no need to work for yourself, why do it? If you spend your time working for others, you meet with nothing but ingratitude. I grudge the time I have to give to the management of my own affairs, but I am always deeply grateful that I was never tempted to dabble in politics. I am training up young men, and in five years' time I shall be free from all cares. When that time comes, I shall lie like a lizard in the sun of good fortune. I will never write a letter and seldom read a newspaper."

"I thought that all Germans were politicians by instinct, from their cradles upwards," Lord Yeovil remarked, smiling.

"Not in these days," Blunn replied, helping himself to his third cake. "My father, of course, was a rabid politician, but he lived in terrible times. A prosperous Germany is so much to the good, of course, but her sons naturally lack the inspiration of what used to be known as patriotism. The fact of it is," he went on, "that industrially Germany has come in for a great heritage. If she had been as prosperous in nineteen-fourteen as she is to-day, that wicked old Kaiser of ours might have rattled his sabre forever and no one would have listened. What people have often failed to understand about my country is that we are not seekers after glory. We want money and the ease and comfort and happy days that money brings."

"You don't think that Germany wants another war, then?" Bobby Lancaster asked.

"My dear young man," Blunn assured him emphatically, "there isn't a leader living or a cause in existence which could induce the German of to-day to exchange the loom for the sword. There isn't a nation which rejoices so thoroughly in the Pact. I thought that this was absolutely understood by now. Even the English sensationalists have begun to trust us."

He smiled around upon them all. Somehow or other he seemed to feel the inspiration of the circle of interested auditors.

"There is only one thing needed," he continued, "which my friends the politicians tell me would end the last hopes of the militarists, and that is that the Pact of Nations, over which my honoured friend here, Lord Yeovil, so ably presides, should induce the United States of America to join them and abandon forever her present aloofness. I do not understand myself the means by which this could be done or the etiquette necessary, but as a representative German citizen, my hand of comradeship is ready at any moment."

"I wonder," Lord Yeovil speculated, "whether you really do speak as a representative German citizen."

"Believe me, I do," was the earnest reply. "My simple tastes in life are shared by millions. What the German of to-day wants is his beer, his wine, his music and his womankind. He wants to spend his spare time with his children and to be able to buy his little home early in life. I am not a great traveller; I don't know how it is with other nations. I know how it is with my own. We want to live out our days comfortably and pleasantly. We are natural human beings, filled with natural desires. I have eaten too many cakes. I shall walk for a little time or I shall have no appetite for this wonderful dinner, which our gracious host has promised us. Princess, will you do me the honour?"

Gertrude rose from her place.

"I am not a great walker, Mr. Blunn," she warned him, "but for ten minutes I will be your companion."

"That ten minutes," he rejoined, "will be the crown of my day."

They all looked after him a little curiously as he stepped out upon his promenade. Lord Yeovil was very much interested.

"I am delighted, Grant," he said to Slattery, "that you have given me an opportunity, through your friend the Princess von Diss, of meeting Mr. Blunn. I find him an extraordinary intriguing personality."

"For a multimillionaire he seems to be a very simple creature," Rose Lancaster observed.

"'Multi' is inadequate," Grant interposed. "He is reputed to be worth anything from forty to sixty million pounds. It is hard to see how any one could have handled such wealth and have remained so apparently ingenuous."

"Do you distrust him?" Susan asked a little bluntly.

Grant hesitated. He seemed to be watching Gertrude and Blunn as they walked together,—Gertrude superbly beautiful, walking with the perfect grace of her long limbs and exquisite poise, Blunn striding along cheerfully by her side, a figure, by contrast, almost of absurdity.

"Well, I don't know," he acknowledged. "You remember what our own Ambassador said many years ago. 'Trust everybody but a German, and trust a German when he is dead.'"

Lord Yeovil smiled.

"Nevertheless, Grant," he confessed, "I have a leaning towards Mr. Blunn. I am almost sorry that he is not a politician. I would rather have him seated at the Conference table than our friend Lutrecht. What about a rubber of bridge until cocktail time? We can play on deck."

Blunn stopped short in his promenade.

"Bridge?" he repeated, with a broad smile. "Did I hear some one say anything about bridge?"

"Mr. Blunn is a fanatic," Gertrude declared. "Grant, you will have to come and entertain me, unless you are very anxious to play."

He rose at once to his feet and gave an order to the steward whom he had summoned.

"I will show you the chart room," he suggested. "There are plenty to play without me."

They strolled off together. Susan sat watching them with interlaced fingers. Suddenly she became aware that Blunn's eyes were upon her.

"Lady Susan and I against any two," he proposed jovially. "Take me out if I double 'no trumps' with your best suit, partner. Discard from weakness. Always support me when you can, and we'll win all the money there is on the yacht. Between ourselves, I have a yacht almost as large as this, lying up in Kiel

Harbour even now. I daren't use her because of the socialists."

"Socialists!" Lord Yeovil repeated. "One never hears of them nowadays."

"They've all come to Germany," Blunn confided. "They are like mice,—they always go for the ripening cheese. They are just a slur upon our too great prosperity. One 'no trump,' partner. I knew it. You have brought me luck. I am going to hold every card in the pack."

CHAPTER X

GERTRUDE's interest in the intricacies of nautical science abated as soon as she found herself alone with her host in the chart room. They sat on cane chairs, and she swiftly brushed aside his explanation as to the problems suggested by the compass.

"My dear Grant," she laughed, "I don't care a bit how you set the course of your yacht or where you go to. What I should really like to know is why you don't hold my hand?"

"I am placing a great restraint upon myself," he assured her. "My captain is on the left-hand side of the bridge there, and my first officer on the right."

"Why you have a room with all these silly little windows, I can't imagine," she complained. "I am feeling unusually gracious this afternoon. It was really very sweet of you to arrange this party and to let me bring Cornelius Blunn. He was most anxious to meet Lord Yeovil."

"I wonder why?" Grant remarked. "He appears to hate politics and most serious matters."

"He does, but he loves men," she explained. "Men, and women, too, for that matter. A new type interests him. He has more friends than any man I ever met, and the number of his women acquaintances is scandalous."

"He seems quite a simple person. I should never have believed that he was the Cornelius Blunn one reads so much about,—the great capitalist, the huge speculator, the man who controls the brains of so many great enterprises."

"Mostly newspaper talk," she observed carelessly. "He holds the majority of the shares in a great many of these companies by inheritance, but he takes no active part in their management. I wonder what Lord Yeovil thought of his suggestion that America ought to be asked again to join the Pact of Nations."

Grant's expression was one of bland indifference.

"I have no idea what Lord Yeovil's own views on the matter may be," he confessed. "We seldom talk politics. How does a man like your friend Blunn, now, get on with politicians, say of the type of Prince Lutrecht?"

"Well, they are entirely different," she said thoughtfully. "Lutrecht is a born statesman. He comes from a stock of diplomatists. He would never have the broad views of Cornelius Blunn."

"This matter of America, for instance?" Grant hazarded.

"How should I know anything about it," she queried, a little impatiently, "and why do we waste time talking politics? You're not nearly so nice as you were yesterday. Have you nothing more interesting to say?"

"And if I have, what would be the use?"

His tone seemed full of bitterness, his glance was certainly reproachful. She leaned towards him and took his hand boldly.

"Can't I make up, just a little, Grant?" she whispered.

"Do you want to?" he demanded.

"I think so."

"And then go back—to Berlin?"

"Who knows?" she sighed. "You yourself have had proof that I am a creature of impulse. When I feel strongly enough I have no will."

There was a knock at the door. A steward brought in a message scribbled on a piece of paper. Grant glanced at it and nodded.

"We had better go down," he said, turning to Gertrude. "The captain wants to consult me about the course. I have promised Lord Yeovil that he shall be back at ten o'clock. And I have an appointment myself later."

"What sort of an appointment?" she asked a little jealously.

"Nothing of any moment," he assured her.

They descended the steps, Grant pausing to speak for a few moments with the captain.

"I'm tired of all these people," Gertrude declared abruptly. "Take me into your music room and I'll play to you."

He shook his head. Lymane was glowering at them from the rail, and Rose Lancaster was sitting alone.

"Alas!" he murmured. "You must remember that I am a host."

"I shall flirt with Arthur Lymane," she threatened.

"You've done that already," he answered drily.

"Nonsense, I've only trifled with him," she laughed. "He's a nice boy but conceited. Walks in his master's shadow and fancies himself a diplomatist. He is as some one once said of a war time Prime Minister,—full of small reticences and bubbling over with ingenuous disclosures."

"How did you discover that?"

"When I talk to him I have to pretend to be interested in politics," she replied evasively. "There is nothing else he can talk about."

Susan cut out of the rubber and Rose Lancaster took her place. Grant crossed over and sank into a chair by the former's side.

"Any luck?" he enquired.

"Thirty francs, thanks to Mr. Blunn. He's a daring caller but he plays the cards wonderfully."

"A most interesting character," he remarked.

"Father seems to like him," she agreed. "The only German he ever has liked."

"And you?"

"I like him, too, or rather I think I do," she replied, after a moment's hesitation. "There are just odd moments when he gives me rather a quaint impression of insincerity. I dare say that's fancy. Grant, you're giving us a wonderful day."

"I want it to be," he answered. "It's very nice to get you all here, and I fancy it must be rather a relief to your father to be right away for a few hours. No messages or cables possible. Hullo!"

He looked up at the masthead. Susan followed his example. There was a little crackling of blue fire there.

"I'm afraid I spoke too soon," he pointed out. "The wireless is evidently working. I meant to have had it disconnected."

Lord Yeovil, who was playing a hand, paused for a moment and looked up curiously.

"I should like to have been Prime Minister to Queen Elizabeth," he grumbled. "One might have had a chance of a few hours' holiday then."

"Not you, Dad," Susan exclaimed. "You'd have found making love to her all the time much more strenuous than law-making."

"My knowledge of history is slight," her father rejoined, "but I don't fancy that Queen Elizabeth showed much amorous interest in elderly widowers."

The Marconi operator presented a message to Lord Yeovil. He tore it open, nodded, and waited till the young man had retired. Then, after a moment's hesitation, he glanced across towards Gertrude, who was leaning against the rail, with Lymane by her side.

"My news is official," he said, "but there is, I imagine, no secrecy about it. It will probably interest you, Princess."

"Me!" Gertrude exclaimed, looking genuinely surprised.

"It is a cable from Berlin," Lord Yeovil continued, "which Andrews has wirelessed on to me. 'Baron Katina left this morning with cabled credentials to take Naga's place here. I am informed that he is accompanied by Prince von Diss.'"

"Otto! My husband!" Gertrude cried.

Lord Yeovil assented.

"Is your husband, by any chance, a Japanese scholar, Princess?" he asked.

"He understands Japanese," she replied. "He learnt it at Tokio years ago. He has been over there once or twice since on missions."

"That probably explains the matter," Lord Yeovil pointed out. "Katina has the reputation of being a great diplomatist, but he has only just commenced the study of European languages. The Prince is probably coming with him as interpreter."

Gertrude's face was, for a moment, scarcely beautiful. She was looking across at Grant. Susan intercepted the glance and laughed, for her, a little maliciously.

"What a catastrophe!" she murmured.

A steward handed round cocktails. Blunn looked at the beautiful glasses, with their slight frosting, and rose to his feet, as he accepted one.

"To my friend and host," he said, addressing Grant. "I drink to you fervently, sir. You are the prince of hosts. Three minutes ago I felt that slight uneasy sensation, that faint but insistent desire for alcoholic sustenance, which sometimes prompts me at about seven o'clock to press the bell for my own butler, or if I am in an hotel or at my club, to make certain suggestions to the waiter. The feeling comes and within three minutes it is gratified. Wonderful!"

He raised his glass to his lips and drained it.

"Have another," Grant invited; "there's a shakerful behind."

"I will," Mr. Blunn assented, without hesitation. "I like your cocktails, sir. I like the time and manner in which they are served. I like everything about them. It is indeed a very happy day. I am going two 'no trumps.'"

Gertrude raised her glass.

"Well," she said, "I suppose I must drink to the end of my grass-widowhood."

She looked across at Grant. He smiled inscrutably.

"You anticipate," he reminded her. "The Prince cannot arrive until the morning after to-morrow."

She paused.

"In that case," she decided, "I shall drink to something else."

Dinner, served as they crept at half-speed towards the harbour, was a wonderful meal. Grant's chef, who had ransacked Monte Carlo on the previous day and motored over to Nice to collect the materials for one of his favourite sauces, had surpassed himself. Every one except Gertrude seemed in the highest possible spirits. Cornelius Blunn, growing pinker with every course, sat like an overgrown and over-filled child, — sometimes witty, sometimes ingenuous, always amusing. Rose Lancaster on one side and Susan on the other were admirable and appreciative foils for his gallantries. Gertrude, on Grant's right, was a little silent and intense; Lymane, on her other side, sulky and inclined to be melodramatic. He was continually endeavouring to inveigle his neighbour into a whispered conversation which she, as persistently, discouraged. She declined altogether to take him seriously.

"My dear man," she protested, "don't you understand the situation? I cannot flirt with you any longer. My husband will be here within a few hours. I must bring myself into the necessary state of mind to receive him. It is a calamity, perhaps, but it must be borne."

"You have the whole of to-morrow," he muttered.

"It will take me the whole of to-morrow to find myself," she assured him. "Here have I been encouraging Mr. Slattery and, at any rate, listening to you, with all the licence of a fairly respectable but susceptible grass widow. Otto is very jealous and I am a very dutiful wife. I have little more than twenty-four hours to forget you both. I must be left entirely alone. I have promised to dine with Mr. Slattery to-morrow night, and a promise is a thing I never break. I warn him, however, that it will be — well —— "

"I rather understood," Lymane interrupted bitterly, "that you were dining with me and coming somewhere to dance afterwards."

"That was the night after, my friend," she replied. "And, alas! there's nothing in the least modern about Otto. I'll give everyone fair warning that while he is here I shall not be allowed to dine or flirt with any one. To-morrow night is my last evening of freedom. Don't be surprised, Grant, if I lead you a terrible dance."

"Why should they have a dinner to themselves?" Cornelius Blunn exclaimed, turning to Rose Lancaster. "I will give a dinner party to-morrow night. I invite everybody. I have some other friends, over at Nice. I will wire for them. Prince Lutrecht and his wife shall come. I will spend the whole of to-morrow arranging it. I cannot equal this festival but I will see what can be done. Accept quickly, please, every one of you."

There was a little affirmative chorus. Cornelius Blunn looked across at Gertrude. She set her lips and shook her head.

"I shall not give up my own dinner," she declared, defiantly, "and I decline to let Mr. Slattery off."

"Very well," Blunn acquiesced good-humouredly. "I shall either alter the date of mine or it shall be an opposition. I shall probably have refinements which have never been thought of before. I shall have the roof removed from the Hotel de Paris for a quarter of an hour only and presents dropped down from aeroplanes for every one. I shall have Mademoiselle Lebrun from Nice to sing to us and Coquinet to tell us stories. I shall —— "

"Don't give it all away," Gertrude interrupted. "If you are trying to tempt me, I am quite firm. If you give your dinner to-morrow night, I shall dine with Mr. Slattery."

"My attitude towards your husband in this matter," Blunn declared, "will be one of pained but remorseful silence."

"So long as it really is silence," Gertrude laughed.

"I have ordered coffee and liqueurs on deck," Grant announced. "We are just entering the bay and the moon is up. You ladies may need your wraps but it is quite warm."

They trooped up the companionway. Grant looked for Susan, but she had hurried on with young Lancaster. On deck they found that they were already headed for the narrow opening between the red and green lamps of the harbour. The great sweep of the bay was outlined by a glittering arc of lights; the towering hillside in the background was bespangled with little points of fire. The Casino flared out in front. The moon, yellower and fuller at every moment, seemed to give a note almost of artificiality to the little scene; they could even hear the sound of music from the open windows of the Concert Room. Susan and Lancaster found their way into the bows and stood watching the phosphorus. Lymane brought coffee to Gertrude where she sat close to the rail.

"Do you really mean it about to-morrow?" he asked.

"Of course I do. Why not?"

"You were not engaged to dine with Grant Slattery," he complained. "You made that up."

"What if I did?" she answered coolly. "Mr. Slattery is an old friend, he is very amusing and he talks about things that interest me."

"Don't I?" he demanded.

"To be quite frank, you don't," she confessed. "You are very young, you know, and you think because you are private secretary to the Prime Minister that you have to wrap yourself in a mantle of impenetrable reserve. I'm positively ill at ease talking to you. I am so afraid that I shall ask something which will provoke one of your diplomatic replies."

He leaned a little nearer to her.

"Come out to supper with me to-night," he begged. "And I'll talk about anything you like in the world."

"Supper, to-night," she repeated, a little dubiously. "But sha'n't we be tired?"

"No," he answered eagerly, "you can rest for two or three hours. Let me call for you, say, at twelve o'clock."

She considered the matter for a moment. Then she nodded.

"Well, you can come and see me at twelve o'clock, anyway," she agreed. "You're a very nice boy, and I didn't really mean to be angry with you. You remember our bargain?"

"Rather!" he answered rapturously.

She looked over her shoulder. Grant had descended from the bridge and was coming down the deck. For once the young man was quick to understand.

"I sha'n't say a word about it, of course," he assured her.

She laughed back at him.

"I see there are hopes for you, after all," she declared.

CHAPTER XI

GRANT walked into the Carlton at a quarter past twelve that evening, the exact hour mentioned by Cleo in the note which the commissionaire at the Sporting Club had given to him. He left his coat and hat in the coat room, made his way inside the restaurant, which was as yet sparsely occupied, and, ignoring the efforts of the *maître d'hôtel* to provide him with a table, strolled across to where Cleo was seated alone. She welcomed him with a bare uplifting of the eyebrows, the sparsest possible smile.

"You permit me?" he asked, with his hand on the back of her chair.

"Certainly," she assented. "Sit down if you wish, but I have changed my mind. I have nothing to say to you."

He summoned a waiter and ordered some wine.

"That seems unfortunate," he remarked. "May I have the pleasure of providing you with your accustomed beverage?"

"You can order some tea for me," she said shortly, "and as many cigarettes as you like. But, alas, you will be wasting your kindness. I have nothing to say to you."

"Perhaps," he suggested, "I should not be considered unreasonable if I were to ask why this change? I am here at your invitation."

"It is permitted always to a woman to change her mind," she reminded him. "I believe you're one of those with whom frankness is best. I have changed mine because Itash —— "

"Sometimes called Sammy," he murmured.

"—has changed his attitude towards me."

"All up with the little lady from the Café de Paris?" Grant queried.

"He has finished with her," she confided. "It was nothing but a passing fancy, ministered to by her lies. I wish, instead of talking nonsense to you, I had killed her."

"But, my dear lady, consider how different everything would have been," Grant pointed out. "Things having happened, as they have, behold ourselves seated — friends, I trust — in this very pleasing place of entertainment, alive and well, and with perfectly robust futures. If you had killed that rather impossible young lady, where would you be now? In that uncomfortable-looking edifice which these wise people of Monte Carlo keep absolutely out of sight, awaiting your trial and not in the least sure what was going to happen to you."

"I am satisfied, if you are," she said shortly.

"Of course, as a patriotic American," he went on, "there are drawbacks to the situation. You were going to explain to me, if I remember rightly, exactly how to save my country from her impending doom, and you were also going to reveal to me various nefarious schemes directed against her."

"Imagination!" she declared. "Nothing that I said was true. It was just spite."

"Well, I don't know that it much matters," he observed, sipping his wine. "I didn't believe it, anyhow."

"Why didn't you believe it?" she demanded.

"Because," he told her, "I have had some conversation with Count Itash. I have come to the conclusion that that young man is not a fool. Under those circumstances I do not see how he could possibly have confided important political secrets to you. Nor can I conceive any sane reason for his having put them upon paper in such a fashion that you could have stolen them. Therefore, the existence of any means by which you could have read the riddles of Itash's brain does not seem to me possible."

"So, to put it in plain words," she suggested——

"I think that you were romancing."

She looked at him half mockingly, half in admiration.

"Really," she confessed, "I find you, for quite an ordinary person, unusually quick of perception."

"And to be equally honest," he rejoined, "I find you only attractive inasmuch as you are entirely removed from the commonplace. You are not good-looking enough to be a danseuse here. I am not sure that you dance well enough. You just have qualities that go to the ordinary man's head. And therefore shall we have one dance before I make my disappointed way back to the hotel?"

Again there was the beginning of that smile, which she seemed never to finish. They moved away to the music. When the dance was finished they found their way to two easy-chairs in a far corner of the Bar. She looked at him sombrely. The smile was no nearer breaking into fruition upon her lips.

"If I were not in love with Sammy," she acknowledged, "I think that I should rather like you."

"A pity about that subjunctive," he sighed. "I am not at all sure that he deserves you."

"If a man really deserved a woman," she said, "it is perfectly certain that the woman would not care for him. That always happens."

"It sounds platitudinal for you," he commented.

"Pooh!" she scoffed. "We all have to be reminded of the things we know best. I am, as you have suggested, plain, dull, altogether ordinary. Yet I have gifts. Sammy, at one time, loved me desperately. If he ceases to love me and puts another in my place, I shall destroy him. At present his passion has returned. He has been very sweet to me for many hours, and so, *Monsieur l'Américain,* let us say good-bye. He does not like you and it would do me no good to have him come here and find us together."

Grant rose to his feet and bent low over her fingers.

"Mademoiselle," he said, "I do not think that this is the end. You would doubtless prefer, under the circumstances, that I quit the restaurant."

"It would be to my advantage, in case Sammy should come," she admitted. "If you were with a party of your friends it would be another matter."

Twice, during that few hundred yards down to the front, Grant stopped, fancying that he was followed. Each time, if there had been a shadow behind, it faded away. He entered the Casino, which he seldom visited, without exactly knowing why, avoided the *Cercle Privé* and hung about the tables near the entrance where the stranger visitants to Monte Carlo congregate. He drew near a table and threw a louis on his favourite number. It lost the first time. He repeated his stake and won. He turned abruptly around, with his winnings, and was not in the least surprised to find Itash standing behind him.

"You are fortunate," the young man murmured equably.

"They are a small part of life, these games of chance," Grant replied.

Itash's dark eyes glowed behind their spectacles.

"Listen," he expounded. "If you treat life like a science to be lived by the direction of the brain, day by day, year by year, decade by decade, then life is a thing that grows dry as dust in the living. It counts only for the hucksters. But if one only realises — if one treats it as a gamble — a hundred-to-one chance, if you will — then life is entrancing."

"Philosophy on the floor of the Casino," Grant observed, smiling. "You haven't lost all your Orientalism, then, in Berlin and London?"

"I have only learnt to value it the more," was the calm reply. "Without it no man can do more than climb to the middle places. In this world one needs the gambler's instinct."

"You'd be a dangerous fellow," Grant remarked, "to be trusted with the whole of your patrimony within these walls."

Itash glanced at his watch and smiled.

"My whole patrimony, my name, and my honour," he said, "are already at stake, but it is not the spinning of a wheel which decides my fate. Will you take a little supper with me at the Carlton, Mr. Slattery? I have a friend who awaits me there — an acquaintance, also, I believe, of yours."

"With the utmost pleasure," Grant assented. "I only came in here because I was bored."

So they climbed the hill and went back to the Carlton. Cleo was still seated alone at her table. She watched the two men enter together, without change of countenance. Itash was very ceremonious.

"You have, I believe, already met my friend, Mr. Grant Slattery," he ventured.

"I have taken advantage of Mademoiselle's official position

here," Grant hastened to intervene. "I have given myself the pleasure of dancing with her."

"In that case, Mademoiselle will permit us to join her," Itash suggested. "But you have wine already upon your table, Cleo! How is that?"

She glanced at the bottle which Grant had left three quarters filled.

"They come here, these men, after a dance," she explained. "They order wine. The management prefers that I accept."

Itash waved it away impatiently and gave a fresh order. Nevertheless his eyes were sombrely lit.

"Amongst Orientals," he confided, "there is always one trait which survives — the trait of curiosity. Now that I have you here together, tell me, I beg, on what subject did you two converse so earnestly in the corner of the Bar there, last night — or was it two nights ago?"

"I was endeavouring to persuade Mademoiselle," Grant replied, "that the Tango, as a dance, is an incomplete affair. The most perfect dances in the world have been those in which the steps are absolutely registered — the minuet, for instance."

"I was venturing," Cleo murmured, "to disagree with Monsieur."

"It appeared," Itash reflected, "that you took the affair seriously."

"Dancing," Grant remarked, "is the profession of Mademoiselle. It happens to be my chief amusement."

Itash turned upon his guest. His question was asked with rapier-like suddenness.

"Your chief amusement, but not your only one, Monsieur?"

"I play golf, I sail my yacht a little, I am an indifferent hand at tennis," Grant acknowledged.

"You have no more serious occupation in life?" Itash demanded incredulously.

His guest leaned over the table.

"My friends," he told his two companions, "I started life trying to be serious. I was moderately well off. I needed a profession. I embraced diplomacy and then — see what happened to me. I was left seventeen million dollars, the whole of the Van

Roorden estate. Well, I confess it, I fell where many a better man has fallen before. I yielded to the call of wealth. I am an idle man now for the rest of my days."

Itash himself took the bottle from the ice pail, filled his own glass and Grant's to the brim. He appeared to have recovered his composure. The shadow of some fear seemed to have passed from him.

"It is what I have been told," he admitted. "Such wealth might dazzle any one. The spending of it might indeed enchain the imagination of the most ambitious on earth. So I drink to your health, Mr. Grant Slattery. I have had a nightmare. It has passed."

They drained their glasses. Itash was himself again. He leaned towards Cleo.

"You will dance with me?" he murmured.

She rose at once. Just then there was the bustle, in the entrance hall, of new arrivals. Gertrude and Arthur Lymane were being ushered in.

CHAPTER XII

The advantage was distinctly with Grant. His air of hurt reticence was admirably assumed. It chanced that, at the moment of leaving the yacht, Gertrude had confided to him that she had a headache and was going to bed immediately on her return to the hotel.

"My congratulations upon your speedy recovery," he murmured.

She was mistress of herself at once. She raised her eyebrows very slightly.

"Oh, my headache," she remarked. "A hot bath and an aspirin disposed of that. Mr. Lymane was a perfect dear and called just as I was wondering whether I should get up and try my luck at the Club, or go to bed. He suggested some supper and a dance here. I am so glad I came. I love this place, and I haven't been here this season. And you? Where are your friends?"

"I came here with the very interesting young man whom I met on the tennis courts," Grant replied. "They tell me that he plays tennis like a pro. Harris, our new secretary, says that he could give me fifteen and owe fifteen. In the other walks of life he is to be taken a little differently. His name is Itash and he is, I understand, devoted to the little danseuse who sits at this table."

The smile had faded from Gertrude's lips. She was looking into Grant's face as though her eyes would bore their way into the back of his brain.

"I should not have thought that a party of three would be very amusing for you," she remarked.

"The little danseuse is only a temporary addition," Grant explained. "I am certainly not making my host jealous, for he takes his protégée away whenever he chooses, and he insisted upon my coming. Still the position is not without its embarrassments. I am seriously thinking of cultivating one of these ladies for myself. There is a divine being opposite, with vermilion-coloured hair and eyes of the most enchanting shade of blue. I think I had better throw myself upon her mercy."

"Come and sit with us," Gertrude invited shortly.

"Not on any account," was the firm refusal. "I am already a *troisième* here. When I leave it will not be to accept a similar place elsewhere. Go and choose your table, you two. I am hurt, but not offended. I will even come and pay my respects later on. But at present, when my friends here have returned, I have an unconquerable desire to introduce myself to the young person with vermilion hair."

"What shall you say to her?" Gertrude asked.

"I shall say," he confided, "'Mademoiselle, I have these few recommendations to your favour. I am an American, as you see me, a millionaire, with a yacht in the harbour and a cheque book which I too seldom use. May I have the pleasure of this dance?'"

"It sounds interesting," Gertrude admitted. "She will probably refuse you. She will think you have drunk too much wine. Such good fortune would be incredible."

He rose to his feet.

"That remains to be seen," he said, taking leave of them with a little bow.

They watched him approach the girl whom he had pointed out, watched her rise with alacrity to her feet, and the commencement of the dance. Gertrude bit her lip as she followed Lymane to a table.

"Monte Carlo," she observed coldly, "is too small a place for these enterprises."

"Life is too short an affair to take notice of them," Lymane rejoined.

They chose their table, ordered wine and danced. Lymane murmured all the time in his companion's ear. Gertrude sometimes listened, sometimes watched the danseuse with the red hair. She seemed to be interested in Itash, but her eyes seldom left Grant and his partner.

"I wonder whether it is my fancy," she confided to her escort, as they sat down presently, "but it seems to me — I suppose it is because of this Nice Conference going on so near — that there is an electrical atmosphere everywhere. I feel as though there were rumblings underneath the earth, as though we were on the brink, all the time, of portentous events."

He smiled indulgently, yet in a slightly superior fashion.

"I don't think that you need be afraid," he said. "I think I can assure you that there are no cataclysms imminent at the moment."

"How can you tell?" she asked.

"Well," he pointed out, "for one thing, England, France, Germany, Japan, Italy, Spain, and a few of the smaller powers are linked hand in hand to preserve the peace of the world. There is no sign of war, no threat of war anywhere. We are all a little jealous of Germany, but industrially she deserves her success. Now, tell me, what form of cataclysm could descend upon the earth to justify your depression?"

"I think," she sighed, sipping her champagne, "that I am afraid of the end of the world."

"The end of the world," he observed, "is but a picturesque fable. The scientists have the matter well in hand. We are likely to have at least a thousand years of warning. My own apprehensions do not extend thus far."

She looked through the menu, which a hovering waiter had handed to her.

"Notwithstanding our wonderful dinner," she decided, "I should like a sandwich. And as it is not the end of the world which is coming and I honestly don't believe I have indigestion, will you tell me why I am so depressed?"

"I can only suggest," he ventured politely, "that it is because of your husband's arrival to-morrow."

"That," she declared, "is a crude remark, the sort of speech which betrays your youth. A man of the world, like Grant Slattery for instance, would never have made it."

"He would probably have hinted at it," was the somewhat sullen rejoinder, "and it would probably have been the truth."

"Well, I don't know," she murmured. "At any rate I am not going to discuss my husband's coming with you. I prefer a little consolation for these vague fears of mine. Do you honestly mean to tell me," she went on, "that the peace of the world is so wonderfully assured? Take these meetings of the Pact, for instance. Is there nothing there which gives cause for a moment's anxiety?"

"Princess!" he expostulated. "You will remember!"

"Heavens! Am I forgetting again!" she exclaimed. "You see, you're such a child, I always forget that you have an official connection with the great world. Of course you can say nothing. But then, as it happens, I know as much as you do. Prince Lutrecht is my husband's cousin. He came to my rooms for a few minutes this evening. I know all that transpires that can be told without an absolute breach of confidence. And I know that as yet there has been nothing serious."

"But you know there are rumours abroad?"

"Prince Lutrecht gave me a hint to-night. There is just one apple of discord that your Chief might throw upon the board."

"Shall we dance?" he begged.

She rose at once, quite willingly.

"You are a thoroughly irritating young man," she declared. "I shall send for Mr. Grant Slattery to come and talk to me. He seems to pick up a wonderful amount of information, and so does Prince Lutrecht. Even my husband hears things sometimes. No one has refused me information—only you. It is either because you don't like me or you don't trust me."

"I am not my own master," he reminded her, as they started off to dance. "As it is, I have spoken more freely with you than with any one else before in my life."

They danced until the music ceased. Gertrude clapped for the encore, and they went on until the finish. Then, as they walked towards their table, she continued their conversation.

"There is something you could tell me," she said, "because, if it is true, the whole world will know it in a day or so. Does Lord Yeovil mean to once more invite America to join the Pact?"

"You have heard that spoken of?"

"I have heard it stated for a fact."

"I believe it is true," he told her.

Grant's farewell shake of the hand possessed a particular significance for Mademoiselle with the red hair, whose rent was a little in arrears. She felt the crisp paper in her palm and flashed her thanks across at him.

"This is too good of Monsieur," she murmured. "Because he dances so beautifully. He has no need of a lesson. I am always at his disposition."

They separated, Mademoiselle to glance at her note and find her most sanguine hopes more than realised, Grant to rejoin Itash and his imperturbable companion.

"I am in danger here," he declared. "I am of so susceptible a temperament and Mademoiselle *aux cheveux roux* has spoken to me of the loneliness of her life. I think I shall go back to my hotel. The sea air to-day was very invigorating but it also makes one inclined to sleepiness. Besides, I am like an uneasy spirit to-night. Wherever I descend I find myself that terrible third. What happens to him in French fiction and on the stage, one knows. I think I'll depart quickly."

Itash smiled, showing his wonderful white teeth. He was more at ease now, and he was not without a sense of humour.

"Fetch Mademoiselle here," he suggested. "She is a very charming young woman and we will make a *partie carrée*. We will see the night through and end it in my rooms with breakfast."

Grant shook his head.

"I am no longer of the age when such things attract," he sighed. "Besides which, I detest an aftermath. The nights which end with bacon and eggs and coffee offend me. I prefer they terminate with the playing of the violin to the door, the bow of the Commissionaire, the little *voiture*."

"Monsieur has sentiment," Cleo murmured.

"I cling to what remains of it," Grant assured her earnestly. "When sentiment goes, then life is like the dust which the Persian poet tells us about. And so, all you young people, farewell."

He made his bow, collected his hat and coat, and departed. He left the place with the air of a conqueror. He looked back at it, metaphorically shaking his fist.

"This is a sorry triumph," he muttered, as he lit a cigarette. "There is that ass Lymane gassing away to Gertrude — thank heavens he doesn't know much — and Mademoiselle Cleo, back again under the thrall, close-lipped, close-tongued, with enough locked up at the back of her brain to make the way easy for all of us."

"Monsieur desires something?" the Commissionaire asked him wonderingly.

"Nothing in the world," Grant replied, slipping a five-franc note into his hand. "I am perfectly happy. I am going home to bed."

The man took off his hat and bowed.

"A pleasant repose to Monsieur," he said.

CHAPTER XIII

THEY sat in the luncheon room at Mont d'Agel, three very hungry but well-satisfied beings, Lord Yeovil, Susan, and Grant. They sipped their apéritifs and waited for their luncheon, "contented but eager," to use Susan's own expression.

"The match was a good one," Grant conceded, "but no Prime Minister has a right to hole out like your father, Lady Susan. Affairs of state and all that sort of thing ought to interfere and make him raise his head."

"That putt at the sixteenth was sheer robbery," she agreed.

"An excellent match," Lord Yeovil declared. "Placing you at scratch, Grant, and Susan at twelve, men's handicap, the fact that I was able to halve the match against you would seem to indicate my having played somewhere about six. Six is above my form."

"I think, with the exception of the drive which you sliced from the eighth tee, Dad, and which landed in Italy," Susan observed, "you were playing better than six."

"The game has restored my faith in my powers of concentration," her father announced. "I said to myself, every nation in the world may be at one another's throats to-morrow, my resignation may be demanded before I return to England, I may march out of Downing Street, bag and baggage, the day of my return, but I will not take my eye off the ball this morning, and I didn't."

"Plumb in the centre, every time," Grant agreed. "Hurray! Here come the *hors d'œuvres*."

"It is not my custom to drink wine in the middle of the day," Lord Yeovil said, "but I think we must supplement the *vin ordinaire* a little—*Montrachet,* perhaps, or *Château Yquem?*"

"This is a terrible start to a strenuous day," Grant remarked, "To-night I dine with Delilah."

Susan looked across the table at him a little curiously.

"I am glad that you admit the attraction."

"I never found any one who knew her and was willing to deny it," Grant rejoined.

"Quite right," his host assented. "Thank heavens that I am no longer a young man. I fancy that I should find the Princess irresistible."

"When I knew her first," Grant continued reminiscently, "she was a simple American girl, living upon a farm, riding three hours every day, playing a little tennis, doing a little housekeeping. Then she had a season in Washington. After that she became somehow the vogue. A town aunt took her up. It was about that time that Von Diss fell so desperately in love with her."

"She was a fool to marry him," Lord Yeovil declared. "Even now, after all these years, a German or an Austrian woman finds it difficult to hold her own. In Berlin the aristocracy, especially, at any rate until about ten years ago, have had a hideous time."

"There's a reaction going on now," Grant reminded him.

"As we well know," the older man assented. "Chiefly owing, I honestly believe, to that fascinating youth, Prince Frederick. A most charming lad. I only hope that Lutrecht and our dear friend's husband, Von Diss, and the others of that régime don't get hold of him and spoil him. By the bye, I am breaking my rule by speaking of such affairs in a public place, and Arthur isn't here to correct me. I wonder why you are not English, Grant. You would have made a wonderful secretary for me."

"I'd rather have been an Englishman than belong to any other race, if I hadn't been an American, sir," Grant answered. "As it is, I am naturally content."

"Au revoir to conversation," his host remarked, watching the approach of their first course. "I now become a glutton. Appetite is, after all, a most entrancing thing."

"During this regrettable silence of my father's," Susan observed, as she helped herself from one of the dishes, "you and I had better exchange a few ideas, Grant. You don't seem to have had much time for me lately."

"Dear Lady Susan," he bemoaned, "the amenities of life have

seemed to lie outside the orbit of my jurisdiction the last few days."

"You always pose as being so busy," she scoffed. "What do you do with yourself?"

"Solve bridge problems, inspect my crew on the *Grey Lady*, lose my *mille* or two, eat, drink, and sleep. It is a most enthralling existence."

"You seem to have left out a few little things," she remarked. "There's the Princess, for instance. I thought that it was rather the object of your life just now to entertain her."

"Others have shared that task with me," he replied. "To-night I dine with her. We shall probably be very sentimental. I shall ask her whether she is entirely happy with the man she preferred to me. She will sigh and tears will stand in my eyes as I look through the wall. Then we shall part with a little gulp. I may kiss her fingers and she will go and powder her nose, put on a becoming *peignoir* and listen for the train. I foresee a sentimental evening."

"Something has happened to you," Susan declared. "You used not to be so sentimental, or so cynical."

"A great deal has happened to me," he agreed. "In three days' time, Lady Susan, if you will trust me so far, I will tell you a most entrancing story."

"And, in the meantime," she reminded him, a little coldly, "the tears will stand in your eyes, and you will look through the wall, whilst thinking of the woman you have loved."

"Those things have to be," he apologised.

"For what purpose?" she demanded. "Where is the necessity? Have you anything to gain, for instance, by flirting with the Princess? Or do you do it to indulge in a sort of sentimental debauch—to go through it and then analyse your feelings? Because——"

She was suddenly silent. She felt that, in a sense, she had betrayed herself. Her father glanced at her across the table. Grant saved the situation.

"You read me like a book, Lady Susan," he acknowledged. "You always do. As a matter of fact, a passion for diluted psychology of an analytical type stopped my taking honours at

Harvard, and will, without a doubt, interfere with my complete success in life. I am hideously curious about little things. Still, I offer no apologies. The Princess has stirred colder hearts than mine."

"If I were your age," Lord Yeovil declared, helping himself to omelette unselfishly, and yet with discretion, "there is nothing in this world which would prevent my being in love with the Princess."

"I am glad that you recognise my difficulties," Grant said gratefully.

"Experience has such a charm for the very young," Susan observed, a little sarcastically.

"After all, it's rather a relief," Grant observed, looking round the room, "to be free for an hour or two from this little host of intriguers. Here we are with a crowd of strangers, amongst whom I only recognise our very excellent friend Baron Funderstrom, the Scandinavian. None of the others are here. I fancy that this atmosphere is a little too bracing for them. We are in a different world. Intrigue up here is unknown—except the intrigue of cutting in."

"Dashed annoying intrigue, too, when it comes off," Lord Yeovil grumbled. "Are you two young people going to play again? Because, I tell you frankly that I am not. I'll send the car back for you with pleasure. A nap in my study for the next hour or two is the thing which appeals to me most."

"Just as Lady Susan wishes," Grant said, looking towards her.

"I should like another round, unless it bores you," she decided.

Their final round was played in the brilliant declining sunlight of a perfect Riviera afternoon. The wind had dropped and brought no longer icy reminiscences from the snow-clad Alps. The air, though keen, was sweet and laden with the fragrance of the trees in blossom, which fringed the slopes of the hills. More than once they paused to look downwards. Susan was, for her, a little listless.

"I don't think you're really enjoying the Riviera this year," he remarked.

"I'm not sure that I am," she admitted. "Somehow or other, from the moment we arrived, we seem to have lived in an unfamiliar atmosphere. I can't explain it. Baron Naga's death seemed to be part of it. Dad bluffs most beautifully but he is all the time nervous and on edge. You — although I don't know what you have to do with it all — seem to be living half in this world and half in some other you won't talk about. Arthur has the air of a man about to commit suicide. The Lancasters are the only normal people, and perhaps that is because they are brainless. What's it all about, Grant? Have you really lost your head about this old sweetheart of yours? And is there really any cause for Dad to worry? All these politicians who come to call are so delightfully amiable and polite that one can't realise that they may not be absolutely sincere."

"I'm not going to try and bluff to you, Lady Susan," Grant said seriously. "I'm afraid there may be trouble afoot. We can't quite get to grips with it, but it's there. We have indications of it, and warnings from all sorts of unsuspected quarters. Personally, I think your father is in a very awkward position. You see the great difficulty is that, however hard he tries, he can't find out exactly how things really do stand. When the Pact was inaugurated, all the nations started trusting one another. They dropped secret treaties and secret understandings and swept the whole of their Secret Service departments into the four corners of the world, — that is to say, the honest ones did. Consequently, now there's trouble about, we don't know where to turn."

"But you?" she protested. "You're out of it all. You're not even English. Why are you so disturbed?"

He smiled as he watched his ball go travelling over a bunker.

"Let it alone, Lady Susan," he begged. "You're the one person outside it all. Stop outside for a time. If the trouble comes you will know of it fast enough."

She was not altogether satisfied.

"Is it my fancy," she asked, "or am I being treated like some one just emerged from the nursery?"

"My dear Lady Susan," he pointed out, "it wouldn't do you a bit of good to be let into your father's worries or mine. And they very likely don't amount to anything, after all."

She shrugged her shoulders.

"Do you talk like this to the Princess?" she queried.

He smiled.

"I should certainly not tell the Princess the things you are asking me," he assured her.

"I suppose I am a cat," Susan reflected, "but I don't like the Princess."

"You'll like her when you know her better," he ventured.

"I don't want to know her any better," she declared. "She seems to me the sort of woman who makes use of people. That's what I can't help thinking about you, and her, and Arthur."

"What use can she make of us?" he asked.

"She wants to get to know things, for the sake of that husband of hers, I suppose. It's all very well for you, but I do think Arthur ought to be more careful. Father never says much but I fancy he's thinking a good deal."

They finished the round almost in silence, and their conversation over tea was negligible. On the way down, Grant was conscious of a sudden fear. Susan, after all, was a creature of impulse. These purgatorial days through which he and the others were passing, meant nothing to her. She might fail to make allowance for them. She was always surrounded by young men, and, for the moment at any rate, she was seriously annoyed with him.

"Lady Susan," he began.

"Mr. Slattery."

"I thought it was generally 'Grant'," he remonstrated.

"I have heard myself called 'Susan'," she reminded him.

"Look here, then, Susan," he recommenced. "We seem to have got wrong somehow. I don't like it. I want to be friends."

"My dear man," she protested, "have I shown any signs of quarrelling with you?"

"You're annoyed, and I don't want you to be."

"Does it really make any difference?" she asked a little bitterly.

"Of course it does."

"Do something to please me then, will you?"

"Anything," he declared, with foolish optimism.

"Don't dine with that Von Diss woman to-night."

He was distressed.

"My dear Susan!" he expostulated. "I can't get out of it."

"Had you asked her to dine with you or did she invent that on the yacht?"

"She invented it on the yacht," he admitted. "At the same time I accepted it, and, to tell you the truth, Susan, for certain reasons, I really am anxious to dine with her."

"The certain reasons being, I suppose, that she may go on making love to you in the flagrant way she did on the yacht."

"Do you mind whether she does or not?"

"Not in the least," she declared untruthfully.

"Then it wouldn't be any use my asking you——"

She turned suddenly towards him with a touch of her old manner.

"You can ask me anything you like, Grant, if only you'll promise not to dine with her to-night."

He was half embarrassed, half irritated. She was, after all, such a child.

"Susan," he begged, "be reasonable."

"What a horrible suggestion!" she scoffed. "I'll be reasonable when I'm middle-aged,—when nothing matters. I'm a very foolish person, of course, but it does happen to matter a good deal to me that you insist upon dining with that woman to-night. To prove how unreasonable I am—*voilà!*"

The car had been crawling round the corner of the Square, and Susan jumped lightly onto the footpath. She waved her hand to Grant.

"Thanks so much for the game," she said. "I'm going to talk to Bobby and Rose."

She waved her hand once more and started off to join her friends. Grant stopped his car by the pavement.

"Look here, you can't leave me like that," he protested. "Your father left you in my care."

"Can't help it," she replied. "You were beginning to bore me, so I had to escape."

"But how are you getting out to the Villa?" he asked.

"Bobby will take me. Won't you, Bobby?"

"Rather!" that young man promised. "Push off, Grant! You've had a pretty good innings, old chap. We haven't seen anything of

Susan all day. Come along! We'll have mixed vermouths over at the Café de Paris, gamble for half an hour, then we'll get rid of Rose, and I'll take you home in a *petite voiture*."

"It's a desperate enterprise, but I accept," she declared. "Good-by, Grant! Hope you enjoy your dinner."

"I shall do my best," he answered, with a little unnecessary emphasis.

CHAPTER XIV

"WELL!"

The monosyllable was suggestive, almost illuminative. Gertrude had paused for a moment on the threshold of the little salon, which she was entering from her bedchamber. Her unexpected visitor, Mr. Cornelius Blunn, looked across at her with a deprecating smile.

"I am a monument of apologies, Princess," he said.

"We will take them for granted, then," she replied. "What do you want?"

He glanced at the clock.

"Five minutes' conversation," he begged, "or, if by any fortunate chance, you are disengaged —— "

"You know quite well that I am dining with Mr. Slattery," she interrupted.

"I had imagined so," he assented. "It is about that dinner engagement that I venture to come and see you."

"You will, I trust, avoid impertinence."

"I shall try," he assured her. "Princess, your mission here was a difficult one. So far you have performed it with much skill."

"I am flattered," she murmured, with latent irony.

"I may or may not share your opinion as to Mr. Grant Slattery," he continued, "but, in other respects, you have done well. I am here to beg you not to spoil the good effects of your work."

"Will you please say what you want to in as few and as plain words as possible," she invited.

"I obey," he answered, with a little bow. "You came here to try and solve for us a somewhat vexed question concerning this young man, Mr. Grant Slattery. You think that you have arrived at the truth concerning him. I am going to be frank with you and tell you that I am not so sure. But I am convinced of one thing, — you have gone as far as Otto would approve in your investigations."

"You think that I am likely to lose my head about this man?" she asked.

Blunn made no reply. She waited for a moment and then glanced towards the clock.

"Otto is my friend," he went on, "and Otto, as you know, is of a very jealous temperament. I think you would be wiser to cancel your dinner engagement for this evening."

"For a clever man," she said deliberately, "I think you are the biggest fool I ever knew."

"I am your husband's friend, and yours," he reminded her quietly.

"Listen," she continued. "Otto sent me here and you know my mission. I shall perform it in just the way I think best. What there is to be said about my methods can come from him. You mean well, I think, but anything which you said would be useless."

"Princess," Mr. Blunn remonstrated, "you're a young woman and you have the strong will of your nationality. I am an elderly man and I claim the right of speaking to you frankly. You are going to spend the evening with a man whom three years ago you treated disgracefully. The instinct for atonement is a very dangerous thing."

"Perhaps," she admitted. "At any rate, I am my own mistress. What I choose to give, I give, and nothing that you could say, no threat that you could utter, would induce me to change."

"Your mind is made up, Princess?"

"My mind is utterly and finally made up."

There was a knock at the door. A messenger from below announced the arrival of a gentleman for Madame la Princesse.

"You can show him up," Gertrude directed.

The man bowed and left the room. Blunn looked across at her and frowned.

"You will receive him here, in your salon?" he asked.

"Certainly," she replied. "If it pleased me to do so I should dine here. I am responsible to no one for what I may choose to do."

Still he made no movement to depart.

"It seems to be my hard fate to anger you, Princess," he regretted. "And I can assure you that such is not my desire. Yet this I must tell you, that I am used to men, and watching men, and turning them inside out, judging them from their characters and actions and the trifles which escape other people. I have never yet been wrong. This man Slattery is, in my opinion, all that we believed him to be. In my opinion, he is playing a game of his own with you. You think that you have discovered him harmless; you think that his devotion to you is real. You are wrong. You are wrong in both conclusions."

She smiled. At that moment she was praying that the confidence which her smile was intended to indicate really existed in her heart.

"I think," she declared, "that a woman is the best judge of a man's affection for her. I may put Mr. Slattery's to the test. If I do, I have no fears."

There was a knock at the door. Grant was ushered in. Gertrude gave him her fingers. He raised them to his lips and turned towards Blunn.

"Have no fear," the latter said. "I am an uninvited guest and I was just taking my leave. Princess, you will allow me once more to assure you that I never make a mistake."

She laughed a little scornfully.

"The Kingdom of Fools is peopled by the men who never make mistakes," she answered.

The door closed upon Blunn. She came a little nearer to Grant.

"What did that fellow want?" he demanded.

"To warn me against you," she replied.

"What a busybody!"

"He has disappointed me," she remarked. "I never dreamed that he was the sort of person who would come and talk to a woman as her husband's friend. Such a terribly obvious attitude."

"And how ignorant he showed himself of you and your capacity for resistance."

She came a little nearer to him, raised her eyes, and stood for a moment silent.

"Do you remember the last time you kissed me, Grant?"

"Perfectly well," he answered. "I stayed with you half an hour after we got back from the opera. I must have interfered with your packing, I'm afraid."

He saw her wince, but he remained unmoved. He was smiling at her pleasantly, regarding her with genuine admiration.

"You look wonderful to-night, Gertrude," he said.

"Then why don't you want to kiss me?" she asked.

"A psychological problem insoluble before dinner," he assured her with faint irony.

"Then you don't want to," she persisted.

He leaned forward, holding her for a moment in his arms, yet gently resisting the abandon of her swaying body. He kissed her on the eyes, drew her hand through his arm, and turned towards the door.

"Five minutes later and Louis would never forgive me," he said. "He is preparing for us——"

The sentence was never finished. The door was suddenly opened without a knock or any form of warning. A man, in travelling clothes, and carrying a small despatch case, entered.

"Otto!" Gertrude exclaimed, disengaging her arm from Grant's. "How on earth did you get here—to-night?"

He frowned irritably.

"I sent a telegram," he replied. "You did not, perhaps, receive it. We found a quicker route. May I be presented to this gentleman?"

"It is Mr. Grant Slattery," Gertrude murmured. "My husband, Prince von Diss."

The two men bowed. Neither extended a hand.

"You can scarcely expect me to bid you welcome very heartily," Grant said, with a secret strain of thanksgiving in his heart. "I was to have had the pleasure of taking your wife out to dinner."

Prince von Diss glanced around him. He had a most unpleasant face, short, fair moustache, carefully trimmed, well-cut features, a wicked mouth, and cold, unprepossessing eyes. He was very nearly bald.

"I was not aware, Gertrude," he observed, "that it was your custom to receive your friends in your salon at an hotel of this description."

"I do as I think well in such matters," she answered calmly.

There was a moment's hectic silence. The Prince seemed about to speak but controlled himself with an effort.

"You are probably fatigued with travelling," she continued, "and would prefer to dine here. In that case I can keep my engagement with Mr. Slattery."

"On the contrary, I shall beg you to break it," the Prince declared emphatically. "It is a peculiarity of mine, but I do not permit my wife to dine alone with any man so long as I am within reach. I shall hope to have another opportunity of cultivating Mr. Slattery's acquaintance."

"I will provide you with one gladly," Grant answered, without hesitation.

Gertrude laid her hand upon his arm.

"I do not allow my friends to quarrel with my husband," she said. "I am very sorry indeed about our dinner, Grant. When will you come and see me?"

"Whenever you choose, Gertrude."

"To-morrow at four o'clock. You will take tea with me here. In the meantime I cannot tell you how much I regret our dinner."

Grant was suddenly conscious of the ridiculous side of the situation. He pulled himself together and turned to the newcomer courteously.

"Perhaps you, as well as your wife, would do me the honour of dining?" he suggested. "Dinner is ordered downstairs. Half-an-hour's delay will be of no consequence."

The Prince bowed coldly.

"I thank you very much, sir," he replied, "but to-night I shall prefer to dine tête-à-tête with my wife. I have affairs to attend to. We shall without doubt meet again."

Grant dined alone in a distant corner of the restaurant, somewhat to his own satisfaction, but very much to the disappointment of the *maître d'hôtel* to whom he had confided his orders. Just as he was finishing, Gertrude and her husband entered the room. The latter had changed his clothes but appeared to be in no better humour. He scowled at Grant and ignored his wife, both when he ordered the dinner and the wine. She leaned back in her chair, fanning herself lazily. Her eyes continually sought Grant's. On the way out he paused for a moment at their table. She made a little grimace of apprehension, but Grant only smiled.

"You have made a very greedy man of me, Princess," he confessed. "I have had to try and eat the dinner I had ordered for two."

"I wish you'd sent me my share," she said. "I have not been consulted about our own, anyway, and I seem to have heard the name of every dish I detest."

Her husband spoke for the first time.

"The marital feast cloys, I am afraid," he sneered.

"I have no doubt but that you are right," Grant assented, with a little bow of farewell. "I'm not married myself, but one seems to discover these things."

He passed out into the hall and stood for a moment smiling to himself. Then, prompted by a sudden impulse, he opened one of the telephone boxes and rang up the Villa Miranda. In a minute or two Susan came to the telephone.

"What on earth do you want?" she enquired. "You ought to be in the middle of dinner."

"I am supplanted," he replied.

"What do you mean? Arthur?" she asked with some excitement.

"Worse! Her husband! The Prince arrived twelve hours before he was expected. It was most awkward."

"So you haven't dined with her?"

"He refused to let me. Gertrude did her best but it was quite useless. You should see him, Susan. He's an insufferable little bounder."

"You would have dined with her, then, if he had not arrived?" she asked, after a moment's pause.

"Naturally."

"Well, good night."

"Stop a minute," he insisted. "If I came around —— "

"Don't come to-night," she interrupted. "Father's going to bed in a few minutes, and I'm going round to the Lancasters. They've some friends in to dance."

"Why didn't they ask me?" he grumbled.

"You're supposed to be engaged," she reminded him. "Good-by."

"Aren't you a little —— "

The instrument whirred in his ear. He was disconnected.

"Little cat!" Grant shouted down the instrument. But he was too late. There was no reply.

Grant, who was living on the yacht, had already commenced to undress when the sight of the moon through the porthole window brought him up on deck again. He sank into a basket chair, filled his pipe and sat smoking. The gangway which connected the stern of the yacht to the dock had been pulled in and there was no sound of any movement on board. The Casino was in darkness, but the Sporting Club was still brilliantly illuminated, and here and there on the hillside lights shone out from the villas. A sort of violet curtain of twilight seemed to brood over the place. An automobile with flashing lamps swung around the corner and dashed along the road to Nice. A *voiture* came down the steep incline towards the harbour. Momentarily curious, Grant watched it. It came along the dockway to within fifty yards of the yacht. Then it stopped. A woman descended and came swiftly along the jetty. The light from an electric standard flashed upon the jewels in her hair as she passed, and Grant sprang suddenly to his feet. He walked hastily towards the stern. The woman had paused, looking at the little chasm of water. She moved out of the shadows and he recognised her.

"Gertrude!" he cried.

"Please put down the gangway," she called out. "I want to come on board."

A sailor on night duty hurried forward. Grant gave a brief order and a gangplank was lowered. It was he, however, who made use of it. He met Gertrude at the shore end and gently led her on one side.

"Gertrude," he told her firmly, "it is impossible for you to come on board at this hour of the night. Tell me what has happened."

She was looking very white and very determined. She put her arm through his and clung to him.

"Grant," she said. "He took me away from you once, and he wasn't altogether honest about it. If you like you can take me back again."

"My dear Gertrude!" he exclaimed.

"I mean it," she went on. "I know everything that is in your mind. I don't care. If I am worth having, take me. Otto has brought it upon himself. I think that I dislike him more than any human being upon the earth."

All the time he was leading her back slowly towards the waiting *voiture*.

"Gertrude," he insisted, "this is not a possibility."

"Why not?" she demanded. "You're your own master. You could steam away to-morrow morning before any one was about. You told me only the other day that you were always ready for an emergency."

"Quite true," he agreed. "But not this emergency."

"He has insulted me," she declared, "and he's insufferable. No self-respecting woman ought to marry a German. She becomes a worse chattel than the plaything of a Mohammedan."

"I am terribly sorry for you," Grant assured her, "but what you are contemplating now would only make matters worse. You must remember this, too. Your husband is a Roman Catholic. He would never divorce you."

She was silent.

"You don't want me," she muttered.

"Perhaps I don't want you in the spirit in which you have come," he answered gently. "You simply want to revenge yourself upon your husband and you offer me the chance of revenging myself, too. It isn't quite a big enough feeling, Gertrude. The satisfaction of it wouldn't last for the rest of our lives."

"Since when have you learnt to preach?" she scoffed.

"A man doesn't need to preach to hesitate about taking another man's wife," he rejoined. "This is just an impulse of yours, Gertrude."

She tried to drag him back toward the gangway.

"Let me come on the yacht," she begged. "I mean it. I don't care even if he won't divorce me."

"You're not coming on," he insisted. "Not to-night, at any rate."

She looked at him with quick suspicion.

"Have you any one else there?" she demanded.

"You know very well that I have not," he answered indignantly. "Adventures of that sort do not appeal to me."

"Very well," she said. "You won't let me yield to one impulse. You can't prevent my yielding to another. I have a disclosure to make. I came to Monte Carlo to spy on you."

"I knew that quite well," he replied.

"Knew it? How could you?"

"Because the newspaper you showed me with my name on bore the yellow pencil marks of your Secret Service."

"Well," she went on, "I haven't made much of you,—I've learnt more from Arthur Lymane. But I've found out a few things and my people are content with what seem to be trifles. You won't let me give myself away. I'll give them away. They know that Lord Yeovil is going to propose an invitation to America to join the Pact. They'll pretend to acquiesce. In reality they're going to vote against it."

"Three of them, perhaps," Grant interposed quickly. "Which one have they induced to be the fourth?"

"That is what I am going to tell you," she said. "Baron Funderstrom."

"The Scandinavian!" Grant exclaimed.

"It has cost them fifty thousand pounds," she continued, "but they have his promise. Four votes and the motion is lost. Those four are arranged for. Now do you believe that I am in earnest when I tell you that I hate my husband? Do you still forbid me to come on the yacht?"

"Yes," he answered.

He was standing with his hand upon the rail of the gangplank. She came close to him. Her eyes were filled with tears. "Let me come, Grant," she begged. "I will be content just to be cared for as you used to care for me. I don't mind what happens to me. You can hide me away, if you like. You can come back here alone if you want. I won't complain. Only I must have some one kind to me. Let me come, please."

His arm barred the way.

"Gertrude," he said, "this may hurt but it's best. I care for some one else. I couldn't have you on the yacht. It wouldn't be honest."

"Some one else!" she muttered. "Well, why not?"

She stood away for a moment, on the edge of the dock. She was looking down at the waters of the harbour. He caught her by the arm.

"Gertrude," he asked, "do you think that they will have missed you yet?"

"I don't think so," she answered dully. "They were all talking in Blunn's rooms. Some one else, Grant! Why didn't you tell me?"

"We were both playing a game," he declared. "You were trying to learn my secrets. I was trying to learn yours."

"Who is she?"

"That doesn't matter, does it? I'm not in the least sure of her or about her, but you see — well, I had to tell you, hadn't I?"

He led her towards the *voiture*. Even when they reached it she looked longingly back at the yacht.

"It would have been such wonderful freedom," she sighed. "You used to care, Grant. I thought that you used to care quite a great deal."

He handed her into the carriage and tucked the rug around her. The hand which he touched was cold.

"The Hotel de Paris, '‚he told the man.

She leaned back without another word. He listened to the horses' hoofs ringing on the hard macadam road. As they turned the corner she waved her hand, — a pitiful little salute.

CHAPTER XV

THE spray came flashing back like drops of crystal sunlight from the bows of the *Grey Lady* as she rose and dipped, ploughing her way southwards in the teeth of a stiff breeze. The rolling blue of the Mediterranean was crested with multitudinous little white caps. Sometimes the wind lifted the foam bodily from the breaking waves and dashed it like a shower of April rain across the white decks. Susan, holding fast to the rail, tossed her head back to let the wind sweep through her hair.

"It's wonderful, Grant," she exclaimed. "This is the best day we've ever had on the *Grey Lady*. The wind's getting up, too, isn't it?"

"It's freshening a little, I think," Grant admitted. "Thank heavens, you're all good sailors."

"Upon me, when sailing," Cornelius Blunn declared, "the sea has a pernicious and devastating effect. It gives me appetite, it gives me thirst, it fills me with the joy of life. Yet no sooner do I set my foot upon an ocean steamer than I am incapacitated. It is amazing!"

"I'm glad you mentioned that—the little matter of thirst," Grant observed, smiling. "It is a long time between afternoon tea and cocktails. We must introduce Baron Funderstrom to my famous Scotch whisky. Let's go into the smoke room. They've got the fiddles on the table."

Baron Funderstrom, a tall, gloomy man, grey-haired, grey-bearded, grey-visaged, of neutral outlook and tired manners, accepted the invitation without enthusiasm or demur. He drank two whiskys and sodas quite patiently.

"It is good whisky," he pronounced.

"It is wonderful," Blunn agreed. "It reminds me of what I used to drink in my younger days."

"It is not so potent as our own," Baron Funderstrom remarked. "One could drink a great deal of this without discomfort."

His eyes were upon the decanter. Grant refilled their glasses.

"Wonderful!" Blunn repeated. "Mr. Slattery, you are the best host in the world. Never shall I forget our first picnic on board this yacht. It is amazing that you should invite us again so soon. Tell me—you will not think I am presuming, I am sure—but our invitation, as I received it, was a little vague. Do we dine on board to-night, or are we to be landed?"

"You dine on board most certainly," Grant announced. "If this wind continues, we may not be able to land you until quite late in the evening. However, I think that I can promise that my larder and my cellar will be equal to any demands we can put upon them."

"So far as one can judge," the Scandinavian observed, "they are capable of anything. It is a great thing to own a yacht like this. It's the acme of luxury. Speaking of returning, though, Mr. Slattery, you will not forget that we have to leave for Nice at nine o'clock to-morrow morning."

"That's all right," Grant assured him. "The wind always goes down with the twilight."

"When shall we change our course?" Cornelius Blunn enquired, looking out of the porthole.

"Presently. It's pleasanter to make a straight run out."

Prince von Diss swaggered into the smoke room. He seemed smaller than ever in his nautical blue serge, and he was perhaps not quite such a good sailor as the others. He was certainly looking a little pinched.

"Mr. Slattery," he said, in a loud and important tone, "I have been talking to your navigator. Isn't it almost time we altered our course? We have been out of sight of land for an hour and more."

"I expect Captain Martin knows what he's about," Grant observed coolly. "Come and try this whisky, Prince, or would you prefer a brandy and soda?"

"I never drink spirits," was the prompt reply. "Wine, if you have any."

"I have some Clicquot—a very excellent year."

"I will drink some Clicquot," Prince von Diss decided.

They all sat down again while the steward produced an ice pail. There was a disposition on Blunn's part to forget that they had been drinking whisky and soda. Grant managed to slip away. He reached the deck and sat down by Gertrude's side.

"Really," she observed, with her eyes fixed upon the horizon, "we might almost be taking that sea voyage."

He smiled.

"A marvellously favourable wind!"

"Are they all right?" she asked, dropping her voice a little.

"Perfectly contented, so far! They've begun on champagne now after whisky and soda. I'm hoping that they may feel like a nap before dinner."

"Champagne!" she murmured. "That's Otto, I'm sure. He never drinks anything else. I don't think, though," she went on, "that you'll ever get him to drink enough to make him sleepy. When do you think the trouble will come?".

"Not until after dinner," Grant assured her. "I shall set the course a little differently before then. As soon as it is necessary to get steam up, I shall be sent for down to the engine room."

"Really, life might have been very amusing," she sighed, "if only——"

"It will be amusing enough presently," he interrupted. "I can see that your husband is already in rather an uncertain mood,—ready to make trouble at the slightest provocation."

"Our friend the Baron, I should think, will remain perfectly philosophical, especially if he has already touched the fifty thousand pounds," Gertrude declared. "He's the most colourless person I have ever met."

Cornelius Blunn came out of the smoking room and walked towards them. His expression was inclined to be thoughtful. He stood for a moment watching their course. Then he looked at the sun.

"You'll have a long beat back," he remarked to Grant.

"I shall steam back," the latter told him. "We're sailing now—for one thing, because it's so much pleasanter, and the women enjoy it so."

"I'm not a nautical man," Blunn confessed, "but I presume it would be impossible to get back under canvas."

"With this wind it would take us at least twenty-four hours," Grant acknowledged. "I don't think we should make it then. Nowadays every yacht of any size has auxiliary power of a sort."

"We would wish to avoid even the appearance of interfering with your arrangements," Blunn said, "but you will not forget that our friend, Baron Funderstrom, is a delegate; that means he must leave for Nice at nine o'clock to-morrow morning."

"He'll be back before midnight."

"It is rather a pity Lord Yeovil was not able to join us. We should have felt quite safe with him here."

"He and Lymane are hard at it, getting things ready for to-morrow," Grant explained. "It isn't very often he misses a day on the sea. What about a rubber of bridge before dinner? I'll order a table."

He strolled away. Blunn turned towards Gertrude. He looked at her for a moment thoughtfully.

"Has anything about this cruise struck you as being in any way peculiar?" he asked.

"Why, no," she replied. "It all seems very pleasant. Mr. Slattery is a wonderful host."

"Marvellous!" he assented. "Still, I don't quite see why he's standing such a long way out or why he was so particularly anxious to have Funderstrom as a guest. Funderstrom is not an attractive man."

"As a matter of fact, it was I who suggested him," she admitted. "And having once mentioned his name, I suppose Mr. Slattery was trying to be civil."

"It was you who suggested him," Blunn repeated thoughtfully. "Ah, well, we shall see. I expect I'm being very foolish. We shall soon know."

"I don't know about being foolish but you're very mysterious," Gertrude said, with slightly uplifted eyebrows.

"It is because I am on the scent of a mystery," he replied. "A crude mystery, a clumsy affair, without a doubt—but still a mystery. We shall see."

It was a significant fact to Cornelius Blunn that cocktails were introduced before the accustomed time and pressed upon every one to the limits of hospitality. Grant, himself, who was, as a rule, exceedingly moderate, set an example by drinking one every time they came round, and when they descended into the saloon for dinner, there were magnums of champagne upon the table.

"When we get on deck after dinner," he announced, "we shall be headed for the land and under steam."

"At what time do you propose to get rid of us?" Gertrude asked.

"In time for a final flutter at the Casino, if you're keen about it," he assured her.

The service of dinner proceeded. The wine circulated, conversation, which had languished at first, soon became gay, even uproarious. Cornelius Blunn alone seemed to be scarcely in his usual spirits. He looked often out of the porthole; more than once he glanced at the clock.

"What about the course, now?" he asked his host once.

"We are round by this time," Grant answered. "You'll hear the engines directly."

Another half an hour passed, however, and the engines remained silent. Then one of the junior officers came in and whispered in Grant's ear. He laid down his table napkin.

"May I be excused for a minute?" he begged. "A matter of etiquette. My engineer always has to consult me. A perfect bluff, of course."

He was gone about ten minutes. When he came back they all looked at him a little curiously. It was Gertrude who became spokeswoman.

"Is anything wrong, Grant?" she asked. "We're not going to be shipwrecked or anything, are we?"

"Not a chance of it," he assured her. "I wish there were. I'd show you what an Admirable Crichton I should make. As a matter of fact, there's a little trouble with one of the pistons. We may not be able to get going for an hour or so."

There was a brief silence. Then Susan laughed gaily.

"What fun! Shall we have to sleep on board?"

"Not so bad as that, I don't suppose," was the cheerful reply. "If you do, though, I fancy we can manage to make you comfortable. Bad luck it's a head wind, or we could beat in. We're gaining a little all the time, as it is."

Baron Funderstrom finished his glass of champagne and looked to see if there was any more in the nearest bottle.

"There will be no doubt, I trust, about my being landed in time to get to Nice to-morrow?" he enquired.

"Not the slightest," Grant promised, making a sign to the steward. "Now, gentlemen, we must just finish this champagne. Then I'm going to introduce you to my Madeira. Vintage port I can't offer you, but my Madeira—well, I bought it on the island myself, and I believe there is nothing else quite like it."

They sat for the best part of an hour round the table. The women went out on deck, but Susan soon returned in glistening oilskins.

"Dark as pitch," she declared, "and little spits of rain all the time. Really, Mr. Host, you do provide us with lots of variety, even in the way of weather."

Grant rose to his feet.

"We'll have a look round," he proposed. "I thought we should have heard the engines before now."

They trooped out on deck. One of the stewards was busy handing out oilskins and sou'westers. They walked up and down for a moment or two. There were no lights in sight, and they seemed to be doing little more than drift.

"I'll go and have a talk to Captain Martin," Grant suggested. "Perhaps I'd better look downstairs first, though, and see what Henderson can arrange, in case we have to give you a shake-down."

"I'd like to come with you," Cornelius Blunn, who had

been curiously silent for some time, proposed. "Which way are your quarters?"

Grant led them along the oak-panelled passage and threw open the door of his own little suite. Blunn, who was following close behind, suddenly pushed against him, so heavily that Grant slipped. The Prince, who had joined them on the stairs, slammed the door. Grant felt the cold pressure of a pistol against his forehead.

"If you utter a sound," Blunn threatened, "as sure as I'm a living man, you'll be a dead one. Hold up your hands and back away there."

Grant held up one hand and stooped and picked up a cigar with the other.

"I give you my word of honour that I am not armed," he said, "and I haven't the faintest intention of quarrelling with a man who is. Now what's it all about?"

"Will you give the order to start your engines?" Blunn demanded.

"I'll see you damned first," was the emphatic reply.

CHAPTER XVI

CAPTAIN MARTIN and Chief Engineer Nicholson were smoking a pipe together in the latter's very comfortable but somewhat out-of-the-way quarters when, to their surprise, the door of the cabin was abruptly opened to admit two of the ship's guests, Cornelius Blunn and Baron Funderstrom.

"Good evening, gentlemen," the captain said, in some surprise.

Cornelius Blunn was not wasting words.

"We want to know, Mr. Engineer, what is wrong with your engines. Why can't you start up and get us back to Monte Carlo according to promise?"

"My engines! Who said there was anything wrong with my engines?" Nicholson demanded.

"Mr. Slattery has told us so," was the curt reply. "He told us not a quarter of an hour ago that you were afraid to start them for fear of an accident to one of the pistons."

"Well, if Mr. Slattery said so," the chief engineer observed, "he's doubtless right."

"I do not believe it," Blunn declared. "We have reason to suspect that Mr. Slattery is trying to keep us out here all night for a purpose of his own."

"If you think that, it's Mr. Slattery you'd better talk to, sir," Nicholson suggested. "My job on board this boat is to take orders from the owner. You'd better go and complain to Mr. Slattery, if there's anything not to your liking."

"We have complained to Mr. Slattery," Blunn rejoined. "He has refused to order you to start the engines."

"Then that's all there is to be said about it," the captain intervened. "They'll start all right as soon as Mr. Slattery says the word, and not before."

Cornelius Blunn's hand left his hip pocket. He was a good judge of men, and he realised that threats were not likely to help him.

"Look here," he said. "You two are sensible men. I'm sure of that. I want to tell you that Mr. Slattery is playing a very dangerous game. He is pretending to be broken down to keep this gentleman, Baron Funderstrom, from attending the Nice Conference to-morrow."

"Aye, aye," the engineer observed. "He has some good reason, no doubt."

"I am not going to threaten you with what may happen if this conspiracy is persisted in," Blunn went on. "I want to put the matter to you another way. Start your engines up and get us into Monte Carlo before morning and you shall have a draft for five thousand pounds, during the day."

"Five thousand pounds!" Chief Engineer Nicholson exclaimed.

"Five thousand pounds!" the captain echoed.

"It's an enormous sum," the former declared.

"It is yours, if you'll do as I have asked," Blunn assured them.

"What's the matter with Mr. Slattery giving me my orders?" Nicholson demanded.

"Mr. Slattery has already given you his orders, and we don't approve of them," Blunn replied.

"It's a pity, that," the chief engineer regretted, "for Mr. Slattery's are the only orders that are likely to receive any attention on board this ship."

"If to that five, I were to add another two?" Blunn suggested.

"Seven thousand pounds! Why, man alive, it's a tremendous sum," the other gasped. "I'd not know what to do with such a fortune."

"That is for you to decide," Blunn said impatiently. "You can make your own arrangements with the captain. All we ask of you is to start your engines, and of the captain, to take us into Monte Carlo. Come! This shall mean your fortunes, both of you. It shall be ten thousand pounds between you, paid in cash to-morrow morning."

"Ten thousand pounds!" the engineer repeated. "Did you

hear that, Captain Martin? Five thousand apiece! Why, mon, the money would be a temptation to us. Like as not we would stay on land and get drunk, instead of coming to sea, like decent seafaring men should."

"Will you do it, or won't you?" Blunn demanded, suddenly suspicious of the other's attitude.

The chief engineer knocked the ashes from his pipe.

"I'm thinking," he said, "that neither of you gentlemen are much used to the sea and the ways of seafaring folk, or you'd know that there isn't a self-respecting officer born who'd take his orders from any except his skipper. You're simply wasting your time here, gentlemen. If you'll excuse me, I'll be getting along. I've a fancy for a word with Mr. Slattery."

"You'll stay here for the present," Blunn declared coolly. "Don't make a fuss about it, please. No one wants to hurt you, but there's a great deal at stake, and a few men's lives won't make much difference."

The engineer looked in blank and genuine amazement down the black muzzle of Blunn's automatic.

"Take your finger off that trigger, you blithering idiot," he shouted. "Don't you know it might go off at any minute?"

"It's very likely indeed to go off if you move," Blunn assured him. "Just as you are, please, both of you."

Baron Funderstrom stepped backwards, and Blunn followed his example. Outside, they shut the door and locked it. The two officers stared at one another open-mouthed.

"So that's the game," the engineer exclaimed. "We're keeping that warmed-up corpse of a lop-eared German from going to the Conference. Abductors! That's what we are."

The captain helped himself to whisky and passed the decanter.

"Fill up, Jim," he invited, "and then you'd better press the bell."

Nicholson did as he was bid. Then he shook his head.

"The fat chump wasn't quite such a flat as all that," he remarked. "Wire's cut outside."

Captain Martin leaned back in his chair and laughed.

"If this doesn't beat the band!" he exclaimed. "To think that I've been going to sea for thirty years, and have never been in a hold-up before! Drink up, Jim, and we'll get busy. There must be something we can do."

The chief mate, Henry Fosbrooke, was standing, his back to the rail, watching the somewhat erratic antics of an uncertain wind in his main-sail. The yacht being for a watch under his control, he was indulging in some mild speculation as to the reason for the curious instructions he had received. To him, out of the gloom, came Blunn, bulky, ponderous, slow-footed, followed by Funderstrom, grey and cold, silent as a dead man.

"Are you the officer in charge?" the former asked.

"I am, sir, for my sins," was the civil reply. "We're giving you a queer sort of entertainment to-night."

"My friend here, Baron Funderstrom, and I are the victims of a practical joke," Blunn continued. "We have a proposition to make to you."

"A proposition," the officer repeated, watching the slow bellying of his sail. "If it is anything to do with getting busy down in the engine room, I shall be glad to hear it, anyhow. I don't fancy this flopping about like a lame duck, with squalls in the offing."

"To tell you the truth, neither do we," Blunn declared. "We want to turn the tables upon Mr. Slattery. Is there a second engineer on board?"

"There he is, sir," the mate answered, pointing to a gloomy figure standing with his hands in his pockets a few yards away.

"I should like to speak to him for a moment. Please call him."

The appearance of the second engineer, who at once obeyed the summons, was distinctly encouraging. He was a youngish man, with shifty eyes and a furtive manner.

"Are five thousand pounds apiece any use to you young fellows?" Blunn asked, addressing them both.

Neither of them answered. They could only stare.

"Get down to your engine room, start up and head this yacht back for Monte Carlo," Blunn continued, "and the money is yours."

"Without Mr. Slattery's orders?" the officer of the watch gasped.

"Mr. Slattery, at the moment, is not in a position to give orders," was the terse reply.

"What about my chief?" the engineer demanded.

"He is in the same position. You have got the run of the ship for a time. Do as I say and I swear before God you shall have the money."

"The devil!" the mate exclaimed. "I thought there was some queer work afoot. What's wrong with Mr. Slattery?"

"Nothing serious," Blunn assured them. "I have locked him up. He is trying to play a trick on us. It is perfectly fair and just to defend ourselves. He is endeavouring to keep us from making land before dawn. We are determined to get there, somehow or other. It is five thousand apiece. There's some fun to be got in the world for five thousand, you know."

"I'm on, anyway," the second engineer decided. "We can't be getting any one into bad trouble."

"You will not be getting any one into trouble at all," Blunn declared. "My friend here is Baron Funderstrom, Scandinavian delegate at the Nice Conference. All Mr. Slattery is trying to do is to prevent his attending the meeting to-morrow morning, for political reasons. We intend that he shall be there."

"But what's become of my chief?" his subordinate asked anxiously.

"Locked up in his own room," was the blunt reply, "and the captain with him. That can't last long, I know, but it won't take us very long either to get back to Monaco, with a full head of steam on."

"All right," the officer of the watch announced. "I'll take her in charge. We've scarcely any sail on her now. We'll get rid of that directly. Five thousand pounds each, mind!"

"It is a bargain," Blunn assured them.

They disappeared in different directions. Blunn, followed by

Funderstrom, his silent and almost ghostly shadow, strolled along the deck. Away aft Rose Lancaster and her brother, Susan and Gertrude were still laughing and talking. Susan looked up as they approached.

"Where's every one?" she asked curiously. "They all seem to have gone to sleep."

"Where is Mr. Slattery?" Gertrude demanded. "And what have you done with my husband?"

"They are all trying to solve the problem of this slight breakdown," Blunn explained. "It seems to be a more intricate affair than we thought."

"I don't care when we get back," Susan declared recklessly. "I've been to look at the cabins downstairs, and I never dreamed of such luxury in my life."

"Odd thing about Slattery, though," Lancaster observed. "Is he really down in the engine room?"

"I left him there," Blunn told them. "Like every owner, I believe he fancies that his presence encourages *les autres.*"

"By Jove, it has, too!" the young man exclaimed. "Can't you hear the thud? The engine's started."

There was a chorus of exclamations. Susan rose from her place and glided unnoticed to the other side of the deck.

CHAPTER XVII

Susan passed unseen down the companionway and into the saloon. A single steward was there, busy at the sideboard.

"Where are all the others?" she enquired.

"They are having supper, your ladyship."

"Do you know where Mr. Slattery is?"

"He is in his room with another gentleman."

Susan hesitated for a moment and then continued on her passage through the saloon. The man deferentially but effectively barred the way.

"If your ladyship will excuse me," he said, "Mr. Slattery gave instructions that he was not to be disturbed."

"You're telling me a lie," she answered promptly. "Mr. Slattery gave no such orders."

The man faltered.

"Well, the gentleman with him did, your ladyship."

"That isn't at all the same thing," Susan declared. "Stand aside, please."

The man hesitated. He was a somewhat undersized person, and Susan, just then, felt herself possessed with the strength of half a dozen such. She swept him on one side, and passed along the passage beyond the saloon. At the second door, which she knew to be Grant's, she paused, knocked in vain and then tried the handle.

"Who is there?" Grant's voice enquired.

"Curse you, shut up!" Von Diss muttered angrily.

"Grant, is anything wrong?" Susan called out.

"A great deal," he answered, "and you seem to have been the only person with common sense enough to find it out. Can you get hold of Captain Martin and tell him there is a mutiny on the ship? I'm locked in here."

The door was stealthily opened. A hand flashed out and caught her by the wrist. She felt herself being dragged into the room. And then pandemonium. The sudden opening of the door showed her what had happened. Grant, lounging on his bunk, covered by Von Diss's weapon, took advantage of that sudden turn to make the spring which he had been contemplating for some time. Von Diss's right arm was knocked up by a cruel undercut; one barrel of the pistol went off harmlessly into the wall. With the other hand, Grant struck him on the side of the head. He collapsed with barely a groan, half on the floor and half on the sofa. Grant stooped and picked up the pistol.

"Bless you, my child!" he said to Susan, who was standing, amazed but unshaken, on the threshold.

"What does it all mean?" she demanded wonderingly.

"Oh, we asked for trouble, all right," he admitted. "We're abductors, pirates, whatever you like. I don't blame these chaps for not taking it lying down. But I think they might have put up a better-class fight. Now let's get on deck. I want to find out who the mischief gave orders to start the engine."

"What about him?" she asked, pointing to the floor where Von Diss lay moaning and half conscious.

"I'll send a steward down," Grant promised. "He's got lots of nerve, I will say that for him. He got me covered and his hand was like a rock. He'd have shot me all right if I'd moved. He made the mistake of his life when he took his eye off me to pull you in. Now we'll have to see about these engines."

She slipped her arm through his. They made their way through the deserted saloon, up the companionway, and out on to the weather side of the deck. A young officer came along, smoking a cigarette. He saluted as Grant spoke to him.

"Who's on the bridge, Simpson?"

"Fosbrooke, sir. It's my relief but he preferred to go on for another hour. Said he had some special orders."

"What's our course?"

"Almost due north, sir," the youth answered. "We shall fetch Monaco in about two hours."

Grant nodded and walked forward to the steps leading to the

bridge. The lookout man stood behind the white canvas. A solitary figure was pacing back and forth.

"Stay here," Grant whispered. "There's probably some one else lurking about to see that this fellow isn't interfered with."

"Not I!" she insisted. "I'm coming up with you. You haven't another pistol, have you?"

"No, but you can have this one," he answered, pushing it into her hand. "They won't suspect your having one and I'm pretty useful with my fists. Got it? Good! Now, go around the other side and tell Gertrude to look after her husband. See what's doing, and then come forward. I can't think what's become of Martin and the chief engineer."

She nodded and glided away through the darkness. Her slippered feet were noiseless upon the deck, and in her black gown she was almost invisible. Grant mounted the steps rapidly. There was no sign of any unauthorised person upon the bridge. The words of stern enquiry were already framed upon his lips. Then, just as he stood on the last step, something swung out from behind the canvas protection. He felt a crashing blow on the side of his head, a sudden sensation of fury, followed by one of darkness. He fell down the steps and collapsed on the deck below. Cornelius Blunn, an ugly block of wood still in his hand, peered over and looked at him.

"A pity," he muttered. "I hate violence."

The seaman had turned round from his shelter on the bridge. He glanced anxiously towards the officer in charge.

"What's going on here, sir?" he asked.

"Only one of the commander's guests run amok," was the answer. "Had too much to drink and wanted to come and sail the ship. Get back to your post, Burgess."

The man looked uneasily below. He was not at all satisfied.

"Seems to me they've treated him a bit roughly, sir," he said.

"Not our job."

"Hadn't I better go down and have a look at him?" he persisted.

"Stay where you are, damn you!" was the angry reply. "We're doing twenty-six knots with a cloud of rain ahead, and thirty fishing boats somewhere about. Attend to your job."

There was a certain irony about Susan's reappearance aft. Grant's string quartette band, of which he was so proud, had begun to play soft music. Funderstrom had rejoined the little group and was sitting upon the outskirts, cold and silent as ever. Gertrude and Rose were listening to the music, but the latter was clearly uneasy. She welcomed Susan eagerly.

"Susan, where is everybody?" she exclaimed. "I never knew anything so mysterious. Mr. Slattery hasn't been back all the time. Prince von Diss has disappeared, and now even Mr. Blunn has deserted us."

"I suppose it's the trouble about the engines," Susan observed. "I don't think there's anything to be alarmed at, though. The sea's quite calm even if we do break down."

Mr. Cornelius Blunn suddenly came into evidence. He stepped through the companionway with the obvious air of having something to say.

"There is no cause for alarm," he assured them; "the whole affair is a mere trifle, but Mr. Slattery has met with a slight accident. He seems to have slipped coming down the steps from the bridge. We've taken him into the saloon. If one of you ladies, who is accustomed to bandaging——"

Gertrude and Susan both rose to their feet. Susan, however, was halfway down the stairs before the others had started. Grant was lying upon a sofa, and a steward was bathing his forehead. He looked up as Susan entered. She hurried over to his side and waved the steward away.

"Are you hurt, Grant?" she whispered eagerly.

"Not I," he answered. "I'm making the worst of it, but I shall be all right in half an hour. It's a fair enough fight, Susan, but these fellows are in earnest, especially Blunn. Look here, Nicholson and Martin must be locked up in the chief engineer's quarters. All the bells are cut, but the captain's boy is certain to find them within half an hour. The worst of it is, we shall be in sight of Monaco in an hour or so if they keep this speed up."

"They sha'n't," she declared. "Tell me. Who's my man? Where shall I go, the engine room, or the bridge?"

Grant smiled.

"Bravo, child!" he muttered. "Look out! They're coming. The bridge!"

Susan turned away with a little shiver of excitement. Gertrude, who had just hurried in, knelt down by Grant's side and called to the steward.

"Some more hot water and lint," she directed. "Some disinfectant, if you have it, and a sponge. Please leave this to me, all of you. I'm used to bandaging but I hate to have too many people round."

Susan left the saloon stealthily and made her way back on deck. She walked up the lee side and climbed the stairs down which Grant had been thrown. The officer in charge was standing, looking steadily at a light far ahead. He suddenly felt a touch on his arm and turned round with a start to find Susan by his side.

"Do you mind my talking to you for a minute," she whispered. "We're all so scared — so afraid that we're going to break down or something."

"We're quite all right," the young man declared, a little thickly.

"Shall we get back to Monaco to-night?"

"In about two hours' time. We shall see the lights presently."

"What is our course just now, then?" she enquired.

"Almost due north," he replied. "There's just a point or two of east in it. You'd better get down, your ladyship. Mr. Slattery doesn't allow any one on the bridge unless he brings them here himself."

She edged a little away from him.

"Where do you give your orders to the engine room?" she asked.

He pointed to the chart house behind. She nodded.

"I have brought you a message from Mr. Slattery," she said.

He looked at her suspiciously. There was something stealthy and guarded in her attitude. The wind was blowing her hair back from her face. It was a very strong capable face, — a stronger face than his own. Her eyes, too — soft and brown, but compelling — seemed to hold him.

"Mr. Slattery's message," she went on, "is that you alter the course to due south. It is his wish to go no nearer to Monaco. Will you please ring down to the engine room at once and reverse your course."

"I can't do that, your ladyship," he declined. "I have my orders. I must stick to them."

"And I have mine," she said, "from Mr. Slattery. I have never broken my word in my life and you can take this from me, just as though I were a man. I'm not going to risk killing you outright but I'm going to shoot you first through one leg and then through the other, unless you do as you're ordered."

"Pooh! Don't be silly," he exclaimed, moving towards her. "I'm twice as quick as you are and a great deal more used to firearms."

"Quick, I say!"

The muzzle of her pistol gleamed wickedly in the light which shone from the chart room. The young man stood and looked ahead of him miserably.

"What a night!" he groaned.

"I can't wait," she declared. "We might be interrupted. Get into the room and ring down at once. If you don't I swear I will keep my word. I will keep it before I count five. One, two, three——"

"Stop!" he begged. "I've had enough of this business. I don't suppose we should have touched the five thousand anyhow."

He swung round and entered the chart house. She listened to his brief conversation, covering him all the time. Soon they began what seemed to be a huge turn. The light on their port bow disappeared. Now it was abreast of them. Presently it was aft. The officer in charge finished his directions and came out of the chart room.

"We're back on Mr. Slattery's original course," he announced. "What will happen when that little fat man finds out, I don't know. Or what will happen to me, either."

"Stick to it now," Susan enjoined, "and I'll do the best I can with Mr. Slattery. You've done all you could to make amends anyhow."

"I can't make out what it all means," he muttered. "What's become of the Skipper and Mr. Nicholson?"

"Locked in the engineer's room," she told him. "I can't understand why they couldn't make themselves heard, though."

The young man grinned weakly.

"They're behind solid mahogany," he declared. "All the doors in the officers' quarters are three inches thick. What's that?"

He swung round. Coming towards them, stealthily and sombrely through the darkness, was Blunn, walking on tiptoe, and behind him gaunt and grey, yet even more menacing, was Funderstrom.

"Give me the gun," the young man begged. "I'm fed up with this."

Susan looked into his face and gave it to him. He turned towards the intruders, and the hand which held the pistol was as steady as a rock.

"Look here," he shouted. "Off my bridge, both of you! Not a word, or by God, I'll shoot you both."

They came to a standstill. The sailor on lookout duty stepped from his canvas shelter and stood staring at them.

"You have altered the course," Blunn complained.

"And if I have, what the hell is that to you?" the young man retorted.

"I take it that you don't want your five thousand pounds, then?" Blunn enquired viciously.

"Not a penny of it," was the prompt reply. "I want you off this bridge and damned quick too, or as sure as I'm a living man I shall shoot."

Cornelius Blunn stood for a moment, irresolute. No braver man than he breathed, but he was also a philosopher.

"Bo's'n," the mate added, swinging round towards the lookout man, "hurry round to my quarters. Get the key of the officers' mess. You'll find that it will unlock the chief engineer's room. The captain and the chief engineer are both there. Ask the captain to step this way. And listen to me," he went on, "if either of your two interfere with that man, I'll shoot, and shoot where it kills, too."

The bo's'n saluted and hurried off. Cornelius Blunn shrugged his shoulders. He leaned against the rail but he made no further movement forward.

"My young friend," he said, "forgive me if I suggest that you are introducing an unwelcome note of melodrama into this little affair. It has been a game of wits between your owner and ourselves. I fear that the young lady," he added, bowing to Susan, "has played the winning card. We will voyage with you, sir, in whatever direction you choose. Funderstrom, I am very thirsty."

The two men disappeared. Susan smiled reassuringly up at the young officer by her side.

"That's all right, now," she declared. "You've seen the thing through, after all. It has been rather a mix-up, you know. I'm afraid Mr. Slattery has been behaving very badly."

He looked steadily ahead into the windy darkness.

"Your ladyship is very kind," he rejoined shortly. "A sailor ought to remember that he only has to obey orders."

She left him a moment or two later and walked down the deck. It was hard for her to believe that the whole thing had not been a dream. A steward was handing round glasses of champagne, and Cornelius Blunn, with an apologetic grin, was holding a glass in either hand. The Prince, looking very pale and malicious, was seated back in the shadows. Grant, with his head bandaged, was standing on the threshold.

"My dear guests," he announced, waving his hand to Susan, as she came up. "I regret having to tell you that the worst has happened. There is no longer any hope of our reaching Monaco to-night. The captain, who has just gone up on the bridge, has assured me that it is impossible."

"There will be a heavy reckoning," Funderstrom warned him solemnly.

"Under the circumstances," Grant went on, ignoring the remark, "I have ordered supper to be served in the saloon."

"Supper," Mr. Cornelius Blunn said thoughtfully. "God bless my soul! That's what's the matter with me. I'm hungry."

CHAPTER XVIII

The landing was a perfectly carried out farce. Everybody appeared to be in high spirits and even Prince von Diss managed to infuse a little cordiality into his thanks for the delightful hospitality he had experienced. Grant was very apologetic about the slight trouble with his engines. Everybody assured him, however, that the few extra hours at sea had been a pleasure and studiously avoided any mention of the mingled farce and drama which they had evoked. On the subject of his dinner, which, after two postponements, had been fixed for the following night, Mr. Cornelius Blunn was eloquent.

"If a single one of you denies me," he declared, "I shall be hurt. It is going to give me the greatest possible pleasure to feel myself, for once, a host, to endeavour to repay a little the sumptuous hospitality I have received. We meet at the Hotel de Paris at eight o'clock. I have, by the bye, asked His Majesty, the King of Gothland, to meet you. His Majesty is most agreeable and his presence will in no way interfere with what I hope is going to be a cheery evening."

Susan and Grant exchanged amused glances more than once, during this somewhat drawn out business of leave-taking. Once she drew near enough to him to whisper.

"What a gorgeous farce! Aren't we all clever?"

"Blunn is the man I admire," he confided. "The Prince can't get away with it. He looks as though he wanted to stick a knife into some one."

There was a little sprinkling of journalists upon the quay, who had come down on the report that an accident had happened to the *Grey Lady*. They attached themselves especially to Baron Funderstrom, who had, however, one reply to them all.

"It was unfortunate that I could not attend the meeting of the Conference," he said, "owing to the slight accident to the engines which happened when we were some distance out at sea. As a matter of fact, however, I know quite well what the agenda consisted of and there was nothing in which my views did not coincide with the majority."

"You know," one of the journalists asked him, "that the Conference has decided to invite America to join the Pact?"

"I imagined that would take place," he admitted, without change of countenance. "The decision to forward the invitation was, I presume, unanimous?"

"The discussion took place in private session," the journalist pointed out. "But one understands that there was no opposition."

Grant glanced at his watch.

"I wonder if your father is back from Nice?" he said to Susan.

She shook her head.

"He doesn't usually arrive at the Villa until six o'clock. Now that the regular sessions have commenced, it may be even later."

"I will come up with you, if I may," he suggested. "I want to see him as soon as possible after he returns. Besides, I want to escape from these people."

"Come along," Susan agreed. "We had better take a carriage. They may send the car down when they see the yacht coming in, but as Peters will be over with Dad at Nice I should think it's doubtful."

They drove off and the remainder of the little company melted away from the pier, all apparently in the highest of spirits.

"I must say one thing about Blunn," Grant declared, as they looked backward for a moment from the top of the hill. "He's an unprincipled scoundrel, of course, but he's a sportsman."

"He's much better than that Prince von Diss or that terrible Scandinavian," Susan assented.

"I suppose you realise," he went on, "that you were the pluckiest person on board."

"Nonsense!" she answered, colouring with pleasure. "It was really a tremendous rag."

"I'm not quite sure what that misguided young officer of

mine thought about it when he found himself held up by a girl," Grant observed drily. "They'd have brought it off but for you."

"I'm very glad," she murmured. "Next time you give a party like that I hope I'm there."

He looked at her for a moment a little wistfully. Youth had certainly befriended her. Gertrude had risen that morning with dark lines under her eyes and her manner on the dock had been almost spiritless. There was nothing in Susan's happy face and smiling expression to indicate a night of anxiety.

"I wish you weren't such a kid," he said suddenly.

"What on earth do you mean?" she retorted. "I'm nearly twenty. Surely that is old enough for—for anything. Are you trying to insinuate that I am unintelligent or unformed or something?"

"You are very sweet as you are, Susan," he assured her. "It was a foolish wish. I wouldn't have you a day older. And here comes your father. They must have been back from Nice early."

Susan scarcely showed her usual joy at welcoming her parent. They all arrived at the Villa together and Lord Yeovil at once drew Grant into his little sanctum.

"I am inclined to think that you must have found a mare's nest, young fellow," he announced. "You can guess my news?"

"You have received the consent of the Pact to forward the invitation to America," Grant replied.

"Not only that, but my motion was supported by Prince Lutrecht."

"Were there no votes against it, then?" Grant asked incredulously.

"There were three black balls," Lord Yeovil admitted. "That was somewhat of a surprise to us, I must say, but, as you know, three was not sufficient to affect the result."

"Well," Grant told him, "I should like you to realise this. It is entirely due to Lady Susan that you had your own way in this matter. You have won the first step towards breaking up what I am convinced now to be a very malevolent conspiracy, and it was your daughter who made it possible."

"My daughter! Susan!" Lord Yeovil exclaimed. "What do you mean, Grant?"

"I mean that I was right—just as right as I knew I was, all the time. Lutrecht voted against it, as he had always meant to, whatever he may have said at the Meeting. So did Katina. That's why he was rushed down from Berlin and why poor old Naga had to go. So did Gortz, the Russian. And, if I hadn't abducted Funderstrom and kept him away until too late to go to the Meeting, his would have been the fourth vote."

"Abducted Funderstrom!" Lord Yeovil repeated wonderingly.

"That's just what we did, sir," Grant assented. "I kept him on the yacht until it was too late for him to go to Nice. There was a tremendous row," he went on, "practically a free fight, and, at one time, Blunn and Prince von Diss were having things their own way, and they very nearly got Funderstrom back. If it hadn't been for Susan, who took command when I was *hors de combat* and, with an automatic in her hand, frightened one of my navigating officers to death, they would have done."

"You'd better not tell me anything more, Grant," Lord Yeovil decided, a little gravely, though there was a twinkle of delight in his eyes. "This sort of thing is outside the sphere of practical politics. All I can say is that, whatever you did, I personally am convinced that you did it for the best—and I thank you."

"What I did," Grant said earnestly, "I did incidentally for the sake of the world's peace, but chiefly for the sake of my own country. We're only halfway through the trouble yet, though. The invitation may be sent. As yet it isn't accepted."

"I hope to God it will be!" was the fervent response. "If it isn't, I tell you, Grant, no man, even though he had the tongue of a god and all the angels, will be able to induce any future Meeting of the Pact to send another invitation."

"I realise that absolutely," Grant acquiesced. "I can assure you of one thing. All that stands for the best in my country will be in favour of accepting, but there is a great deal there that stands for the worst. There will be plots, and bribery, and intrigue, any quantity of it. And yet we are going to win. The invitation shall be accepted."

A servant brought in cocktails and Grant was easily persuaded to stay and dine.

"I sha'n't change," his prospective host told him. "You can send for your things, if you like, or change afterwards if you are going on anywhere. What I want you to do is to sit down in that easy-chair, and tell me — unofficially, mind — the whole story of your adventures on the yacht."

Grant lit a cigarette and accepted the invitation.

"When we all wished one another good-by this morning," he said, "I had to pinch myself metaphorically to realise that I wasn't dreaming. The whole thing seemed too improbable and fantastic. However, here's the story."

CHAPTER XIX

THE dinner given by Cornelius Blunn was the most talked-of function of a very brilliant Riviera season. The writing room on the left of the lounge at the Hotel de Paris had been transformed into a private banqueting apartment, at one end of which a small stage had been erected for artists who came from Nice and even Cannes to entertain the guests, and whose fees were a record in munificence. Despite the slight formality of the opening stages of the gathering, owing to the presence of the Scandinavian monarch, the keynote to the whole party seemed to be set and adequately maintained by Blunn himself, —reckless, brilliant lightheartedness. Gertrude sat on his right, jealously watched from across the table by her husband. Grant, with curious disregard for precedence, was seated at her other side. On Blunn's left was a lady of royal birth, whose exploits had been the talk of Europe,—a woman still beautiful and witty, who was supposed to be devoting the remainder of her years and a portion of her colossal fortune to the entertainment of the monarch who sat on her left. Lord Yeovil, persuaded to be present with great difficulty, at the last moment, was in the vicinity, with the Princess Lutrecht for a neighbour. Several of the Monte Carlo notables in addition to the originally invited guests were present. There was no one there who did not acknowledge the genius of Blunn as a host. Europe had been sought for gastronomic delicacies. Wines were served which had become little more than a memory. The greatest violinist known lifted them all, for a moment, into the rare atmosphere of the world to which he held the pass-key. The most popular humourist in Paris offered the wittiest creations of his brain.

The only person who seldom smiled was Gertrude. She had already been accepted in the little principality as the reigning beauty of the season, but her appearance to-night had created a positive sensation. She had justified to the fullest extent the old contention that beauty is not a permanent and unchanging thing, but an effect of chance, an evanescent quality, possessed one minute and gone the next. This might have been the moment of her life. She seemed to carry with her a nameless and unanalysable perfection of grace, of figure,—all those nameless qualities which come so wonderfully to the aid of features not really perfect in form. The violet of her eyes was distracting. Even the slight fatigue which was sometimes apparent in her languid tones seemed to bring her distinction. Susan, at the first sight of her, and more than once since, had been conscious of a little sinking of the heart. It seemed impossible that any man could look at her without desire.

Grant himself was moved by the unfamiliar side of her beauty,—the beauty which, for this one evening, seemed to have taken to itself a certain appeal, a helplessness, a demand for something which perhaps no one else but he could realise. Once or twice, at a whispered word from her, he had felt his pulses leap as in the old days, had felt, indeed, some touch of the old folly back again,—the folly of which he had deemed himself purged. He had permitted himself to think for one moment of a few nights ago when she had stood on the edge of the quay, looking down to the yacht, looking wistfully at the gangplank, passage across which he had so strenuously forbidden. It had been comparatively easy then. He wondered whether any man in the world would have found it easy now.

"Are you quite at your best to-night, Grant, or is it my fancy?" she asked, during a pause in the conversation.

"If I am not," he rejoined, "it is because you surpass your best."

Almost for the first time, she laughed happily. There was real meaning in his tone and it was the sort of speech for which she craved.

"You really think that I am looking well to-night? You see, I never know where I am between the two extremes. Ottilie declared that I was a vision of delight. Otto snarled out something about the Montmartre."

"It is a most unfortunate circumstance," Grant declared, "that every day I am learning to dislike your husband more."

"You may hate him if you want to," she replied. "I shall not quarrel with you."

"Well, I hope he is much kinder to you at home than he appears to be in public. I can't stand the man who scowls at his wife's beauty because it naturally attracts admiration and doesn't himself endeavour to offer her his homage."

"Otto is thoroughly German," she replied. "Some Englishmen are the same, they say. They buy their wife with their name or money or simulated affection, and when they have her it is finished. She is their chattel, she is their singing bird or dancing girl, to perform for their pleasure. There are times, nowadays," she went on, "when such methods fail, and they bring disaster. But even then the man is generally selfish and brutal enough to see that some one else shares that disaster."

Cornelius Blunn leaned a little forward in his place with uplifted glass.

"Before I forget it—Bon Voyage, Mr. Slattery," he said. "May your trip across the Atlantic provide you with as much amusement as our recent cruise. And may its result be as satisfactory."

Grant bowed pleasantly and drank.

"I shall miss you all," he acknowledged, smiling.

Grant saw the white shoulder, so close to him, quiver for a moment,—a queer little habit of hers in times of emotion. She remained silent, however, for some time. Perhaps she knew that her husband's eyes were upon her, as well as Blunn's. Under cover of a great chorus of laughter, evoked by one of the latter's stories, she turned at last to Grant.

"That is just one of the sweet little stabs," she confided, "which I have learnt to expect. Cornelius has been saving that up for me. I think that you might have spared me the shock."

"I only made up my mind twelve hours ago," he assured her. "I can't imagine how he knew."

"I'm glad to hear that. I think that I should have been the first to be told."

"You probably would. Next to the Yeovils, of course."

"Lord Yeovil or Lady Susan?"

"They are equally my friends," he replied.

"Are you in love with Lady Susan, Grant?"

He was a little startled, both by the question and the thrill which it brought.

"I happen to be thirty-one years old," he reminded her. "Lady Susan is nineteen."

"That is rather a recognised standard," she remarked, "according to present ideas. The older a man gets the more he leans towards the kindergarten. In any case it doesn't answer my question."

"I have no time to be in love with any one just at present," he said. "I have work to do."

"You men and your work!" she exclaimed bitterly. "You drag it around with you like a closet of refuge, into which you can step whenever you are hard pressed. Honestly I can't imagine why there are any good women in the world. There certainly is no encouragement for them. When do you sail, Grant?"

"To-morrow or Thursday."

"Are you going straight to New York?"

"I may stay at Gibraltar to coal," he replied. "I shall probably have to."

She turned a little towards him. She had a trick of dropping her voice almost to a whisper. Her little question barely reached his ears.

"Are you taking me with you?"

"I can't do that, Gertrude," he said firmly, "neither would you come. And it isn't a fair question to ask me when you know that you are looking more adorable than you ever looked in your life."

"I tried to make myself look nice to-night because I wanted to ask you that question, or something like it. Isn't it terrible, this gift of frankness I have developed? I think out a course of complete dissimulation and I find myself suddenly the very personification of candour. Why won't you take me, Grant? Are you afraid of Otto? He is a very small man and not very strong. And duels have gone out even amongst us now."

"I thought," he remarked with a smile, thankful for the note of banter in her tone, "that your beloved young Prince was trying to bring them in again."

"They say so," she admitted. "That is because he got them reinstated when he was at the University, and, amongst his young friends, he is President of what they call their 'Court of Honour.' But I do not think you would be afraid to fight with any man, Grant, for anything you cared for. The great question is, or would be, whether you cared enough."

"It isn't entirely a question of caring," Grant declared. "There are two contemptible rôles in the world. One of them is the rôle of Joseph. I tell you frankly, Gertrude, that that is a part I never intend to play. Therefore if I am placed in the position of that unfortunate young man — which I trust I never shall be — I shall probably fall gracefully."

"Thank heavens," she murmured. "I may remind you of that some day."

"The other," he went on, "is the man who takes away another man's wife. Frankly, I hate that a great deal worse. I suppose, during my thirty-one years, I have behaved neither worse nor better than other men. But I have never poached. I don't understand the morality of it exactly, but it happens to be how I feel."

"I suppose you will admit," she said, "that circumstances alter cases. What do you think, for instance, of Otto persuading me to run away with him the day before we were to be married, by telling me something about you when you were in Berlin which I afterwards found to be an utter falsehood?"

"That was a contemptible action," he acknowledged, "but —— "

He paused significantly. She half closed her eyes.

"Yes, I know," she confessed drearily. "I was just as much to blame. More so, perhaps — but how I have suffered for it!"

He lowered his voice.

"Your husband," he warned her, "seldom takes his eyes from us. Blunn, too, watches. We must speak of other things."

"It is always like that," she muttered under her breath. "Eyes seem to follow me everywhere. Ears are listening. Life is like that in Berlin. Everybody seems to have espionage on the brain."

Suddenly they all had a surprise. Blunn rose to his feet. His action was so unexpected that they all stared at him. He beamed around at their expectant faces. He had the trick of smiling at a score of people so that each one thought the smile specially intended for him.

"My dear friends," he began, "have no fear. This is not a speech. This is merely the expression of a quaint desire which has just come into my mind to express my joy and pride that, to-night, amongst all of you dear people who have come at my bidding, there has come one who, I think, within the next few days or weeks, will be acknowledged the greatest benefactor, the most far-seeing diplomatist, the most beneficent statesman of this generation. I am referring, of course, to Lord Yeovil."

Everyone smiled. The idea, even the words, were still, from an ordinary point of view, curiously out of place. Yet, spoken by Blunn, just as he spoke them, they seemed natural and reasonable.

"I will tell you what Lord Yeovil has done," he went on. "He has had the courage of a great man. He has braved possible opposition,—and opposition to the Chairman of the Pact of Nations can only mean one thing, where the personal dignity of that functionary is concerned. He has, I say, braved opposition, and he has pointed out to all of us the weak link in the chain of our hope for eternal peace. I mean the standing out of your great country, sir," he added, bowing to Slattery, "the United States of America, from the Pact of Nations. Some of us have felt that by her repeated refusals she did not deserve any further invitations. Some of us have selfishly felt that we, ourselves, are in a better position for her being outside of it. Lord Yeovil swept aside all these pettinesses. He spoke to us as only a great man speaks. He saw the truth, and he made us see it. We ratified that invitation. I ask you to drink the health of Lord Yeovil with me. There is no other statesman living to-day who could have done this great thing. I am a proud man that he sits at this table. I only ask you to forgive the unassailable impulse which has prompted me to make this public apologia. For, behind my words, you will guess the truth,—that I was one of those who hesitated. That is finished. I am a man convinced. I do homage to a greater brain. My dear friends — I don't say 'Ladies and Gentlemen' — let us drink to Lord Yeovil."

"Amazing!" Grant murmured, with genuine admiration in his tone.

Lord Yeovil, whose face was as still as the face of a graven image, raised his glass. He took the only means possible of showing his opinion of his host's action. He remained seated.

"My friends," he said, "any reply of mine to our host's kindly words would give undue significance to his friendly outpourings, and would invest a few remarks, spoken at a private dinner, with a semi-official significance. I think that what we have all done together is a great and a good thing. I should have liked every representative who was present at Nice to have thought the same. Those three anonymous dissentients, whose votes were recorded against me, still rankle just a little. However, the thing is accomplished. I thank you, Mr. Blunn, for your appreciation, and I thank you more especially still for the most wonderful entertainment at which I have ever been privileged to assist. There is one thing, however, which, at the present moment, seems of more vital importance to me, and I am sure, to all of us, than any unexpected and unofficial discussion of a political matter. We should all be made supremely happy if Mademoiselle Lebrun would sing to us once more."

There was a gleam of admiration for a moment in Blunn's eyes. He was just the man to appreciate the aptness which had minimised as far as possible the importance of his pronouncement. He despatched an emissary at once for the famous soprano.

"When Mademoiselle has sung," he announced, "His Majesty has asked permission to retire to the Rooms."

The King smiled.

"This is an amazing place, with an amazing atmosphere," he declared. "Even when one entertains like an ambassador — as no ambassador of to-day could — always in the background there is that little god calling. We leave our seats at the opera to tempt chance. We forget sometimes, watching the spinning of that wheel, that the most beautiful woman of our desire is waiting for us. How is it with you, Mr. Blunn? They tell me that you are one of the richest men in the world, but I have seen you standing watching that table as though nothing but an earthquake could move you until the little ball had found its place."

"I feel it," Blunn acknowledged. "I have even gone so far, following out the trend of your thoughts, as to try to appreciate the psychological side of it. It isn't always the money that counts. Your Majesty has, if I might be permitted to say so, exaggerated when he speaks of my wealth, but still it is not the money at all which one thinks of. There is a personal sense of triumph when your number turns up. You feel that you have backed yourself against a mighty organisation and won. You are supremely indifferent to the fact that chance has aided you. You have an absolute conviction that it is your own cleverness. That is the secret of the thrill when your number turns up and the croupiers fill your pockets."

Mademoiselle Lebrun sang, and afterwards there was a little movement of departure.

"Will you please escort me up to the Club?" Gertrude whispered to her neighbour.

Grant bowed.

"With pleasure," he assented.

There were other influences at work, however. Blunn turned to her good-humouredly, with the air of one making a pleasing announcement. The Prince was laughing a little in the background.

"His Majesty asks for the pleasure of conducting you to the Rooms, Princess."

"If you will do me that honour," the King murmured, bowing.

"I shall bring you bad luck," Gertrude warned him, her voice trembling a little.

"You will give me, even in that event, what counts, perhaps, for more — very charming company," was the gallant rejoinder.

CHAPTER XX

Susan came up to Grant, smiling, about half an hour later. She had left Bobby Lancaster and his sister seated on a divan.

"Aren't you flattered, Grant?" she exclaimed. You've been labelled dangerous. Kings have been summoned to the help of the terrified husband. Look, they've made the poor woman sit at a table and play roulette, which she hates, with His Majesty on one side, her husband behind her chair, and Blunn, like a patron saint, hovering around."

Grant looked at the little phalanx and nodded.

"Well," he admitted, "I'm half inclined to believe you're right. It does seem to be a plot. Where's your father?"

"Gone home," she answered. "He was very angry with Mr. Blunn."

"All the same, it was clever," Grant observed. "I'll bet he's got a dozen copies of those few remarks of his ready for print and distribution in the States. The audacity of it all is so amazing. There were you and I and Gertrude, to say nothing of the Prince, who knew the whole secret, absolutely within a few yards of him, — knew how he fought to get that gloomy Scandinavian back to Nice in time to vote. He just laughs at us and ignores it all. We're only one or two. It is the millions he wants. It's magnificent!"

"Since I'm afraid it's quite hopeless for you to get anywhere near the enchanting Princess, would you like to talk to me for a few minutes?" she invited.

"We'll find that greedy corner in the Bar," he assented, turning away with her, "where you eat up all the chocolate éclairs."

She sighed.

"I wish I weren't so fond of food. People won't believe that I have sentiment when they watch my appetite. However," she went on cheerfully, "I sha'n't want anything more to eat to-day, nor to-morrow, as a matter of fact."

"It was a great dinner," he acknowledged. "We'll have an orangeade and go through the courses. They were something to dream of."

"If you're going to talk about food," she began peevishly,——

"Not necessarily food," he interrupted, as they selected their easy chairs. "There were the wines—that Château Yquem, for instance. Terrible to drink it after champagne, but it was a dream."

"How long are you going to stay in the States?" she asked.

"Until you're grown up," he replied. "Then I'm coming back to see what sort of a woman you have become."

"You will probably find me married to Bobby Lancaster," she warned him. "He proposed to me to-night in an entirely different way and I was really touched. I don't see why one should wait forever for a man who never asks one, and who talks about going to the other end of the world as though he was slipping into Corret's to have his hair cut."

"Meaning me?"

"Meaning you."

For a single moment Grant felt that he had exchanged his thirty-one years for her nineteen. She was smiling at him with all the gentle *savoir faire* of a woman of the world. He himself was embarrassed.

"Aren't you by way of being an extremist?" he enquired. "Even if one might hesitate to ask you to leap into sedate middle age, it seems rather a pity for you to marry into the nursery."

"Bobby is twenty-four," she declared indignantly.

"You amaze me," he confessed. "But consider those twenty-four years. We will leave out the perambulator stages. Fifteen to nineteen at Eton—cricket and rackets. Twenty to twenty-four, a guardsman—rather more cricket, rather more rackets. It is a full and busy life, child, but it makes for youth."

She smiled serenely.

"You don't understand," she remonstrated. "Cricket is almost our religion. I asked the Captain of the Australians to marry me when I was fourteen."

"He spared you?"

She nodded.

"He gave me his daughter's photograph. She was much older

than I was, very thin and she squinted. It wasn't really a romance — it was cricket."

"Is Bobby any good?" he asked.

She sighed.

"That's rather the pity of it," she admitted. "He very seldom makes any runs and he has ninety-five different excuses, or rather explanations, for the way in which he got out."

"I don't think I'm missing much in cricket," Grant reflected. "I played halfback for Harvard. Football isn't a bad game, you know."

She looked at him sympathetically.

"That must have been back in the dim past," she observed. "Long before the sedate middle-aged feeling came upon you."

"Susan, I want to tell you this. You're a delightful child and an amusing tomboy and I've often wished that you were just a few years older."

"Why?" she demanded breathlessly.

"Never mind. But, in addition to youth, you have a brain, and you're one of the pluckiest girls I've ever had with me in a tight corner. Don't think I've forgotten it, because I haven't."

"Rubbish!" she laughed.

"And I'm going to say this to you," he continued, turning towards her, so that she suddenly saw that he was in earnest, and became very still indeed, "I've got a half-finished job on my hands, and how it will turn out I don't know. It will be a matter of six months before I'm through. When I'm through, I'm coming right back. And, Susan, I don't want to say too much, but I don't think those boys are going to be quite what you deserve in life. It's horrible to feel a little too old."

She suddenly gripped his hand.

"Idiot!" she murmured. "You're not a bit too old. I wouldn't marry Bobby Lancaster if he were the last man on earth."

She was looking at him with a suspicious mistiness in her eyes. Her mouth was quivering just a little. And then it all passed. She was herself again, — slim, girlish, delightful, with the audacity of a child and the certain promise of the woman's beauty in her delicate immaturity.

"I don't know how I can trust you to cross the Atlantic alone," she laughed. "How many of the crew of the *Grey Lady* have you sacked?"

"Not one," he admitted. "I've forgiven them all. You don't think Blunn is going to smuggle himself and a few desperate plotters on board, do you? Or put an infernal machine there to blow me sky-high?"

She shook her head.

"I'm half honest," she said thoughtfully, "when I tell you frankly that I don't like letting you go alone. You, in your sedate middle age, do need a little looking after, sometimes, you know — somebody with the commonsense of youth. However, it's just an idea, I suppose. I wish you luck in America, Grant."

"Will you wish me a safe return?" he asked.

Once more she looked at him. He felt the peace of a great understanding in his heart. Those were not the eyes of a child.

"Yes," she answered. "I hope you will come back safe and soon."

At a few minutes after ten the next morning the Blue Peter was flying from the masthead of the *Grey Lady* and the last of a little stream of tradespeople were leaving the yacht. There was the usual crowd of loungers upon the dock to watch the departure, and on the bridge Lord Yeovil and Grant were standing a little aside, talking.

"If anything could make me a convert to your somewhat alarmist point of view, Slattery, Blunn's behaviour last night would do it," the former acknowledged, after a little desultory conversation upon the events of the evening before. "I still don't understand what was at the back of his mind."

"I can tell you," Grant said. "You'll find a copy of that speech will appear broadcast throughout America. 'Cornelius Blunn, the great shipping magnate, entertains Prime Minister of Great Britain, to celebrate invitation to the United States to join the Pact of Nations.' That's the sort of headline you'll see in every paper which counts. Every word he said will appear verbatim. It's wonderful propaganda for Germany."

"He stole a march on me, I'm afraid," was the somewhat rueful admission.

"Never mind," Grant consoled him. "We've won the first

bout, after all, and Blunn knows it. For all his carefully laid scheme to prevent it, America is invited to join the Pact of Nations. Now we'll have to strip for the second bout. We shall have to fight like hell to get that invitation accepted. You don't follow our domestic politics, sir, I expect."

"How can I?" Lord Yeovil protested. "I've problems enough of our own to deal with all the time."

"The opinion of the educated and intelligent citizen of the United States upon any vital subject," Grant expounded, "is sometimes, unfortunately, an entirely different matter to her voting force. That is our only danger. Cornelius Blunn and his friends know quite well that if America accepts the invitation of the Pact, all those grandiose schemes which have been formulated and brought to maturity by Germany and her friends fall to the ground. Peace is assured to the world for an indefinite period of time. Germany must abandon her hope of revenge. Japan must reconcile herself to the permanent subordination of the yellow races. Therefore, strenuous efforts will be made in America to prevent her acceptance."

"I can quite believe that," Lord Yeovil assented. "The peace lover will have German-American interests and the Japanese influence to fight. Still, I can't help thinking that on a question like this the commonsense of the country will carry all before it."

"I am with you there," Grant agreed, "and yet it is a fact that there have been, even within my memory, laws passed by the legislature which were in absolute opposition to the will of the people. The voting power of America is a chaotic and terribly uncertain quantity. Our friend Blunn will be over there before a month is passed. Prince Lutrecht will be visiting at Washington. I shouldn't be surprised if Baron Funderstrom takes a little tour there, too. Headquarters will be moved from Monte Carlo to Washington and New York, and we haven't any reasonable means of coping with all the flaring, misleading propaganda which will be let loose to induce America to refuse this invitation within the next few weeks. The only hope will be if, by any remote chance, one of us is able to discover proof of the subsequent intentions of Germany and her jackals. Otherwise I honestly believe that there is a serious possibility that the United States in the most courteous possible tones, will decline your invitation."

"If they do," Lord Yeovil remarked grimly, "I must resign at once from my position as Chairman of the Pact and probably from the Premiership of Great Britain. A refusal under the present circumstances would be little less than an affront. You have this matter very much at heart, Grant."

"I'm an American and I am fond and proud of my country," Grant answered. "I pose as being an idle millionaire. You know I'm not. I never worked so hard in my younger days, when I was Second and eventually First Secretary, or went through so many disagreeable moments as I have during the last eighteen months. I don't fancy my next six months will be any easier. I am going to do my level best to bring the truth home to the American people and to show up the plot which I am convinced is being organised against us. If I succeed I shall come straight back to Europe and, if I may, I shall come and pay you a visit."

Lord Yeovil held out his hand. Probably at that moment the same thought was in the minds of both men.

"You have my best wishes, Grant," he said cordially.

Grant walked with his departing guest to the gangplank and waved his farewell as they backed away into the harbour and swung round. Very soon they were heading for the open sea. The wonderful little bejewelled principality of intrigue, of fierce excitements and strange happenings, grew fainter but not less beautiful. The sun was streaming down upon the snow-streaked mountain peaks, the white-faced villas, the deep masses of green, the garish but curiously attractive front of the great Casino. Grant breathed a sigh of relief as the coast line faded away and the west wind took them into its embrace. There were ten days at least of freedom,—ten days in which to rearrange his thoughts, to prepare for the next stage of the struggle.

He lunched early, dozed for an hour in the afternoon, read for a little time, and discussed the question of coal supply with the chief engineer. They made careful calculations and to Grant's relief, came to the conclusion that a call at Gibraltar would not be necessary. He was suddenly feverishly anxious to reach New York, to see his friends at Washington, to gauge for himself exactly the feeling which would be created by this fateful invitation. The solitude of the open seas appealed to him immensely. He sat on deck for a while after dinner, in a sheltered place, listening to the rush of the wind and watching the stars make a fitful appearance. As the breeze stiffened they altered their course slightly and showers of spray sometimes swept the deck. He turned in early and slept soundly although every now and then he was haunted by a queer sense of some unusual sound, — unusual yet not sufficiently distinct to waken him. In the morning, he turned out at his usual hour, quite unconscious of the fact that he was so soon to be brought face to face with tragedy. He took his bath of warm and then cold sea water, strolled on deck, breakfasted in a sunny corner, and lit a pipe. After an hour or so he strolled aft on his way to the chart room. As he passed the companionway he glanced in, gripped at the door, stood stupefied, speechless, aghast. Still wearing her wonderful cloak, her satin shoes and slippers, her eyes weary but passionately questioning, came Gertrude.

CHAPTER XXI

"If you please, Grant," she said, "I want my clothes."

His words, even to himself, sounded pitifully inadequate. "How on earth did you get here?" he demanded.

"It was rather difficult," she admitted. "I had a lot of luck. Can I have some coffee or something? I haven't had anything since I came on board."

"When was that?" he asked.

"Four o'clock yesterday morning. I'm starving. I was afraid you'd hear me crying in the night."

"Good God!" he groaned. "Come down to my room. You mustn't let them see you like that."

She followed him down to his own quarters. He shut the door, watched her sink into a chair, and stood over her.

"Tell me about it," he said simply.

"After we got home," she began, "—and they made me play roulette until two o'clock—Otto was simply brutal. I couldn't bear it any longer, and the thought of your going. I gambled once before in life, you see. I gambled again. I gave Ottilie, my maid, all the money I had. She packed a trunk for me and addressed it to you. It came on board with a lot of other things. It must be somewhere about. That was easy enough. The difficulty was to get here myself. I borrowed a chauffeur's overcoat, put it on over all my things and a cap that hid my face. I walked up and down the docks for an hour, until I saw a chance. Then I came down the gangway, slipped along the empty side of the deck, got down the companionway—I had to hide twice behind doors—but eventually I got to the door of the stateroom which you said you kept for any special guest, and which I knew wasn't to be used this voyage. I crawled in, locked the door, and lay down. I hid there and waited. It must have been about four or five o'clock yesterday morning. I heard all the people come on with stores. I heard Lord Yeovil come on board. I heard your voices as you walked up and down with him. All the time I lay there in terror. Then I heard the rush of the water and the anchor come up. I heard the engines and knew we were out at sea. Still I dared not show myself. I was afraid."

"Afraid," he repeated mechanically.

"I was afraid you'd send me back. I knew there was only one chance — to stay on board long enough. I hid all day, terrified lest some one should look in the stateroom. At night I felt so ill that I almost gave up, but somehow or other I dropped off to sleep. When I woke I felt faint, and I found myself crying. I went to sleep again, though. This morning, as soon as I heard your voice on deck, I crept up the stairs and here I am. I am here, Grant. You are not going to be cruel?"

He rang the bell.

"Some coffee, an omelette, quickly," he ordered from the astonished steward. "Serve it here. Let me have the coffee at once."

"Don't keep me alive unless you are going to be kind to me," she begged hysterically. "I couldn't bear it, Grant. Tell me you are not going to land me anywhere. Why are you looking at me like that?"

"I was thinking," he answered.

"Grant, you cared for me once," she went on. "I know I must look perfectly hateful now, but I'm not hateful. I'm really rather wonderful. I could be. Otto was killing me, and all the horrible things he made me do. Grant, say something to me. Feel my hands, how cold they are. Be kind to me."

"My dear, who could be anything but kind to you?" he exclaimed. "But you must realise — you must know — this is a terrible thing you have done."

He took her hands and held them in his for a minute. The steward brought in the coffee. The boy followed behind, a moment or two later, with an omelette and cold meats. Grant felt suddenly stifled. He turned towards the door.

"I'm going to leave you for a short time," he announced. "You must drink your coffee and you must eat something. I'm going to try and find out where your things are. I will have them put in a room for you and a bath got ready. We can't talk until you are yourself again."

She looked at him wistfully.

"I'll do just as you tell me, Grant," she promised.

"Then first of all drink your coffee while it is hot," he insisted.

He made his way on deck. For a moment he could scarcely realise that this was the same cruise, the same ship, the same deck he had walked a few moments ago. He tried to face the matter calmly. She had been on board since the night after Blunn's party, the remainder of that early morning, and all the next night. By this time every one in Monte Carlo probably knew, — probably *she* knew. No one would ever believe the truth. No one could ever be told the truth. There was no explanation, no defence. She was there alone on the yacht with him. Before they could land anywhere, two nights would have passed. A sudden storm of anger seized him! Then he remembered her, as she had almost crouched in her chair, her gorgeous clothes bedraggled, her eyes searching his like the haunted eyes of a dumb animal in fear. What way was there out of it? He had faced problems before, difficult problems. How could he deal with this one?

Presently he returned to his quarters and sent for his own servant.

"Brookes," he asked, "did you know anything about a lady being on board?"

"Nothing, sir, until a few minutes ago when I saw her coming up the companionway," the man assured him.

"Have you heard any one else allude to it in any way?"

"No one, sir."

"It appears that she sent a trunk here, or a package addressed to me, containing her clothes," Grant continued after a moment's pause. "Kindly search for it and have it taken to the Empire suite aft. Prepare a bath there and everything that is necessary. Find the lady and let her know. She will lunch with me in the saloon."

"Very good, sir," the man replied.

And after that! He busied himself for an hour or so in the minor affairs of the ship. The captain found him studying the chart.

"When should we make Gibraltar, Martin?" he enquired.

"Sunday morning, sir, as early as you like. I'll guarantee the coal, though."

Grant nodded.

"I may decide to put in," he said. "I'll let you know."

Gibraltar! A hopeless place. How could he possibly leave her there amongst strangers? And yet, if not, it must be Madeira, worse still, or New York. Eight days alone with the woman with whom he had once been in love,—the memory of whose kisses had never altogether passed. It all seemed very hopeless. His own marked attentions to Gertrude during the last week or so—attentions persisted in partly to lull her suspicions and partly to keep her away from Arthur Lymane—came back to his mind. There was probably not a soul in the world who would hold him blameless for what had happened. A diabolical trick of fate!

He came down the deck a few minutes before lunch time and found Gertrude established in a long chair,—a very changed and resuscitated Gertrude. She was wearing a white serge costume; her hair—she wore no hat—shone in the warm light with the colour of cowslips in a sun-soaked meadow. She was herself again, *soignée,* as perfect in the small details of her toilette as though her maid had spent the morning by her side. Brookes appeared with two cocktails on a tray, just as Grant arrived. She took one readily and smiled at her distracted host.

"This is wonderful," she murmured. "I never wanted anything so much in my life. The epoch to which my reputation belongs is finished," she went on, a moment or two later. "You can put me off somewhere if you want to and make me appear ridiculous. I do not think that you will be so cruel as that, though."

"No," he admitted. "I do not think I shall. But, in the name of God, what made you do it?"

"I have tried to explain," she answered. "Perhaps presently I may be more coherent. Am I allowed to lunch with you?"

"By all means. The bugle has just gone. Let me help you out."

Her fingers clung to his, and she took his arm as they passed down the companionway and entered the beautiful little saloon. She looked round her almost affectionately.

"I didn't think I should be here again so soon," she murmured.

"Neither did I," he answered.

"I missed most of the fun the other night," she went on ruminatingly. "If I had known what was going to happen, I shouldn't have been so careful. Your little friend, Lady Susan, really won the trick, didn't she?"

"She did," Grant assented. "She brought that youthful navigator of mine to his senses. I think if it hadn't been for her, your husband and Blunn would have got Funderstrom back and that invitation to America would never have been sent."

"In which case, I suppose you would not have been on your way to America now?"

"I certainly should not," he acknowledged.

"And you would have been spared this terrible thing which has come upon you!"

"The voyage would never have taken place," he remarked stonily.

The service of luncheon proceeded amidst flickers of conversation of a general character, chiefly prompted by Gertrude. Afterwards they took their coffee on deck.

"To leave our unimportant selves for a moment or two," she said sadly, yet with an effort at lightness, "What are you going to do in America?"

"I shall find work there," he answered.

"You certainly will," she agreed. "I believe you are going back with the right idea. If not, you can hear it from me. All that speech of Blunn's was sheer and unadulterated bluff. Germany will do its very utmost in the States to get the Senate to refuse the invitation from the Pact. They have more power than you would imagine."

"You have reason to believe this?" Grant asked.

"I know it," she assured him. "They talked before me freely enough — Blunn, Lutrecht, Otto. I was only Otto's wife, his chattel. I didn't count. I shouldn't be likely to dare to breathe a word of which my lord and master did not approve. Oh, they are fools, those men, the way they treat their womankind."

"Have you any idea as to the means they intend to use?" Grant enquired.

"Propaganda, first and foremost," she declared. "They are all prepared. Whom they cannot convince, they will buy. They reckon that the bill for assenting to the invitation will be fought inch by inch in the Senate. They will go any lengths to stop it."

Grant's face darkened.

"I know what that means," he muttered. "I know what a political fight in my country means, alas!"

"I might be able to help," she suggested a little timidly. "I have seen something of life in Berlin."

He made her drink her coffee and afterwards lie down and rest. He himself spent a restless afternoon. The situation tormented him. A man of fixed and changeless purposes, as a rule, he found himself all the time looking at the matter from varying points of view. There were moments when his old tenderness for Gertrude seemed to some extent revived when, for the sake of bringing the happiness once more into her face, he felt a queer incoherent impulse to bid her close the gates of memory upon her past,—to assure her of his unchanged devotion. And then he shook with terror at the thought that such an idea could possibly have occurred to him. He was running a risk of ruining his own life and perhaps Susan's for the sake of a sentimental impulse of pity. He kept to himself most of the afternoon. At dinner time the strain began again. She wore a simple but beautifully fitting black net gown, and the way her eyes sought his as though for his approval would have seemed pathetic to a harder-hearted man than Grant. She drank more champagne than usual at dinner time and regained some of her spirits. She seemed less timid, some of her constraint appeared to pass. Afterwards they sat out on deck in a sheltered place. A clear, windy night, a star-strewn sky and a moon in its last quarter. They smoked, drank coffee, and every moment conversation became more difficult. Suddenly she leaned towards him and caught at his hands.

"Grant," she murmured, pleading, "can't you pretend, even if you don't feel anything any more? Don't keep me at arms' length like this. We're alone. There isn't any one in the world to interfere, and my heart is dry. Kiss me as though you cared just a little."

Her arms were around his neck, her head falling back, her lips close to his. A sudden coldness came over him. He remembered how he had longed and fought against the desire to kiss Susan. It wasn't fair, he had told himself. She must have her chance. She was so young. The sort of kiss he would have given her seemed somehow sacrilegious.

"Grant, kiss me."

He obeyed coldly, and with no pretence of fervour.

"Gertrude," he said, "it's a horrible thing. You know I cared once. You know that once I was glad enough to kiss you."

"Is it that girl?" she asked.

"Yes," he answered.

Her arms slid away from him — white, reluctant arms, beautiful in shape and texture — arms with their own peculiar expression of despair, as they fell upon her lap. The life for a moment seemed to go out of her.

"She is so young," she murmured. "Such a child, Grant. She doesn't understand life yet. You could leave her alone and she wouldn't be hurt. And you — you don't realise it, but you need more than that."

"Gertrude," he confessed, "I'm a fool about her. I can't help it. She's one of a type, I know — a very beautiful but not an unusual type. But she's just herself. The way she looks, her voice, her laugh, her little mannerisms — they just sit in my heart, they make me feel tender and wonderful things, and there doesn't seem to be room for anything else."

She lay watching the lazy movements of the yacht as it rose and fell, watching the black tumult of waters, glittering, now and then, in the faint moonshine. For a time she seemed utterly inert. Then she rose suddenly to her feet.

"I have a fancy to walk, Grant," she said. "No, don't come, please. I would just like to walk alone. It is a fancy of mine."

He helped her to her feet. She drew a fur wrap around her shoulders and turned hastily away. He leaned back in his chair, his eyes following her movements. She walked with rapid, unhesitating footsteps, sure-footed and graceful on the sloping deck, walked with her head a little uplifted, as though watching the rolling mast stab upward at the stars, as though she had passed into a world of her own thoughts, as though she were pursuing phantom ideas, seeking comfort in impotent essays of the imagination. The wind blew in her hair but brought no colour to her cheeks. Time after time she passed his chair without a glance, and each time it seemed to him that she was a little paler. At least he stopped her.

"You are tiring yourself, Gertrude," he said kindly. "Take my arm if you want to walk any more."

"You are right," she assented. "I will go down. Good night, Grant."

He kissed her fingers, horrified to find how cold they were. He insisted on taking her down the companionway to the door of her stateroom. She turned round there and smiled at him a little wanly. The suite consisted of a tiny sitting room as well as a bedroom and bathroom, the latter all black and white marble, and gleaming silver.

"You give me so much luxury, Grant," she sighed. "If only you could find a little kindness in your heart for me."

He felt suddenly brutal. He stooped and kissed her hands.

"Dear Gertrude," he whispered, "my heart is full of kindness. So full——"

"So full, Grant?"

"So full that I don't know how to offer it to you," he answered. "You see I'm a clumsy brute, Gertrude, and I've never been able to forget the years when I thought you the most beautiful thing on earth."

"But you don't any longer!" she cried.

He turned away. She listened anxiously to his receding footsteps. Then she threw herself on the sofa with a little moan. Afterwards she prepared for bed, left her door on the latch, wrapped a dressing gown of wonderful, rose-coloured silk around her, lit a standard electric light, drew out a book at random, and made a pretence at reading. She waited until she heard him come down the gangway, heard him pass her door with unfaltering footsteps, on his way to his own quarters, heard him open and close the door of his own room. Then she dropped the book and turned over on her face amongst the pillows.

CHAPTER XXII

THE next morning they passed Gibraltar soon after noon and headed for the Straits. At one o'clock Grant, who had spent the morning on the bridge, descended and walked down the deck. The chair in Gertrude's accustomed place was empty. Brookes came out from the little smoke room with a single cocktail upon a tray.

"Where is Madam?" Grant enquired.

"Her Highness sent word that she would remain in her rooms to-day," Brookes answered. "She begged that you would not disturb yourself on her account. She is simply a little tired."

Grant frowned. He was most unexpectedly disappointed.

"Who is looking after the Princess?" he asked.

"I thought of doing so myself, if you have no objection, sir," the man replied. "If you can manage with Jackson in the saloon, sir, it would perhaps be better."

Grant nodded and went to his solitary luncheon. It was certainly, to some extent, a relief to be spared the haunting question of her eyes, to be made to feel all the time that, in some way or another, he was unintentionally avenging himself for the great slight of his life. Yet the solitude oppressed him. He ate without his usual appetite and even forgot his whisky and soda until the meal was over. He spent the afternoon engaged upon some work. At six o'clock he sent her a little note:

My dear Gertrude, he wrote,

I am so sorry you are not well. Is there anything I can do? Shall I have the pleasure of seeing you at dinner time?

In a few minutes Brookes brought back an answer.

Dear Grant,

There is nothing the matter with me. If it is any pleasure to you, I will come to dinner.

In a sense he hated the satisfaction with which he read the few lines. He turned around and faced himself a little savagely as he realised the feeling. The wind, which had been freshening during the last few days, was now blowing almost a gale. He put on his oilskins, lit a pipe, and walked out on deck. Even he, a yachtsman from his boyhood, had to crawl along for some time, clutching at any support he could find, until he reached the railing. Linking his arm through it, he stood and looked down at the boiling cauldron of waters below. Grey clouds were rolling up all around them. White-capped waves rose one after another, as though to defy their progress. The first officer passed him on the way to the bridge.

"Heavy sea, sir, for the time of year," he observed.

"Is it getting worse, do you think?"

The man shook his head.

"It will blow itself out by dusk, sir," he prophesied. "It's a pleasure to see the way she rides through it."

Grant found his way presently on to the bridge and walked for an hour in the roar of the wind and with the spray dashing continually in his face. Towards the hour of twilight there was a faint yellow line of light westward,—the only parting in the ever-gathering clouds.

"What do you think of it, Captain?" Grant asked.

"I'm thinking she's the grandest little weather boat I've ever been on," the latter replied. "All the same, it's as well we're on the southern route. We might have lost a boat or two. It will be down before morning, sir."

Grant, curiously excited by the storm, changed for dinner a little before his usual time and made his way to the tiny smoke room. Brookes was already there, mixing cocktails.

"We will have a bottle of the special Clicquot to-night," Grant ordered.

"Her Highness is dining, I believe, sir," the man told him. "She said that she felt much better."

Grant nodded, furious with himself that the indifference with which he replied was only assumed. He stood in the swaying room, holding on to one of the fixed chairs, bitterly resenting the sudden access of weakness which made him half long for, half dread her coming. Then he heard an unexpected sound,—the sound of her laughter, silvery, almost gay, as she came cautiously in, holding on to the wall. He stepped forward to meet her and led her to a chair. She looked at him wonderingly.

"Whatever have you been doing, Grant?" she exclaimed. "What a colour you have! You look as though something marvellous had happened."

He shook his head.

"Just the storm," he answered. "It was wonderful this afternoon."

She nodded.

"I watched it from my porthole. In a way it excited me too. I was glad you sent your little message, Grant."

She looked at him and the fingers which held his glass shook. She was wearing a simpler dress even than the night before,—a gown of black and silver brocade, whose only fastening was a girdle around her waist. It was cut low at the throat and she was wearing no jewellery, not even her pearls, to conceal the white softness of her neck. When he looked at her arms he saw that the sleeves were wide and loose.

"I am afraid that I was a little churlish last night," he confessed, "and I didn't mean to be, Gertrude."

She caught at his fingers and held them for a moment.

"You are a dear, Grant," she said, "but you do carry the executioner's knife with you. To-night let us forget. I think I too have the storm in my heart. Let us forget the pain that comes when one remembers—when one passes on to solitude. You shall be my agreeable companion at dinnertime, and we will imagine that afterwards—well, what shall I say?—Otto is waiting for me in the lounge, you are on your way up to solve bridge problems at Lord Yeovil's. But, we dine together."

"If we dine at all," Grant laughed, as the spray suddenly beat against the porthole. "This may put the fires out."

"The bugle has gone anyhow," she answered.

She was forced to cling to him along the passage. He had, even, once to support her. In the saloon everything had been made fast as far as possible, and deep fiddles were upon the table. The service of the meal, however, was unimpaired. Gertrude had found her appetite. So also had Grant. Conversation became suddenly a pleasure. It was as though the whole awkwardness, the whole tragic significance of their presence alone in the middle of the Atlantic had been swept away. She began to talk of Berlin, the efforts of the aristocracy to reinstate themselves, the silent influence of Lutrecht, Blunn and his wonderful love of life and dark background of unscrupulous ambition.

Grant, who was usually so full of reserves, told her what only one or two people in the world knew,—of his visit to Berlin as a traveller in steel, told her how he had stayed at a commercial hotel and dodged the fashionable quarters of the city, of how he had seen her once in the distance, driving. He even told her what she wore. She laughed into his face, with glad eyes.

"You remember my ermines. You remember just what I wore. And yet you pretend that you don't care."

"I have never pretended quite so much as that," he answered.

The wine danced in their glasses.

"Wonderful!" Gertrude declared. "No one ever has such wonderful wine as you, Grant. Or is it drinking with you that makes me think so, I wonder. When you can leave off being severe, when you can look like a human being, something like the dear Grant of only a few years ago—then you make life seem too thrilling. Oh, if only I had the power to soften your heart just a little, to awaken memories in your brain, to make your eyes soften and have you feel—well, you have felt things for me, Grant."

"And you for me?" he ventured.

"As for no one else," she answered; "then and, alas, now."

He felt a sudden rebellious stirring of the pulses, and he set his teeth. She laughed at him, half provocatively, half insolently.

"Grant," she begged, "just this one night may we have some more wine? Hearing the thunder of those seas breaking outside excites me. I had no lunch and I'm hungry and thirsty."

Brookes hastened away. They were alone for a moment. She

leaned towards him. He sat quite still. Her lips rested for a second delicately, yet tenderly, upon his, and passed away.

"The storm," she whispered. "Put it down to that. All the strange things that one can't see at normal times seem to be calling out inside one to-night. Grant dear, do you know you really have got better-looking during the last three years? I like the way you part your hair, and those tiny little bits of grey at the sides."

"Are you trying to turn my head?" he replied uneasily.

"If I could, I would," she confessed. "Why think of it? Why speak of it? I love the excitement of this great motion, the thrill of being here alone with you. We are somewhere in the middle of the Atlantic, aren't we, Grant? Oh, I wonder what Otto is thinking about?"

She leaned back and laughed, showing her perfect teeth, the faint colour once more back in her pale cheeks.

"I think I must have an evil nature," she went on, "because I love to think of him now, tearing his hair and cursing—impotent. If there's anything in the world really detestable, it's a jealous man who takes no pains to keep what he has—a jealous man who thinks that what he has bought—bought at the altar—is his by divine right."

Grant rose to his supreme effort. He braced himself and fought against the personal note which had crept into their conversation. He tried to discuss the future of the nations, but she would have none of that. He told stories, and she suffered herself to be amused. But all the time the atmosphere which she had created seemed to remain. Her eyes were continually seeking his, begging for that answering flash which bespoke a common understanding.

"Ah, Grant," she said once, as they lingered for a moment over their last glass of wine, "how happy I am to-night. You were adorable to fetch me from my solitude. Do you know that, if you had sent me no word, I should have stayed on where I was? I think that I should have died."

"I missed you," he acknowledged simply.

"Dear man!" she murmured. "And yet you were trying all the

time to look as though I were an intruder, as though I had committed some unforgivable sin. I suppose I have really," she went on. "There are some who will never forgive me. An hour or two ago I thought that I should never forgive myself. The greatest shame of life seemed so near."

He had the sudden feeling of a terrified animal. Every door of escape seemed closed, and with it all there was the hateful singing in his blood, the crude insistence of primitive passion. Susan seemed to be receding, to be watching him from afar off, a little sad,—just a dream. Again he swung himself into battle.

"A delightful dinner, and such a dinner as I never dreamed of alone with you," he declared. "Now comes the difficult part. Can we get into the smokeroom?"

"Easily," she scoffed.

They made their way, holding on to the tables. The yacht was plunging and rolling even more than ever.

"I ought to go on deck," he told her, "and see how things are looking."

"Presently," she pleaded. "Come into the music room for a minute or two. That will leave me only a step across to my room. We can have our coffee there."

They made their way into the little rose and white music room. Opposite, through the hooked door, was a glimpse of her own suite. The steward brought them in coffee and liqueurs. He steadied himself with difficulty. Suddenly one of the lights went out. Only the standard was left heavily shaded and obscured.

"The captain told me to say, sir," Brookes reported, "that all was well on deck, but there has been a mishap to the batteries supplying the electric light, and we may be short for an hour or so. The electrician is already at work repairing."

Grant nodded.

"I shall come on deck before I go to bed," he said.

The roaring of the wind seemed louder, and the beating of the great waves over the portholes more insistent. She felt her way to the music stool.

"Now," she announced, "I shall sing to you. You shall hear my singing above the storm, if I have enough voice left. Come near, Grant. Come where I can see you."

Her fingers wandered over the keys, then struck a few familiar chords.

"Hackneyed," she laughed up at him, "but so apposite. Listen, dear man of surpassing strength."

She sang *"Mon coeur s'ouvre à ta voix,"* sang with her voice sometimes drowned by the booming of the sea and wind, sometimes rising clear and insistent through the momentary silences, always with that faint note of an actual passion, which fired his blood. When she had stopped she held out her arms. He took her gently into his but he held her away.

"Don't do this, Gertrude," he begged.

Her head sank back. He saw a look of absolute terror in her eyes. She was like a limp burden in his arms.

"I am faint," she whispered. "Carry me across."

He staggered with her out of the room, across the passageway, unhooked her door, and bent over her, alarmed. Suddenly there was a shock greater than they had felt before. The light in the stateroom went out, the door slammed. He saw her eyes open, blaze up at his through the darkness. Her arms around his neck were suddenly like a vise. She clung to him madly.

"Grant," she cried, "you have to kiss me now. This may be the end!"

BOOK TWO

CHAPTER I

GRANT, returning from an early stroll in the streets of New York on the morning after his arrival, looked with dismay at the three capable and determined-looking young men who occupied chairs in his sitting room, and at the one young lady, who, having placed her notebook upon the table, was deeply immersed in a novel. They all rose at his entrance. Jim Havers of the *New York Letter* was the first to announce himself.

"Glad to meet you, Mr. Slattery."

"Tarleton, of the *Moon,*" his neighbor announced. "Glad to welcome you back to New York, Mr. Slattery."

"Booker, of the *Chronicle,*" the third young man echoed. "Hope we're not too early for you."

"I'm Phoebe Smiles," the young lady told him, with the air of one who imparts information which should be entirely unnecessary. "You know about me, I dare say."

Grant shook hands with all of them.

"Look here," he said, "I'm very glad to see you and to be welcomed back home, but what's it all about? I'm not a novelist, or a politician, or an English nobleman. You can't get head lines out of me."

"Not so sure that we mightn't, sir," Tarleton replied cheerfully. "We thought, as we all arrived in a bunch, we'd better wait and see whether you had any preference as to which section of the Press you talked to. If you haven't you can give it to us all together. We can use the stuff a bit differently."

"But I'm no use to you fellows," Grant protested. "I'd just as soon talk to you all together as singly. In fact, I'd rather. It saves time. But what do you want me to talk about?"

"First of all your voyage home," Tarleton suggested. "Some hurricane you struck, eh?"

"We ran into a terrible storm about two days out of Gibraltar," Grant told them. "The *Grey Lady* behaved magnificently. Captain Martin and every one of my officers really deserve a word of praise. We didn't even lose a boat, and, as you know, some of the big liners got badly knocked about."

"That's interesting," Tarleton admitted, making a few notes. "There's just one other little thing about the voyage, Mr. Slattery."

"Go ahead," Grant invited.

The three men looked at one another. Tarleton appeared to be almost embarrassed,—an unusual situation for a newspaper man. Grant, who had pushed a box of cigars across the table, lit a cigarette and threw himself into an easy-chair.

"There have been some rumours going around," Tarleton said at last, "about a romantic stowaway."

"Really!" Grant remarked. "I haven't heard them. What sort of a stowaway?"

"A lady," Booker interposed, taking up his share of the burden. "A lady who has been missing for some time from Monte Carlo."

"Is that so!" Grant exclaimed. "What was her name?"

"The Princess von Diss."

Grant stared at him for a moment.

"Do you mean to suggest that the Princess von Diss was a passenger on board my yacht?" he demanded.

"That's the story that's been going round," Tarleton acknowledged.

"The idea seems to be that she smuggled herself on board without your knowledge," Havers intervened, "and was only discovered on the third day out."

"A beautiful romance," Miss Phoebe Smiles murmured.

"Of course," Tarleton suggested diffidently, "this might very reasonably seem to be a subject upon which you might not care to talk. Say the word, and we'll quit. Put it to us that on the subject of the missing Princess von Diss Mr. Slattery had nothing to say, and down it goes in our books and we'll pass on to the next."

Grant smiled.

"I think you can go a little further than that," he said. "You can assure the millions in New York, who are interested in this sort of thing, that I dined with the Princess von Diss on the night before I left Monte Carlo, at a dinner party given by Mr. Cornelius Blunn, the multi-millionaire,—a dinner which included her husband, the Prince von Diss, the King of Gothland, the English Prime Minister, and various other distinguished people. Since that evening I have not seen or heard of the Princess."

The pencils were, for a moment, busy.

"One may take it, then," Tarleton ventured, "that these stories of a romantic stowaway on board your yacht are untrue."

"Entirely," Grant assured them. "There was a large black cat discovered when we were three days out. She was the only stowaway I know about."

"Good heading, that," Booker observed.

"ROMANTIC STOWAWAY ON MR. GRANT SLATTERY'S YACHT DISCOVERED. ANSWERS TO THE NAME OF LIZZIE."

"Well, that disposes of the less important object of our visit," Havers declared. "Can you say anything to us, Mr. Slattery, about the Nice Conference of the Pact of Nations, and the invitation which was sent from there to this country?"

"I was at Monte Carlo at the time," Grant replied, "and I had the privilege of meeting Lord Yeovil often. I look upon the invitation as one of the greatest events of this decade. Lord Yeovil ran a great risk in bringing it forward. There was, as you may have heard, opposition."

Pencils were poised and an eager air of expectancy made itself felt.

"Can you," Tarleton asked, "tell us which countries opposed the invitation?"

"The negative votes are recorded by black balls," Grant explained. "I can only tell you that three were given. No one could say who put them in."

"Did you hear any rumours as to which countries probably did oppose the motion?" Jim Havers enquired.

"Nice and Monte Carlo were full of gossip," Grant replied. "But you must remember that very few people knew even what the system of voting was, much less that there were three black balls actually recorded. You gentlemen have made your scoop in being the first to publish that information. I had meant to have it published here. One of my objects in revisiting America is to impress upon my fellow countrymen the absolute necessity of accepting the invitation from the Pact."

"I see," Havers murmured. "You probably have a little more information up your sleeve, Mr. Slattery."

"I have a few more things to say," Grant confessed. "But I think I've given you fellows something to be going on with. I noticed that one of our well-known politicians, in rather a flamboyant speech last night, declared that America has no enemies. It is a foolish statement to make. Those three black balls proved the contrary."

"America has done very well so far by keeping out of the Pact," Booker remarked.

"It has been in accordance with her principles to remain aloof from European affairs," Tarleton put in.

"She occupies a mighty powerful position as a looker-on," Havers declared.

"All that belongs to the past," Grant explained earnestly. "America's policy in keeping out of all these compacts except the Limitation of Armaments may have been a sound one. Personally I am inclined to contest it. However, it is of the future we have to think. Times and conditions have changed. You must remember too that the constitution of the Pact is peculiar. Subscription to its principles and inclusion in its membership makes war between any of the nations belonging impossible. On the other hand any member or members of the Pact may make war against any nation outside the Pact without breaking their covenant. In fact, it would be against its established principles for any nation belonging to the Pact to intervene."

"You're not seriously suggesting, Mr. Slattery," Booker enquired, after a brief silence, "that any nation or combination of nations would actually dream of attacking the United States?'

"I have not said so, but I see nothing absurd in the idea," Grant assured them. "We are a mighty country in wealth, man power and brains, but we have faithfully obeyed the statutes of the Limitation of Armaments and we are to-day no stronger than many a poorer country, either on land or on sea. A combination of any two powers you can name would have the advantage of us."

"It would take a great deal to start a war scare in this country," Havers remarked with a smile.

"There were a great many people who didn't believe war was possible in nineteen-fourteen," Grant pointed out. "It came, nevertheless. The trouble is that the United States of America are governed too much by men who have never left their own country. To them America is omnipotent. To us, who have travelled and seen other things, she is not."

"We've got something more than we expected from this visit," Jim Havers admitted frankly. "I won't promise you that my paper, for one, is going to record your views sympathetically, Mr. Slattery. But whether they put them up like a puppet horse, to knock them down again, or whether they espouse them for their own, there's going to be some big type used."

"I'm quite content," Grant replied. "I'm here to be laughed at, if you will. But I'm here to tell you what I believe to be the truth, and I'm going on to Washington with a few more little facts to lay before some friends of mine up there. I want to see America accept that invitation, naturally, cordially, and freely. Then I am going to throw my hat into the air. And I shall have cause to do it too."

"I'd like a few more of your reasons for adopting this attitude," Havers suggested.

"You won't have them to-day," Grant told them bluntly. "I have an appointment with an important person in the newspaper line later in the day, and I am going to Washington on Thursday. When I get back we'll see how things go. I have some more facts up my sleeve, but I've got to build up my case. Good morning, gentlemen. Take another cigar, won't you, Mr. Havers? Glad to see any of you when I get back from Washington."

They filed out with a handshake and a word of thanks. Miss

Phoebe Smiles lingered behind. She waited until the door was closed. She was very neatly and smartly dressed. She had an appealing air and an exceedingly engaging smile. She smiled now at Grant.

"Mr. Slattery," she begged, "you might tell me the truth about that romantic stowaway."

"My dear young lady," he replied, "I have already told you, you and the others, that the story was a fabrication."

"That's all very well for the others," she pleaded, "you see they're good chaps and sportsmen and they couldn't press the point, with a lady in it. But the story's bound to come out, Mr. Slattery, and I should know just how to handle it. You were once engaged to marry the Princess von Diss, weren't you?"

"Yes, and she jilted me," Grant acknowledged. "What is the object of reminding me of that little episode, Miss Smiles?"

"Now you're angry," she cried regretfully. "I'm so sorry. Only, you see, Mr. Slattery, journalism is so much more difficult for a woman than a man and it would be such a wonderful thing for me if you felt inclined to tell the truth about that stowaway."

He opened the door.

"Miss Smiles," he said, "I can only add this to what I have already told your fellow visitors,—she took milk three times a day and scraps when she could get them. But here is your scoop as you insist upon it. She had green eyes, green passionate eyes, and her name was not Lizzie at all, it was Henrietta. Come back when the others come, won't you, Miss Smiles."

The young lady smiled and pouted a little.

"You look so nice and yet you're so hard," she complained, lingering on the threshold.

"You are mistaken. I am really very susceptible," Grant assured her. "That is why I am going to lock my door as soon as you are out of sight."

She heard the key turn in the lock as she made her way towards the passage from which the lift descended. Whilst she waited she looked at herself in the glass and gave a little sigh. She was not used to rebuffs.

"It must be this hat," she decided, giving it a little push on one side. "I was never sure about it. Down, please."

CHAPTER II

GRANT, a little later in the morning, presented himself at the office of the newspaper in New York which was generally considered to be the most influential and weighty in the Metropolis. Its correspondents were to be found in every capital of the world. One of the editors was received weekly at the White House. It stood for what was sane and beneficent in American legislation and the cause which it espoused was seldom known to languish. The editor, Daniel Stoneham, was an old friend of Grant's, and on sending up his card he was shown at once into his presence. The two men shook hands warmly.

"Good man, Grant!" Stoneham exclaimed. "Glad to see you back again. One hears of you hobnobbing with Kings and Prime Ministers and the great people of the earth. Quite time you showed a little interest in your own country."

"Well, I'm here on the old job," Grant declared sinking into the easy-chair to which his friend had pointed and accepting a cigarette.

"The deuce you are!" the other observed, with some surprise. "I thought since you had become a millionaire you'd turned slacker. I haven't heard anything of you for a year or so."

"I've been doing much more difficult and unpleasant work than ever before in my life," Grant confided. "I've been doing Secret Service work which is only half official. That is to say, that if I get into trouble I'm not acknowledged and if I do any good work the Department gets the credit. That doesn't matter, though. The point is that I've made a scoop on my own. There's trouble brewing."

"What sort of trouble?" Stoneham demanded. "Do you mean anything in connection with the invitation from Nice?"

"Well, I'll tell you this for one thing. That invitation would never have been sent but for me."

"Say, you're not pulling my leg, are you?"

"I was never more in earnest in my life. It was touch and go with Lord Yeovil's proposition. There were three votes against it. Four would have barred it. The fourth man had been bought for fifty thousand pounds. I imitated the methods of the adventurous novelists and abducted him. I kept him out at sea all night and the voting took place without him. If he'd got there in time, Lord Yeovil's motion would have been defeated, America would never have been invited to join the Pact and the trouble which is even now brewing against her would have developed very rapidly."

"Serious business this, Grant," Stoneham remarked.

"The most serious part of it is that it's the truth," Grant rejoined drily. "However, the first stage in the battle has been won. The invitation has been despatched to Washington. Now I tell you where the second stage of the battle begins and where America will need the aid of every one of her loyal citizens. There will be, without the slightest doubt, an immense and cunningly engineered propaganda to prevent America's accepting that invitation. I want to fight that propaganda, Daniel. I want you to help me."

The editor sat back in his chair and his thoughtful grey eyes studied Grant's face. He was a short man, clean-shaven, with smooth black hair streaked with grey. Whenever any one wished to annoy him they called him the Napoleon of journalism. Still the likeness was there.

"Whose were the three votes against the invitation being sent to America?" he enquired.

"Germany, Japan, and Russia."

"And the one which would have been given but for your intervention?"

"Scandinavia," Grant replied. "That of course has no political significance. It was simply that the man himself was bought."

"And what do you suppose is the reason for Germany and Japan voting against the United States being allowed to join the Pact?" Stoneham asked.

"I believe it is their intention to attack us," Grant pronounced. "The Pact only forbids aggressions between the countries belonging. She has no jurisdiction even over her own members who find cause to quarrel with an outside country. We've been a little too high and mighty, Stoneham. If we'd decided to adopt the attitude of remaining outside the affairs of the world, we should never have subscribed to the Limitation of Armaments. To-day, for all our great wealth, our immense man power, and our supreme civilisation, the combined armaments of Japan and Germany are precisely double our own."

"Of course," Stoneham said, "if any other man in the world were to come to me and talk like this, I should say that he was a lunatic."

"I am no lunatic, Dan," Grant declared. "I know very well what I am talking about."

"Have you any proofs?"

"I sent them to Washington an hour after I landed. You don't need them, Dan. You believe me, I know."

"Yes, I believe you."

"And you'll help? You'll put that in the forefront of your whole policy, the acceptance by the United States of this invitation from the Pact? You'll press it home to the people, Dan? Remember, it's our last chance. We've refused twice."

Stoneham was curiously silent. He was looking for a moment out of the uncurtained window, away over the skyscrapers and chimney pots to where little flashes of the blue Hudson, with its tangle and burden of sea and river-going craft were visible. There was something smouldering in his eyes.

"Grant," he said at last, "you've brought me news. I have some to give you. In a way, although I never realised it before, my news bears upon yours."

"Get along with it," Grant begged.

"A commanding interest in this paper — three quarters of the shares in fact — was signed away last night. The control of the paper has gone out of our hands altogether."

"Who is the buyer?" Grant demanded eagerly.

"Felix Pottinger," was the quiet reply.

"And who's behind him?"

"They tried to keep that secret. But I found out by an accident. The real buyer is Cornelius Blunn of Berlin."

Grant was thunderstruck.

"Fifteen days ago," he confided after a brief silence, "I was a guest at a dinner party given by that man. A few days before that we were scrapping on my yacht. He tried to start a mutiny. Offered ten thousand pounds to some of my youngsters to get the yacht back in time for his Scandinavian friend to vote at the Nice Conference. Blunn and I have had the gloves off all the time. He sent some one down from Berlin to spy on me at Monte Carlo. My God! This comes of our hospitality to foreigners. This is where we make the laughing stock of ourselves for all the world. Cornelius Blunn! The German multimillionaire! The man who hates America, her industries and her politics, is calmly allowed to come here and buy the only great American newspaper which represents no other interests save those of America."

"There is a certain amount of irony in the situation," Stoneham admitted. "You know what happened, I dare say. The Chief, after fifteen years of wisdom, went on to Wall Street a few months ago. He lost between five and ten millions and had a stroke. I suppose this will just see him through."

"I thought the old man wouldn't have done it if he'd been himself," Grant muttered. "I suppose I'd better go and see Dawson."

"You'll have a hard nut to crack. I heard Dawson speak only last night at a dinner. His references to the invitation were very perfunctory indeed. He's one of the men who believe in America for the Americans. You needn't look so depressed, though. What about me? I shall be out of a job within a week."

"Come and have some lunch?" Grant invited.

Stoneham shook his head.

"I guess not. We're all in a state of nerves here. Waiting to hear what's going to happen. The sale seems to have been a lightning-like affair. We're expecting a visit from Pottinger in a minute. Shouldn't be surprised if he takes us over within twenty-four hours."

"Couldn't you get one article in?" Grant suggested.

"I'll try," Stoneham assented. "Where are you?"

"The Great Central. They're getting my flat ready at Sherrey's if I stay on. Things seem a trifle uncertain at present."

"I'll ring you up," Stoneham promised.

Grant lunched at his club, where he met many of his friends and acquaintances to whom he was simply a rather restless, much to be envied millionaire. Whenever he could, he brought the subject of conversation round to the Nice invitation. To a certain extent he was dismayed by the prevalent criticisms.

"Guess there's no one in the world so thick-skinned as a Britisher," one man declared. "You can't keep him in his place unless you tie him there. What does America want, sending her best men away from home and spending her time and money on these wearisome conferences? They don't amount to anything, anyway."

"England's got a scare about something or other and wants to hold her big relation's hand," another usually well-informed man remarked. "For all their strength, there was never a less self-reliant nation."

"It's just like English statesmanship to make it difficult for them down in Washington," a third occupant of the room pointed out. "It simply puts our Government in an embarrassing situation. Nobody wants to seem ungracious, and it won't be easy to say no. At the same time, I can't see that a shadow of good can come of acceptance. They're always squabbling at the Pact meetings, like they are at the Limitation of Armaments. The latest *canard* now is that Japan has secretly built some flying ships which could destroy any fleet afloat."

Grant remained a listener only. He left the club about the middle of the afternoon, and, after a few minutes' anxious deliberation, was driven to the Hotel des Ambassadeurs.

"Is the Princess von Diss staying here?" he asked the clerk at the desk.

"Not at present, sir," the young man replied, with a curious glance at Grant.

"I saw by the newspapers that she was in Newport," the latter persisted, "and was coming here."

"We have been asked for no reservation at present," he was assured.

Grant scribbled the name of his hotel and the number of his suite on the back of a card and passed it across.

"If the Princess should arrive," he begged, "will you let her have this?"

"With pleasure, sir."

Grant went back to his sitting room and considered the situation. If he approached Dawson, the editor and part-proprietor of the next most important paper to the *New York*, he was absolutely sure of an unsympathetic hearing. Dawson, already prejudiced, would believe nothing without proofs, and such proofs as Grant possessed were, by this time, in the hands of his official sponsor in Washington. He changed early, dined at another of his clubs and wandered into two or three more of which he was a member. He found nowhere any particular interest in the subject which was to him such a vital one. Everybody was hugely concerned with his own affairs, the price of American stocks, the latest singer at the Opera, the winning of the amateur golf championship of the world by an American, the success of the American tennis players on the Riviera. A few people seemed to regard Lord Yeovil's proposition as a kindly act, but altogether unnecessary. America was splendid in her isolation, strong and secure as the Rock of Gibraltar. No wonder there was a desire on the part of the other nations to fasten like limpets upon her. One didn't wish to hurt England's feelings, but it would have been better policy to have enquired first whether such an invitation would be acceptable.

"And how the mischief," Grant was driven at last to observe, "could America have replied to that? We haven't an official, even the President, with sufficient authority. The matter now is put on a definite basis. The Senate must decide."

"Sure," the young man to whom he had been speaking agreed listlessly. "Look here, Grant," he went on with a sudden accession of interest, "you must have seen the Hoyt brothers play over at Monte Carlo. Is it true what they say, — that the elder's getting stale? I've a thousand dollars on their match against the Frenchmen."

"I saw very little tournament tennis," Grant answered. "The Hoyts are great favourites for the match, anyhow."

He found his way back to his rooms comparatively early. There was no telephone message from the "Ambassadeurs," — only a scribbled note from Stoneham.

DEAR GRANT, it said,

Thought you'd like to know Pottinger took us over at six o'clock, asked to see the leading article for to-morrow's paper and tore it into small pieces. He's in possession. We're out, lock, stock, and barrel. You'd better get to work.

Dan.

Grant tore the note thoughtfully across and put through a long distance call to Washington. Then he threw himself wearily into an easy-chair. The roar of the city, abating but slightly as night advanced, still mercilessly insistent, soothed him. He closed his eyes, mindful of sleepless nights. The tinkle of the telephone bell awoke him. In a few moments he was through to Washington.

"Brendon, Secretary, speaking," a voice announced. "Is that Mr. Slattery?"

"Grant Slattery speaking," was the prompt rejoinder.

"Can you come to Washington to-morrow? The Chief would like to see you."

"I'll catch the ten o'clock train," Grant promised.

He went to bed better satisfied. The struggle had commenced.

CHAPTER III

GRANT felt that on the whole he was well received at Washington. A very great man indeed vouchsafed him his confidence.

"I am going so far as to tell you, Mr. Slattery," he said, "that I, personally, am in favour of accepting the invitation of the Pact of Nations. I have met Lord Yeovil once or twice and I am perfectly certain that he is sincere in his friendship for this country. The attitude of isolation, which some of our most brilliant statesmen have acclaimed, is not, in my opinion, a sound one in these days of practical politics. I would welcome a decision of my Government which brought us into line with the great Powers of Europe. At the same time, to be equally frank with you, I cannot for one moment believe that there exists any Power in the world or any combination of Powers which would dream of flaunting the world's desire for peace and making an unprovoked attack upon this country."

"Neither should I, sir," Grant answered hastily, "unless I had lived in the shadow of these people and had imbibed their hopes and ambitions. Take, for one moment, Japan. I have lived in Tokio, and other cities of the country, for a year. I lived there not as an American but as an Englishman. Japan is a very proud country. The sons of her over-populated Empire have penetrated with difficulty but still without vital resistance into most quarters of the world. It has remained with America to place an embargo upon her citizenship, to enunciate the great principle of the inferiority of the yellow races. There, sir, lies the cause of the undying enmity of the people of Japan for the Government of this country."

"It was really an affair of state, not international legislation," his host reminded him.

"That has not affected the question," Grant insisted. "The

feeling is there. Then take the case of Germany. She cannot strike against England or France. They are members of the Pact. But do you think that twenty years, or two hundred years, would quench that desire for revenge which has been part of the birthright of every living German to-day? There remains of her foes only America. Do you realise, sir, the anomaly of subscribing to the Limitation of Armaments and refusing to accept the protection of the Pact of Nations?"

"Theoretically, again, yes," was the considered reply. "But, practically, I am entirely with my advisers. I do not believe in the possibility of any hostile action against this country. At the same time, you will see that I am quite frank with you, for I admit I should prefer to be associated with the Pact of Nations. My efforts will be devoted in that direction."

"I beg that you will make them strenuous efforts, sir," Grant enjoined. "You have read the memoranda I addressed to the Secretary?"

"With great interest and some amusement," was the smiling reply. "Am I really to accept the account of the happenings on board your yacht as being authentic?"

"They are not even exaggerated, sir," Grant assured his auditor earnestly. "If I had not kept Funderstrom out all that night, Lord Yeovil's motion would have been lost."

"I must accept your word, of course. On the other hand you must admit that the whole thing reads like a piece of opera bouffe. Before we leave this subject, Mr. Slattery, I should like to ask you one more question. You have spoken of the hostile intentions of Japan and Germany against this country. Have you ever come to any conclusion as to the manner in which this hostility was to be displayed?"

"Sir," Grant replied, "I am a wealthy man, so this is of no moment, but I have spent a hundred thousand dollars trying to get hold of a perfectly simple document which I know to be in existence. There is an elaborated scheme agreed to by Japan and Germany, which is intended to strike at the very heart of our existence, and for which I have the strongest reasons for believing that Mr. Cornelius Blunn is responsible. There are two people from whom I hope to obtain it. Both have, so far, disappointed me.

Nevertheless I shall get it some day. As regards the part of the conspiracy dealing with direct warfare, that, without a doubt, is to be conducted by sea,—the German fleet coming from eastwards to the Atlantic seaboard, the Japanese fleet, to San Francisco. I might point out, sir, that the American fleet, honourably kept within the Limitation of Armaments Statutes, would be utterly unequal to dealing with both adversaries arriving from opposite directions."

"You drive me to the conclusion, Mr. Slattery, that I am devoid of imagination," his host observed, smiling. "I cannot conceive the spectacle of those two fleets approaching our shores with a hostile purpose. You need not take it as a cause for alarm that I am unable to embrace your theory. So far as you are concerned, I am with you on the practical side of the matter. My influence will be directed towards securing an acceptance of Lord Yeovil's proposition."

Grant rose to his feet. His companion laid a detaining hand upon his shoulder.

"My wife desires that you will give us the pleasure of lunching with us," he said. "Her mother and yours were friends, as you may know. And I, myself, was at Harvard with your uncle. I knew your father, too, although he graduated a year or two before me. You are, I hope, free?"

"I shall be honoured," Grant acceded.

Luncheon was an informal meal. A few officials were present, two ladies who were distant relatives of the host, a recent arrival amongst the diplomats and a newly elected senator. The presiding genius of the establishment took Grant under her special protection.

"I'm not going to pretend to be tactful, Mr. Slattery," she declared, "because you know that Gertrude's mother and I were great friends, and I was, at one time, very fond of Gertrude. I think I was one of the first to notice her friendship with Otto von Diss, and certainly one of the first to disapprove of it. I'm a terrible gossip, and I read all the society papers. So of course I know that you have been meeting at Monte Carlo. Tell me, has she changed?"

"She is as beautiful as ever," Grant said, "but she has certainly changed. She has gained a great deal, and I think lost something."

"She can't possibly be still in love with that ridiculous little husband of hers."

Grant was silent for a moment. Under ordinary circumstances he felt that his hostess's lack of reserve was really the truest form of tact. But the things she did not know were burning in his brain.

"I did not see a great deal of Gertrude in Monte Carlo," he confided. "Her husband arrived unexpectedly, and I think that he is of a very jealous temperament."

"Were you speaking of Gertrude von Diss?" one of the women from across the table interposed. "I see from the paper that she is in Newport, just arrived from Europe."

His hostess turned enquiringly towards Grant.

"I heard the same rumour," the latter remarked, "but I scarcely think that it can be true. I enquired in New York, but no one there knew anything about her. At the same time it is certainly a fact, as I learned this morning, that her husband's friend, Cornelius Blunn, who was with us all at Monte Carlo, landed in New York two days ago. The Von Disses may have come with him."

Grant's host frowned for a moment.

"Blunn seems to have a great many friends in this country," he observed. "He appears to spend half his time going back and forth."

"His present visit seems to have been to some purpose," Grant declared a little bitterly.

"In what respect?"

Grant was, for a moment, taken aback.

"You know about Mr. Cornelius Blunn's purchase, sir," he ventured.

"I've heard nothing," was the somewhat impatient reply.

"I am sure I beg your pardon, sir. It would have been my first item of news, but I never imagined that Gordon Marsham would have acted without giving you notice."

"What's Gordon Marsham got to do with it?"

"Just this much, sir," Grant pointed out. "He has sold the *New*

York to Cornelius Blunn. A man named Pottinger is the new editor. Stoneham's article which should have appeared this morning, welcoming the invitation from the Pact, was torn into small pieces."

Grant's host was more perturbed than he had been during the whole of the morning.

"Marsham's action," he declared, "is absolutely unbelievable. He knows perfectly well that the *New York* has become almost the mouthpiece of the Government. It was practically a subsidised journal. To dispose of it secretly, just now, to a German-American, without even advising us, is an amazing proceeding. You are sure that you are not misinformed, Mr. Slattery?"

"Absolutely certain," was the confident reply. "The discourtesy to you, sir, can only be explained by Mr. Marsham's breakdown in health."

"It is a very serious event," was the grave acknowledgment. "The *New York* was the one great American paper—a paper which, when things really mattered, brushed aside minor issues and preached the gospel of real things. One of the editors used to be here every week. I always treated him with the utmost confidence."

"Have you ever met Cornelius Blunn, sir?" Grant enquired.

"Once only. A genial, simple fellow he seemed, for such a master of industry. I could scarcely believe that I was talking to the owner of so many gigantic commercial undertakings."

"He is outwardly the most simple and good-natured, and actually the most inscrutable person I ever came across," Grant confided. "There is a rumour about him that he carries wherever he goes, night and day, locked and padlocked in a little casket of gold, a letter written by his father on his deathbed."

"How romantic!" one of the women murmured.

"Has any one any idea as to its contents?" some one else asked.

Grant shook his head.

"I was once told," he said, "that if one could read that letter one could read the riddle of Blunn's life. I have formed my own idea about it."

"A secret?" his hostess enquired.

"Not amongst us," Grant replied. "I believe that it is an injunction from Blunn senior — who died, they say, of a broken heart, some years after the signing of the Peace of Versailles — to his son to devote his life towards avenging Germany's humiliation. Personally, I believe that that is the motive before Blunn day and night. I believe that with that end in view he is deliberately working to upset the peace of the world."

Grant's pronouncement was received, as he had expected, with disfavour. His host merely smiled. The senator from the west, who had been waiting impatiently for an opportunity to join in the conversation, cleared his throat and leaned a little forward.

"Sir," he said, "I guess every man in this country is free to express his opinions. Those may be yours, but I'd like just to tell you how the people down in my State look upon such talk. They say that trouble is made by talking about it, that most of the wars of the world have come about through newspaper discussion in advance and mischievous people going about putting belligerent thoughts into the minds of peaceful people. If I heard you, sir, make such a statement as you have just made on a public platform, I should conceive it to be my duty to use every gift of oratory with which I have been endowed to demonstrate to your audience the futility, the absurdity, and the immorality of such a statement. Hearing it under this roof, sir, I say no more than this. War and the desire for war is dead amongst the civilised nations of the world. We are every one of us grappling hard with social and economic problems of far greater consequence. The whimper of a person like Cornelius Blunn, for all his millions, is less than the voice crying in the wilderness, when one considers the majesty and colossal power of the chief nation against whom that voice is raised."

Grant inclined his head courteously. The bombast of the senator's words had appealed slightly to the sense of humour of most of them. Yet Grant was perfectly well aware that the man had spoken the truth when he declared that he was voicing the views of the people of his State. It was a representative expression of opinion. He could even see a qualified but vital assent to it in the faces of most of the little party. His host applied the closure.

"Well," he said, "we must not drift into too serious argument. We shall all have an opportunity of expressing our views presently upon this subject."

"In the meantime, sir," Grant begged, "might I ask Mr. Senator Ross one question?"

"By all means," was the prompt assent.

"Would you, sir," Grant went on, turning towards the senator, "vote for the United States accepting the invitation of the Pact of Nations to join them?"

"I should not," was the decided reply. "The Pact of Nations may have need of the United States. The United States has no need of the Pact. As a citizen of the United States I am prouder of the present isolated attitude of my country than I am, even, of her undoubted supremacy in every field of economics and civilisation."

The senator's sonorous statement was the signal for the breaking up of the little party. Grant was accompanied to the door by one of the secretaries with whom he had some previous acquaintance.

"The old type remains, I see," the former remarked, with a smile.

"It's the type beloved of the semi-professional politician," the young man declared. "We have one of them to lunch every week. The chief can't stand them in larger doses. But you know they have an enormous backing."

Grant felt the warning behind his friend's words, as he walked slowly back towards the club where he was staying. It was the West, the big, brawny West, with its polyglot population and immense material prosperity, which he chiefly feared.

CHAPTER IV

GRANT left Washington with a curious mixture of impressions. He had spent a fortnight in the political capital of his country and yet he came away with a strange conviction that he had been somewhere on the edge of real things, that he had talked of vital events with men whose interest in them was chiefly academic. Washington might be the furnace, but impulse took him where the fuel lay. He spent four days in Chicago. He went on to St. Louis and Minneapolis. Then he crossed the continent to Boston, where he breathed an entirely different atmosphere. The editors of two great newspapers believed in him and were ready to preach his doctrine. Nevertheless when, after six weeks' absence, he found himself back in New York, it was with a feeling rather of discomfiture than of self-satisfaction that he viewed his progress. The magnificent self-assurance of his country seemed impregnable. Even where he had been listened to most kindly he felt that he was receiving the indulgence accorded to a crank.

Arrived in the sitting room of his hotel he took up his pile of letters and sorted them through. One by one he passed them by. He had commenced his task with a sinking heart. He finished it with a curious admixture of feeling. There was no letter from Gertrude. He rang up the Ambassadeurs. They had received no news of any projected visit from the Princess. He felt himself face to face with a new situation. The problems with which he had expected to be confronted seemed to have melted away. Yet to him there was something ominous and disconcerting in this state of negation, something which seemed like the corollary of his own threatened failure in the larger enterprise which he had embraced. He was not an abnormally temperamental person but a fit of black depression suddenly swept over him. The thought of Susan, her sweet, girlish charm, her ingenuous appeal, tugged at his heart strings with swift and passionate little bursts of memory. He cursed himself for the hesitation which had kept him that last night at the Villa, when they had stood alone upon the balcony, and the chance had been his, from taking her into his arms. That one kiss which he had craved from her would have clad him in the armour of a gigantic selfishness towards every other claim or appeal. She had been right. The difference between their ages was a trifling matter, something to be reckoned with if she had been a simpering schoolgirl of her years, but for Susan — with her understanding, her insight, her delightful womanliness — a thing not worthy of consideration. What was she thinking of him now, he wondered? There had been a certain guardedness in the Press but the story of Gertrude's flight had blazed along the Riviera, the more ardently believed in because of the mystery surrounding it. Lord Yeovil's letters, kindly still and even friendly, betrayed signs of it. There was no mention of Susan or any message from her, a certain restraint in dealing in any way with personal topics. Grant moved restlessly to the window. Although it was his own city, the loneliness of a stranger in New York seemed to have enveloped him in a cloud of deepening depression. The magnitude, the sombre magnificence of it all, the towering buildings, the height from which he looked down at the streets like illuminated belts, the tangle of distant lights upon the river, the dull roar of ever proceeding traffic, seemed almost terrifying. A city honeycombed with people, moving on at the hand of destiny; a contemplation for the philosopher, an invitation towards lunacy to the lonely individual. Grant momentarily lost his courage. He seemed cut off from his friends, the destroyer of his own happiness. The sight of a familiar face, the sound of a cheery voice at that moment, would have been a joy to him. He answered almost eagerly the knocking at his door. A man entered, a man with the two things for which he had felt himself craving — a smile and a cheerful face — but the last person in the world from whom he was expecting to receive a visit.

"Blunn!" he exclaimed.

The newcomer laughed cheerfully as he deposited his silk hat and Malacca cane upon the table and withdrew his evening gloves.

"Well, well," he said, "I thought we might meet over here. I'm not offering to shake hands although I'd be very glad to. I've come for a chat, though, and when I chat, I like to be comfortable. May I have an easy-chair, a whisky and White Rock, and a cigar? I have just left the Opera, and I am a little exhausted with the wonder of it. Your new prima donna is marvellous."

Grant rang for the waiter.

"What on earth have you come to see me about, Blunn?" he asked.

"My dear fellow, what a question!" the other replied, looking round the room and finally selecting his chair. "Enemies always visit one another. It lends spice to combat. Now the one of us with the keener brain will leave this interview the gainer. Which of us will it be, I wonder? A most interesting speculation. By the bye, might I suggest a little ice with the whisky and White Rock?"

Grant gave the order. He was in the frame of mind to welcome the presence even of Mr. Blunn.

"After your magnificent banquet in Monte Carlo my last evening there," he observed, "I think that you are making very slight demands upon my hospitality."

"I shall make larger ones upon your patience, perhaps," Blunn declared. "You're not looking well, Mr. Slattery. This rushing around from one big city to another, these alarmist conclaves in Washington, do not agree with you so well as the sunshine of the Riviera."

"You seem pretty well-informed as to my movements."

"Naturally. We do not keep a large and expensive Secret Service going here for nothing. I could give you a most faithful record of your movements on every day since your arrival, starting with your visit to your friend Stoneham of the *New York,* your luncheon at the club and your subsequent visit to the Hotel des Ambassadeurs and winding up with the telephone message which called you to Washington."

"Wonderful!" Grant murmured, affecting unconcern, but in reality a little staggered. "Here's your whisky and White Rock," he added, as the waiter entered. "Will you help yourself?"

Mr. Blunn prepared his highball with care, lit his cigar and leaned back in his chair.

"I am thankful," he confessed, "that prohibition in this country was before my time. It did some good, they tell me. Swept away the saloons and kept the alcoholic strength of spirits down. On the whole, however, it must have been very uncomfortable."

"The statute was modified almost out of existence before I took an interest in such things," Grant remarked.

Blunn was silent for a moment or two. He had completely the air of a man steeped in the atmosphere of the music he has enjoyed and dropping in for some slight refreshment with a friend.

"Mr. Slattery," he said, a little abruptly, "one of the objects of my visit is to congratulate you upon your failure."

"My failure," Grant repeated.

"Precisely. At Monte Carlo you scored a daring and well-deserved victory. There were a dozen ways by which we could have outwitted you, but luck was on your side. You brought off one of the crudest pieces of amateur, melodramatic brigandage I ever remember to have read of in the pages of your most flamboyant novelists. Still, you brought it off. You scored the trick. Dazzled a little, shall we say, by success, you start off now to attempt the impossible. Here, my young friend, you are, in plain parlance, up against a hopeless proposition. You want to drive home to the statesmen and people of the United States the fact that a certain combination of forces, with Germany, of course, as the villain of the play, is planning a warlike enterprise of some sort or another against this country in revenge for their intervention in nineteen-seventeen. You cannot do it."

"Can't I?" Grant murmured.

Cornelius Blunn smiled. Very reluctantly he knocked the ash from his cigar.

"Well, ask yourself how far you have succeeded at present,"

he went on. "You have had every possible advantage. You have visited Washington as a *persona grata,* you have talked with officials and statesmen to whom you are personally well known, and whom your high character and reputation must influence largely in your favour. You had a very pleasant time socially, everybody was very nice to you. How much progress did you make?"

"Go on, please."

"You have since visited most of the principal cities in the States. You have interviewed a great many newspaper proprietors. You have given four lectures. The only place where you really created an impression was in Boston and there the ground was already prepared for you. I do not think that I am far from the mark when I offer you my congratulations upon your failure."

"But why congratulations?" Grant asked. "Why not sympathy?"

Mr. Blunn pinched his cigar and smiled thoughtfully.

"If you had been a real danger to us," he confided, "we should have had to take steps—very regretful steps. You can scarcely imagine that a completely organised Secret Service, of whose existence I have just given you proof, can be without agents who are prepared to go to any lengths which necessity might demand."

"You mean that you would have had me assassinated?"

Blunn shrugged his shoulders.

"We should have tried to avoid melodrama. You would probably have met with an accident."

"This is very interesting," Grant admitted. "I am alive on sufferance, then?"

"Don't put it like that, I beg you."

"Supposing I become dangerous?"

"Why conjure up these disagreeable possibilities," Cornelius Blunn expostulated. "I do not see any immediate prospect of your becoming dangerous. You have no organisation, no definite propaganda, no real evidence of the things which you fear. For your information I may tell you this. Short of an absolute upheaval, there is not the slightest doubt but that the Senate will refuse their sanction to the President to accept this invitation of the Pact of Nations."

"Why are you so anxious that America should not join the Pact?" Grant asked.

Mr. Blunn smiled.

"If you knew that," he announced, "then perhaps we should have to label you dangerous, which, as I have previously explained, would not be good for your health. Now, my young friend, we have had a pleasant talk. Shall I tell you what I really came to see you about?"

Grant glanced at the clock. It was long past midnight.

"Perhaps it would be as well."

"I came," Blunn said, "to ask whether you can give me any information as to the whereabouts of my friend Von Diss's wife."

"I have not the slightest idea as to her whereabouts," Grant assured him coolly. "In any case, why come to me?"

"There is an impression upon the Riviera and elsewhere that the Princess left Monaco on your yacht."

"The impression is ridiculous," Grant declared.

"Is it?" Blunn murmured. "Well, well! The Princess——"

Grant stopped him with an imperative gesture.

"Do you mind leaving the Princess out of this conversation?" he interrupted. "I do not care, at any time, about discussing women. The Princess is an old friend of mine, a new friend of yours. Some other subject of conversation, if you please, or I shall be forced to remind you that the hour is late."

"Quite a sound attitude," Mr. Blunn remarked reflectively. "Still, you might remember that I am her husband's oldest friend, and domestic relations in Germany are treated, I think, a little more sacredly than in most countries. I might even go so far as to say that I represent the Prince."

"As to the Prince's representative," Grant retorted, "there is the door. To Mr. Cornelius Blunn, my enemy, I know, but whose conversation and sense of humour attract me, I would suggest another whisky and White Rock."

Blunn helped himself sparingly and rose to his feet. He

knew his man, and the ostensible object of his visit remained unfulfilled.

"*À propos* of our former subject of conversation, Mr. Slattery," he said, "take my advice. Don't become too prominent in your propaganda, and, above all, don't be too inquisitive. There are some things which you would give a great deal to discover, but the discovery of which would mean death. You are a young man and reasonably fond of living, I am sure."

"Not only that," Grant replied, "but I mean to live until my work is done."

Mr. Blunn finished his highball slowly and thoughtfully. Then he rose, put on his hat, and hung his overcoat over his arm.

"A very pleasant chat, Mr. Slattery," he concluded. "I like you, you know. You are a young man of imagination and spirit. I wish that you were a German."

Grant held open the door.

"If you had been endowed with a conscience at your birth, you wouldn't have made a bad American," he reciprocated.

CHAPTER V

Cornelius Blunn had in no wise exaggerated the mighty Juggernaut of propaganda which had already been set in movement in every city and in every State. Its extent and the magnitude of its operations were almost inconceivable. There was scarcely a magazine or review published which did not contain an article by some brilliant writer, preaching the doctrine of American independence and self-determination. A small army of lecturers were at work upon the same theme. There were letters to the newspapers, public meetings, and a vast distribution of free literature. Stoneham, who had been taking a brief vacation, was brought back to New York by an urgent cable from his friend. They discussed the situation, dining at a famous club, on the night of his return.

"I am with you, Grant, you know that," the newspaper man said, "both from conviction and as a pal. But you're up against a simply absurd proposition. Plenty of us over here know that for twenty years Germany has been preparing for this sort of thing. She has a perfect machinery of propaganda which only needed a touch of the finger to set it going. Blunn has set his hand upon it. Look at the result. There is scarcely a magazine of repute into which they haven't bought their way. They have their own newspapers and they are hanging on to the fringe of a good many others. They're well in with the reviews, they have a strong hold in the colleges, the book counters are flooded with their practically free literature. On the other side there are a fair number of thinking people who would advocate America's joining the Pact. But there is no organisation, nothing to bring them together, no means of spreading their opinions. You've done as much as one man could do. Five thousand of you might have made a little headway. As it is, Cornelius Blunn and his friends are absolutely convincing the great majority of the inhabitants of the United States that America will sacrifice her independence if she accepts this Pact, that Great Britain is jealous of America's supremacy in commerce and finance, and that this invitation is merely a trap. People can't help believing a thing they are always being told. That is the first principle of successful propaganda."

"I know, Dan," Grant acknowledged. "But we're not going to knuckle under without a fight. We are late starters but fortunately I've got a few millions to spare. I want you to look round and collect as many young writers and lecturers as you can who are inclined to come in on our side. Take those who agree with us from conviction where possible, but pay them well. We may be late starters, but remember this thing won't be voted on finally for two or three months to come yet. I was talking on the 'phone with Entwistle at Washington only this afternoon. It's a complicated procedure and, after all, you know, we have something on our side. The President and most of his *entourage* are with us. That must count for something."

"There are drawbacks to democracy," Stoneham sighed. "Also a ridiculous side to it. The German confectioner in the next street has exactly as much voting weight on this or any other matter as a Harvard professor who has made a study of European politics and probably visited every capital. Decision by votes is always bound to have its fallacies. Look at prohibition, for instance, imposed upon the people of America against their wish, by votes. I'm not at all sure that in a thousand years' time absolute monarchy won't be recognised as the only sane form of government."

"In the meantime," Grant suggested, "let's get busy. I'll open an account for you to-morrow at any bank you say. Put yourself down for any salary you like and pay for contributions just what you think they're worth. Scour round the city for the young men who can write what we want—lecturers, magazine writers. We may be late starters, Dan, but we've a great gospel to preach. We've logic on our side, too. America was the first of the nations of the world to propose a reduction of armaments and to strip herself of the means of offensive warfare, just at the time when she, better than any other in the world, was able to afford it. She is still the leading spirit in the Limitation of Armaments. Why, then, should she remain outside the Pact? She lays herself open to conspiracies galore. She refuses the protection of the Pact and accepts the restrictions which her own generosity imposed upon her. And, Dan, let them rub it in. Let them ask where all this stream of literature on the other side is coming from. Tell them straight it's coming from Germany. Ask them if they think Germany has forgotten."

They made many plans and Grant succeeded in awakening a measure of enthusiasm in his companion. On their way out they met an acquaintance, laughing over a cartoon in a weekly newspaper. He held it up for them to see. There was a little circle of diners, Lord Yeovil in the middle, and before him one miserable chicken, on which the eyes of the sixteen seated around the table were fixed hungrily. A short distance away the allegorical Jonathan was seated alone at a table with a magnificent turkey in front of him. Lord Yeovil, risen to his feet, was addressing an almost plaintive invitation.

"Won't you come across and join us, Brother Jonathan, and bring the bird?"

"Propaganda," Stoneham murmured. "It's damned clever, too. That sort of thing impresses."

On their way up town they passed a procession. They stopped for a while to see it go by. There was a long line of youths marching in fours, dressed in the uniform of boys scouts, with several bands playing. They carried banners, on most of which was inscribed the same or a similar message:

EUROPE AND EUROPE'S TROUBLES
FOR EUROPE.

AMERICA AND AMERICA'S PROSPERITY
FOR AMERICA.

"I know that Association," Stoneham remarked. "They call themselves the 'National Scouts of Free America.' They have free uniforms, free bands, about six excursions into the country in the year, also free, and the treasurer to the fund which keeps them going is a Mr. Hans Klein. More propaganda!"

"Oh, our enemies are thorough enough," Grant agreed bitterly. "They take their disciples from the cradle and rub it all in with the alphabet. And, yet, you know, carefully though they were prepared for it, although they chose their own time, had every advantage science and preordination could give them, they lost the Great War. Their detail was wonderful enough, but you can't win on detail alone. I'm optimist enough, Dan, to believe that, as these people failed once before, so they will fail again, and for the same reason."

"You're rather inspiring to-night," Stoneham confessed. "Expound!"

"I do not believe in the ultimate success of any cause," Grant continued earnestly, "which is utterly devoid of spirituality. The Germans started out in nineteen-fourteen with every advantage, but with a boldly proclaimed battle cry of material gain. They were opposed by a nation, fighting for their own land and womankind, and there is no cause which can provoke a greater spirituality. They were opposed too by the British, fighting with no shred of self-interest, with no possible hope of aggrandisement, fighting to redeem their word to Belgium, and fighting against the principles which threatened the very foundations of civilisation. Then we came in. It took us a long time, but it was very far from being our quarrel. Anyhow we came in. And Germany, who started with every advantage, lost. I know as certainly as we walk here side by side, Dan, that Germany means to go to war again, partly a war of vengeance, partly a war of aggrandisement. Well, I think that we shall stop her. There's no soul to her cause. Nothing can flourish or live without a touch of the spirit."

"It isn't argument, Grant," Stoneham observed, "but I see your point. To a certain extent it's convincing."

"Argument is not the infallible solution of any subject," Grant persisted, "any more than the brain is the only adjudicator. Take the hereafter, for instance. We all have a feeling that something of the sort exists. But argument with a nonbeliever would be impossible. We set too much store by our brains."

They had emerged into Broadway, with its medley of blazing lights, its throng of people, its indefinable but ever existent fascination. Grant stopped short and pulled his companion up as they watched a couple descend from an automobile and cross the pavement towards a famous supper place.

"Some one you know?" Stoneham enquired.

His companion nodded.

"Slightly. The man was at Monte Carlo, in attendance upon the Japanese Ambassador. Itash, his name is. The girl was one of the dancers at the Café de Paris. That's rather a coincidence seeing them here."

"Why?"

"Because," Grant explained, "I very nearly got hold of some wonderful information from the young woman who used to be the sweetheart of Itash before he took up with this girl. How she got it from him I don't know, but she got it. She was half mad with jealousy and she sent for me. By the time I got there, though, Itash had made it up with her, and she would tell me nothing. Now—if one could only get hold of her now, there might be something doing."

Stoneham shrugged his shoulders.

"A Japanese diplomatist," he said, "even the youngsters, are not noted for their ingenuousness. I can't imagine that young man, Itash, as you call him, giving much away."

"Neither can I," Grant agreed, "but she was very positive, and she did tell me one or two things."

"Then if I were you," Stoneham suggested, "I should get into touch with her as quickly as possible. Send her a cable and tell her what's going on. She wouldn't be the first jealous woman who's saved or lost an empire."

They passed away from Broadway again and reached Grant's hotel. They sat in the sitting room, discussing plans till the small hours of the morning. Just as they were separating Stoneham put his arm round the other's shoulder.

"Grant, old fellow," he said, "I am with you right through this business. But there's just one thing I want to tell you before you go too far. We're on a loser. America will decide against the Pact. I saw a first forecast of the voting yesterday. The majority for rejecting the invitation was more than two to one."

"I should put it down as even less favourable than that," Grant replied. "And still I don't despair. I've a few more irons in the fire, Stoneham, than I've had time to tell you about yet. I've a capital fellow out in Japan, going on with the work I began. The British police patrols are on the scent of something there, and I paid rather an interesting visit to Archangel a few months ago. I'm not relying on our propaganda alone, Dan. Before that vote is taken in the Senate, I'm hoping to launch a thunderbolt or two from very unsuspected places. We've got to have the propaganda going, but don't you be surprised, old fellow, if, at any moment, I find you a new sort of fuel."

"We can do with it," his friend assured him. "These things that you are talking about concern chiefly the Limitation of Armaments Congress. I'm afraid a few surreptitious ships here and there won't have much effect on public opinion."

Grant smiled.

"You wait until the first of my thunderbolts is launched," he enjoined.

CHAPTER VI

GRANT met Cornelius Blunn on Fifth Avenue one morning a week or so later,—Cornelius Blunn resplendent in a light grey suit, with a waistcoat cut very low, a carefully arranged white tie, white spats, and a white Homburg hat. He had the air of a man pleased with his appearance.

"Well, my young friend," he exclaimed, stopping Grant. "How goes it?"

"I think you are winning," was the frank reply.

"That's a sure thing," Blunn declared. "I mean, how do you amuse yourself?"

"Indifferently," Grant confessed. "Your accursed organisations are getting on my nerves."

"To tell you the truth, you're getting on mine a little," Blunn confided. "You know, I'm not thin-skinned, but you've been getting a trifle savage lately. I should very much dislike anything to happen to you, but it has been suggested to me once or twice that New York would be a healthier place without you."

"The old threat," Grant rejoined lightly. "By the bye, why shouldn't two play at that game? I look upon you as one of the greatest enemies to the world's peace at present existing. Why shouldn't I kill you?"

"Too risky, my young friend. You're not in touch with the criminal organisation of this city, and to attempt anything of the sort yourself would be madness."

"I'm not so sure about the madness," Grant replied. "I think that I could prove justifiable homicide."

Blunn smiled.

"That's just your trouble," he expostulated. "You can't prove anything. You've got some very sound ideas in your head. You've insight all right. You can trace the natural sequence of events. But the trouble is you're short of facts."

"Perhaps I am," Grant acknowledged. "Perhaps I know a little more than you imagine."

Blunn looked thoughtfully along the crowded pavement.

"I should hate very much to think that you did," he said. "It would leave me only one alternative."

"I wonder," Grant meditated, "how much you understand of the science of bluff."

"Nothing," was the emphatic reply. "I have always treated you with the utmost candour. I tell you everything that may be for your good. Now I'll tell you another thing which you probably do not know because for some reason or other it has been kept rather secret. I only knew myself a few hours ago. The next meeting of the nations subscribing to the Limitation of Armaments has been fixed for about five weeks ahead. That will be before a final decision can be arrived at with reference to the matter in which we are interested."

"In Washington?" Grant demanded.

"In Washington."

"Lord Yeovil will be present?"

"Naturally. You will have an opportunity of telling him of the progress you have made. Our friends over here will arrange to finish the meetings of the Limitation of Armaments and bid their guests farewell before the news of their adverse decision with reference to the Pact is known."

"You are really a very interesting fellow to meet," Grant admitted. "You are always full of information."

"We must see more of one another," Blunn murmured. "Meanwhile——"

They saluted with great politeness and passed on. Grant was obsessed with only one thought. Lord Yeovil might be out at any time within the next month and probably Susan. He had written to her once or twice and received no reply. He suddenly swung round and caught up with Blunn again.

"May I ask you a question?" he begged.

"Why, my dear fellow, of course," was the immediate response.

"You have alluded to a ridiculous rumour that the Princess

von Diss accompanied me on my yacht when I left Monaco. Was that rumour — prevalent?"

"From one end of the Riviera to the other. There was scarcely any one who did not believe it."

"Thank you," Grant muttered.

He strode off, furious with the malicious turn of fate, which Blunn's news had brought into the forefront of his mind. Of what benefit to him was Susan's coming? What joy would he find in seeing her? Probably by this time she had cast him out altogether from her thoughts as an adventurer, one of those most hopeless of all people in the world to deal with, — a man with the spirit of a *boulevardier,* a *poseur* in love as in life. He walked rapidly away and back to his hotel. There was a letter to be written that night, — a letter which it would cost him a great deal to write, a letter which from any point of view must mean an accusation against himself. He ascended to his rooms full of his purpose. As he entered the salon, however, he stopped short. The person who had been in his thoughts for days was seated there, smoking a cigarette and, apparently, waiting for his return. A pile of magazines was strewn before her, the pages of which she was turning over a little listlessly. At Grant's entrance she pushed them all away from her with an air of relief. She looked across at him sombrely, yet gladly. There was not a flicker of emotion, not an effort at coquetry. She was just now as she was when they had fought their little duel once before, silent, imperturbable, a trifle contemptuous.

"Mademoiselle Cleo!" he exclaimed.

"Monsieur," she replied. "You have been a long time coming."

"Not so long, Mademoiselle," he replied promptly, "as you have been in keeping your word."

She rose to her feet. More than ever there seemed to be feline suggestions about the way she looked and stretched herself.

"Be so kind," she begged, "as to order me some tea and some more cigarettes. I think — I am almost sure — that I have made up my mind to tell you the things you desire to know."

Grant rang the bell and gave the waiter an order. Then

he pulled up an easy-chair for her and seated himself opposite.

"Did you come with Itash or did you follow him?" he asked simply.

"I followed him," she acknowledged. "What I was told I could not believe. Last night I saw with my own eyes. He has brought Yvonne here, brought her to New York. He, who had promised me a hundred times—but that makes no matter."

"Did you come alone?"

"I came alone. It was an evil day for Itash when I came."

"Tell me this," he said. "You profess to know Itash's secrets, yet Itash is a very clever young man. Did he confide in you, or did you steal papers?"

"Neither," she answered.

"Then will you tell me," he begged, "exactly how it is that you are in a position to dispose of his secrets?"

She smiled.

"That is my affair," she declared. "Some day—very soon—you shall know."

CHAPTER VII

Cornelius Blunn was a guest such as hotel proprietors dream of and very seldom have the chance to entertain. His demands were always on a magnificent scale and no spendthrift prince in the days when there were such beings could have shown less disposition to haggle. At the Great Central Hotel in New York he had a suite of five or six rooms, the most simple of which was his own bedchamber. Notwithstanding his affability and democratic habits, he was a person difficult of approach. In an outer room there were always two or three typists. In the next apartment were the travelling advisers connected with his various enterprises, who, with his direction and lavish cabling, influenced the destinies of his industrial ventures when he was from home. Then came a smaller chamber occupied by his secretary,—a somewhat colourless young woman of twenty-nine or thirty years of age, with thin sandy hair, and intelligent forehead, close-lipped, silent, a woman of deliberate ways and quiet speech. Beyond was a pleasant little reception room, with a lavishly furnished sideboard, plenty of magazines and easy-chairs, and, leading from it, Blunn's sitting room, an apartment with a great writing table, a special telephone and very little else in the way of furniture. The chair occupied by his visitors was a comfortable one enough, but it faced the north light. Even Itash blinked behind his spectacles as he subsided into its depths.

"You have news, my young friend?" Blunn enquired of his caller.

"There is very little," the latter answered, speaking with his usual deliberation. "Four more names have been sent in from our headquarters at San Francisco. They are all vouched for. They all desire places of responsibility. One of them, a fruit grower in California, is well known to me. His father was in the service of our family."

Cornelius Blunn nodded.

"Good," he said. "You have places for them?"

"For the first three," Itash replied. "The man I spoke of last, I have sent for. I propose to take him into the Intelligence."

"You have no other news?"

"There is no other news. May I smoke?"

Blunn nodded his permission. He sat back in his chair apparently studying his visitor. Itash was by no means a pleasant personality. The strength of his face lay rather in its cunning than in any other quality. His mouth was cruel. His eyes, as bright as beads, too shifty. His complexion was yellow even for an Oriental. His black hair reeked of the productions of the barber's shop. The handkerchief which he had been holding in his hand seemed steeped with some powerful scent. The cigarette which he presently began to smoke had a pungent and almost sickly odour.

"Count Itash," Blunn said at last, "you are a very clever young man of the Oriental school, but you have one fault. You are too fond of women."

Itash removed his cigarette from his mouth. He seemed a little uncertain how to take the other's speech. In the end he grinned.

"In your country," he retorted, "it is wine and beer, and food. In mine it is flowers and women."

"You may dabble in horticulture as much as you choose," Blunn observed drily, "but women are dangerous."

"I have learnt to manage them," the young man declared.

"So far as your personal comfort is concerned, no doubt that is so," Blunn acknowledged, "but you must remember that, to me, and many others, you do not exist as a young scion of the Japanese nobility who desires to achieve success as a diplomatist and walk meanwhile in the flowery ways. You are something more vital. You are a part depository of the greatest secret the world has ever known. Itash, if a single bead of the truth has sweated out of your carcass, you shall be looking for your own particular corner in hell before the moon changes."

Blunn struck the table in front of him, not heavily, but with a sharp menacing tap. There were lines in his face now which few people ever saw. His cheeks seemed to have sagged a little, his eyes sunken. His lips had parted, and one of his teeth, always a slight disfigurement, had, for the moment, the appearance of a fang. Itash dropped his cigarette. The sudden attack had paralysed him. He looked like a person stricken through fear into idiocy.

"Pick that up," Blunn directed, "and speak the truth, or nothing that I have ever threatened you with will count by the side of the things which shall surely happen. What have you told Cleo, the dancing girl of Monte Carlo?"

"Nothing, upon the tomb of my fathers!" the young man swore.

He picked up the cigarette. Blunn's questioning eyes still held him.

"Upon the great matters," he went on, "I have never spoken in my life with any human being, and as to women—they are my toys. I have never treated one seriously. It is not our way in Japan. There is not one of them who knows a thought that is in my brain, a feeling that comes from the heart. Not one, not one!"

"You know that this dancing girl has followed you to New York?" Blunn demanded.

"What has that to do with the matters that count?" Itash enquired wonderingly. "She has been the companion of my idle moments, she has never asked a question; she is like the others, a being for the dance, the wine, an hour or so of love. I tire of her and I take another companion. Sometimes you change wine for beer, is it not so? She is a foolish being and my notice has been pleasant to her. She is jealous—women are made like that. What does it matter?"

"I hear your words," Cornelius Blunn said. "Now listen to this, Itash, and tell me what you make of it with your Oriental wisdom. This dancing girl has followed you from Monte Carlo to New York. Two nights ago she visited Grant Slattery, was in his room for two hours. What do you make of that?"

"It is her profession," Itash sneered.

"You think so? That is the Oriental kink in you," Blunn declared. "A man like Grant Slattery doesn't amuse himself with the cast-off mistresses of such as you. Now listen! Of your wisdom answer me this. Why, on the morning after her visit, did Grant Slattery himself interview the managers of the three great steel companies with whom Japan has dealt in this country?"

Itash's face expressed only bewilderment. He seemed utterly unable to read the riddle of Blunn's words.

"I am foolish," he confessed. "I cannot see what distresses you. I cannot understand what Cleo——"

Blunn pulled him up. He was convinced that the young man was at least a harmless agent of his own undoing.

"Listen," he interrupted. "You are one of the few persons in a position to call the attention of people whom it might concern to the fact that Japan, during the last three years, has purchased more steel in the United States than would build her six battleships allowed her by the Limitation of Armaments twice over and re-lay every line of railway she has in Japan. Cleo, your sweetheart, comes to see Grant Slattery, and Grant Slattery interviews representatives of these three steel companies the very next morning."

"Never have I opened my lips to Cleo upon any such subject in my life," the young man asserted fervently. "She knows nothing. She can know nothing."

"Humph!" Blunn grunted. "The puzzle remains then. But I do not understand it. I am uneasy—it is one of the most unfortunate things which could have happened that this annual meeting of the Limitation of Armaments should be fixed for a date just before the question of joining the Pact comes up in the Senate. We keep our secrets well—we, who understand these things—but there are other matters besides the secrets of your country's warships which are there to be discovered, if the fortune went against us. A scare at the Conference might undo all our great work."

"There will be no scare," Itash declared. "Our extra battleships are hidden. No one knows that each one has a sister-ship."

"There remains that visit," Blunn muttered. "I shall brood over it until I have some explanation. I am not happy about you and your hobbies, Itash. Women are best left out of the game. I had rather you collected butterflies."

"I should be as likely to tell the butterflies my secrets," the young man scoffed. "You should know that we do not treat our womankind as you do. They are the marionettes who dance for our pleasure. To treat them seriously would spoil our joy of them."

Cornelius Blunn seemed to be slowly coming back to himself again. His tone was almost good-humoured.

"Listen," he said. "You sup every night with your little lady from the Café de Paris at the Folies Bergères, is it not so?"

Itash was a little startled.

"I am usually there," he admitted.

"To-night," Blunn announced, "I am your host. I remember the young lady. I have danced with her myself. I will dance with her to-night, whilst you look on and are sulky. You need not be afraid," he went on. "I have no designs on your belongings. It pleases me to spend an hour or so with you both. At midnight, at the Folies Bergères! You have always the corner table on the right, have you not?"

"I have never seen you there," Itash remarked suspiciously, as, in obedience to the other's gesture of dismissal, he rose to his feet.

"I have never been there," Blunn acknowledged. "But I know most things that go on in New York."

CHAPTER VIII

THE supper party that night at the Folies Bergères was unexpectedly gay, although, in one respect, the arrangements made by Itash miscarried. Mademoiselle Yvonne had found a friend, a Belgian young lady, who had attained some celebrity in the music halls as Mathilde Leroy, and some notoriety in the Press, owing to the number of her admirers and the eccentricity of her toilettes. Itash, who preferred to retain his own dancing companion, invited Mademoiselle Mathilde to make a *partie carrée*. But though Cornelius Blunn was graciousness itself and the hilarity of the little party was chiefly due to his efforts, he evinced a partiality for Mademoiselle Yvonne which was somewhat disconcerting for her escort, and most disappointing for Mademoiselle Mathilde.

"You will make him jealous, my poor Itash," Yvonne declared, laughing, as, for the third time following, she suffered Blunn to lead her amongst the dancers. "He likes so to dance with me, the poor boy. Mathilde wearies him, for she talks of nothing but her jewels, and her gowns, and her need for money."

"And what do you talk to him about?" Blunn asked.

She sighed a little.

"Of what is there one can speak," she complained, "with such as Itash? Oh, he is a good boy. He never flirts with the other girls, and he gives what he can. But women to him are just things without a soul. Often I wish that I had a friend who lived in the great world and who would speak to me of the things he did, of his triumphs, even of his troubles. That would make life more interesting. Some one, for example, like Monsieur."

"Does Itash never speak to you of serious things?" he persisted.

"Never, one word," she answered fervently.

"Do you think that he ever spoke to Cleo of such?"

"But why?" she demanded. "I have as much intelligence as Cleo, and he preferred me. It was unfortunate for Cleo, but it came about so. It is not all happiness, Monsieur Blunn," she whispered, "to have for a friend a young man often so morose and gloomy. Because I dance with you and he sees that I am happy, he will scarcely speak to me for days. He will not stay away. Oh, no. I shall have no liberty. When he has finished his work he will come, and lie still and smoke, and watch me. I must be there for him to look at, to dance for him, if he wishes it, but of conversation, of companionship, of the good time together,—nothing."

"Yet you came with him, here."

She shrugged her shoulders.

"He is constant," she admitted. "In his way he is generous. What would you have? He deserted another and came to me. When another comes whom I prefer I shall desert him. It is the life."

He leaned and whispered something in her ear. She laughed back at him softly.

"A man like you," she murmured. "That would be paradise for any girl. See, let us sit and talk. Itash is dancing with Mathilde, after all. He swore that he would not again. But there they go. We will sit down. I will have some more champagne. We will talk, yes."

They left the dancers and sat down at their table. Blunn gave an order to the waiter who filled their glasses and departed for more wine.

"He dances well, at any rate," Blunn remarked, watching Itash and Mathilde. Yvonne was looking into her gold mirror, with a little powder puff poised between her fingers.

"He dances well, but like a monkey," she declared, without looking away. "He is what I call a gymnast. He does not make you feel the joy of it."

She suddenly pushed her vanity case on one side. She leaned across towards him; all the coquetry of her nature shone out of her eyes, lured him from her curving lips.

"Ah, Monsieur," she said, "you make me speak unkindly but I think that you make me love you. Shall I? Would you have me love you?"

"Mademoiselle, it would only be fair," he replied. "For you I adore."

"It is true?" she whispered, leaning a little closer. "You assure me that it is true?"

He smiled at her. Then he patted her hand.

"It is true, Mademoiselle Yvonne," he assured her, "yet listen to me. I shall not treat you as my young friend Count Itash does. I shall speak to you as a woman of understanding, of sympathy, of sweetness."

"Proceed, Monsieur," she begged. "You intrigue me very much."

"The memory of you will remain with me," he went on, "until the time comes when I may remind you of to-night, and we may, perhaps, look for happiness. But I am a man who is living through these days with one thought. I have a purpose from the accomplishment of which I never swerve. When that is finished, then my feet press the earth again. It is then I seek Yvonne."

"You seemed like that," she murmured. "All the time I knew that you played with words. I am disappointed. You make me unhappy, Monsieur."

"On the contrary," he declared, "I am going to make you happy. I have a little surprise for you — if you will do me the honour of accepting it — a little present."

"Monsieur!" she exclaimed.

She shook with eagerness. A present! The most appealing word in the language to one of her order.

"I am faced with a problem," he explained, "which I think that you can solve. If you can I shall beg your acceptance of this trifle. If you cannot — well, I shall ask you to accept it all the same."

She looked at the morocco case which he held in the hollow of his hand, saw the lid fly open, and gave a gasp of delight. She was a good judge of jewellery, and diamonds set in platinum appealed to her.

"But it is magnificent!" she cried.

Blunn replaced the case in his pocket. A touch of his foot spelt out a warning.

"This is not for Itash," he murmured. "Later on."

Itash, morose, but intensely polite, returned. Mademoiselle Mathilde certainly did her best to further his wishes. Besides, she very much preferred Cornelius Blunn.

"You are not fair," she whispered to him. "All the time you talk and dance with Yvonne, and poor Count Itash—he bores himself with me, shaking with jealousy. I am disheartened."

Blunn poured out the wine.

"Mademoiselle," he invited, "you will dance with me, perhaps, next time. You must remember that Yvonne is an older friend, and when one nears fifty one does not offer oneself so readily as a partner to acquaintances. One lacks the courage."

"But you dance wonderfully," she assured him. "Come, the music is beginning. I have been impatient for an hour to get you to myself. The time has come."

They danced, talked nonsense, and danced again. Mathilde would have been more than content to have spent the whole of the evening with her partner. Itash, too, would very much have preferred it. And yet, by some means or another, the master-mind of the four had his own way. Without the slightest apparent effort things came to pass as he desired. Professedly a little weary, he found himself sitting with Yvonne. Mathilde and Itash, with the precision of dancing dolls, were performing a tango.

"This is my question, Yvonne," Cornelius Blunn said simply, as he drew the case from his pocket. "By some means or other Itash, who I believe is an honourable man, has betrayed to Mademoiselle Cleo, the young lady whom you supplanted, a secret of great importance. I do not believe that he wilfully communicated it to her. I do not believe that he has ever committed a word to writing. Yet she knows. Now, can you, dear little friend, give me any idea how this has come to pass?"

For a moment Yvonne looked utterly blank. She seemed genuinely perplexed. She began to shake her head. And then a sudden light flashed across her face. She threw herself back in her chair and laughed for a moment heartily. She laid her hand on Mr. Blunn's shoulder. She drew his head down to hers.

"Mon Dieu!" she whispered. "It is easy. I have heard strange things myself, to which I have paid no attention. He talks in his sleep — talks — talks — ah, how he talks — sometimes all through the night!"

The little case was in her fingers. She dropped it into her bag. Cornelius Blunn sat by her side, grim and silent, a veritable Nebuchadnezzar, brooding over the terrible writing. Thirty years of his own toil, thirty years of a nation's agony, a stealthy creeping forward through the ages, the brains of two greedy empires concentrated upon one end, building and toiling and planning, — these things were all imperiled, because a dancing girl had known jealousy!

CHAPTER IX

STONEHAM returned from a lecturing tour in the West, dispirited, and with a frank confession of failure. He presented himself at Grant's rooms just as the latter was finishing breakfast.

"I've bad news, old chap," he declared at once. "I've done my best, and I guess I've made about as much impression upon my audiences as if Pussyfoot Johnson had come back to life and were preaching prohibition once more. They won't have it at any price."

Grant pushed a box of cigars across the table and rang for a waiter to remove his tray.

"'America outside' still their motto, eh?" he observed, as he drew a chair up to the open window.

"You see," Stoneham went on, "they've never forgotten what a triumph it was for American diplomacy that our people, in those days, refused all invitations to join the Genoa Conference. We scored immensely all round by remaining outside, and you know what a general muddle that affair ended in. The fact of it is," he continued, selecting and lighting his cigar, "our people over here have never regained their faith in British diplomacy since those days. They can't see that they stand to be hurt in any way by remaining outside, and they can see that they might be drawn into a lot of trouble if they got involved in some of these economic disputes. We make our own rules now and play our own game, and we're the richest country in the world. It's a pretty hard situation to shake, Grant."

Grant was less perturbed than his companion had imagined possible.

"I've talked with Cornelius Blunn, since you've been away," he announced, "I've heard the same story from him. I believe he's right. I believe you're right. I believe that if the matter were to be decided upon to-day, the invitation to join the Pact would be rejected by an overwhelming majority. Fortunately, the meeting of the Limitation of Armaments is to come first."

"Sure, but what difference does that make?" Stoneham enquired.

"It's going to make all the difference," Grant assured him. "I'm on the track of things already, and the Conference doesn't take place for another month."

"Am I to be wise to this?"

"You are. But we've got to move warily. Blunn can afford to be good-natured about our fight against him so far as it has gone. He knows very well that his propaganda department is in perfect order. He can practically count his votes. He knows that on a fight as things are at present, we haven't a chance. The moment he realises that we are getting round his flanks, though, he'll be dangerous. Dan, you remember my telling you about Cleo, the little dancing girl, who used to go about with Count Itash?"

"Quite well."

"Well, Itash has brought the other girl over here. Cleo has followed, and Cleo paid me a visit the day before yesterday. She gave me a hint and I verified it. She is coming here again this morning."

"Do you trust her?" Stoneham asked doubtfully. "Do you think it really likely that a man like Itash would have told her secrets."

"Of course he wouldn't," Grant agreed. "But this is the point. Itash has a habit of which he is ignorant. He talks in his sleep. Cleo admits that she thought nothing of it, at first;—that she did not even listen. Then some of the things he said struck her as being strange. Finally she understood. He was worrying over a failure of his to keep secret two great contracts for steel given last year and the year before. I followed this up. It happened to be rather in my line. What about this for a bombshell, Dan? Japan bought steel plates enough in Germany during the last two years to build every scrap of naval armament to which she was entitled. She also bought from different firms in America, some in the name of China, and some in her own name, three times the same quantity of steel, all of which was shipped."

"But, say, how could she get away with a thing like that?" Stoneham asked incredulously.

"Largely bluff. The steel plates from Germany she declared faulty and announced her intention of using them for factory construction. Germany, with unusual complacency, actually admitted at the last meeting of the Limitation of Armaments that the plates were unfit for battleships, and, nominally, received a large compensation. This is the first little hint Mademoiselle Cleo has given me, Dan, and by the time I get my despatches in from Japan—I have a good man out there, thank God—I think I shall be able to give the Limitation of Armaments Conference a shock. Cleo has a few other little matters to tell me about, too."

"Say, this is great!" Stoneham exclaimed. "Pity you couldn't have got her to make a complete disclosure while she was about it."

"I did my best," Grant assured him. "I offered her everything in the world except my hand and fortune, and I don't think she'd have accepted those. She's simply crazy over this fellow Itash. She's going slowly in case he relents."

Stoneham, with a start, sat upright in his chair. A sudden recollection had flashed into his brain.

"My God!" he cried. "Whatever have I been thinking about? What did you say her name was?"

"I've never heard her called anything but Mademoiselle Cleo. What about her? Don't tell me anything's happened already."

Stoneham caught up one of the newspapers from the table and pointed to a paragraph on the first page.

"Haven't you read that, man?" he demanded.

"Haven't looked at a paper," was the feverish reply. "I hadn't finished my mail when you came in."

Grant read the paragraph eagerly. It occupied only a short space but the headlines were thick and prominent.

ATTEMPTED MURDER ON BROADWAY

Famous French Danseuse Shot by a Rival

At a few minutes before two o'clock this morning, what seems to have been a deliberate attempt at murder took place on the corner of Broadway and Thirty-seventh Street. It appears that Count Itash, who is here on an official mission to the Embassy of his country at Washington, was leaving Mason's Restaurant with Mademoiselle Yvonne, a well-known French dancer, when two shots were fired from amongst the crowd of passers-by. Mademoiselle Yvonne was slightly wounded but was able to return home in a taxicab. The assailant was distinctly seen by several of the passers-by, but managed to temporarily escape during the confusion. Her identity is known, however, and her arrest is momentarily expected.

Later:

Count Itash, on being interviewed, declared himself wholly unable to account in any way for the incident. He was not aware that the young lady by whom he was accompanied had any enemies in New York or any acquaintances at all. He was inclined to believe that the shot might have been intended for himself. Mademoiselle Yvonne, who is in a state of nervous prostration, declines to be interviewed at present. Her wound is apparently very slight but she is suffering from shock. Mademoiselle Yvonne was première danseuse last season in the Café de Paris in Monte Carlo, and has many friends both in Paris and over here. Her photograph appears on another page.

Later:

Mademoiselle Yvonne has denounced Mademoiselle Cleo, of Monaco, a rival danseuse, as her attempted murderess.

"Fool!" Grant exclaimed. "We are done, Dan. The police will have her, and if I know anything of Mr. Cornelius Blunn, she won't see daylight again until it's too late."

His companion was thoughtful for a moment.

"I'm not sure," he reflected, "that the best thing in the world for us won't be to have her safely under arrest. Blunn's gang can't get at her in prison anyhow. And she can be seen there."

"Blunn has a terrific pull with the police," Grant reminded him.

Stoneham moved towards the telephone.

"I'll ring up Police Headquarters and see if she's been arrested," he announced. "I know a man there who'll look after this for us."

His hand was already upon the telephone when there was an imperative knock at the door. He glanced around. Grant rose to his feet. Before either of them could say a word, the door was thrown open and closed again. Cleo stood there, with her back to it, holding tightly to the handle, panting for breath.

"They're after me," she cried. "There's scarcely a minute. Ring up Itash. Quick! 1817 Plaza."

Stoneham asked at once for the number.

"What do you want to say to Itash?" Grant demanded. "Tell me the rest quickly. You're French. Itash is in league with the Germans."

"Bah!" she sobbed. "He could be in league with the devil if he would come back to me. Listen. I ask him. He shall hear what I know. Then he shall choose. He shall take me and my silence and leave her for ever, or I will kill her and I will tell you his secrets."

"Is that 1817 Plaza?" Stoneham enquired.

"It is Count Itash who speaks," was the slow rejoinder.

"Mademoiselle Cleo is here in 940, Hotel Great Central, the apartment of Mr. Grant Slattery. She desires you to come."

Cleo sprang across the room. She snatched the receiver in her own hand. She broke into a stream of incoherent French, rocking herself back and forth all the time, as though distracted with pain.

"I heard you speak those things," she cried. "I know the

great secrets. I know what they would give me the price of a kingdom to have me tell. Very well, then, very well. Come here, then, before the police can touch me. Come to me here. Give up Yvonne for ever, and there shall be a seal on my lips as though the finger of the Virgin rested there. I have never deceived you, I am always faithful. I am always true. I am racked with pain and jealousy, Itash. Take me back. I have spoken the word. It shall be as though Her finger rested upon my lip."

She threw down the receiver. She turned towards them with a smile of triumph upon her lips.

"He comes," she announced. "Now we shall see!"

CHAPTER X

CLEO threw herself into a chair, sprang up again, listened for a moment at the door, her hand pressed to her side.

"Mademoiselle," Grant said to her soothingly, "consider. You're in no such great danger. Mademoiselle Yvonne is, I understand, unhurt. Even if you should be arrested the charge will not be a serious one."

"They will keep me in prison a month, perhaps two months," she cried. "And all that time he will be with her. It is not to be borne. I meant to kill her. I wish I had killed her."

He tried to reason with her.

"Mademoiselle Cleo," he pointed out, "you are young, extremely attractive, a wonderful dancer. I will take an apartment for you and have you appointed principal danseuse at one of our best restaurants here. You shall have two thousand dollars a month and an automobile. I will present to you the young men of the city. Why worry about that faithless Itash? I will do all this for you, if you will tell us in these few seconds, while you still have time, those things which remain in your memory."

"In five minutes you will know," she replied. "In five minutes if Itash will not promise to give up Yvonne, I shall tell you all for nothing. Then we will see."

"You will trust to his promise?"

"If he lies, he knows that this time I shall kill him. I am not a girl who can be treated as he has done. He shall learn that."

There was a slow and somewhat ponderous knocking at the door. She turned towards it, breathless, expectant. Then suddenly she gave a little cry.

"It is too soon," she exclaimed. "It must be those others.

Protect me. For heaven's sake, don't let them take me before Itash comes."

The knocking was repeated, and this time the door was instantly opened. There was no doubt about the character of the two men who entered; detective was written on every feature. One stood by the door. The other advanced a little into the room.

"Mr. Slattery, I believe," he said. "Sorry to intrude upon you, sir, but I have a warrant for the arrest of that young woman. You're Mademoiselle Cleo?" he went on.

"What do you want with me?" she demanded.

"I'll have to take you to the police station, young lady," was the brusque reply. "Charge of shooting with the intent to murder. You'd better keep your mouth closed till you get to headquarters."

She looked around her a little wildly.

"Can't you make them wait until Itash comes?" she begged of Grant. "He will, perhaps, arrange with them. I didn't mean to hurt her. All that I want is Itash."

"Say, young lady," the detective interposed, "our orders are that you are not to talk. We've an automobile outside and if you'll just allow me to run you over first for arms, I guess we can let you walk ahead of us and no fuss."

"I have no weapons," she declared, holding out her arms. "You can search me if you like."

"Who's this Itash she's talking about?" the detective enquired, as he passed his hands over the girl's quivering body.

"Count Itash. The Japanese gentleman who was with the girl she is supposed to have shot at," Grant told him.

"So he was the cause of the trouble, was he?" the man observed. "Well, young lady, he'll be able to see you at Police Headquarters after you've been examined."

"Before I go," she began——

"Stop it!" the detective insisted. "My orders are strict. You are not to be allowed to talk. Special orders from the Chief of Police. I don't want to do anything harsh and I don't wish to lay hands on the young lady," the man went on, turning to Grant, "but she's got to cut out the gab. This way, young lady."

They had already taken a step towards the door when it was suddenly opened. The second detective stood on one side, as Itash walked in. He was looking very pale and solemn, but, as usual, neatly and correctly dressed. Cleo would have rushed towards him, but for the restraining hand upon her shoulder.

"Sammy!" she cried. "You see what they're doing to me. They are taking me to prison. Tell them about it, Sammy. It was not really my fault. Send them away, please. Give them money. Tell them I am sorry. Anything. And tell me that it is finished with Yvonne. Take me away with you, Sammy."

He looked at her without changing a muscle of his countenance. Then he turned to the detective.

"Where are you taking her?" he enquired.

"To Police Headquarters," the man replied. "And it's about time we were off."

"Do not let me detain you," Itash said coldly. "Police Headquarters is a very good place indeed for that young lady. She was once a friend of mine, but she is so no longer. She tried to murder the young lady who was my companion last night. I have no wish to stand in the way of her punishment."

Mademoiselle Cleo seemed to have become suddenly calm. Only her eyes burned as she looked towards Itash.

"It is thus you speak to me?" she moaned. "You have no pity. No longer any love."

"It is finished," he pronounced.

She beckoned to Slattery, who stepped quickly forward. The officer would have thrust his hand over her mouth but he was too late. She whispered for a moment in Grant's ear. Then she turned to the detective.

"I am quite ready," she announced. "This time you have only a small charge against me. I shot to frighten, not to kill. There is a time coming before very long when I shall kill. Farewell, Itash. You have done an evil day's work for yourself. If you knew how many of your secrets still lurk in my brain besides those which I have shared with our friend, Mr. Slattery, here, you would not stand like a piece of marble and watch me being led away to prison while you go to take the *déjeuner* with Yvonne. You would be shaking in every limb, Itash,—shaking,

I tell you. For in your heart you know very well that you are a coward."

"Secrets!" Itash repeated scornfully. "What secrets could you know? I have given you my caresses—never my confidence."

She threw her head back and laughed.

"So you did not understand me over the telephone? Go and call on your friend, Mr. Cornelius Blunn," she jeered. "He knows."

"Say, young lady, I have been very patient, but orders are orders," the detective declared savagely. "Out of this room you go and if you utter another word you go with my hand over your mouth."

"It pleases me to depart," she replied haughtily. "Au revoir, Mr. Slattery. Come and see me in prison. There is more to be——"

The detective's patience was at an end. His hand closed upon her lips. He pushed her from the room. In the hallway they heard her muffled laugh.

"Gentlemen," Itash said, "I am sorry that you should have been troubled in this matter. I did not know that it was to the apartments of Mr. Grant Slattery that I was coming."

"Mademoiselle Cleo is an acquaintance of mine from Monte Carlo," Grant reminded him. "You doubtless remember our little supper party there."

"With much pleasure," Itash assented. "Nevertheless, Mr. Slattery, a word of caution may not be out of place. The young lady is not altogether trustworthy. Her tempers are violent. She is not truthful. She is, indeed, dangerous."

"Then we are both well rid of her, Count," Grant observed drily.

"It grieves me to speak ill of one of her sex," the young man continued, drawing on his gloves. "Mademoiselle Cleo was once my very good friend. I tire of her and take another, and she will not accept the situation. It was foolish."

"Very foolish indeed," Grant assented.

"The situation," Itash proceeded, "was probably clear to you when I had the honour of inviting you to supper at the Carlton at Monte Carlo. You are a man of the world, Mr. Slattery. I have been told that Mademoiselle has made scandalous talk of me. You will understand from whence comes the idea to speak evil."

"The whole situation," Grant assured him, "is most transparent."

Itash bowed low.

"I should not mention this matter at all," he went on, "but we, who are in the Diplomatic Service of our country — you, Mr. Slattery, I believe were once thus engaged — can so easily have mischief made around us — a malicious word, a suggestion of a confidence betrayed, it is sufficient to do much harm. You will bear this in mind, Mr. Slattery, if, by chance, Mademoiselle should have come here with mischievous intent."

"I will bear it in mind," Grant promised.

"No word concerning the affairs of my country, no single sentence of political import of any sort whatsoever has ever passed my lips when in the presence of Mademoiselle Cleo," Itash declared. "Therefore what she says she knows, she invents. I wish you good morning, gentlemen."

He made a dignified and leisurely exit. They heard the door close behind him, heard him pass down the corridor towards the lift.

"What did she whisper to you?" Stoneham asked.

"She was a trifle cryptic," Grant replied. "She spoke in French. What she said was simply this — 'The secret of the world is to be found in two small volumes hidden in the box of gold, in number twelve hundred and eight.' Box of gold! What the mischief was she driving at?"

There was a sudden change in Stoneham's expression.

"Why, Grant," he exclaimed, "haven't you ever heard the story about Cornelius Blunn's father?"

"I've heard one version of it," Grant acknowledged. "Tell me yours."

"You remember his history, of course. He was a great friend of the Kaiser Wilhelm's — one of the war party, one of those who really believed in Germany and her divine right to rule the world. The Treaty of Versailles broke his heart. On his deathbed he wrote a letter, which he placed in a gold casket which the Kaiser had once given him, containing the freedom of the city of Berlin. The idea always has been that that letter was a charge upon his son to see that some day or other Germany was avenged. Cornelius Blunn carries that casket always with him. If there really does exist any document in the world, any secret treaty or understanding between Germany and, say, Japan, having for its object a consummation of this injunction, why that's the likeliest place in the whole world to find it."

"What about the twelve hundred and eight?" Grant asked.

"That was what put me on the scent," Stoneham replied. "Twelve hundred and eight is the number of Cornelius Blunn's suite on the twelfth floor of this hotel."

CHAPTER XI

Itash proceeded to pay his morning call upon the person whom the newspapers had christened "The Mid-European Napoleon of Modern Finance and Diplomacy." He was passed through into the presence of the great man within a very few minutes. He entered courteous, self-assured, dignified. He was reduced within a few seconds to a state of abject collapse. For years afterwards he remembered the horror of those moments. Cornelius Blunn's opening words filled him with blank amazement, his final ones stripped him of every shred of confidence and self-respect.

"I have been associated at different times," the latter concluded, "with rogues and hucksters, thieves, liars and fools. I have never yet entrusted the destinies of a great nation to a man who cannot keep his mouth shut, even in his sleep."

"But how could I tell?" the young man gasped. "How do I know even now that what you tell me is true?"

"Let me remind you of this," Blunn went on. "We talked for hours one night in Monte Carlo on the matter of steel. With two companies over here we are all right. Over the third we have no control or any influence. We discussed the possibility of this third company adding up the amount of your contracts with their two rivals — even leaving out the steel plates we sent you from Germany — and of presenting a report to the Limitation of Armaments Conference. You remember that conversation?"

"I remember it perfectly," Itash groaned.

"You left me with your mind full of the subject. It was at the time when Mademoiselle Cleo was your fancy. Very well, the other day Mademoiselle calls upon our friend Grant Slattery, and the next morning he visits the representatives of each one of those steel firms. Can't you see that trouble or suspicion at the Conference might upset everything we have done?"

"I know," Itash muttered. "Still, they will not discover anything that counts in time. We have been very clever. We have four secret harbours and two secret dockyards, besides the one in China. Each battleship we built was duplicated. The two were given the same name. We kept even the work people in ignorance. The flying ships are safe. They are up in Ulensk. Now I shall send a cable. The four battleships which have been launched must steam away northward. The four that are ready to be launched under the same name must take their place. Everybody will believe that it is the same ships returned. I am not afraid. There are American spies in Tokio, but our secret harbours have never been visited."

"Go and send your cable and come back again," Blunn directed. "Warn your people that without a doubt investigations will be made. Let your fleet be manœuvred in every way so as to confuse undesired onlookers. But remember, nothing must interfere with its final assembly. You know the date."

Itash smiled for the first time.

"On November the first," he said, "we have the most complete and wonderful plan of movement. Units of the fleet will appear from all sorts of unexpected places. They have their final meeting place only five days' steaming from San Francisco."

Blunn nodded.

"Go and send your cables," he ordered. "Then return here. I suppose you can rely upon your code?"

"My code is undecipherable to any human being except the person to whom it is addressed," Itash declared. "It is based upon the ancient priests' language of my country, two thousand years old, and untranslatable save by a Japanese scholar. That again is coded and has never left my person."

He opened his coat and waistcoat and showed a band around his underclothes. Blunn waved him away.

"Good!" he approved. "Be back within two hours. You will not sleep before then!"

For a few moments after the departure of Itash, Cornelius Blunn sat motionless in his chair, his eyes fixed upon the calendar which stood on his table. Finally he rose to his feet, opened the door and called to his secretary.

"Miss Herman," he enjoined, "for half an hour I am engaged. You understand? Not even a telephone message."

"I understand perfectly, sir," she replied. "It is as usual."

She returned to her place. Blunn reëntered his sitting room, carefully locking the door behind him. The apartment, before the changes necessitated by his demands, had been an ordinary hotel sitting room, with heavy plush furniture and curtains. There were two windows, across which he carefully drew the curtains until every scrap of daylight was excluded. He then turned on the electric light and made his way to the ponderous safe, which looked as though it were built into the further wall. He undid his coat and waistcoat and released the chain which was wound around his body. At the end of it were two keys. With one, after a few minutes' adjustment, he opened the safe. From underneath a pile of papers he drew out a curiously shaped and heavy box fashioned of beaten gold. On the left-hand side of the lid were the arms of the city of Berlin. On the right the arms of the Hohenzollerns. In the middle was an inscription in German——

> To Cornelius Blunn, the faithful servant of this city and friend of his Kaiser,
>
> WILHELM.
>
> Nineteen-thirteen.

Blunn closed the door of the safe and returned to his place at the desk, carrying the box with him. He lit the electric lamp which stood upon the table and, with the other key, unlocked the casket. Its contents were simple enough in appearance — two small morocco-bound volumes resembling diaries at the top and a few sheets of parchment on which were several great seals; underneath a letter, yellow with age, crumpled a little at the corners, and showing signs of slight tear in one of the folds. With careful fingers Cornelius Blunn spread the latter out on the table before him. At either end he placed a small paperweight. Then he folded his hands and read its contents to himself in a very low undertone. The roar of the city seemed muffled by the closely drawn curtains. One thought of a dark and silent mosque in the middle of a sunlit Oriental city. Here was a man at his devotions,—and this was what he read:

My Beloved Son,

I write you this message from my deathbed with the last fragment of strength with which an inscrutable Providence has endowed me. I go before my work is accomplished, and, for that reason, a heavier burden must rest upon your shoulders. You will bear it worthily because of the purpose. My son, the chosen people of God were often called upon to face suffering—aye, and humiliation. But in the end they triumphed. Greatness will always survive, and the greatest thing upon this earth is the soul of the German people.

Have nothing to do, Cornelius, with those who would write her apologia. The empires of the world were built up with blood and sacrifice, and the knowledge of these things was in our hearts,—we, who planned the war and believed that we should see Germany the ruling power of the world from Palestine to London. We struck too soon or too late. History may, perhaps, tell you. Next time the hour must be chosen so that failure is an impossible element.

All that shall happen in the future and the way to our glorious goal has been discussed between us many a time. My charge upon you is this. Remember the maxims of those who made Germany. The man whom you forgive will never forgive you. The man to whom you show a kindness will owe you a grudge for it. Hate your enemies in life, in death, and after death. When the time comes, every man and woman of the United States of America, of France, of England is your enemy. Never did the Philistines oppress and humiliate the children of Israel as these people have done the nation of His later choice. Show no mercy. Strip them,—those whom you leave alive—of wealth, women and honour. Let them feel the iron in their souls which that accursed Treaty of Versailles has brought into the souls of our own people. When Germany strikes again see that she climbs for ever to the highest place amongst the peoples of the earth. By the sword Germany came into being, and by the sword she shall fight her way to the chosen places. Farewell, Cornelius, and remember my last words. NEVER SPARE AN ENEMY OR MISUSE A FRIEND.

CORNELIUS BLUNN.

The sound of the man's low voice ceased. Yet for several moments he sat quite still. A breath of wind, coming through the opened upper part of the window, moved the curtains an inch or two, and a thin sharp shaft of sunlight fell like a glancing rod of gold across the table, resting for a minute upon his face. All that there was of coarseness, even the humanity of good-fellowship and humour, seemed to have vanished. Cornelius Blunn had become the prototype of his country, fashioned according to his father's mandate of blood and iron. He might indeed have posed, in those few moments, for a statue of the great avenger. There was implacable hatred in every feature and line of his face, unforgiving, unmerciful. He was the incarnation of a real and living spirit.

The ceremony was over. With reverent fingers the letter was restored to its place at the bottom of the box. For a few minutes he pored over the contents of the two morocco-bound volumes. Finally he returned everything to the box, carried it to the safe, reset the latter's combination, and carefully locked it. Then he turned out the lights, drew back the curtains, lit a cigar and unlocked the door.

"Business as usual, Miss Herman," he said.

"Mr. Gurlenheim from the new London Steel Company is waiting to see you, sir," she announced.

A shadow of anxiety rested for a moment on Blunn's face.

"I will see him at once," he decided. "Count Itash too, immediately he returns."

Mr. Gurlenheim was a short, rather pudgy man, with flaxen hair streaked with grey, a guttural voice, and a fussy manner. He accepted a chair, but got up again directly.

"My friend," he exclaimed, as soon as he had shaken hands, "it is a serious matter on which I have come to see you. We have received a communication signed by the Secretary of the Limitation of Armaments Conference requiring a statement of all steel sold to Japan for the period of the last two years. We are asked to prepare it at once, as it may be referred to at the next meeting of the Conference."

"Nothing to worry about," Blunn declared, pushing a box of cigars across the table. "The Conference have accepted the position so far as the steel supplied from Germany is concerned—faulty plates. Our people conceded—on paper—an enormous reduction in price. As regards the steel from America—well, Japan over-bought. That's all she can say. There seemed a possibility of shortage in steel and she decided to cover herself. We're only limited to building, not to making provision for building."

"But what about the building, my friend?" Mr. Gurlenheim enquired anxiously. "Japan has gone a little beyond her specified limit, eh?"

"We are not fools, we and those others," Cornelius Blunn told him calmly. "What has been done in Japan it is better for you not to know. But whatever has been done has been accomplished in such a manner that it would take a year to discover anything, and before then the time will have arrived."

Mr. Gurlenheim drew a very large silk handkerchief of florid design from his pocket and mopped his forehead.

"This year will seem like ten to me," he confessed. "It is all very well for you, my friend. You will be in Germany when the storm bursts. Supposing the people should take it into their heads to wreak vengeance upon us here? They might—if they knew."

Cornelius Blunn smiled scornfully.

"If you feel like that," he said, "you'd better go to the Riviera for a few months, and leave some one else your share of the plunder here. Only you must let me know quickly. You are down for very unimportant work, nothing that exposes you to the slightest risk, but I want to be sure of even the weakest link in the chain."

"I shall stay," Gurlenheim declared. "I know what I have to do. But, supposing—supposing for one moment, Blunn, that anything went wrong. Say, for instance, that things came out at the Limitation of Armaments Conference and that America decided to join the Pact?"

"In that case there would be a postponement," was the grim

acknowledgment. "The end might not come in your days or mine."

"No fear of the whole scheme leaking out with names and that sort of thing?" Gurlenheim persisted.

"There is no fear of that," Blunn assured him. "The only complete list of names and stations in this country never leaves my possession. I have been looking at it to-night. No one else ever sees it."

Mr. Gurlenheim began to feel a man again,—or as much of a man as nature intended him to be. He accepted the cigar which he had previously ignored, pinched it carefully and admired its quality.

"It is a great thing to be a very rich man like you," he sighed. "Money comes fast enough over here, but not fast enough for the years. I am fifty years old and I have barely a million."

Blunn smiled.

"Before this time next year you can call it ten," he promised. "The wealth of the world is coming to us, Gurlenheim. It is coming because we're going to take it. To-night, at dinner, drink a glass of wine to the memory of the men who drew up the Treaty of Versailles, and who thought that war could only be made with ships and men."

"That war could only be made with ships and men!" Gurlenheim repeated, as he rose to his feet. "Good! I will drink that glass of wine. I will drink that toast."

CHAPTER XII

GRANT drew a little sigh of relief as, in response to his invitation, the door of his room was opened and his long-expected visitor arrived. He rose at once to his feet. For a person whose enthusiasms were chiefly latent, his manner was almost exuberant.

"Colonel Hodson," he declared, "you're the one man in the States I've been longing to have a chat with ever since I landed. I'm afraid I'm responsible for bringing you back from your vacation."

The newcomer smiled slightly as he shook hands. He was a tall, fine-looking man, with strong features and a dignified carriage. His eyes wandered from Grant to Stoneham who was seated at the table writing a letter.

"This is my friend, Mr. Dan Stoneham, late editor of the *New York*," Grant explained. "He is with me up to the eyes in this business. Dan, come here and shake hands with Colonel Hodson, head of the—well, what do you call your department now, Hodson? Home Secret Service it used to be before the word 'Secret Service' became taboo."

"'Service A' we call it now," Hodson confided. "Nothing much in a name, anyway. And nothing much in the job lately. I'd been over in Honolulu a month when they cabled for me."

Grant pushed up an easy-chair, produced cigars, whisky and a syphon, and rang for ice.

"I was afraid they weren't going to send for you after all," he observed. "They didn't seem in any way anxious to put me in touch with you. Tell me honestly, Hodson, what do they think of me in the Department?"

"They are interested," the latter acknowledged, stretching himself out and lighting a cigar. "They have a great respect for your insight on all ordinary matters, but in the present instance they are inclined to think that you have a bee in your bonnet."

"I was afraid so," Grant admitted. "I'm not surprised at it."

"They think that you've been mixing with the foreigners, and especially with the British, pretty freely, over on the other side," Hodson continued, "and that you've got a lot of un-American stuff in your blood. You know Secret Service and foreign plots and all these 'German *cum* Japanese' scares don't cut much ice in Washington these days. You should hear Senator Ross on the subject."

"I've heard him," Grant groaned. "I know the spirit, too, and I know perfectly well, Hodson, that if I'd been living in America for the last twenty years and hadn't been out of it except as a tourist, I should probably be feeling exactly the same way. Ross is wrong. I should have been wrong. There's a very terrible crisis looming up before us. You and I, Hodson, are going to avert the greatest calamity with which the world has ever been threatened."

"Let me warn you," Hodson said, "my instructions are to go dead slow with you. I am to do nothing which will make a laughing stock of the Department or which will evoke even questions from nations with whom we are upon friendly terms."

"I quite understand your position," Grant assured him. "When you're convinced, as you will be soon, you'll be with me body and soul. Until then, I'll take you by the hand carefully."

"Let's get to work then," Hodson suggested. "Give me an outline of your suspicions and show me the loose threads that you can't lay hold of yourself."

"Right!" Grant declared. "First of all then. In Monte Carlo I came across a plot to prevent that invitation being sent to America to join the Pact of Nations. I frustrated it. Over dinner some time I'll tell you how. That doesn't matter for the moment. The information upon which I acted came partly from the Princess von Diss, who was sent from Berlin to Monte Carlo to see what I was up to there, and partly from a dancing girl, the sweetheart of Count Itash, a young man who has held various diplomatic positions in Japan and whom I should describe as Japan's arch intriguer, just as Cornelius Blunn is Germany's. The information she gave me was correct."

"Is this man Itash the sort of person who gives away his secrets to his feminine companions?" Hodson asked quietly.

"Not in the least," Grant acknowledged. "As a matter of fact, we have only just discovered the truth. He talks in his sleep. The girl unfortunately is madly in love with him and only gives him away piecemeal. A few days ago in a fury of jealousy — Itash has brought another woman out here — she told me that he was worried about Japan's contracts with the steel houses here, in addition to their importations from Germany. I spoke to Washington on the telephone. They have agreed to take the matter up. They have already applied to their own steel companies for particulars of steel supplied to Japan during the last two years, and when they get it, which they will before the Limitation of Armaments Conference, if will be a staggerer. That's only a tiny little link in the chain, though. Japan's clever enough to wriggle out of that, or to keep the thing going until it's too late. It just helps, that's all. Last night the girl was fool enough to try and shoot her rival. She escaped arrest and came to me. She declared that unless Itash promised to give up the other woman she would tell me wonderful things. We telephoned Itash, who was still ignorant of his nocturnal indiscretions and who came round at once. His attitude towards the girl was brutal and I am convinced that she was on the point of making a full disclosure of all she knew. Cornelius Blunn, however, had discovered the leakage, and Blunn, I am sorry to tell you, Hodson, is, I believe, on very friendly terms with certain members of your police organisation here. They managed to effect the girl's arrest just as Itash had reduced her to a state of fury, and they did their best, acting under special orders, to prevent her saying a word to me. She told me one thing in French. She whispered that the whole secret of a great internal conspiracy against America could be discovered in a little gold casket which never leaves Blunn's possession. It is at present in room twelve hundred and eight of this hotel."

"Has she anything more to tell?" Hodson asked.

"I know that she has," Grant assured him. "But, although the charge against her can scarcely be a very serious one, as the girl was uninjured, they refuse to allow me, or even a lawyer, whom I engaged, to see her at all. She is at present in the Tombs. The charge against her, I suppose, could be handled in many different ways, but can she be kept legally from seeing either a lawyer or a friend?"

"She cannot," Hodson declared.

"Then let this be your start," Grant begged. "Go to the Tombs this minute. You have the right to insist upon seeing her. Do so. Tell her you come from me. Here is my card."

"Accompany me," Hodson suggested after a moment's reflection. "We will interview the young lady together."

Colonel Hodson, it appeared, was after all a little sanguine. At Police Headquarters he left Grant in the waiting room while he made his way to visit a personage in authority. Instead of the few minutes he had mentioned, however, he was gone nearly half an hour. When he returned there was a marked change in his manner. He seemed, subconsciously, to be treating Grant with a little more respect.

"Well, you're right, so far, Slattery," he confessed. "There's a conspiracy here to keep that young woman from communicating with anybody at all, a conspiracy which is entirely against police regulations and which is going to lead to a whole heap of trouble later on. However, there it is, and they're in it deep enough to run a pretty considerable risk. They've tried every mortal bluff they can think of, but their present attitude clean gives the show away. In an hour's time they will be compelled to let me visit her. Until then we'll take a drive round and I'd like to hear a little more of your story. I'll frankly admit, Slattery," he acknowledged as they left the place together, "that my interest is growing."

They drove about for an hour, and Grant confided to his companion a great deal of the result of his wanderings and investigations during the last two years. Hodson listened imperturbably. He realised the note of conviction in his companion's tone but he himself kept an open mind. Notwithstanding his official position, he had the instincts and the outlook of a citizen. Deliberate warfare with its hideous wastage of human life and its ghastly uncertainty seemed to him a visionary idea, a phantasy of the disordered and over-imaginative brain. A single person of disordered mentality might brood upon such a cataclysm; no normal group of persons in these sober days was likely to tolerate the idea. All these little happenings and tendencies to which

Grant alluded might so easily be traced to lesser things. He made only one comment.

"Supposing for a moment," he said, "that there was the least truth in your prophecy and that a naval attack from outside was to be supplemented by an enormous and wide-reaching internal conspiracy, do you realise what a terrible reflection that would be upon my Department?"

"I can't help it, Hodson," Grant declared. "Of course I realise it. I'm not going to blame you. No one can be blamed for not searching for what they don't believe exists, but I do beg you to remember that if there's a thousand to one chance that my view of things is correct, you ought not to leave my side until we're through with this business. And so far as you personally are concerned, now listen. During the last two years I have submitted between forty and fifty reports dealing with this matter to the Department in Washington. Have those reports been handed on to you?"

"Not one of them," Hodson replied. "I had no idea, even, that you had ever made them."

"Then you must remember," Grant pointed out, "that at the worst, the chief responsibility rests with those higher up. My reports should every one of them have come to you, and you should have made the investigations on this side to which they pointed. Can you tell me offhand whether there are any great patriotic societies formed to keep Germans together in this country?"

"There's one," Hodson acquiesced. "'Brothers in Love,' they call it — kind of Odd Fellows affair. It exists chiefly for charity and does an enormous amount of good. It must have two or three million members."

"Anything with the Japanese?"

"There is one, but I don't know much about it," Hodson confessed. "It is rather a different class thing, founded to teach the lower classes the arts of agriculture and to keep the others in touch with Japanese culture and literature."

"Quite so," Grant murmured. "I haven't the faintest doubt that those societies are on the surface everything they appear to be. Neither have I the slightest doubt that behind them, committee behind committee, are the people who deal with Blunn and Itash."

Hodson smiled a little doubtfully.

"I'm in a receptive frame of mind, Slattery," he admitted, "but don't try me too high. Processions, brass bands, and picnics are all I can think of in connection with the 'Brothers in Love.' The Japanese I never quite understood. Here we are back again. I see the governor's car here. Now we ought to have some fun."

Grant again waited for his friend, who this time was gone for a little more than ten minutes. When he returned there was a steely glint in his eye.

"Slattery," he announced, "you win all round, so far as this girl's concerned. They've had her up before headquarters while we've been away, discharged her, and they have the effrontery to assure me that they let her walk out of the court without asking where she was going to, or without having her followed. They've just turned her loose in New York and left us to hunt. I don't like it. Come along!"

"Where to?" Grant asked.

"To see some friends of mine, who can tackle this job," was the stern reply. "We ought to be able to find her before many hours are passed."

CHAPTER XIII

HODSON and Grant dined together that evening in the latter's room, and Grant was in the middle of his promised story of Funderstrom's abduction when the telephone rang. A man's voice asked for Colonel Hodson. Grant passed over the receiver.

"An urgent call for you, Hodson," he announced.

Hodson spoke a few brief words and listened.

"We'll be along in ten minutes," he said as he laid down the receiver.

"Slattery," he went on, "that was a man from Poynter's Detective Agency speaking. They're the people we called on this morning about this young woman. They think they've found her. Will you come along with me?"

"Sure," Grant assented. "Anything wrong, do you think?"

"I rather gathered so," was the grave reply.

They jumped into a taxi and Hodson gave the man an address on the other side of the Park. In about twenty minutes they pulled up outside what was evidently a second-class lodging house. On the steps a young man was waiting.

"Colonel Hodson?" he asked.

"Right," Hodson answered. "Are you from Poynter's?"

"Yes, sir. Mr. Poynter's upstairs himself. He left me here to wait for you. Will you go up to the top floor?"

They climbed six flights of stairs — narrow stairs, and dark — passing through mixed atmospheres of cooking, stale tobacco, of beer and patchouli. There were theatrical cards stuck on some of the panels; now and then a door was stealthily opened and the intruders scrutinised. On the sixth floor Mr. Poynter, the famous detective, who had once been in the Government service, stood waiting. He shook hands with Hodson and nodded to Grant.

"We're up against a nasty piece of business, Colonel," he announced. "I wanted you to see exactly how things stood for yourself before the police got hold of it."

"Get on with the story, Poynter," Hodson invited.

"In the first place," the detective pointed out, "the girl's bell is cut. You see the wire there. It's a clean cut, been done with a pair of nippers, within the last hour or two. Now come inside, sir. But," he added, his hand upon the handle of the door, "you must be prepared for something unpleasant."

"The young lady?" Grant exclaimed.

"She is dead," Poynter answered gravely. "The scene is set for suicide. Personally I think there is not the slightest doubt but that she was murdered. The door of her room was locked and the key is nowhere in her room. I picked the lock after I had tracked her down. This way, sir. The smell is still bad, but I have had the window open an hour."

They entered what was little more than a garret bedroom. On the bed lay the body of Mademoiselle Cleo. Mr. Poynter raised the sheet which he had drawn over her face and let it drop almost immediately. Above the girl's head was the gas jet and from it a small piece of tube hung downwards. The remains of the imprisoned gas were still escaping by the open window.

"She was quite dead when I picked the lock," Poynter told them, "and for the moment I thought that the gas would get me. I managed to make a rush for it to the window, though."

"But surely all this points to her having committed suicide?" Grant queried.

"I am perfectly certain all the same that she did not," the detective replied. "Not only has her bell been cut but the telephone is cut too. She was lying half across the floor, trying to reach it or the window when I found her, and the window was fastened down with a nail which had only recently been driven in. There is not the least doubt but that some powerful person entered her room, held her down until the last moment, then rushed out, locking the door behind him. There are marks upon the girl's throat which could not possibly have been self-inflicted."

Grant searched the room for a note or letter, but in vain.

"What she knew," Hodson decided at last, "she has taken with her. You had better notify the police, Poynter, and stand by while they take note of the things you have pointed out to me. You can say that we two have seen them."

"And don't let them take her away," Grant insisted. "I will be responsible for the funeral arrangements."

"There's just one thing," Mr. Poynter said, casting his professional eye once more around the room. "I have a perfectly definite idea of my own as to the type of person who was following this poor girl. Am I to go on?"

"Absolutely," Hodson replied. "You can treat it as a Government affair, Poynter, and take your orders from me. The young lady was suspected of having political secrets in her possession."

"I'll make a report in a few days," Poynter promised.

They descended to their taxi and drove away. Both men were silent. Grant was filled with a sense of horror. The sordidness of the little scene, its atmosphere of tragedy, its cruelty, had brought the tears into his eyes.

"If ever I get my fingers on the throat of that brute Itash," he muttered, "I think that I shall kill him. What did you think of the matter, Hodson?"

"I think that Poynter was entirely right," was the confident reply. "And every moment I am coming round to your point of view. I am beginning to believe that this conspiracy really exists."

"You're coming in?" Grant enquired, as the taxi drove up to the Great Central Hotel.

Hodson shook his head.

"You'll see nothing of me for twenty-four hours or so," he announced. "I am going to work in directions you can't approach. You and Stoneham go on with your propaganda, even though the thing looks hopeless. Let your friends think that's all you've got to depend upon. Don't go away from your rooms for more than an hour or two without leaving word where you're to be found. There may be some big things doing when I get started."

Grant made his way through the crowded vestibules of the hotel and down the main lobby. On one side was the supper and dancing room, and, as he passed the entrance, he came face to face with Itash, who had apparently just arrived. A few yards away Yvonne was handing her cloak to the attendant. Grant hesitated for a moment and then came to a standstill, affecting not to notice Itash's outstretched hand.

"I have a piece of information which may be of interest to you, Count Itash," he said.

"You are very kind to trouble," was the studiously courteous reply.

"I have just come from a very sorry apartment in a squalid part of the city," Grant went on. "I was summoned there to identify the dead body of Mademoiselle Cleo."

If Itash felt anything, he effectually concealed it. He passed his fingers over his sleek black hair and bowed slightly. A gesture of his hand kept Yvonne from advancing.

"This is very terrible news," he said. "I had noticed that the young lady seemed to be in a very depressed state. It is to be feared, perhaps, that she took her own life?"

"Nothing of the sort," Grant answered bluntly. "She was murdered."

Then, for the first time, Itash showed signs of feeling. His eyes glittered, his lips seemed to grow tight against his teeth.

"That is very terrible," he confessed. "In Japan we do not think so much of suicide. One leaves life when one is tired. But a murder is a terrible thing. Who, in this country, would dream of murdering poor Cleo? She had no money, but little jewellery."

"She might have had something more valuable than either," Grant observed.

Itash shook his head.

"Oh, no," he murmured. "I know what you mean, but those were fancies of hers. If she has ever imagined that she heard anything from my lips of import she has been mistaken. My country has no secrets, neither have I. I grieve for your sad news, Mr. Slattery. I thank you."

"You are dancing?" Grant enquired.

"I am dancing," Itash acknowledged, offering his arm to Yvonne. "This is the last night in New York of my friend, Mademoiselle Yvonne. She is summoned back to Paris and sails to-morrow."

Grant remained perfectly immovable, regardless alike of

Yvonne's proffered greeting and Itash's low bow. They passed together into the ballroom. Grant watched them with a strange inexplicable disgust, a disgust which seemed to be born of his passionate but silent anger. In his mind he saw Cleo followed home from the Police Court to her dreary apartment, saw her walk into the little chamber of death, into the toils prepared for her. She was, after all, very young, and she loved. She was still lying in that little chamber, with a sheet over her face,—and Itash danced.

"I think," Grant said to himself, as he turned away, "that I shall certainly kill Itash."

The next morning there were no sensational headlines, even in the most melodramatic of the newspapers. In two or three of them was a short paragraph, headed:—

"SAD SUICIDE OF A FRENCH DANSEUSE."

Not a single newspaper gave more than a few lines to a description of the event. The *New York* was perhaps the fullest. It told how, after being very leniently treated by the judge at the Police Court, she had been discharged, on a promise to leave the country within a week, and not to molest Mademoiselle Yvonne again. She had then, the paragraph continued, apparently gone straight back to her apartments, had locked the door, turned on the gas, attached a piece of rubber to the jet, fastened the window, and lain down to die. A more determined suicide, the police reported, they had very seldom come across.

CHAPTER XIV

It was three whole days before Grant saw anything more of Hodson. Then the latter appeared in his room about seven o'clock in the evening and demanded a cocktail.

"Glad you've remembered my existence," Grant grumbled good-humouredly, as he gave the necessary orders. "Stoneham and I have been pegging away. There are heaps of things I want to know about."

Hodson nodded.

"There are big events close at hand," he announced. "A great deal of what you suspect is true, with a few other trifles thrown in. Can you go to England to-morrow?"

"England!" Grant exclaimed. "Why, the Limitation of Armaments Conference starts here in a little over a fortnight."

"You'll be back for it," the other assured him. "I want you to catch the *Katalonia* to-morrow morning. She sails at eight o'clock. Let me see, to-morrow's Saturday. You'll be in Plymouth Wednesday, and in London Wednesday night. Lord Yeovil will be expecting you. You can sail back on Saturday in the *Sefalonia*. You'll probably return with Yeovil and his staff."

"What am I to do in England?" Grant asked, trying to keep back an alien and most disturbing thought.

"Deliver despatches from Washington," was the prompt reply. "I have them in my pocket. I came through from Washington to-day. Great Britain polices the eastern waters for the Limitation of Armaments Conference, and we want a sea-plane patrol over certain specified districts. There are a few other little matters to be enquired into, too."

"Look here," Grant expostulated. "You're not sending me over to play messenger boy, are you?"

"Not likely!"

"What's the game then? Do you want to get me out of the way?"

"Not precisely that. Where are you dining?"

"With you, anywhere. I was going up to the Lotos Club. Stoneham generally drops in there."

"I'm tired," Hodson confessed. "I'd like to hear some music and look at some pretty women. I'll go round and have a bath and change and call for you in half an hour. We'll get a corner table at Sherry's. I think, as we're saving empires, we can afford some terrapin and a bottle of champagne."

"You're serious about that trip to England—because I must have my fellow pack?"

"Serious! My God, I am!" was the emphatic answer. "You'll be the chief spoke in the wheel for the next ten days. You won't miss anything here, either. I'm gathering up some wonderful threads but I'm doing it silently. I'll come round in half an hour. I'm on your floor."

A fit of restlessness seized Grant. He gave his servant the necessary orders, interviewed the travel manager in the hotel and secured the best accommodation possible on the steamer. Then he permitted himself to think deliberately, opened up the closed chambers in his mind, welcomed reflection and memory. He would see Susan. He would find out what her silence really meant, what she thought or believed about him. In a sense, it was all very hopeless. He had been forced into an accursed position. He scarcely knew even now how to appraise it. And yet the big thing remained unaltered and still seemed to tower over everything else,—he loved Susan. There was not a grain of affection in his heart for anybody else. She was his only possible companion. Was he so much less fit for her than any other of the young men by whom she was surrounded? He tried to judge himself and his position fairly. The trouble was that it could never be represented to any one else in the same manner. He remembered and brooded with gloomy insistence over that slight vein of prudery in Susan, something altogether unconnected with the narrow ways, or any unduly censorious attitude towards life, which seldom in fact expressed itself in speech, but was more a part of herself, a sort of instinctive and supercilious shrinking from the small licences of a world which she never judged in words. Perhaps he had fallen for ever in her esteem; perhaps the one sin recorded against him would have cost him already what he had sometimes fancied that he had won. Now that he was going to see her so soon, he wondered how he had been content to wait to know the truth. Next Thursday he would be in London. It was the height of the season and she would certainly be there. Next Thursday or Friday they might meet. He told himself that he would know in the first ten seconds whether his disaster had been irredeemable.

The two men dined at Sherry's in a retired corner. They dined, as Grant complained, like profiteers and gourmands. Hodson ordered caviare and lobster Newburg, terrapin, saddle of lamb, asparagus and champagne.

"A disgraceful meal," Grant declared, as he sipped his cocktail. "Do you really think we shall get through it?"

"Of course we shall," Hodson laughed. "To tell you the truth I've scarcely eaten anything for two days. They were a tough lot on the trains to Washington and back. I can manage better in the cities."

"What do you mean?" his companion asked curiously.

"Well, the same powers that murdered that poor girl and translated it into suicide were out for me," Hodson explained. "If they had known that it was you who started me off, I expect you'd be in the same position. My own little crowd are pretty useful though. And Poynter's men are wonderful. There are two of them at the next table. They look all right, don't they?"

"They look just like two successful business men talking over a deal," Grant observed.

"Well, they aren't," Hodson assured him. "They're two of Poynter's shrewdest detectives. They've got guns in their pockets and their job is to see that no one tries to steal a march on me from the lounge. One of my men is down in the kitchen. I dared not eat anything on the train, for they were in with the chef there. I've been shot at twice in the last twenty-four hours. They nearly got me, too. It's a great storm that's gathering, Grant."

"Exactly why are you sending me to England?"

"Listen," was the earnest reply. "This is official. It comes from the White House. You know who owns the *New York* now. You know the power at the back of the greater part of our Press. They want to make bad blood between Great Britain and this country. You can guess why. They're at it already, and the British Press, quite naturally, is beginning to take it up. Use all your influence with Lord Yeovil. Tell him the truth. Get him to take you to see his own big newspaper people and try to keep the feeling down. Beg him to disregard any attacks upon him personally, either before he comes or directly he lands. It's all part of the game. It will all be over, tell him, in two months, and for heaven's sake do what you can to stop trouble."

"I certainly will," Grant promised. "I used to have a certain amount of influence with Lord Yeovil."

"That's why we're sending you. One reason, at any rate. Then — Hullo! another farewell party, I see."

"Why farewell?" Grant asked, looking curiously at the newcomers.

"I hadn't come to that. Cornelius Blunn is sailing for England to-morrow. He'll be your fellow passenger."

"Where the devil is he off to?"

"A dozen of the most astute brains in the States, besides my own, have tried to solve that question," Hodson replied. "At present, I must frankly admit that we don't know. I have a theory. He's getting a trifle shaken up in New York. Not exactly scared, but nervy. He wants to reëstablish confidence. There's a dinner of German bankers in London at which he is advertised to take the Chair. He imagines that his attendance at that function just now will put us off the scent. He'll probably come back by your steamer."

"Is he taking the casket with him, I wonder," Grant reflected.

"I may consider some day," Hodson said deliberately, "that within the last few hours I have made the mistake of my life. That girl's whisper to you was probably the vital part of all that she had to tell. I honestly believe that the key to the whole conspiracy — and there is a great conspiracy, Grant, I'll tell you that — is in that casket, side by side, no doubt in affectionate communion, with that letter from old man Blunn, the present man's father, which we know he always carries with him. They'll risk a lot for sentiment, these people. I honestly believe I ought to have raided his private room with a dozen picked men, broken open his safe and casket and shot myself if I found nothing. I believe it was a fair risk. Honestly, Grant, it wasn't that I funked it. It was just because I knew all the time how Cornelius Blunn would have laughed at me if the thing had been a fake, how the Department would have laughed at me, how the Press would have poked fun, and the novelists pointed to me in triumph as one who carried the skein of fancy farther even than their imaginative brains had ventured. The fact of it is, Slattery, that ridicule is a much more powerful factor in our daily lives than we are willing to acknowledge. A great many men are susceptible to ridicule who are immune to fear."

"All the same," Grant proposed a little doggedly, "give me a dozen men and a plan of campaign and I'll run the risk."

"As a last resource," Hodson declared, "it is always open to us. Personally, I have some hopes in other directions. Now, let us see whom our friend, Cornelius Blunn, is entertaining. H'm! A respectable lot but suggestive. The two great steel men, Pottinger, the new editor of the *New York*, Admiral Purvin —he's all right but inclined to be talkative—and Doctor Sinclair Forbes, the great Jewish educationalist. A respectable party but a dash of the Teuton about most of them. A farewell party that amounted to anything would have been given in his rooms. By the way, Grant, if you speak to Blunn on the way out, don't tell him you're sailing to-morrow. I've arranged for you to be quarter of an hour late. They'll put the gangway down again for you. I'm beginning to have great faith in Blunn's organisation. If he considered your presence in England likely to prove inconvenient, I think it's very doubtful whether you would reach the steamer in time. Now he's seen us. Wave your hand, Slattery. Play his game. Love your enemies on the surface. Be glad to see the people you wish were at the bottom of the sea. It's a great game as Blunn plays it. How he must hate to see us together. And yet, behold! A great honour is coming to us."

Blunn had risen to his feet, with a word of excuse to his

guests, and came across the room to them. He beamed upon Grant and shook hands with Hodson cordially, reminding him of a previous meeting at Washington.

"I am giving a little farewell party," he announced. "I have decided, rather at the last moment, to accept an invitation to visit London."

"Didn't I once hear you say that you seldom visited England?" Grant queried.

"Your memory is excellent, Mr. Slattery," Blunn admitted. "To tell you the truth, I do so now more from a sense of duty than with the expectation of any pleasure. The whole world knows that my father hated England, and, in a milder form, I have inherited his dislike. But, in these days of settled peace, what can one do? What good does it do to ourselves or to the world to keep open the old sore? I have been asked to preside at the Anniversary Dinner given to celebrate the reopening of the German banks in London. I must confess that at first I refused but strong pressure has been brought to bear upon me. I have decided to go. Naturally my presence on such an occasion must mean the burying forever of all feelings of ill will."

"I think you are quite right," Hodson remarked.

"So do I," Grant echoed. "Your presence there will be of great significance. By the way, are you returning to the States?"

"I am not sure. My friend Lutrecht, who is coming over to represent us on the Limitation of Armaments Conference, is very anxious that I should be here, but, personally, I think it exceedingly doubtful. My affairs in Germany require my presence, and I have promised to visit Hamburg within the next few weeks. I will only say 'au revoir', gentlemen. Mr. Slattery and I, at any rate, are citizens of the world, and we are likely to meet in most unexpected places."

He returned to his table and the two men exchanged a smile.

"Even Cornelius Blunn," Hodson murmured, "has a knack of telling the truth sometimes."

CHAPTER XV

THERE was humour rather than tragedy in the inevitable meeting between Cornelius Blunn and Grant on the *Katalonia.* On the morning after their departure, Grant, while promenading the deck, heard a feeble tapping against the glass which enclosed the small promenade of one of the magnificent private suites, for which the vessel was famous. Inside Mr. Cornelius Blunn, almost unrecognisable, swathed in rugs, with a hot-water bottle at his feet and a servant by his side, was gazing out at the world with lack-lustre eyes. Grant obeyed his summons, pushed back the sliding door, and stepped inside.

"So you are here, my young friend," Cornelius Blunn said weakly. "What does it matter? I am sick in the stomach. I do not think that I shall live till we reach Southampton."

"Not so bad as that, I hope," Grant ventured.

"It is worse," Blunn groaned, "because I am beginning to hope that I shall not. Go away now. I am going to be ill. I wanted to be sure that I was not already seeing ghosts. If this were only your yacht!"

Grant hurried out with a word of sympathy.

"An object lesson in proportionate values," he reflected, as he walked down the deck,—and then, his little effort at philosophy deserted him. He himself found great events dwarfed by small ones. His heart was pounding against his ribs. He was face to face with Gertrude von Diss!

His first impulse was ludicrously conventional. He hastened to relieve her of the rug she was carrying. Behind her came a maid with coat, pillows, and other impedimenta of travel.

"Gertrude!" he exclaimed, as he stood with the rug upon his arm. "Where have you come from? Where have you been?"

"Stateroom number eighty-four," she replied, "and I am on

my way to that chair, and please don't ask me whether I have been ill. Come and tuck me up as a well-meaning fellow passenger should."

He obeyed at once. The maid assisted his efforts, a deck steward supplemented them. Presently Gertrude declared herself comfortable and her *entourage* faded away. Grant sat by her side.

"I am going to break orders," he said gently. "I am afraid that you have been ill."

There were hollows in her cheeks. The freshness of her exquisite complexion had departed. Her eyes seemed to have receded. She was thin and fragile.

"Yes," she admitted. "I have been ill. A nervous breakdown, accompanied by great weakness of the heart was all that the doctor could find to say about it. I might have helped his diagnosis."

"Don't, Gertrude!" he begged.

"My dear man, don't be afraid that I am going to break into reproaches! There is nothing more illogical in the world than the position of the woman who complains of a man because he doesn't care for her. It is no sin of yours that you didn't love me, Grant. It was most certainly no sin of yours that, for a few hours, I made you pretend to. That was entirely my affair,—entirely my cunning scheme, which went wrong. Some idiot once wrote that 'love begets love!' I thought that with my arms around your neck I could have brought about a sort of transfusion, forced a little of what was in my heart into yours,—and you see I couldn't. In the morning I knew. You were very dutiful. Your lips were there for me if I wanted them. Your arms were ready for my body if I had been content to come. You were prepared to take advantage of all the nice and proper little arrangements which the circumstances had placed at my disposal. And of love there was not a scrap. I had made my venture and lost."

"Gertrude, this is terrible," he groaned.

"It is terrible because it is the truth," she continued. "We have that much in common, we two. We both love the truth. I have prayed for this moment, that it might come about just as it has done, that these few plain words might be spoken, and that for the rest of our lives, we should know!"

"I was a brute," he muttered. "I tried, Gertrude."

"What a horrible condemnation," she laughed bitterly. "And so true—so damnably true. You did try. I watched you trying hour by hour. I watched you drink champagne at night. You tried to pretend. It was I who had to make the excuses—because I knew. I who had to pretend not to see your look of relief. You never deceived me for a single moment, Grant. It was I who gambled and lost."

"I am sorry."

"Don't be sorry," she enjoined. "Now, I will tell you something. Notwithstanding the great humiliation through which I have passed, I am glad. I am glad that it all happened. When this pain is lightened, I shall be more glad still. I was restless and unhappy whilst I believed that I could reawaken your love. Now, I am every day more rested, more content. And here is the wickedness of me, Grant—I am glad about it. I do not regret for a single moment my experiment. The only regret I have is that I failed."

"You know why?" he ventured.

"You were very frank about it," she admitted, "but somehow or other I couldn't believe that you knew, yourself. You are a man of parts, even a little older than your years, and Susan Yeovil, for all her charm, is young. I used my brain upon the matter—foolishly—the one thing brain has nothing to do with. Finished, my dear Grant! That rug a little more closely round my left foot, please. And don't imagine for a moment that I am going to offer you my eternal friendship. About some matters my sentimentalism is not of the sloppy order. There's a jagged edge about our relations and always must be. But that's no reason why you shouldn't make the deck steward bring me some of that delicious *bouillon*."

"Where have you been and where are you going?" Grant asked, as soon as he had ministered to her wants.

"I've been in New Hampshire," she told him, "staying with one of the neglected aunts of my family. A wonderful spot amongst the hills. Incidentally I was ill there."

"And now?"

"Well—I have plans but they are not concluded. My book, please, and then you can continue that swinging walk of yours. Afterwards pay me the little attentions one fellow passenger may offer to another, if you like. But rest assured that your liberation is complete."

Grant chose another deck for his promenade. The magnificent and primitive selfishness of his sex had asserted itself. He found nothing but relief in this meeting with Gertrude. He could, at least, go to Susan with his hands free, so far as he ever could be free. The trouble of it was that, for all her worldliness, he feared her standards, feared that vein of idealism which he had once or twice detected in her. Of course there was something artificial about the whole outlook. A thing which she knew, that everybody else knew, ranked a little differently to that nebulous past which, by common consent, was somewhere locked away in the back chambers of a man's life. Yet, with it all, Susan's common sense was admirable. There was her father to guide her.

Later in the day he revisited Cornelius Blunn and found little improvement in his condition. The only moment when a spark of his old spirit showed itself was when, with a pitiful groan, he murmured:

"And to think that I must return!"

"You are coming back to the States, then?" Grant asked quickly.

For a single moment the man's self-control reasserted itself. He shook his head feebly.

"I have too many affairs on hand," he said, "to make plans. Maybe at once, maybe in many months.

"One thing is very certain. I shall not stay in England long. My own country I love. America I love. But England, no. Excuse me, Mr. Slattery. I can talk no longer. I find it exhausting. Your look of health offends me. You look as though you were on your way to eat a hearty meal, and that offends me more. Come and see me when I am stronger. Müller!"

Grant strolled away, smiling. It was a very harmless and helpless Cornelius Blunn, this. But for how long?

CHAPTER XVI

THE preliminaries of Grant's mission to London seemed to him, eager to get into touch with the vital things, monotonous and a little wearisome. He paid his respects to his own Ambassador and received the entrée to the Embassy. Afterwards he made a formal application for an appointment with Lord Yeovil, and, after a brief delay, was accorded an interview in Downing Street at six o'clock that evening. The interval he filled up by calling with the Naval Attaché of his Embassy upon the Admiralty, and with the Military Attaché upon the War Office. At six o'clock precisely he was received in Downing Street by Arthur Lymane, who welcomed him with a certain amount of surprise.

"Glad to see you and all that, Slattery," he said, "but I never thought of you as being on the official side of anything. I thought you'd absolutely chucked the service some years ago."

"I'm on a special mission," Grant explained. "They've sent me over to see one or two people here and especially Lord Yeovil. I'm going back on Saturday."

"We shall all be fellow passengers then," Lymane observed. "Do you think America will be able to stand the troupe of us? Because we're all coming—even bringing our own little typists this time."

"Is Lady Susan—" Grant began hesitatingly.

"Yes, Lady Susan's coming along."

"She's all right, I suppose," Grant enquired. "I don't seem to have heard anything of her for some time."

"In the pink. She's been doing the honours for her father this season and doing them wonderfully, too."

"Engaged yet?" Grant ventured with a ridiculous affectation of carelessness.

"Nothing announced," was the cautious reply. "There are three or four of them running neck and neck. Bobby Lancaster's fallen behind a bit, although he's as keen as ever. Lord Glentarne's chief favourite for the moment, and there are a lot of rumours going about that Buckingham Palace has its eye on her. No matrimonial news about you, I suppose, Slattery?"

"None."

A little bell rang, and Grant was ushered into the presence of the man who, a few months ago, notwithstanding the difference in their ages, had been his most intimate friend. From the moment of his entrance, however, he understood that those days were past. Lord Yeovil was courteous, even friendly. Nevertheless the change in his demeanour would have been apparent to a man of fewer perceptions than Grant.

"Very glad to see you again, Slattery," the Prime Minister said, motioning him to a seat. "It seems a long time since we used to sit cudgelling our brains about those bridge problems."

"History is giving us something much more serious with which to occupy ourselves, sir," Grant replied. "All the things which you and I used to speak about in those days are coming to pass."

Lord Yeovil nodded.

"This time, I gather, you come to me officially."

"That is true, sir. I am the bearer of a message and representations from my Government to yours. May I beg for your serious attention?"

"By all means," the Prime Minister acquiesced. "My car is ordered for seven o'clock. Till then I am at your service. I will just give Arthur a few messages and leave word that we are not to be disturbed."

Until a quarter to seven Lord Yeovil was an attentive listener. When his visitor had at last finished, he was looking very grave.

"I have always felt a premonition of something of this sort," he confided. "My invitation to the States was practically founded upon it. But I must confess I had no idea that things were so imminent. Nor even at the present moment is it quite clear to me how Germany and Japan propose to work this thing."

"There is a great deal that we have to discover yet, sir," Grant declared. "We're reconstructing the scheme more thoroughly, day by day, but, from the facts we have, it seems as though the central idea is that the Japanese fleet, which we have reason to believe is much larger than it should be, will approach the west coast of America at exactly the same time that the German fleet approaches the east coast,—the German fleet, by the way, augmented, without a doubt, by the Russian. We in America, as you know, sir, being the instigators of the Limitation of Armaments, have been most scrupulous in keeping zealously to our official tonnage in every class of battleship, and the consequence seems to be that the American fleet, even if it could meet either of these others undivided, would be greatly inferior in numbers, and the idea of dividing it to meet these two opposing forces simultaneously would be simply to court disaster."

"This, of course, is all supposition," Lord Yeovil observed.

"Founded upon a certain amount of proof, which I shall presently produce," Grant went on. "The most urgent matter, however, which I was begged to discuss with you, sir, was the attitude of certain portions of the American Press towards yourself and this country. I shall offer you presently an explanation of that attitude and I am to beg you most sincerely, in the name of the President and the Government, to use your influence with the Press of your own country to avoid, so far as possible, recrimination and reprisal."

"It is true, I suppose," Lord Yeovil enquired, "that the *New York* is no longer conducted in the interests of your Government?"

"The *New York*," Grant replied, "has been purchased by Cornelius Blunn, and is the most dangerous organ in the States to-day."

The Prime Minister glanced at his watch.

"I fear that, for the present, we must postpone our discussion," he announced. "It has been a great pleasure to see you again, Slattery, and to receive you in an official capacity. No one could have been more welcome—as a representative of your people."

Grant felt a sudden chill. He took his courage into both hands, however.

"I fear, sir," he ventured, "that I seem to have forfeited in your eyes the position of which I was once very proud — the position of being a friend of your household."

Lord Yeovil hesitated. The young man's directness was almost disconcerting.

"I would not say that," he rejoined, a little more kindly. "I am naturally a man of the world, and I am not a hard judge of any man's actions. This is a matter, however, which, if you choose, we will discuss at another time."

Grant rose to leave. There was again a very perceptible hesitation on his host's part.

"To-night," he said, "I am giving a reception at Yeovil House, a sort of farewell before I leave for Washington. Most of the diplomatic people will be present. If you care to attend, it will give me great pleasure to see that you have a card. You are staying at the Embassy?"

"At Claridge's."

"You will have a card within an hour."

Grant once more summoned all his courage.

"Shall I have the pleasure of meeting Lady Susan?" he asked.

"My daughter has made her début this season as a political hostess," was the polite but somewhat cold reply. "She will be assisting me to-night."

It was gone, then, the old cordiality, the easy terms of familiarity on which Grant had stood in the household. Lord Yeovil had become to him — as he was to most of the world — a courteous and polished diplomat, kindly and gracious in words and demeanour, but a person who seemed almost outside the amenities of life. And, if the change was so noticeable in him, what had he to expect from Susan?

He was in a somewhat depressed frame of mind when he called in at Carlton White's, selected the most beautiful roses he could find, and sent them to Yeovil House. Afterwards he went back to the Embassy and was kept there until eight o'clock. There were many questions raised over the despatches he had brought, which were full of vital interest to various members of the staff. Grant could not help contrasting the atmosphere here and the atmosphere in Washington. Geographically the two were not so far apart. The Press, cables, wireless, rapid travel had, in the language of the journalists, brought the two hemispheres side by side, and yet there was an extraordinary difference in outlook, in political perspective. Things which in Washington seemed far away, phantasmal, hatched in the brain of the alarmist, inconceivable in near life, here assumed a different appearance. Here, at any rate, it was realised that Europe had become once more a huge whispering gallery of intrigue, that the curtain might at any moment be raised once more upon the great drama of war and bloodshed. Facts were the same in both capitals. The atmosphere alone was different. The incredible in one place was the grimly possible in the other.

CHAPTER XVII

It was after half-past ten when Grant, in the suite of his own Ambassador, mounted the stairs of Yeovil House and waited for some time in the block which had collected at the entrance to the reception rooms. From where he stood he suddenly recognised Susan, recognised her with a little shock of mingled pleasure and apprehension. His first impression was that she had changed, had grown older in some marvellous fashion, without the loss of any of her beauty or freshness. She wore the gown in which, only a few months ago, she had been presented. Her hair, in the midst of a galaxy of brilliant coiffures, was arranged as simply as in the old Monte Carlo days, and the jewellery she wore consisted only of a simple rope of pearls. Yet she seemed to have assumed without effort and with perfect naturalness a becoming dignity and ease, wholly in keeping with her position as the hostess of a great gathering, and having a certain piquant charm when associated with her extreme youth. She talked gaily and without embarrassment to every one, passing them on with that tactful little word which is sometimes a hostess's greatest difficulty and having always the air of thoroughly enjoying her position, of finding real joy in welcoming individually members of the distinguished crowd which streamed slowly by. More than once Lord Yeovil, who in his court dress and dazzling array of orders was himself a striking figure, found time to glance for a moment, half in amusement, half in delight, at the girl by his side, whom the society papers of to-morrow were all to acknowledge as one of London's most promising hostesses. Step by step they moved on. Glancing upwards, Grant fancied once that she recognised him. If so, there was no change in her expression. She welcomed the Ambassador, talked for a moment with his wife, exchanged some jest about a golf match with the Naval Attaché, and finally turned away, to find Grant standing before her. She gave him her hand and smiled as frankly as ever. There was no trace of self-consciousness in her manner. Yet Grant was aware of a great chill of disappointment.

"Welcome back to London, Mr. Slattery," she said. "You really are a globe trotter, aren't you? I hope you've brought some new bridge problems with you for father. He needs a little distraction, poor dear, with all those terrible newspapers of yours hurling thunderbolts at his head."

"Glad to see you, Slattery," Lord Yeovil added. "You'll find Arthur in the room to the left. If dancing amuses you, he'll introduce you to some good partners."

And that was the end of it. Grant found himself one amongst seven or eight hundred people, meeting an old acquaintance occasionally as he strolled about, introduced by Lymane to one or two young women with whom he danced, and all the time conscious of a vague but sickening sense of disappointment. This was the meeting to which he had looked forward so eagerly. He was judged and condemned, wiped out, finished with. And why not? Who in the world would believe that Gertrude had come to him as a stowaway? And, worse still, whom could he tell? It was a little trap of fate, into which he had fallen, a problem to which there seemed no solution.

Later in the evening Arthur Lymane sought him out and presented him to a white-haired, lean-faced man, in the uniform of an admiral.

"Admiral Sullivan would like to have a word or two with you, Grant," he said. "Unofficially, of course. The Admiral is head of our Naval Intelligence Department."

"I have heard of Admiral Sullivan often," Grant declared, shaking hands. "Once in Tokio, where he wasn't very popular, and again in Archangel."

"Don't mention that," the Admiral begged, with a little grin. "Tokio I don't mind. I hear you fellows are getting the wind up on the other side of the pond."

"We're shaking in our shoes," Grant assured him. "Can we find a place to talk?"

"I know the runs of this house," was the cheerful reply. "Come along."

They passed outside the formal suite of reception rooms into an apartment opening from the billiard room,—a small den, in which were a few easy-chairs, a quantity of sporting literature, several decanters, and some soda water.

"This is Arthur Lymane's little shanty," Grant's cicerone explained. "Can I mix you one? Say when."

They subsided into easy-chairs. The Admiral's blue eyes were still twinkling.

"By the bye," he confided, "I'm the man who handled your reports from Archangel and Berlin."

"You didn't throw them into the wastebasket, I hope?"

"Not on your life," was the prompt assurance. "I acted upon them, and jolly quick too. They tell me you've been doing S. S. work for Washington for the last two years."

"Two years and a half, to be exact," Grant admitted. "I'm beginning to piece things together now."

"Interesting!" his companion murmured. "There have been rummy things going on all over the world—heaps of loose threads we've got hold of ourselves. I wonder whether your conclusions are the same as mine?"

"There is no secret about my conclusions, so far as you're concerned," Grant replied. "I am convinced that there is a most venomous plot brewing against my country. That is why I am so thankful that the question of our joining the Pact has been raised again. My only fear is that it's a trifle late."

The Admiral selected and lit a cigar with deliberate care.

"Well," he said, "the world knows my opinion of Pacts and Limitation of Armaments Conferences, and all that sort of twaddle. They are started by philanthropic fools to be taken advantage of by rogues. I've given Yeovil seven questions to ask the Japanese representative at Washington, and I tell you that there isn't one of them which he will be able to answer."

"Thank heavens the Conference comes before the matter of joining the Pact is voted on by the Senate," Grant exclaimed fervently.

"Damned good job, I should think," the other agreed. "It's easy enough to see that your country's being riddled with propaganda. As regards that Conference, how long is it supposed to last?"

"Usually about a fortnight."

"Well, I'll tell you something. This time it won't last for twenty-four hours."

"Go on, please," Grant begged.

"There'll be a most unholy row," the Admiral confided. "The only two countries who have kept to their programme are yours and mine. France has built twice her allotted number of submarines, and, to be frank, we've winked at it. Germany and Russia between them, as you found out, have kept on exchanging ships and building ships for one another till even the experts can't keep pace with conditions. If you take my advice, Slattery — and they tell me you've got the ear of your Government — you'll cable home and urge your administration with all the eloquence you can pump out of your brain, to accept Yeovil's invitation and join the Pact and fight it out with the Senate afterwards. You people have got lots of the right stuff in you, I know, and you can't believe that anything on God's earth could hurt you, but you take it from me, there's a hell of a lot of trouble brewing. Get 'em to sign on to the Pact, Slattery. We shall all have a finger in the pie, then, anyway."

"I went straight back to Washington from Monte Carlo," Grant confided, "and I can assure you that I have done my best. The trouble of it is — just as you pointed out a few minutes ago — there's a propaganda going on over there which one can't deal with, unless something happens which will drive the truth home to the people. That fellow, Cornelius Blunn, has founded an organisation, with branches in every city in the United States, and that organisation exists primarily to stop America joining the Pact, and secondly, I am convinced, for her destruction. The Press has been tampered with. Blunn has even succeeded in buying the *New York*."

"But surely your Government can't be absolutely blind to what's going on?"

"They've only just begun to realise it," Grant assured his companion. "That's why for this visit they've given me an official status. If the vote were taken to-day, I think the Senate would reject the proposal to join the Pact by a majority of three to one."

The Admiral nodded sympathetically.

"It's a filthy business," he admitted. "I hate this underground work, myself. All the same, you don't need to worry. When you people really are waked up, it doesn't take you long to get going, and the first few hours of the Limitation of Armaments Conference will send all Cornelius Blunn's propaganda sky high."

"I must say you put heart into a man," Grant declared gratefully.

The Admiral rose with a glance at the door and a welcoming smile.

"Well," he said, "here comes the young lady who's taken the heart out of a great many of us. Lady Susan, we've made free with Arthur's room and we've drunk his whisky. I don't know what's going to happen to us. My only excuse is that your father told me off to have a chat with Mr. Slattery."

She laughed.

"Why should you need an excuse? There isn't a room in the house where you're not welcome, Admiral. I was scouting round with Arthur to see if there were any shirkers from the dancing room. We're so short of men. And, Mr. Slattery, my father wishes to see you before you leave."

"I'm quite at his service," Grant replied, rising.

By some means or other the thing he had so greatly desired came to pass — he was left a few yards behind with Susan. She neither avoided nor sought for this contingency. She walked by his side, humming slightly to herself, entirely at her ease.

"Lady Susan," he began, with less than his usual confidence, "may I remind you of our parting at Monte Carlo, of something I said to you?"

She looked at him with slightly uplifted eyebrows.

"I should consider your doing so in atrociously bad taste," she replied.

He winced a little. Perhaps she saw that he was genuinely suffering. Perhaps that love of fair play, which was so strong in her, rebelled against the idea of any possible misunderstanding.

She slackened her pace. She made sure that they were well out of hearing of the other two.

"I detest hearsay evidence," she said. "I shall ask you a question. A terrible thing to do, I suppose, but I shall ask it all the same. Did the Princess von Diss accompany you on your yacht from Monte Carlo to America?"

"She did," Grant admitted.

"And was she not also a passenger on the steamer from which you landed yesterday?"

"She was, but——"

"Please do not continue, Mr. Slattery," she begged. "I hated asking you these questions, but I was determined that there should be no risk of any misunderstanding. I do not wish to quarrel with you. I found you a very pleasant companion at Monte Carlo. I hope that we shall continue friends. We can only do so if you will remember that, although I do not think that I am a prude, I should consider any reference to our last conversation at Monte Carlo as an insult. Angela dear, what luck to meet you here! I want to present Mr. Grant Slattery, who is dying to dance,—Lady Angela Brookes. Mr. Slattery is an American, Angela, and I will vouch for his dancing. He used to try and teach me complications, but I am not nimble enough. And, Angie, I don't think you'd better lose your heart to Mr. Slattery. He makes love to single ladies most fluently, but he runs away with the married ones. And I never thanked you for your roses, Mr. Slattery. Goodnight, all of you. I must go back to my post of duty."

Grant offered his arm to the very pretty girl to whom he had been introduced.

"I suppose we must obey orders," she said.

"Part of them," he answered, a little desperately. "Part of them I hope you will forget."

She laughed up at him. He had seemed very grave, but perhaps after all he was going to be amusing.

"I'll see how well you dance," she promised.

CHAPTER XVIII

GRANT was fully aware, on the afternoon before his return, that he had brought his mission to a most successful conclusion. The English Press was receiving the American attacks upon Lord Yeovil and his invitation with good-humoured magnanimity. He had collected more evidence — evidence of a very sinister nature — as to the brooding air of unrest which everywhere prevailed, and, in view of certain contingencies, firmly fixed in his own mind but only half believed in by other people, he had obtained pledges of the utmost value and importance. Yet, so far as he personally was concerned, he felt very strongly that his visit had been a failure. The more he thought of it, the more he became convinced that its failure had been inevitable, that his advertised delinquencies could have been looked upon in no other way. And yet he smarted under the judgment. The man in him rebelled.

In Bond Street that afternoon, he heard his name pronounced by a woman alighting from a motor car just in front of him. He recognised her with some difficulty. It was indeed Gertrude, looking entirely her old self.

"Still in London," he remarked, as he stood by her side for a moment.

"Still here," she assented. "I had orders to wait — to meet my husband."

"Your husband!"

She smiled with faint irony.

"My husband. Are you surprised? He arrives to-day. He is quite excited at the idea of seeing me again."

"I can well believe it," Grant observed, a little bewildered.

"But you," she went on. "You have not the appearance of

amusing yourself at all. You are worn to a shadow, my dear Grant. Why do you worry so about this little game of politics? Believe me, for all your efforts, the world will be very much the same in five or ten years' time."

"The philosophy of sloth," he reminded her, smiling.

"Perhaps so. But you seem, indeed, very miserable," she continued, studying him for a moment. "What is the matter? Are your love affairs progressing ill?"

"I have no love affair," he answered.

She looked at him for a moment searchingly, and her lips slowly parted. She laughed—laughed the more as his frown deepened.

"You poor man!" she exclaimed. "And after all your sacrifices! Perhaps it was not so much of a sacrifice, though," she went on, glancing unconsciously at her reflection in the plate-glass window of the shop in front of which they were standing. "I suppose I have gone off. What do you think, Grant?"

"You looked ill upon the steamer," he told her. "To-day you look as well as you ever have done in your life."

"I hope I do," she murmured. "Otto would feel at once that he had been cheated out of something if I had lost my looks. I can never quite make up my mind," she went on reflectively, "how much of my appearance I owe to my clothes. I have a wonderful flair for clothes, you know, Grant, and for wearing them."

"People have remarked upon it," he agreed a little drily.

She smiled.

"You're getting bored," she declared. "The trouble about me is that I'm so self-centred. I'm always talking about myself, and, of course, I ought to be sympathising with you. But how can I, Grant? You fix your mind and affections upon an ingénue of the most British type and then you nurse a broken heart because the inevitable happens."

He broke away from the subject.

"May I take it, then," he asked, "that you and your husband are reconciled?"

"We are about to be," she admitted. "It is very amusing. I made the first overtures, or rather Mr. Cornelius Blunn made them on my behalf. He pleaded my cause most eloquently. I have been given to understand that I am forgiven. My husband arrives to-day. We are staying at the Ritz. I think I will not ask you to call."

She saw the displeasure in his face. For a moment she faltered. She was gripping her little gold purse tightly with the fingers of her left hand.

"I seem to you flippant?" she went on. "Well! — you must make allowances for me. This is not exactly the happiest day of my life. I suppose really I should look for happiness in other ways — trying to do good and all that sort of thing. If I were to play the much admired part of long-suffering heroine in the cinema romance of life, I should, of course, put on my plainest clothes, wait mysteriously upon your young ingénue, confess the whole truth to her at the cost of my own undying humiliation, and not leave her until I had shown her the truth. Then I should telephone you. You would leap into a taxi and drive to Yeovil House. I should take a last look at your photograph and an overdose of veronal. Curtain to slow music!"

Grant's feelings had suddenly changed. He realised the state of strain in which she was.

"You're talking a great deal of nonsense, Gertrude," he said. "I am glad to have seen you. I am glad to hear your news. If I may be allowed to say so, I do indeed wish you happiness. I wish that I could have had my share in bringing it to you."

He passed on a little abruptly, and Gertrude made her delayed entrance into the establishment where hovering satellites had been eagerly awaiting her. To Grant, the interview had been, in its way, a painful one. From a material point of view, Gertrude's reconciliation with her husband was certainly the best thing that could have happened to her. Yet, during the whole of their conversation, he had been conscious of an uneasy environment of misery. The meeting, notwithstanding a certain sense of relief which it brought him, had only increased his depression. He strolled on without any particular idea as to where he was going. At the corner of Bond Street and Piccadilly he heard a familiar voice and felt a friendly hand upon his shoulder.

"Why so woebegone, my young friend? You ought to be up in the seventh heavens to think of all the excitement you are causing."

Grant was suddenly down again in the world of real things. He shook hands heartily with his new friend.

"Good morning, Admiral," he said. "Do I look as though I were indulging in a fit of the blues?"

"If I hadn't been a brave man," Sullivan declared—"we're all brave in the navy!—I wouldn't have ventured to speak to you. Come along and lunch."

Grant hesitated. His companion took him by the arm.

"Ritz Grill Room—my favourite corner table," he insisted. "We ought to have heaps to talk about—except that I am too hungry to talk at all. I've been up since five o'clock on your business—in the Marconi room at the Admiralty, most of the time."

"Any news?"

"Not much that's fresh, anyway. We're getting things into shape for the moment we receive word from Washington. There's a Cabinet Council to-day, you know. Lucky some of our friends can't get hold of the agenda. We should have the whole world by its ears to-morrow."

They descended the stairs and remained for a moment in the lounge of the Grill Room, while Sullivan ordered luncheon from an attentive *maître d'hôtel.* The barkeeper was content with a nod.

"You like your cocktails dry, of course," Sullivan went on. "I brought you here instead of the club because all the fellows would want to meet you and talk, and we're not loquacious, just at present, except to one another."

"Very thoughtful of you," Grant approved. "I had an idea that you might be coming across with us."

"Can't be done. We shall work the show from here. All the same, I must confess I had rather be in Washington. Have you sent that cable?"

"I've sent one a yard long. The trouble is the Government are pretty well convinced already. It's the voters we want to get at. What I'm afraid of all the time is that the trouble will commence before the President has been empowered to sign."

The Admiral rose to his feet in reply to a summons from the *maître d'hôtel* and led his guest towards the table which had been prepared for them.

"Don't worry too much about that, young fellow," he enjoined cheerfully. "I'm a sailor, not a politician, but I can see my hand before my face in the daylight. If half the members of the pact go on the rampage — well, I shouldn't be surprised if the other half didn't follow suit. Now then, sit in that corner and try an English lobster."

"Another thing that rather puzzles me," Grant remarked, as they proceeded with their luncheon, "is why our friends, the enemy, should have chosen for their enterprise the year in which England is policing the Asiatic seas on behalf of the Limitation of Armaments Committee. If it had been Germany's year, for instance, they could have done what they liked."

"Well, there are two reasons for that," his companion explained. "The first is that the most important year, so far as secrecy is concerned, was last year, when some of their phantom ships were actually laid down. Last year, as you know, Germany policed the whole of the eastern waters and reported everything O. K. Then, their second reason, no doubt, is that England polices very strongly, and it means at least two capital ships and subsidiary craft detached from the main fleet. They think they've got rid of those units in case, by any chance, we should break the Pact and intervene. As a matter of fact, we have made a few changes," he went on, lowering his tone. "Our best battleship and three destroyers are on their way home now. Australia's replacing them for us."

"I am going to ask you the most improper question a person in my position could ask of a person in yours," Grant declared. "If the German fleet entered the Atlantic steaming westwards, before America had had time to join the Pact, should you interfere?"

Sullivan grinned merrily.

"The politicians have to decide that," he reminded his guest. "But a look round our naval ports to-day would probably surprise you."

"How would your strength work out?"

"A trifle to their advantage on paper," the Admiral admitted, "if you count the Russians in. But there might be a little difficulty about Russia keeping her appointment. They have just been served with a notice to receive a police patrol of inspection for a report to the Limitation of Armaments Committee. They will either have to show their hand or stay in their harbour. Then there's another point to be borne in mind. I am a terribly pig-headed and prejudiced Britisher, and I swear by our own forces, but the French submarines have gone one or two ahead of us. I had sooner face the devil himself than the flotilla which is collecting in Cherbourg harbour."

Grant's eyes flashed for a moment.

"You mean that France——"

"Pooh! My dear fellow. I don't mean anything," Sullivan interrupted. "I'm a sailor, not a politician. But I'll tell you this. France is very often misjudged. Thirty years ago the world thought her self-centred, selfish, neurotic. So would any of us have been after what she went through. You wait. Jove! There's our hostess of last night. Ripping, isn't she? She'll be the *partie* of the season. They say young Suffolk's making the running. Makes one wish one were young again. Why not an international alliance, Slattery? Why don't you go in with your millions? Old Yeovil thinks no end of you."

Grant endured his companion's careless banter without moving a muscle. Susan, the centre of a gay little party, looked round as she entered the inner room and nodded to the two men. There was a smile for each—the smile of a happy, light-hearted girl, who has nothing but good will for the whole world. And yet somehow or other it was a smile which Grant hated. He felt that it put the seal upon his ostracism.

CHAPTER XIX

Grant was conscious of a queer presentiment as he stopped to speak with Cornelius Blunn on the first day out from Southampton. Blunn was occupying his usual suite and was lying in splendid isolation in his own little portion of the deck. He had come on board the day before, to all appearance his usual self. Now, within twenty-four hours, he was again writhing in misery. There was something in his look of misery, as he glanced up at Grant, which touched the latter.

"Sit down and talk to me for a minute, my young enemy," he invited. "The doctor tries to tell me that part of this seasickness is nervousness. One should seek distraction, he says. Tell me how you succeeded in London."

"Admirably," Grant replied, accepting his invitation. "But I'm not going to cure your seasickness by telling you my secrets."

Cornelius Blunn smiled faintly.

"You're a nice lad," he said. "Pity you aren't a German. I'd have made a great man of you."

"I am very glad I am not a German."

"Why?"

Grant shrugged his shoulders.

"Well," he pointed out, "of course every nation has its characteristics, bad and good. Your people are industrious, domesticated, subject to discipline, and full of courage. On the other hand they are the most egregiously selfish and egotistical race upon the face of the earth. It is Germany first, and let any one else exist that may. That is what I don't like about your people."

Cornelius Blunn did not reply for a moment.

"It may seem so to the world," he conceded presently. "You see we are a nation of individualists."

"Why are you alone?" Grant enquired, after a moment's pause.

The troubled look returned to Blunn's face.

"A chapter of accidents has befallen me," he explained. "Müller, my body servant, and Felix, my secretary, who came over with me, missed the boat at Southampton. Both were executing commissions for me late in London, and I sent them down by car. They had an accident, twelve miles from Guildford, and both were too injured to continue the journey. The steward does his best, but I am not used to being alone. If any other boat could have got me over in time for the Conference, where my presence in an advisory capacity is required, I should have postponed my departure."

Grant murmured a few words of sympathy and presently departed. On the deck he met Lord Yeovil, with whom he turned and walked.

"Blunn seems to be quite ill," he confided.

"Unfortunately men do not die of seasickness," the other rejoined. "It sounds a brutal thing to say, I suppose, but, in my opinion, it would be a great benefit to the world if Blunn were to be removed from it. I have come to the conclusion within the last few weeks, Slattery, that, more than any other man living, Cornelius Blunn represents the spirit of warfare and unrest. He is the personification of all that is evil in the German system. I can quite believe your story that he carries with him day and night a famous letter of hate, inscribed by his father on his deathbed. He not only carries the letter, but he carries the spirit."

"One is so often tempted to like the man," Grant remarked. "And yet I know that you're right. If all that we suspect of his domestic intrigues in America is true, he is a very terrible person. I hope Lady Susan is keeping well. I haven't seen her about."

"She is playing deck tennis forward," her father replied. "A pleasant game but a trifle energetic for this warm weather. Lutrecht and his faithful henchman, Von Diss, are playing écarté in the smoke room. Did you know, Slattery, that Von Diss was to be one of the German *entourage?*"

"I had no idea of it," Grant answered hastily and with perfect truth. "I met the Princess in Bond Street the day before we sailed and she told me that her husband was arriving in London that afternoon. She gave me no idea that it was for the purpose of proceeding to the States or that she was accompanying him."

"They keep their secrets well, these Germans," Lord Yeovil mused. "They have method and reticence. I must go and spend my usual hour with Arthur. I don't think I ever had such a mass of material to master in my life — pretty terrible, some of it, too."

Grant strolled on and threw himself into a chair close to the rail. "Method and reticence!" He thought for a moment of Cleo's whispered words. If they were true, and he had never doubted them, the whole secret of the poisonous domestic conspiracy, as much or more to be dreaded than any avalanche of foreign aggression, was contained in two small valumes — neat, they would be; precise, they would be; venomous, they would surely be — and never so nearly within his grasp as now. He fell to studying the ethics of the much debated problem of justification by result. Cornelius Blunn, at the present moment, was probably more helpless than he would ever be found again. Was it worth the risk of failure, the plan that was slowly forming itself in his mind? . . .

Von Diss, very neat and dapper in white flannel trousers and blue serge coat of nautical cut, came up and touched Grant on the arm. He always made a show of being very friendly with the rival whom he hated.

"I saw you talking to our friend, Cornelius Blunn," he said. "His condition puzzles me. It is a terrible thing to suffer so from such a simple cause. Incomprehensible, too! He enjoys sailing as much as any man, and yet directly he gets on a big steamer, he collapses altogether."

"He was very ill coming over," Grant remarked. "Yet he was himself again the night after landing. His speech at the Whitehall Rooms was an admirable production."

Von Diss nodded.

"He is not old," he went on, half to himself. "He is a strong man. His mentality is amazing. Yet this simple illness seems to have thrown him into a strange disorder. I made a harmless request to him this morning, and he ordered me away."

"A harmless request!" Grant felt a sudden inspiration. "A harmless request!" Bearing in mind Cornelius Blunn's unprotected state, Von Diss had probably asked for the care of the casket or that it be deposited in the ship's safe. It was a perfectly reasonable suggestion.

"I expect you will find him better to-morrow," Grant observed. "The Princess is, I trust, not suffering?"

"She is a little tired, but she has no *mal de mer,*" her husband replied. "I go now to fetch her. Presently I shall talk with our friend, Cornelius Blunn, again."

He wandered off and Grant made his way to where the deck tennis was proceeding. He sat down and watched the players for a time. Presently, without noticing who her neighbour was, Susan came and shared his seat. She gave a little start as he spoke and made an involuntary movement. Grant rose at once to his feet.

"Pray let me go away," he begged. "I am sorry that you find my presence so utterly distasteful."

He was angry with himself directly he had spoken. She only laughed at him and settled herself down more comfortably.

"Don't be absurd," she said lightly. "Only I didn't happen to notice who it was. Don't you play any of these games?"

"Sometimes."

"We're having a competition," she confided. "So far Charlie Suffolk and I have beaten everybody. Oh, I must go," she added, slipping off. "I see there is another couple ready for us."

He watched her for a moment or two and turned away. He tried other parts of the ship, but some fascination seemed to draw him always back to that little enclosed space where Cornelius Blunn lay with half-closed eyes. He had lost a great deal of his natural colour and seemed somehow to have shrunken. Grant hesitated at the round glass door for a moment or two, wondering whether or not to enter. Then he realised that Blunn was asleep. He stooped down, withdrew the key from the lock of the door, and placed it in his pocket. Afterwards he walked away.

CHAPTER XX

AFTER resisting the impulse at least half a dozen times, Grant finally found his way, after dinner that evening, to the dancing deck aft. It was a very beautifully arranged space, given over in the daytime to various games, and at night covered with a specially prepared floor for dancing. The windows opened all the way round, and in hot weather the roof rolled back. From one of the window seats he watched for some little time. Susan was, as usual, surrounded by admirers, but she was unlucky in her partners. Three or four times he saw her finish a dance a little abruptly and stroll with her companion on the open portion of the deck. After watching a particularly unsuccessful effort, he made his way towards her. Although he concealed his condition admirably, no neophyte fresh from boarding school and attending his first dance could have been more nervous.

"May I have a dance, Lady Susan?" he asked.

She looked at him without immediately replying. For a moment she was more like the Susan of Monte Carlo, even though there was something faintly resentful in her expression. It was at least feeling of a sort.

"I'm so sorry," she said, "but do you know I really can't get my feet to go to-night? I think I must have played too much tennis. Tell me, have you heard how Mr. Blunn is this evening?"

"I haven't enquired since dinner," Grant replied. "I will let you know if I hear later."

He turned away and walked out on to the open deck. There was nothing more to be done. He was in a hopeless position. There was nothing he could say to her, no complaint he could make, no excuse he could offer. He drew a wicker chair to the side of the rail, threw himself down, lit a pipe, and began to smoke. Somehow or other the tobacco tasted wrong, even the beauty of the night seemed to increase his depression. Presently he left off smoking, leaned back in his chair and closed his eyes. They were playing a waltz he used to dance with Susan. He lay still and listened.

Susan, crossing the deck in search of her father, discovered him in conversation with the Prince and Princess von Diss. She stopped and was half inclined to retreat. Gertrude, however, had already turned towards her.

"Lady Susan," she said, "I was just sending my husband to look for you. Will you come and sit with me for a moment?"

Susan glanced meaningly towards her father, who she had been told was looking for her. He mistook her appeal for help and smiled acquiescence.

"Do, Susan," he enjoined. "I only sent for you to say that I was going to the smoke room. Von Diss and I will finish our little discussion there."

Gertrude led the way towards a distant corner where there were two comfortable chairs. Susan walked by her side, apparently at her ease, but inwardly fuming. There was something about this woman which always made her feel young and unformed.

"Of course, my dear Lady Susan," Gertrude began, "I know that you detest having to talk to me. But you see it really can't be helped. My husband is meeting your father officially and, so long as my husband has decided to make me so, I am a perfectly respectable woman."

"I have had very little experience in the ethics of such matters," Susan replied. "I am content as a rule to follow my own judgment."

Gertrude settled herself quite comfortably in her chair.

"Ah, well," she sighed, "you're very young. It is just your youth which makes your judgment so absurd. You're very angry with Mr. Grant Slattery, aren't you?"

"Whatever my feelings may be with regard to Mr. Slattery, or any other man," Lady Susan rejoined quietly, "they concern — if you will forgive my saying so — myself alone."

"Very foolish," Gertrude murmured. "Listen to me, please. Poor Grant, he really is in a ridiculous position. If there weren't just a spice of tragedy attached to the situation, I am sure I should never accept the rôle of obvious idiot which seems thrust upon me."

"I hope you're not going to offer me any confidences," Susan begged. "I do not desire them."

"My dear Lady Prig, you're going to hear what is good for you," Gertrude continued calmly. "You can't get up and leave me, because I am an older woman, and it would be very rude of you. You probably think that when Mr. Slattery said good-by to you in Monte Carlo he knew that I was going to America with him. Well, the poor man didn't know anything of the sort."

"He didn't know?" Susan repeated incredulously. "Why, it was the night before."

"Precisely," Gertrude acquiesced. "You see, I was very fond of Grant Slattery, and I couldn't quite believe that he had lost all feeling for me. Sheer vanity of course,—for which I suffered. I knew quite well that if I had asked him to take me away he would have refused point-blank—because I had already asked him and he had refused—but I wanted to go away with him and I took a risk. I went on board his yacht as a stowaway. He hadn't the faintest idea I was there until the yacht was a day and a half out. He wouldn't have known, even then, if I hadn't nearly fainted from hunger."

Susan sat quite still for a moment. She was struggling to emulate her companion's composure.

"It sounds incredible," she murmured.

"It is the truth, nevertheless," Gertrude assured her. "When I disclosed myself, he was aghast. He took no pains to hide from me the fact that my presence there was utterly undesired. For some time he considered landing me at Gibraltar. That, however, would have made the matter no better from any point of view, and I suppose he realised that it would have been a particularly brutal act. So he let me stay. He had to."

There was a pause. Gertrude seemed to be listening to the music. Suddenly she recommenced.

"Of course, the rest of the story is absurd, as well as being humiliating. Why I tell it to you I really don't know. I made an idiot of myself in the usual way, and I forced Grant into the usual hopeless position. I suppose because he was in love with you, he played the Sir Galahad for some time with almost ridiculous perfection. Then one night we ran into a terrible storm. I was frightened, and Grant — he is really very kind-hearted — began to realise that he had been hurting me badly every moment of the time. I became emotional and finally desperate. I will spare you the rest of the story — but I gave Grant no chance. Afterwards I understood how hideous one-sided love can be. If I had wronged my husband I paid in the suffering of those three or four days before I could get Grant to land me at Newport. I only saw him for a few minutes at meal times and afterwards when he used to come and try to make polite conversation to me, but the whole affair was ghastly. I had done the most absurd thing a woman could possibly attempt. I had tried to secure for myself the man who was in love with another woman. There were those few hours I spoke of during the storm. After that — nothing. I did not see Grant again until we met by accident on the steamer coming back to England. I had been ill in a little country place in New Hampshire and he had no idea even where I was. I wonder whether you would be very kind now and go and ask my husband to give me his arm. I think we must be somewhere near the screw. I am beginning to feel the motion."

Susan rose to her feet. Something in her expression warned Gertrude.

"My dear child!" she exclaimed, "if you say a single word of what I can see in your face I shall scream. I am an impossible person who has told you an impossible story for an impossible reason. Please do as I ask you."

Susan rose to her feet and conveyed his wife's message to the Prince. Then, for a moment, she hesitated. Two or three young men moved towards her but she waved them away.

"In a minute," she called out. "I am coming back."

She walked out on to the open part of the deck. A few yards away Grant was still seated, gazing gloomily across the sea. She drew nearer and nearer to his chair. He heard the sound of her hesitating footsteps and turned around. Suddenly he sprang to his feet. He could scarcely believe his eyes. She was smiling at him, a little plaintively, with just a touch of appeal about her mouth.

"I was stupid, Grant," she whispered. "Would you care to dance this?"

"Susan!" he exclaimed.

"Very stupid indeed," she went on. "Let's have a good long dance like we used to and then do something terribly obvious — go and look at the bows or something."

He had sense enough to ask no questions, to accept what came to him. Gertrude watched them for a moment as she passed along, leaning on her husband's arm.

"Really," she remarked, "I suppose the papers are right when they call that young woman beautiful. I used to think she lacked expression."

The Prince looked at the young couple through his horn-rimmed eye-glass.

"She does very well," he agreed. "They have the looks, these young Englishwomen, and the figure — sometimes the wit. They move all the time, though, in a very narrow world."

Gertrude continued her walk.

"I suppose the stony and narrow way has its compensations," she sighed.

CHAPTER XXI

The *Sefalonia* was due in New York on Wednesday morning, and, on Tuesday night Grant and Susan sat out on deck together until almost eleven o'clock. Susan glanced at her watch reluctantly.

"If this voyage were going on any longer, Grant," she said, "I should have to tell people that we were engaged in self-defence. We really do such outrageous things. Do you know that I didn't dance with any one else to-night?"

"I know I am getting very unpopular," Grant observed, smiling, "and, curiously enough, I don't care a bit."

"Nor do I, really," she agreed.

"The one thing I am glad about," he went on, "is that we are approaching a country which has most civilised ideas as regards matrimonial arrangements. No putting banns up and waiting three weeks and that sort of thing."

"You don't suppose I'm going to be married over here, do you?" Susan exclaimed.

"I am hoping so," he replied patiently. "I thought a quiet little wedding in Washington would round off proceedings there,—if we are any of us left alive."

"You've some very serious work to do first, Grant," she reminded him.

"Very," he assented. "So has your father. Mine may lead me into more trouble, perhaps, but your father's is the greater responsibility. I don't think there is another man in the world who would be able to handle the situation he will have to handle in a few days. There is a terrible crisis closing upon us, Susan."

"The thought of it makes our little affairs seem almost unimportant, doesn't it?" she sighed.

He leaned over and kissed her daringly.

"Just for luck," he murmured.

On his way to his stateroom Grant passed the entrance to Cornelius Blunn's suite. He raised the curtain. The steward was seated outside the closed door.

"How's Mr. Blunn to-night?" he enquired.

"He's been a little easier, I think, sir," the man replied.

"I wonder whether he'd like to see me?"

"I don't think I'd disturb him, sir. He's locked the door and he seems quite quiet now."

"Are you going to sit there all night?"

"Mr. Blunn's giving me ten dollars a night not to move, in case he wants me. The chief steward's put another man on to look after some of my rooms. Lucky I'm used to sleeping in a chair."

"Goodnight," Grant wished him.

"Goodnight, sir."

Grant made his way to his own stateroom, exchanged his patent shoes for some dark-coloured ones with rubber soles, his dinner jacket for a blue serge coat which buttoned close up to his throat, slipped the latest thing in automatics into his pocket, and went up on deck again by a roundabout way. It was nearly midnight now, and only a few people were still in evidence. He drew a chair into the recess close up against the glass-enclosed space in front of Blunn's suite and waited until one by one they dispersed and he was entirely alone. Then he rose to his feet, opened the sliding door to which he had the key, and found himself in the little sheltered portion of the deck allotted to the suite. The door opening into the outer room was left upon a hook. There was no sound to be heard inside, although a light was burning. Softly he lifted the hook and peered in. The apartment was evidently the sitting room of the suite and was untenanted. He stepped inside and listened. Opposite to him was another door, also on the hook, leading to the sleeping room, from which a thin gleam of light shone. He approached it noiselessly. There was still no sound to be heard, not even the breathing of a sleeping man. For some seconds he paused, puzzled by the unbroken silence, then slowly, and with the utmost care, he lifted the hook and pushed the door open, inch by inch. At last the opening was wide enough to admit the upper part of his body. He leaned forward and stood quite still gripping the side of the door. The bed was empty, although in disorder. Cornelius Blunn was seated on a chair before a round table, leaning forward, his head resting upon his arms. He was wearing a heavy dressing gown over his pyjamas, and was apparently in an extraordinarily deep sleep. His left hand was stretched out across the table, and gripped between its fingers was the end of a chain and some keys. A few inches farther away still was a box of dull yellow metal.

The seconds crept on. Grant could almost feel his own heart thumping. He stepped into the room, hooked the door again, and drew nearer and nearer to the silent figure. Then, as he bent over it, a new horror faced him. He forgot for a moment the great object of his search,—forgot that the secrets of a world's salvation were there within his grasp. He stooped down to peer into the stricken face. Human nature, all his powers of restraint, failed him. He gave a little cry. It was a terrible thing to look thus into the face of a dead man. He recovered himself at once. The cry, he realised, had been almost fatal. The steward outside had heard him. There was a heavy knocking at the door. He took no notice. The knocking continued. Then Grant made the effort of his life. He seized the stiffening fingers and dragged from them the end of the chain, unbuttoned the other end from the belt underneath the pyjama jacket, slipped it into his pocket and took the casket into his hands. With stealthy footsteps he stole away, unhooked the door and hooked it again, crossed the sitting room, reached the little glass-enclosed deck, passed through on to the main deck, and went staggering towards the farther end. He stood for a moment in the wind to recover himself. They were making about thirty knots an hour through a tumbling sea with little showers of spray thrown glittering into the air. Grant felt the sting of them on his face and in a moment he was himself again. He walked round the bows, descended the gangway from the other side and hurried to Lord Yeovil's suite. There was still a light in the sitting room. He knocked at the door and entered. Lord Yeovil, half undressed, was finishing a whisky and soda. He looked at the intruder without saying a word. Grant slipped the bolt through the door.

"I've got it," he announced breathlessly. "I've got the casket and the key. I want you to put it at once into one of the official boxes."

"Any struggle?" Lord Yeovil asked.

"None," was the awe-stricken reply, "but it was horrible all the same. Cornelius Blunn is dead."

CHAPTER XXII

THERE was pandemonium on the *Sefalonia* for the last four hours before she reached dock. The horror of a death on shipboard was deepened by the fact that Cornelius Blunn, who had consistently declined to allow any doctor to examine him, had shown no signs whatever of the heart disease which had ended his life so abruptly. But apart from the tragedy itself there were two men on the steamer, Prince Lutrecht and Prince von Diss, whom the event seemed to have reduced to an almost hysterical state. The captain scarcely knew how to deal with the situation which their importunities created. They refused even to leave his room. Their persistence was becoming intolerable.

"Commander," Prince Lutrecht said earnestly, "you are an Englishman, and I know that you are a lover of fair play. I tell you that last night there was stolen from Cornelius Blunn's room a casket containing political documents of the most vital importance to the future of the world. Those documents, if they fell into the wrong hands, might lead to a terrible and disastrous war. They were carried about by Cornelius Blunn in defiance of our wishes and it might very well be that he has met with his death in defending them. But they have been stolen and are, at the present moment, concealed upon this ship, and I appeal to you, as the one responsible person here, to assist us towards their restoration."

"But what can I do, Prince?" the captain expostulated. "I have nine hundred and seventy-five passengers on board. Do you wish every one of them searched?"

"Not every one," Prince Lutrecht replied. "The person who must be responsible for this robbery is Mr. Grant Slattery. He and Cornelius Blunn were enemies, yet he was always stopping to speak to him. He learned the way into his suite. Without a doubt Slattery was the thief."

"I have already done more than I have any right to do in that matter," the commander pointed out. "I have had Mr. Grant Slattery's rooms searched. Besides, the steward saw him going down into his stateroom at a reasonable hour. I cannot see the slightest evidence against the young man."

"He has probably passed the casket on to some one," Prince von Diss declared. "We must insist upon having the staterooms and baggage of his friends searched."

"Including, I presume, the belongings of Lord Yeovil?" the commander asked with a patient smile.

"The casket must be found," Prince Lutrecht persisted.

"Gentlemen," the commander said, "I will discuss the matter with my officers and see whether any search in conjunction with the Customs examination can be effected. I tell you frankly that, so far as regards the personal and official luggage of the Prime Minister of my country, I should not allow it to be touched. You must excuse me. We shall be taking up the pilot within half an hour."

"Captain," Prince Lutrecht announced in desperation, "I am prepared to give a reward of one million dollars for the recovery of that casket and its contents."

"There is no harm in announcing the fact," was the cold reply. "You must excuse me now. I have my duties to attend to."

Nothing happened. No discovery was made. As the great steamer backed up to her place alongside the dock, she was boarded by a small army of detectives, members of the police force and journalists. The Customs House officials, miraculously worked into a state of intense excitement, made almost savage onslaughts upon the general baggage. There was a rumour—many people declared they had seen it in black and white—that a million dollars would be paid for a small casket of dull yellow metal which had been stolen on board the *Sefalonia.* A great many people thought a million dollars a very useful sum of money and did their best to earn it, the consequence being that the majority of the passengers from the *Sefalonia* were detained many hours before they got away. Grant Slattery, who was met by Hodson, with Lord Yeovil and Susan, were amongst the earliest to leave. They all drove together towards the hotel in Park Avenue at which the latter were staying the night before their departure for Washington. Halfway there, Hodson, who had been looking out of the little window behind, redirected the driver.

"We are being followed," he announced, "by at least two taxicabs. I have told him to drive to Police Headquarters. It is the only safe place for an hour or so. Sorry to detain you and your daughter, Lord Yeovil, but if we had gone on to the hotel there would only have been some shooting on the sidewalk. There'll be some trouble here, but we'll do it on the rush."

The only luggage they had with them were two official-looking black boxes on which the name of the Right Honourable the Earl of Yeovil was painted in white letters. These had not been subjected to search and were inside the car with them.

"Which one?" Hodson asked.

Grant touched the box nearest to him with his foot. Hodson picked it up.

"It is just three steps across the sidewalk," he said. "Even if they wing me I'll get there. Don't let the young lady move. We won't hang round many seconds. They'll probably try a rush."

Susan passed her arm through Grant's.

"You must stay and protect me," she insisted.

He patted her hand. The light of battle was in his eyes.

"It may take both of us to get that safely inside," he warned her.

They swung round the last corner. Hodson held the box under his arm. Grant, with his automatic in his right hand, crouched by his side. Before they had drawn up against the curb, Hodson had flung the door open and made his spring. A taxicab from behind came crashing into the back of their car, without, however, doing serious damage. Hodson, quick on his feet, was halfway across the sidewalk before the first shot was fired. He staggered for a moment and Grant, rushing past him like a footballer who takes a pass, snatched the box from under his arm and, bending low, dashed past the astonished bystanders into the shelter of the building. Hodson stumbled after him. Policemen and detectives came running up, closing around them.

"Get those fellows in the taxicabs, if you can," Hodson cried, stooping down to feel his leg. "Green and his gang, by the looks of them. This way, Grant!"

They penetrated into the heart of the building, Hodson limping slightly from the effects of the bullet which had grazed his shin bone. They entered without ceremony an inner room. An astonished-looking secretary jumped up from the table and his Chief, recognising Hodson, looked more astonished still.

"My God, we've done it!" the latter exclaimed. "Sorry, sir. We've got the material here to hang a thousand men. Cornelius Blunn's handbook to the German Empire in America, and all the rest of it."

The functionary stood up.

"You'd better get to work," he advised. "Your last report was perfectly true, Hodson. I shouldn't be surprised if they attempted to bomb the place."

Grant produced the key to the casket, and Hodson drew out the books. The police official spoke on the telephone and half a dozen detectives with automatic pistols guarded the door, while a small corps of policemen guarded the entrance to the building.

"Now," Hodson said, "I think we can get to work on this little business."

Grant left Police Headquarters half an hour later to find Lord Yeovil and Susan still waiting. They drove off towards the hotel, and Grant at once unburdened himself.

"It is the most amazing scheme that's ever been conceived," he declared. "Scores of names in every city in the States, every one with their exactly assigned task on an exactly stipulated day. They all had their station, all their peculiar functions. Brooklyn Bridge, for instance, would have been blown up the day the German fleet appeared in sight. So far as we could see, there wouldn't have been an important bridge left in the country. The Japanese programme out west was worse. There will be over two hundred arrests to-day. There will be trouble in the city to-night, though, if the news gets about."

They arrived at the hotel.

"You're staying here, Grant?" Lord Yeovil enquired.

Grant shook his head.

"I will come and dine, if I may, sir," he replied. "I haven't got a scrap of writing now of any sort, but I'm a marked man. I'm best away from your hotel."

"How absurd!" Susan exclaimed. "Why, we're in this as much as you are. We brought the box away."

"To tell you the truth," Grant confided, "I think we are all quite safe for the moment. They must know that our object in going to Police Headquarters was to leave the documents there."

The car drew up at the hotel in Park Avenue. Grant walked across the pavement first and back again.

"All clear," he announced. "No one's bothered even to follow us. Listen."

They stood at the entrance to the hotel, listening. Away down towards the city, they heard the sound of three or four dull explosions, following one another quickly.

"That is the end of the civil war," Grant said grimly. "Or the beginning of it."

CHAPTER XXIII

THE opening session of the Limitation of Armaments Conference was held in an environment outwardly calm, but with mutterings of the storm very clearly audible to those who knew something of the real position. The actual surroundings all made for peace, — a stately and dignified chamber, with carefully shaded windows, cool white walls, and oaken furniture, massive, and beautiful with age. There were twenty-six representatives present and six secretaries at the side table, amongst whom Slattery, by special appointment, found a place. He was next to Itash, but the two men exchanged no greetings. At the appointed hour the President entered the room and spoke a few words of welcome. His allusions to the world's desire for peace seemed to contain, perhaps, a faint note of irony; otherwise there was nothing to indicate any foreknowledge of untoward events. After he had extended his usual formal invitation to luncheon he left the room, and his place was taken by the Secretary of State, who embarked at once upon the proceedings. He declared that on a matter of urgency he had given permission to the English representative, Lord Yeovil, to make a statement before the agenda was entered upon. There was a little movement, a rustling of papers, as Lord Yeovil, on the right-hand side of the Secretary of State, rose to speak, a slim, dignified figure in the cool, soft light. He spoke slowly and very gravely, and his words seemed chosen to attain to the essence of brevity.

"Mr. Secretary and members of the Conference," he said, "as you know, certain of the Powers have assumed year by year the duty of policing the waters and lands of the earth, in order to satisfy ourselves that the regulations imposed by you, gentlemen, are dutifully and honourably carried out. I have to present to you a report from the Commander of the English flotilla in eastern waters to the effect that Japan, by a system of duplication, described in the papers which I have the honour to lay before you, has during this and the preceding year, exceeded her allowance of marine tonnage by two hundred and fifty thousand tons, and also that, in the harbour of a port on the Chinese coast, leased to her, or on an adjacent island, there have been constructed and are now ready for flying, a score of flying ships of a new type, obviously designed for offensive purposes. The papers containing particulars of this divergence from the principles and ordinances of the Conference, I had the honour to hand to Mr. Secretary of State last night, and a copy has, I believe, been prepared for the inspection of each of you."

There was a tense silence. One of the young men from the side table arose, with a little pile of papers in his hand, which he distributed around the table. The Secretary allowed a few minutes to elapse while everyone studied the very simple document laid before him, translated in each case into the language of each separate representative. Then he rose to his feet.

"It is my duty," he said, "to call upon the representative of Japan, His Excellency Prince Yoshimo, to afford us an explanation and reply to this very serious charge."

Itash moved silently from his place and stepped behind the representative of his country, who was also the Ambassador to the United States. Prince Yoshimo rose slowly to his feet. He seemed imperturbable and wholly unembarrassed.

"Mr. Secretary," he said, "and gentlemen, the charge of Lord Yeovil has come as a surprise. I can only say that, as has happened before, a little too much zealousness has been shown, a little too great—great——"

"Credulity," Itash whispered.

"—credulity displayed," the Ambassador went on. "The so-called duplicate ships are nothing but coal barges, and the flying boats are for commercial purposes. That is my reply."

Lord Yeovil rose once more to his feet.

"The statement of His Excellency Prince Yoshimo," he announced, "is in direct contradiction to my information."

Once more Prince Yoshimo rose, calm and soft-tongued.

"Mr. Secretary," he said, "I have afforded you the explanation you desired. Let others go and see. Our harbours, and the harbours of such part of the Chinese coast over which we have influence, are free to the vessels of any one of the powers here present."

The Secretary turned to Lord Yeovil, who rose once more to his feet.

"I desire, sir," the latter begged, "a postponement of any further discussion for two days."

The routine business of the Conference was continued, but it was very hard to secure the close attention of any of the members. The questions which they were called upon to decide seemed of infinitesimal importance compared to the magnitude of the issues which had already been raised. The morning session drifted away, however, and the afternoon session, without further incident. The proceedings terminated about five o'clock. Slattery, leaving the place alone, came face to face with Itash in one of the lobbies. No form of salutation passed between them, but Itash stopped and the beginnings of a smile curved his lips unpleasantly.

"Is this wonderful information," he asked, "part of the babble I am supposed to have talked in my sleep and Mademoiselle Cleo to have repeated?"

"And for repeating which she was murdered?" Grant added.

Itash was unmoved.

"I so seldom read the newspapers," he said. "I understood that she had committed suicide. That was quite reasonable. Why not? We each have the right. But you do not answer my question."

"Nor do I intend to," Grant replied. "But I will be very rash indeed and tell you this. It was Mademoiselle Cleo who conveyed to us your fear that Mr. Cornelius Blunn yielded too much to sentiment. The deepest vault in the Safe Deposit Company of the City should have held that little casket of gold."

Itash drew a queer little breath. It was as though he had been attacked suddenly by asthma. No thunderous exclamations or furious expletive could have contained half the feeling of his simple words, each one detached from the other, slow and pregnant of a certain agony.

"What — do — you — mean?"

"Ah!" Grant murmured. "Explanations are so tedious. I will leave you a little puzzle with which you may occupy the rest of the day. Prince Lutrecht is sharing your anxiety. So, I think, is Prince von Diss. Very soon you will know."

"The casket contained nothing but the letter of Cornelius Blunn, the elder, to his son. A personal letter of no importance."

Grant passed on with a little smile. Itash watched him down the long corridor, watched him disappear. Then he turned back and hurried to the room where Prince Lutrecht and Von Diss were still talking.

"Prince," he confided, drawing Lutrecht on one side, "I have just spoken with Slattery, the man who has been doing all this evil work for America. He either jibed at me or the books were in the casket."

Prince Lutrecht shrugged his shoulders. He was a philosopher and a man of great mind.

"My friend," he said, "everything that could be done to recover that casket was done. It escaped from our hands. We did our best. I refuse to believe that Cornelius would have trusted himself upon the ocean, carrying such a treasure, without a bodyguard. Besides, two or three days have passed, and nothing has happened. There would have been a thousand arrests and the papers would be seething with their discovery, had the books been there."

"But," Itash began——

Prince Lutrecht waved him away.

"I will not be worried with possibilities," he declared. "We have others matters to face."

Slattery spent a wonderful hour in a quiet room of an official building, talking through a private wire to Hodson in New York. Afterwards he dined at the British Embassy, where all official entertainment had been postponed. He was able to sit alone with Susan on one of the broad piazzas afterwards, watching the rising of the moon, and the fireflies in the meadow at the bottom of the garden.

"Your father was splendid," Grant told her. "He said just enough. The day after to-morrow will come the bombshell. Hodson has done splendidly too," he went on. "They have raided thirty or forty mansions in New York, St. Louis, and even Philadelphia, and discovered documents which afford them absolute proof. They are trying to keep the Press muzzled until after to-morrow, but I'm afraid it will be difficult."

"It seems an amazing tangle," she murmured.

"We're making history at express speed," he replied. "I wonder whether we couldn't walk down and see if those really are fireflies."

She rose to her feet, took his arm, and they passed down the broad walk, through the ornamental gardens, to the little wood beyond. After which they talked no more of politics.

CHAPTER XXIV

On the Wednesday morning, the day but one after the opening Conference, the members assembled at the same time and place, with one notable absentee. At the appointed hour for commencing the proceedings the Secretary of State made a momentous announcement.

"Gentlemen," he said, "I have to announce that Prince Yoshimo, the representative of Japan, has sent me formal notice on behalf of his Government that he desires to withdraw from this Conference."

There was a little murmur of excitement. Prince Lutrecht rose to his feet.

"Mr. Secretary, and Gentlemen," he began, "I am not in any way an apologist for the action taken by my distinguished confrère on the instigation of his Government. On the other hand I must point out to you that the charges brought by Lord Yeovil against the honour of a great nation, publicly and before you all, were of a nature to provoke most intense and poignant reprisals. I regret very much that they were made. I foresee from the retirement of the representative of Japan from this Conference — a retirement which I fear may be final — a serious blow to its utility. The item upon the agenda for discussion this morning deals, I see, with a supposed secret naval and military understanding between Russia and my country to the exclusion of other members of the Pact. If it is proposed to interfere in any way with the arrangements which I admit exist between the Russian and German naval forces, for joint practice and manœuvres, I desire to tell this meeting at once that I offer my strongest protest and shall follow the example of my friend, the Japanese Ambassador, in retiring from participation in the Conference."

Prince Lutrecht resumed his seat. Lord Yeovil glanced towards the Secretary of State. The latter nodded and rose once more.

"I think," he announced, "that Lord Yeovil has a reply to make to Prince Lutrecht, but before we proceed with what is the apparent business of this Conference, I desire to make an unofficial announcement to you all, which you will learn when you leave this room, but which it was the President's wish that you should know of in conjunction with such events as are now taking place. The Japanese Ambassador last night tendered to the Government of the United States a formal demand that all persons of Japanese birth, desiring to do so, shall be permitted to acquire land and American citizenship on an equality with other nations."

Monsieur Lafayel, the French representative, for a moment, lost his head.

"Mon Dieu!" he exclaimed. "A declaration of war!"

"My distinguished friend technically anticipates," the Secretary observed. "But the attitude of the United States of America to such a demand is, perhaps, too obvious for any other construction to be placed upon the situation."

Lord Yeovil rose once more to his feet. He looked around the table before he spoke with the air of one who desires to impress on his mind the memory of a scene destined to become historical. He spoke slowly and with unflurried tone.

"Mr. Secretary and Gentlemen," he said, "I address you once more in reply chiefly to the remarks of my distinguished friend, Prince Lutrecht. I speak to you, not only as the representative of Great Britain, but as the representative of the Power chosen in rotation for the duty of policing the seas and enforcing the regulations imposed by this Conference. I have to announce to you that I am in possession of absolute proof of the ill-faith of the seceding nation — Japan — from this organisation. I have to-day received cabled information from the Admiral commanding the police forces of the organisation in eastern waters, that he has, in accordance with instructions received, destroyed the four or five battleships built in excess of Japan's rights and also the nest of flying ships lying in the harbour of Yulensk, and built and armed without the cognisance of this Assembly."

It is, perhaps, doubtful whether spoken words have, at any time, produced a greater effect upon a gathering of men than these words of Lord Yeovil's. Amazed and half-incredulous interest was the prevailing note. Lutrecht, however, seemed like a man stricken. Every scrap of colour left his cheeks. His eyes burned like dry fires. His tongue was perpetually moistening his lips. He seemed to be trying to speak, but he made no effort to rise to his feet.

"Further," Lord Yeovil continued, "and in reply to Prince Lutrecht, I have to inform him that the evidences as to the secret understanding between the naval forces of Germany and Russia are not in accordance with the terms of this Conference, and I have ventured, on behalf of the powers with which I am endowed, to anticipate your permission to act according to our statutes. A small portion of the British fleet has surprised the Russian battleships lying at Archangel and, on behalf of the Conference — not, I beg you will understand, in any way on behalf of Great Britain, but acting simply in the interests of all — has taken possession of those ships and disarmed them, pending a satisfactory settlement. I may add that we found them provisioned and ready to sail to join the German fleet at a rendezvous off the north coast of Ireland."

Prince Lutrecht rose a little heavily to his feet. All his effrontery had deserted him.

"Mr. Secretary," he announced, "I have no alternative but to follow the example of His Excellency, the representative of Japan, and sever my allegiance to this Conference."

"A course which I naturally follow," the representative of Russia declared, rising in his place.

"It will afford my country the greatest regret," the chairman said drily, "that this Conference, for the inauguaration of which America was responsible, and to whose conventions we have zealously, and it seems at great risk to ourselves, been true, exists no longer. But I may add that it is still more to our sorrow that the circumstances of the breaking up of the Conference point clearly to disloyalty on the part of two of the subscribing nations."

Prince Lutrecht made one effort.

"Disloyalty, sir?" he repeated, half-turning on his way to the door.

"I regret to have to use that word, Prince," the Secretary observed gravely. "I shall offer no explanation at this time. If you require one, read the Press of to-night and to-morrow morning. You will find there bad news. This is the last word."

Lutrecht left the room. The Secretary waited until the door was closed.

"I have no other course, gentlemen," he continued, "painful though it may be, than to declare that this Conference has come automatically to an end until some further understanding can be arrived at amongst the nations, based upon principles which seem to have been deserted by the representatives of the two seceding Powers. The United States of America must in future guard their own freedom."

There was a rustling of papers, shuffling of feet, and then every one began to talk at once. The Limitation of Armaments Conference ended, as most similar assemblies had done,—in a mixture of exaltation, confusion, and misunderstanding.

There was a very fateful and wonderful meeting, convened on behalf of his Government by the Secretary of State an hour or so later, and attended by Lord Yeovil, Prince Yoshimo, and Prince Lutrecht. They met in the Secretary's official room in the White House. No one shook hands, no civilities of any sort were offered. The Secretary himself locked the door.

"Gentlemen," he said, "I have asked you to meet me because, whatever our feelings may be, the United States of America, more than any other country, hates war, deprecates revenge, and seeks for the truest expression of civilisation. By a series of fortuitous incidents America has become apprised of the hostile intentions of Japan and Germany. Let me remind you, Prince Lutrecht, that, if you persevere, you are without the aid of the Russian navy, and your fleet will be met, before it enters the Atlantic, by the combined navies of France and England, and probably Italy. The fact that, for the moment, America stands outside the Pact has, thanks to the generous instincts of the nations of the world, been ignored by them, in the face of recent discoveries. You, Prince Yoshimo, have lost that superiority of naval forces by means of which you intended to inflict disaster upon our fleet and coasts, and to impose your will upon our people. If your fleet sails it will be met by the American fleet in its entirety, and I imagine that, under the present conditions, the advantage in material would rest slightly with us. The schemes you produced for disorganising the mentality of our country have been discovered and dealt with. Fifty citizens of this country—some of them citizens of repute—are to-day in jail. Five hundred more are under police supervision. The points of danger from New York to San Francisco which it was their duty to attack have been guarded and will be guarded. Now, gentlemen, you have heard what I have to say. Are you going through with your abortive schemes? If so, you can have your papers within half an hour."

Amazing man of an amazing race, Prince Yoshimo bowed.

"There have been many misunderstandings," he said. "Japan, too, loves peace. I think, under the circumstances, I can anticipate my Imperial Master's decision. I desire to withdraw the documents I had the honour to present to the Government of the United States yesterday."

"And I," Prince Lutrecht added, "desire to assure you, and through you your Government, that gross exaggeration has been used in describing the attitude and aims of my country. It seems to be the hard fate of Germany to be continually striving for peace and to be always suspected of bellicosity. I offer the fullest pledges of our peaceful intentions. On behalf of my Government I acquiesce in the cessation of the understanding between Russia and ourselves. I declare for peace."

The Secretary bowed.

"This," he pronounced, "is not the place or the hour to discuss the future. The Limitation of Armaments Conference has ceased to exist. The Pact, I imagine, must be either dissolved or reconstructed, full account having been taken of the dangerous position in which your two countries, gentlemen, have placed the peace of the world. That, I think, is all we can say at present."

Prince Lutrecht bowed sombrely. Prince Yoshimo followed

his example. They left the room together, undismayed, with little apparent loss of dignity. Lord Yeovil accepted a cigarette and lit it thoughtfully.

"Queer brains, some of these people," he observed.

The Secretary smiled.

"What about a cocktail and some luncheon?" he suggested. "The Chief would like to see you."

Lord Yeovil glanced at his watch.

"I am taking a day off," he announced. "And, by the bye, I shall have to hurry. My daughter is being married to Grant Slattery at one o'clock, and we have a little family party afterwards at the Embassy. Your wife will have received a note by now. I hope we may have the pleasure of seeing you both."

"I am quite sure that you may count upon us," the other replied heartily. "Let me offer you at once, however, my best wishes for your daughter's happiness. Grant Slattery's a fine fellow. Only a very few of us will ever know how much our country owes to him for his work during the last two years."

"Not only your country, but the world," Lord Yeovil acquiesced. "War brings equal disaster to victor and vanquished."

"A relic of the Middle Ages," the American statesman declared, "in which the victors sometimes derived an illusionary benefit from the simple fact that international commerce consisted merely of a primitive attempt at barter, and the complication of exchanges was unknown."

"And yet," Lord Yeovil sighed, "there will always be wars."

THE GREAT IMPERSONATION

CHAPTER I

THE trouble from which great events were to come began when Everard Dominey, who had been fighting his way through the scrub for the last three quarters of an hour towards those thin, spiral wisps of smoke, urged his pony to a last despairing effort and came crashing through the great oleander shrub to pitch forward on his head in the little clearing. It developed the next morning, when he found himself for the first time for many months on a truckle bed, between linen sheets, with a cool, bamboo-twisted roof between him and the relentless sun. He raised himself a little in the bed.

"Where the mischief am I?" he demanded.

A black boy, seated cross-legged in the entrance of the banda, rose to his feet, mumbled something and disappeared. In a few moments the tall, slim figure of a European, in spotless white riding clothes, stooped down and came over to Dominey's side.

"You are better?" he enquired politely.

"Yes, I am," was the somewhat brusque rejoinder. "Where the mischief am I, and who are you?"

The newcomer's manner stiffened. He was a person of dignified carriage, and his tone conveyed some measure of rebuke.

"You are within half a mile of the Iriwarri River, if you know where that is," he replied,—"about seventy-two miles southeast of the Darawaga Settlement."

"The devil! Then I am in German East Africa?"

"Without a doubt."

"And you are German?"

"I have that honour."

Dominey whistled softly.

"Awfully sorry to have intruded," he said. "I left Marlinstein two and a half months ago, with twenty boys and plenty of stores. We were doing a big trek after lions. I took some new Askaris in and they made trouble,—looted the stores one night and there was the devil to pay. I was obliged to shoot one or two, and the rest deserted. They took my compass, damn them, and I'm nearly a hundred miles out of my bearings. You couldn't give me a drink, could you?"

"With pleasure, if the doctor approves," was the courteous answer. "Here, Jan!"

The boy sprang up, listened to a word or two of brief command in his own language, and disappeared through the hanging grass which led into another hut. The two men exchanged glances of rather more than ordinary interest. Then Dominey laughed.

"I know what you're thinking," he said. "It gave me quite a start when you came in. We're devilishly alike, aren't we?"

"There is a very strong likeness between us," the other admitted.

Dominey leaned his head upon his hand and studied his host. The likeness was clear enough, although the advantage was all in favour of the man who stood by the side of the camp bedstead with folded arms. Everard Dominey, for the first twenty-six years of his life, had lived as an ordinary young Englishman of his position,—Eton, Oxford, a few years in the Army, a few years about town, during which he had succeeded in making a still more hopeless muddle of his already encumbered estates: a few months of tragedy, and then a blank. Afterwards ten years—at first in the cities, then in the dark places of Africa—years of which no man knew anything. The Everard Dominey of ten years ago had been, without a doubt, good-looking. The finely shaped features remained, but the eyes had lost their lustre, his figure its elasticity, his mouth its firmness. He had the look of a man run prematurely to seed, wasted by fevers and dissipation. Not so his present companion. His features were as finely shaped, cast in an even stronger though similar mould. His eyes were bright and full of fire, his mouth and chin firm, bespeaking a man of deeds, his tall figure lithe and supple. He had the air of being in perfect health, in perfect mental and physical condition, a man who lived with dignity and some measure of content, notwithstanding the slight gravity of his expression.

"Yes," the Englishman muttered, "there's no doubt about the likeness, though I suppose I should look more like you than I do if I'd taken care of myself. But I haven't. That's the devil of it. I've gone the other way; tried to chuck my life away and pretty nearly succeeded, too."

The dried grasses were thrust on one side, and the doctor entered, — a little round man, also clad in immaculate white, with yellow-gold hair and thick spectacles. His countryman pointed towards the bed.

"Will you examine our patient, Herr Doctor, and prescribe for him what is necessary? He has asked for drink. Let him have wine, or whatever is good for him. If he is well enough, he will join our evening meal. I present my excuses. I have a despatch to write."

The man on the couch turned his head and watched the departing figure with a shade of envy in his eyes.

"What is my preserver's name?" he asked the doctor.

The latter looked as though the question were irreverent. "It is His Excellency the Major-General Baron Leopold von Ragastein."

"All that!" Dominey muttered. "Is he the Governor, or something of that sort?"

"He is Military Commandant of the Colony," the doctor replied. "He has also a special mission here."

"Damned fine-looking fellow for a German," Dominey remarked, with unthinking insolence.

The doctor was unmoved. He was feeling his patient's pulse. He concluded his examination a few minutes later.

"You have drunk much whisky lately, so?" he asked.

"I don't know what the devil it's got to do with you," was the curt reply, "but I drink whisky whenever I can get it. Who wouldn't in this pestilential climate!"

The doctor shook his head.

"The climate is good as he is treated," he declared. "His

Excellency drinks nothing but light wine and seltzer water. He has been here for five years, not only here but in the swamps, and he has not been ill one day."

"Well, I have been at death's door a dozen times," the Englishman rejoined a little recklessly, "and I don't much mind when I hand in my checks, but until that time comes I shall drink whisky whenever I can get it."

"The cook is preparing you some luncheon," the doctor announced, "which it will do you good to eat. I cannot give you whisky at this moment, but you can have some hock and seltzer with bay leaves."

"Send it along," was the enthusiastic reply. "What a constitution I must have, doctor! The smell of that cooking outside is making me ravenous."

"Your constitution is still sound if you would only respect it," was the comforting assurance.

"Anything been heard of the rest of my party?" Dominey enquired.

"Some bodies of Askaris have been washed up from the river," the doctor informed him, "and two of your ponies have been eaten by lions. You will excuse. I have the wounds of a native to dress, who was bitten last night by a jaguar."

The traveller, left alone, lay still in the hut, and his thoughts wandered backwards. He looked out over the bare, scrubby stretch of land which had been cleared for this encampment to the mass of bush and flowering shrubs beyond, mysterious and impenetrable save for that rough elephant track along which he had travelled; to the broad-bosomed river, blue as the sky above, and to the mountains fading into mist beyond. The face of his host had carried him back into the past. Puzzled reminiscence tugged at the strings of memory. It came to him later on at dinner time, when they three, the Commandant, the doctor and himself, sat at a little table arranged just outside the hut, that they might catch the faint breeze from the mountains, herald of the swift-falling darkness. Native servants beat the air around them with bamboo fans to keep off the insects, and the air was faint almost to noxiousness with the perfume of some sickly, exotic shrub.

"Why, you're Devinter!" he exclaimed suddenly,—"Sigismund Devinter! You were at Eton with me—Horrock's House—semi-final in the racquets."

"And Magdalen afterwards, number five in the boat."

"And why the devil did the doctor here tell me that your name was Von Ragastein?"

"Because it happens to be the truth," was the somewhat measured reply. "Devinter is my family name, and the one by which I was known when in England. When I succeeded to the barony and estates at my uncle's death, however, I was compelled to also take the title."

"Well, it's a small world!" Dominey exclaimed. "What brought you out here really—lions or elephants?"

"Neither."

"You mean to say that you've taken up this sort of political business just for its own sake, not for sport?"

"Entirely so. I do not use a sporting rifle once a month, except for necessity. I came to Africa for different reasons."

Dominey drank deep of his hock and seltzer and leaned back, watching the fireflies rise above the tall-bladed grass, above the stumpy clumps of shrub, and hang like miniature stars in the clear, violet air.

"What a world!" he soliloquised. "Siggy Devinter, Baron von Ragastein, out here, slaving for God knows what, drilling niggers to fight God knows whom, a political machine, I suppose, future Governor-General of German Africa, eh? You were always proud of your country, Devinter."

"My country is a country to be proud of," was the solemn reply.

"Well, you're in earnest, anyhow," Dominey continued, "in earnest about something. And I—well, it's finished with me. It would have been finished last night if I hadn't seen the smoke from your fires, and I don't much care—that's the trouble. I go blundering on. I suppose the end will come somehow, sometime.—Can I have some rum or whisky, Devinter—I mean Von Ragastein—Your Excellency—or whatever I ought to say? You see those wreaths of mist down by the river? They'll mean malaria for me unless I have spirits."

"I have something better than either," Von Ragastein replied. "You shall give me your opinion of this."

The orderly who stood behind his master's chair, received a whispered order, disappeared into the commissariat hut and came back presently with a bottle at the sight of which the Englishman gasped.

"Napoleon!" he exclaimed.

"Just a few bottles I had sent to me," his host explained. "I am delighted to offer it to some one who will appreciate it."

"By Jove, there's no mistake about that!" Dominey declared, rolling it around in his glass. "What a world! I hadn't eaten for thirty hours when I rolled up here last night, and drunk nothing but filthy water for days. To-night, fricassee of chicken, white bread, cabinet hock and Napoleon brandy. And to-morrow again—well, who knows? When do you move on, Von Ragastein?"

"Not for several days."

"What the mischief do you find to do so far from head-quarters, if you don't shoot lions or elephants?" his guest asked curiously.

"If you really wish to know," Von Ragastein replied, "I am annoying your political agents immensely by moving from place to place, collecting natives for drill."

"But what do you want to drill them for?" Dominey persisted. "I heard some time ago that you have four times as many natives under arms as we have. You don't want an army here. You're not likely to quarrel with us or the Portuguese."

"It is our custom," Von Ragastein declared a little didactically, "in Germany and wherever we Germans go, to be prepared not only for what is likely to happen but for what might possibly happen."

"A war in my younger days, when I was in the Army," Dominey mused, "might have made a man of me."

"Surely you had your chance out here?"

Dominey shook his head.

"My battalion never left the country," he said. "We were shut up in Ireland all the time. That was the reason I chucked the army when I was really only a boy."

Later on they dragged their chairs a little farther out into the darkness, smoking cigars and drinking some rather wonderful coffee. The doctor had gone off to see a patient, and Von Ragastein was thoughtful. Their guest, on the other hand, continued to be reminiscently discursive.

"Our meeting," he observed, lazily stretching out his hand for his glass, "should be full of interest to the psychologist. Here we are, brought together by some miraculous chance to spend one night of our lives in an African jungle, two human beings of the same age, brought up together thousands of miles away, jogging on towards the eternal blackness along lines as far apart as the mind can conceive."

"Your eyes are fixed," Von Ragastein murmured, "upon that very blackness behind which the sun will rise at dawn. You will see it come up from behind the mountains in that precise spot, like a new and blazing world."

"Don't put me off with allegories," his companion objected petulantly. "The eternal blackness exists surely enough, even if my metaphor is faulty. I am disposed to be philosophical. Let me ramble on. Here am I, an idler in my boyhood, a harmless pleasure-seeker in my youth till I ran up against tragedy, and since then a drifter, a drifter with a slowly growing vice, lolling through life with no definite purpose, with no definite hope or wish, except," he went on a little drowsily, "that I think I'd like to be buried somewhere near the base of those mountains, on the other side of the river, from behind which you say the sun comes up every morning like a world on fire."

"You talk foolishly," Von Ragastein protested. "If there has been tragedy in your life, you have time to get over it. You are not yet forty years old."

"Then I turn and consider you," Dominey continued, ignoring altogether his friend's remark. "You are only my age, and you look ten years younger. Your muscles are hard, your eyes are as bright as they were in your school days. You carry yourself like a man with a purpose. You rise at five every morning, the doctor tells me, and you return here, worn out, at dusk. You spend every moment of your time drilling those filthy blacks. When you are not doing that, you are prospecting, supervising reports home, trying to make the best of your few millions of acres of fever swamps. The doctor worships you but who else knows? What do you do it for, my friend?"

"Because it is my duty," was the calm reply.

"Duty! But why can't you do your duty in your own country, and live a man's life, and hold the hands of white men, and look into the eyes of white women?"

"I go where I am needed most," Von Ragastein answered. "I do not enjoy drilling natives, I do not enjoy passing the years as an outcast from the ordinary joys of human life. But I follow my star."

"And I my will-o'-the-wisp," Dominey laughed mockingly. "The whole thing's as plain as a pikestaff. You may be a dull dog—you always were on the serious side—but you're a man of principle. I'm a slacker."

"The difference between us," Von Ragastein pronounced, "is something which is inculcated into the youth of our country and which is not inculcated into yours. In England, with a little money, a little birth, your young men expect to find the world a playground for sport, a garden for loves. The mightiest German noble who ever lived has his work to do. It is work which makes fibre, which gives balance to life."

Dominey sighed. His cigar, dearly prized though it had been, was cold between his fingers. In that perfumed darkness, illuminated only by the faint gleam of the shaded lamp behind, his face seemed suddenly white and old. His host leaned towards him and spoke for the first time in the kindlier tones of their youth.

"You hinted at tragedy, my friend. You are not alone. Tragedy also has entered my life. Perhaps if things had been otherwise, I should have found work in more joyous places, but sorrow came to me, and I am here."

A quick flash of sympathy lit up Dominey's face.

"We met trouble in a different fashion," he groaned.

CHAPTER II

DOMINEY slept till late the following morning, and when he woke at last from a long, dreamless slumber, he was conscious of a curious quietness in the camp. The doctor, who came in to see him, explained it immediately after his morning greeting.

"His Excellency," he announced, "has received important despatches from home. He has gone to meet an envoy from Dar-es-Salaam. He will be away for three days. He desired that you would remain his guest until his return."

"Very good of him," Dominey murmured. "Is there any European news?"

"I do not know," was the stolid reply. "His Excellency desired me to inform you that if you cared for a short trip along the banks of the river, southward, there are a dozen boys left and some ponies. There are plenty of lion, and rhino may be met with at one or two places which the natives know of."

Dominey bathed and dressed, sipped his excellent coffee, and lounged about the place in uncertain mood. He unburdened himself to the doctor as they drank tea together late in the afternoon.

"I am not in the least keen on hunting," he confessed, "and I feel like a horrible sponge, but all the same I have a queer sort of feeling that I'd like to see Von Ragastein again. Your silent chief rather fascinates me, Herr Doctor. He is a man. He has something which I have lost."

"He is a great man," the doctor declared enthusiastically. "What he sets his mind to do, he does."

"I suppose I might have been like that," Dominey sighed, "if I had had an incentive. Have you noticed the likeness between us, Herr Doctor?"

The latter nodded.

"I noticed it from the first moment of your arrival," he assented. "You are very much alike yet very different. The resemblance must have been still more remarkable in your youth. Time has dealt with your features according to your deserts."

"Well, you needn't rub it in," Dominey protested irritably.

"I am rubbing nothing in," the doctor replied with unruffled calm. "I speak the truth. If you had been possessed of the same moral stamina as His Excellency, you might have preserved your health and the things that count. You might have been as useful to your country as he is to his."

"I suppose I am pretty rocky, eh?"

"Your constitution has been abused. You still, however, have much vitality. If you cared to exercise self-control for a few months, you would be a different man.— You must excuse. I have work."

Dominey spent three restless days. Even the sight of a herd of elephants in the river and that strange, fierce chorus of night sounds, as beasts of prey crept noiselessly around the camp, failed to move him. For the moment his love of sport, his last hold upon the world of real things, seemed dead. What did it matter, the killing of an animal more or less? His mind was fixed uneasily upon the past, searching always for something which he failed to discover. At dawn he watched for that strangely wonderful, transforming birth of the day, and at night he sat outside the banda, waiting till the mountains on the other side of the river had lost shape and faded into the violet darkness. His conversation with Von Ragastein had unsettled him. Without knowing definitely why, he wanted him back again. Memories that had long since ceased to torture were finding their way once more into his brain. On the first day he had striven to rid himself of them in the usual fashion.

"Doctor, you've got some whisky, haven't you?" he asked.

The doctor nodded.

"There is a case somewhere to be found," he admitted. "His Excellency told me that I was to refuse you nothing, but he advises you to drink only the white wine until his return."

"He really left that message?"

"Precisely as I have delivered it."

The desire for whisky passed, came again but was beaten back, returned in the night so that he sat up with the sweat pouring down his face and his tongue parched. He drank lithia water instead. Late in the afternoon of the third day, Von Ragastein rode into the camp. His clothes were torn and drenched with the black mud of the swamps, dust and dirt were thick upon his face. His pony almost collapsed as he swung himself off. Nevertheless, he paused to greet his guest with punctilious courtesy, and there was a gleam of real satisfaction in his eyes as the two men shook hands.

"I am glad that you are still here," he said heartily. "Excuse me while I bathe and change. We will dine a little earlier. So far I have not eaten to-day."

"A long trek?" Dominey asked curiously.

"I have trekked far," was the quiet reply.

At dinner time, Von Ragastein was once more himself, immaculate in white duck, with clean linen, shaved, and with little left of his fatigue. There was something different in his manner, however, some change which puzzled Dominey. He was at once more attentive to his guest, yet further removed from him in spirit and sympathy. He kept the conversation with curious insistence upon incidents of their school and college days, upon the subject of Dominey's friends and relations, and the later episodes of his life. Dominey felt himself all the time encouraged to talk about his earlier life, and all the time he was conscious that for some reason or other his host's closest and most minute attention was being given to his slightest word. Champagne had been served and served freely, and Dominey, up to the very gates of that one secret chamber, talked volubly and without reserve. After the meal was over, their chairs were dragged as before into the open. The silent orderly produced even larger cigars, and Dominey found his glass filled once more with the wonderful brandy. The doctor had left them to visit the native camp nearly a quarter of a mile away, and the orderly was busy inside, clearing the table. Only the black shapes of the servants were dimly visible as they twirled their fans,—and overhead the leaning stars. They were alone.

"I've been talking an awful lot of rot about myself," Dominey said. "Tell me a little about your career now and your life in Germany before you came out here?"

Von Ragastein made no immediate reply, and a curious silence ebbed and flowed between the two men. Every now and then a star shot across the sky. The red rim of the moon rose a little higher from behind the mountains. The bush stillness, always the most mysterious of silences, seemed gradually to become charged with unvoiced passion. Soon the animals began to call around them, creeping nearer and nearer to the fire which burned at the end of the open space.

"My friend," Von Ragastein said at last, speaking with the air of a man who has spent much time in deliberation, "you speak to me of Germany, of my homeland. Perhaps you have guessed that it is not duty alone which has brought me here to these wild places. I, too, left behind me a tragedy."

Dominey's quick impulse of sympathy was smothered by the stern, almost harsh repression of the other's manner. The words seemed to have been torn from his throat. There was no spark of tenderness or regret in his set face.

"Since the day of my banishment," he went on, "no word of this matter has passed my lips. To-night it is not weakness which assails me, but a desire to yield to the strange arm of coincidence. You and I, schoolmates and college friends, though sons of a different country, meet here in the wilderness, each with the iron in our souls. I shall tell you the thing which happened to me, and you shall speak to me of your own curse."

"I cannot!" Dominey groaned.

"But you will," was the stern reply. "Listen."

An hour passed, and the voices of the two men had ceased. The howling of the animals had lessened with the paling of the fires, and a slow, melancholy ripple of breeze was passing through the bush and lapping the surface of the river. It was

Von Ragastein who broke through what might almost have seemed a trance. He rose to his feet, vanished inside the banda, and reappeared a moment or two later with two tumblers. One he set down in the space provided for it in the arm of his guest's chair.

"To-night I break what has become a rule with me," he announced. "I shall drink a whisky and soda. I shall drink to the new things that may yet come to both of us."

"You are giving up your work here?" Dominey asked curiously.

"I am part of a great machine," was the somewhat evasive reply. "I have nothing to do but obey."

A flicker of passion distorted Dominey's face, flamed for a moment in his tone.

"Are you content to live and die like this?" he demanded. "Don't you want to get back to where a different sort of sun will warm your heart and fill your pulses? This primitive world is in its way colossal, but it isn't human, it isn't a life for humans. We want the streets, Von Ragastein, you and I. We want the tide of people flowing around us, the roar of wheels and the hum of human voices. Curse these animals! If I live in this country much longer, I shall go on all fours."

"You yield too much to environment," his companion observed. "In the life of the cities you would be a sentimentalist."

"No city nor any civilised country will ever claim me again," Dominey sighed. "I should never have the courage to face what might come."

Von Ragastein rose to his feet. The dim outline of his erect form was in a way majestic. He seemed to tower over the man who lounged in the chair below him.

"Finish your whisky and soda to our next meeting, friend of my school days," he begged. "To-morrow, before you awake, I shall be gone."

"So soon?"

"By to-morrow night," Von Ragastein replied, "I must be on the other side of those mountains. This must be our farewell."

Dominey was querulous, almost pathetic. He had a sudden hatred of solitude.

"I must trek westward myself directly," he protested, "or eastward, or northward — it doesn't so much matter. Can't we travel together?"

Von Ragastein shook his head.

"I travel officially, and I must travel alone," he replied. "As for yourself, they will be breaking up here to-morrow, but they will lend you an escort and put you in the direction you wish to take. This, alas, is as much as I can do for you. For us it must be farewell."

"Well, I can't force myself upon you," Dominey said a little wistfully. "It seems strange, though, to meet right out here, far away even from the byways of life, just to shake hands and pass on. I am sick to death of niggers and animals."

"It is Fate," Von Ragastein decided. "Where I go, I must go alone. Farewell, dear friend! We will drink the toast we drank our last night in your rooms at Magdalen. That Sanscrit man translated it for us: 'May each find what he seeks!' We must follow our star."

Dominey laughed a little bitterly. He pointed to a light glowing fitfully in the bush.

"My will-o'-the-wisp," he muttered recklessly, "leading where I shall follow — into the swamps!"

A few minutes later Dominey threw himself upon his couch, curiously and unaccountably drowsy. Von Ragastein, who had come in to wish him good night, stood looking down at him for several moments with significant intentness. Then, satisfied that his guest really slept, he turned and passed through the hanging curtain of dried grasses into the next banda, where the doctor, still fully dressed, was awaiting him. They spoke together in German and with lowered voices. Von Ragastein had lost something of his imperturbability.

"Everything progresses according to my orders?" he demanded.

"Everything, Excellency! The boys are being loaded, and a runner has gone on to Wadihuan for ponies to be prepared."

"They know that I wish to start at dawn?"

"All will be prepared, Excellency."

Von Ragastein laid his hand upon the doctor's shoulder.

"Come outside, Schmidt," he said. "I have something to tell you of my plans."

The two men seated themselves in the long, wicker chairs, the doctor in an attitude of strict attention. Von Ragastein turned his head and listened. From Dominey's quarters came the sound of deep and regular breathing.

"I have formed a great plan, Schmidt," Von Ragastein proceeded. "You know what news has come to me from Berlin?"

"Your Excellency has told me little," the doctor reminded him.

"The Day arrives," Von Ragastein pronounced, his voice shaking with deep emotion. He paused a moment in thought and continued, "the time, even the month, is fixed. I am recalled from here to take the place for which I was destined. You know what that place is? You know why I was sent to an English public school and college?"

"I can guess."

"I am to take up my residence in England. I am to have a special mission. I am to find a place for myself there as an Englishman. The means are left to my ingenuity. Listen, Schmidt. A great idea has come to me."

The doctor lit a cigar.

"I listen, Excellency."

Von Ragastein rose to his feet. Not content with the sound of that regular breathing, he made his way to the opening of the banda and gazed in at Dominey's slumbering form. Then he returned.

"It is something which you do not wish the Englishman to hear?" the doctor asked.

"It is."

"We speak in German."

"Languages," was the cautious reply, "happen to be that man's only accomplishment. He can speak German as fluently as you or I. That, however, is of no consequence. He sleeps and he will continue to sleep. I mixed him a sleeping draught with his whisky and soda."

"Ah!" the doctor grunted.

"My principal need in England is an identity," Von Ragastein pointed out. "I have made up my mind. I shall take this Englishman's. I shall return to England as Sir Everard Dominey."

"So!"

"There is a remarkable likeness between us, and Dominey has not seen an Englishman who knows him for eight or ten years. Any school or college friends whom I may encounter I shall be able to satisfy. I have stayed at Dominey. I know Dominey's relatives. To-night he has babbled for hours, telling me many things that it is well for me to know."

"What about his near relatives?"

"He has none nearer than cousins."

"No wife?"

Von Ragastein paused and turned his head. The deep breathing inside the banda had certainly ceased. He rose to his feet and, stealing uneasily to the opening, gazed down upon his guest's outstretched form. To all appearance, Dominey still slept deeply. After a moment or two's watch, Von Ragastein returned to his place.

"Therein lies his tragedy," he confided, dropping his voice a little lower. "She is insane—insane, it seems, through a shock for which he is responsible. She might have been the only stumbling block, and she is as though she did not exist."

"It is a great scheme," the doctor murmured enthusiastically.

"It is a wonderful one! That great and unrevealed Power, Schmidt, which watches over our country and which will make her mistress of the world, must have guided this man to us. My position in England will be unique. As Sir Everard Dominey I shall be able to penetrate into the inner circles of Society—perhaps, even, of political life. I shall be able, if necessary, to remain in England even after the storm bursts."

"Supposing," the doctor suggested, "this man Dominey should return to England?"

Von Ragastein turned his head and looked towards his questioner.

"He must not," he pronounced.

"So!" the doctor murmured.

Late in the afternoon of the following day, Dominey, with a couple of boys for escort and his rifle slung across his shoulder, rode into the bush along the way he had come. The little fat doctor stood and watched him, waving his hat until he was out of sight. Then he called to the orderly.

"Heinrich," he said, "you are sure that the Herr Englishman has the whisky?"

"The water bottles are filled with nothing else, Herr Doctor," the man replied.

"There is no water or soda water in the pack?"

"Not one drop, Herr Doctor."

"How much food?"

"One day's rations."

"The beef is salt?"

"It is very salt, Herr Doctor."

"And the compass?"

"It is ten degrees wrong."

"The boys have their orders?"

"They understand perfectly, Herr Doctor. If the Englishman does not drink, they will take him at midnight to where His Excellency will be encamped at the bend of the Blue River."

The doctor sighed. He was not at heart an unkindly man. "I think," he murmured, "it will be better for the Englishman that he drinks."

CHAPTER III

Mr. John Lambert Mangan of Lincoln's Inn gazed at the card which a junior clerk had just presented in blank astonishment, an astonishment which became speedily blended with dismay.

"Good God, do you see this, Harrison?" he exclaimed, passing it over to his manager, with whom he had been in consultation. "Dominey — Sir Everard Dominey — back here in England!"

The head clerk glanced at the narrow piece of pasteboard and sighed.

"I'm afraid you will find him rather a troublesome client, sir," he remarked.

His employer frowned. "Of course I shall," he answered testily. "There isn't an extra penny to be had out of the estates — you know that, Harrison. The last two quarters' allowance which we sent to Africa came out of the timber. Why the mischief didn't he stay where he was!"

"What shall I tell the gentleman, sir?" the boy enquired.

"Oh, show him in!" Mr. Mangan directed ill-temperedly. "I suppose I shall have to see him sooner or later. I'll finish these affidavits after lunch, Harrison."

The solicitor composed his features to welcome a client who, however troublesome his affairs had become, still represented a family who had been valued patrons of the firm for several generations. He was prepared to greet a seedy-looking and degenerate individual, looking older than his years. Instead, he found himself extending his hand to one of the best turned out and handsomest men who had ever crossed the threshold of his not very inviting office. For a moment he stared at his visitor, speechless. Then certain points of familiarity — the well-shaped nose, the rather deep-set grey eyes — presented themselves. The surprise enabled him to infuse a little real heartiness into his welcome.

"My dear Sir Everard!" he exclaimed. "This is a most unexpected pleasure — most unexpected! Such a pity, too, that we only posted a draft for your allowance a few days ago. Dear me — you'll forgive my saying so — how well you look!"

Dominey smiled as he accepted an easy chair.

"Africa's a wonderful country, Mangan," he remarked, with just that faint note of patronage in his tone which took his listener back to the days of his present client's father.

"It — pardon my remarking it — has done wonderful things for you, Sir Everard. Let me see, it must be eleven years since we met."

Sir Everard tapped the toes of his carefully polished brown shoes with the end of his walking stick.

"I left London," he murmured reminiscently, "in April, nineteen hundred and two. Yes, eleven years, Mr. Mangan. It seems queer to find myself in London again, as I dare say you can understand."

"Precisely," the lawyer murmured. "I was just wondering — I think that last remittance we sent to you could be stopped. I have no doubt you will be glad of a little ready money," he added, with a confident smile.

"Thanks, I don't think I need any just at present," was the amazing answer. "We'll talk about financial affairs a little later on."

Mr. Mangan metaphorically pinched himself. He had known his present client even during his school days, had received a great many visits from him at different times, and could not remember one in which the question of finance had been dismissed in so casual a manner.

"I trust," he observed, chiefly for the sake of saying something, "that you are thinking of settling down here for a time now?"

"I have finished with Africa, if that is what you mean," was the somewhat grave reply. "As to settling down here, well, that depends a little upon what you have to tell me."

The lawyer nodded.

"I think," he said, "that you may make yourself quite easy as regards the matter of Roger Unthank. Nothing has ever been heard of him since the day you left England."

"His—body has not been found?"

"Nor any trace of it."

There was a brief silence. The lawyer looked hard at Dominey, and Dominey searchingly back again at the lawyer.

"And Lady Dominey?" the former asked at length.

"Her ladyship's condition is, I believe, unchanged," was the somewhat guarded reply.

"If the circumstances are favourable," Dominey continued, after another moment's pause, "I think it very likely that I may decide to settle down at Dominey Hall."

The lawyer appeared doubtful.

"I am afraid," he said, "you will be very disappointed with the condition of the estate, Sir Everard. As I have repeatedly told you in our correspondence, the rent roll, after deducting your settlement upon Lady Dominey, has at no time reached the interest on the mortgages, and we have had to make up the difference and send you your allowance out of the proceeds of the outlying timber."

"That is a pity," Dominey replied, with a frown. "I ought, perhaps, to have taken you more into my confidence. By the by," he added, "when—er—about when did you receive my last letter?"

"Your last letter?" Mr. Mangan repeated. "We have not had the privilege of hearing from you, Sir Everard, for over four years. The only intimation we had that our payments had reached you was the exceedingly prompt debit of the South African bank."

"I have certainly been to blame," this unexpected visitor confessed. "On the other hand, I have been very much absorbed. If you haven't happened to hear any South African gossip lately, Mangan, I suppose it will be a surprise to you to hear that I have been making a good deal of money."

"Making money?" the lawyer gasped. "You making money, Sir Everard?"

"I thought you'd be surprised," Dominey observed coolly. "However, that's neither here nor there. The business object of my visit to you this morning is to ask you to make arrangements as quickly as possible for paying off the mortgages on the Dominey estates."

Mr. Mangan was a lawyer of the new-fashioned school,— Harrow and Cambridge, the Bath Club, racquets and fives, rather than gold and lawn tennis. Instead of saying "God bless my soul!" he exclaimed "Great Scott!" dropped a very modern-looking eyeglass from his left eye, and leaned back in his chair with his hands in his pockets.

"I have had three or four years of good luck," his client continued. "I have made money in gold mines, in diamond mines and in land. I am afraid that if I had stayed out another year, I should have descended altogether to the commonplace and come back a millionaire."

"My heartiest congratulations!" Mr. Mangan found breath to murmur. "You'll forgive my being so astonished, but you are the first Dominey I ever knew who has ever made a penny of money in any sort of way, and from what I remember of you in England—I'm sure you'll forgive my being so frank —I should never have expected you to have even attempted such a thing."

Dominey smiled good-humouredly.

"Well," he said, "if you enquire at the United Bank of Africa, you will find that I have a credit balance there of something over a hundred thousand pounds. Then I have also—well, let us say a trifle more, invested in first-class mines. Do me the favour of lunching with me, Mr. Mangan, and although Africa will never be a favourite topic of conversation with me, I will tell you about some of my speculations."

The solicitor groped around for his hat.

"I will send the boy for a taxi," he faltered.

"I have a car outside," this astonishing client told him. "Before we leave, could you instruct your clerk to have a list of the Dominey mortgages made out, with the terminable dates and redemption values?"

"I will leave instructions," Mr. Mangan promised. "I think

that the total amount is under eighty thousand pounds."

Dominey sauntered through the office, an object of much interest to the little staff of clerks. The lawyer joined him on the pavement in a few minutes.

"Where shall we lunch?" Dominey asked. "I'm afraid my clubs are a little out of date. I am staying at the Carlton."

"The Carlton grill room is quite excellent," Mr. Mangan suggested.

"They are keeping me a table until half-past one," Dominey replied. "We will lunch there, by all means."

They drove off together, the returned traveller gazing all the time out of the window into the crowded streets, the lawyer a little thoughtful.

"While I think of it, Sir Everard," the latter said, as they drew near their destination, "I should be glad of a short conversation with you before you go down to Dominey."

"With regard to anything in particular?"

"With regard to Lady Dominey," the lawyer told him a little gravely.

A shadow rested on his companion's face.

"Is her ladyship very much changed?"

"Physically, she is in excellent health, I believe. Mentally I believe that there is no change. She has unfortunately the same rather violent prejudice which I am afraid influenced your departure from England."

"In plain words," Dominey said bitterly, "she has sworn to take my life if ever I sleep under the same roof."

"She will need, I am afraid, to be strictly watched," the lawyer answered evasively. "Still, I think you ought to be told that time does not seem to have lessened her tragical antipathy."

"She regards me still as the murderer of Roger Unthank?" Dominey asked, in a measured tone.

"I am afraid she does."

"And I suppose that every one else has the same idea?"

"The mystery," Mr. Mangan admitted, "has never been cleared up. It is well known, you see, that you fought in the park and that you staggered home almost senseless. Roger Unthank has never been seen from that day to this."

"If I had killed him," Dominey pointed out, "why was his body not found?"

The lawyer shook his head.

"There are all sorts of theories, of course," he said, "but for one superstition you may as well be prepared. There is scarcely a man or a woman for miles around Dominey who doesn't believe that the ghost of Roger Unthank still haunts the Black Wood near where you fought."

"Let us be quite clear about this," Dominey insisted. "If the body should ever be found, am I liable, after all these years, to be indicted for manslaughter?"

"I think you may make your mind quite at ease," the lawyer assured him. "In the first place, I don't think you would ever be indicted."

"And in the second?"

"There isn't a human being in that part of Norfolk would ever believe that the body of man or beast, left within the shadow of the Black Wood, would ever be seen or heard of again!"

CHAPTER IV

Mr. Mangan, on their way into the grill room, loitered for a few minutes in the small reception room, chatting with some acquaintances, whilst his host, having spoken to the *maître d'hôtel* and ordered a cocktail from a passing waiter, stood with his hands behind his back, watching the inflow of men and women with all that interest which one might be supposed to feel in one's fellows after a prolonged absence. He had moved a little on one side to allow a party of young people to make their way through the crowded chamber, when he was conscious of a woman standing alone on the topmost of the three thickly carpeted stairs. Their eyes met, and hers, which had been wandering around the room as though in search of some acquaintance, seemed instantly and fervently held. To the few loungers about the room, ignorant of any special significance in that studied contemplation of the man on the part of the woman, their two personalities presented an agreeable, almost a fascinating study. Dominey was six feet two in height and had to its fullest extent the natural distinction of his class, together with the half military, half athletic bearing which seemed to have been so marvellously restored to him. His complexion was no more than becomingly tanned; his slight moustache, trimmed very close to the upper lip, was of the same ruddy brown shade as his sleekly brushed hair. The woman, who had commenced now to move slowly towards him, save that her cheeks, at that moment, at any rate, were almost unnaturally pale, was of the same colouring. Her red-gold hair gleamed beneath her black hat. She was tall, a Grecian type of figure, large without being coarse, majestic though still young. She carried a little dog under one arm and a plain black silk bag, on which was a coronet in platinum and diamonds, in the other hand. The major-domo who presided over the room, watching her approach, bowed with more than his usual urbanity. Her eyes, however, were still fixed upon the person who had engaged so large a share of her attention. She came towards him, her lips a little parted.

"Leopold!" she faltered. "The Holy Saints, why did you not let me know!"

Dominey bowed very slightly. His words seemed to have a cut and dried flavour.

"I am so sorry," he replied, "but I fear that you make a mistake. My name is not Leopold."

She stood quite still, looking at him with the air of not having heard a word of his polite disclaimer.

"In London, of all places," she murmured. "Tell me, what does it mean?"

"I can only repeat, madam," he said, "that to my very great regret I have not the honour of your acquaintance."

She was puzzled, but absolutely unconvinced.

"You mean to deny that you are Leopold von Ragastein?" she asked incredulously. "You do not know me?"

"Madam," he answered, "it is not my great pleasure. My name is Dominey—Everard Dominey."

She seemed for a moment to be struggling with some embarrassment which approached emotion. Then she laid her fingers upon his sleeve and drew him to a more retired corner of the little apartment.

"Leopold," she whispered, "nothing can make it wrong or indiscreet for you to visit me. My address is 17, Belgrave Square. I desire to see you to-night at seven o'clock."

"But, my dear lady," Dominey began——

Her eyes suddenly glowed with a new light.

"I will not be trifled with," she insisted. "If you wish to succeed in whatever scheme you have on hand, you must not make an enemy of me. I shall expect you at seven o'clock."

She passed away from him into the restaurant. Mr. Mangan, now freed from his friends, rejoined his host, and the two men took their places at the side table to which they were ushered with many signs of attention.

"Wasn't that the Princess Eiderstrom with whom you were talking?" the solicitor asked curiously.

"A lady addressed me by mistake," Dominey explained. "She mistook me, curiously enough, for a man who used to be called my double at Oxford. Sigismund Devinter he was then, although I think he came into a title later on."

"The Princess is quite a famous personage," Mr. Mangan remarked, "one of the richest widows in Europe. Her husband was killed in a duel some six or seven years ago."

Dominey ordered the luncheon with care, slipping into a word or two of German once to assist the waiter, who spoke English with difficulty. His companion smiled.

"I see that you have not forgotten your languages out there in the wilds."

"I had no chance to," Dominey answered. "I spent five years on the borders of German East Africa, and I traded with some of the fellows there regularly."

"By the by," Mr. Mangan enquired, "what sort of terms are we on with the Germans out there?"

"Excellent, I should think," was the careless reply. "I never had any trouble."

"Of course," the lawyer continued, "this will all be new to you, but during the last few years Englishmen have become divided into two classes—the people who believe that the Germans wish to go to war and crush us, and those who don't."

"Then since my return the number of the 'don'ts' has been increased by one."

"I am amongst the doubtfuls myself," Mr. Mangan remarked. "All the same, I can't quite see what Germany wants with such an immense army, and why she is continually adding to her fleet."

Dominey paused for a moment to discuss the matter of a sauce with the head waiter. He returned to the subject a few minutes later on, however.

"Of course," he pointed out, "my opinions can only come

from a study of the newspapers and from conversations with such Germans as I have met out in Africa, but so far as her army is concerned, I should have said that Russia and France were responsible for that, and the more powerful it is, the less chance of any European conflagration. Russia might at any time come to the conclusion that a war is her only salvation against a revolution, and you know the feeling in France about Alsace-Lorraine as well as I do. The Germans themselves say that there is more interest in military matters and more progress being made in Russia to-day than ever before."

"I have no doubt that you are right," agreed Mr. Mangan. "It is a matter which is being a great deal discussed just now, however. Let us speak of your personal plans. What do you intend to do for the next few weeks, say? Have you been to see any of your relatives yet?"

"Not one," Dominey replied. "I am afraid that I am not altogether keen about making advances."

Mr. Mangan coughed. "You must remember that during the period of your last residence in London," he said, "you were in a state of chronic impecuniosity. No doubt that rather affected the attitude of some of those who would otherwise have been more friendly."

"I should be perfectly content never to see one of them again," declared Dominey, with perfect truth.

"That, of course, is impossible," the lawyer protested. "You must go and see the Duchess, at any rate. She was always your champion."

"The Duchess was always very kind to me," Dominey admitted doubtfully, "but I am afraid she was rather fed up before I left England."

Mr. Mangan smiled. He was enjoying a very excellent lunch, which it seemed hard to believe was ordered by a man just home from the wilds of Africa, and he thoroughly enjoyed talking about duchesses.

"Her Grace," he began——

"Well?"

The lawyer had paused, with his eyes glued upon the couple

at a neighbouring table. He leaned across towards his companion.

"The Duchess herself, Sir Everard, just behind you, with Lord St. Omar."

"This place must certainly be the rendezvous of all the world," Dominey declared, as he held out his hand to a man who had approached their table. "Seaman, my friend, welcome! Let me introduce you to my friend and legal adviser, Mr. Mangan—Mr. Seaman."

Mr. Seaman was a short, fat man, immaculately dressed in most conventional morning attire. He was almost bald, except for a little tuft on either side, and a few long, fair hairs carefully brushed back over a shining scalp. His face was extraordinarily round except towards his chin, where it came to a point; his eyes bright and keen, his mouth the mouth of a professional humourist. He shook hands with the lawyer with an *empressement* which was scarcely English.

"Within the space of half an hour," Dominey continued, "I find a princess who desires to claim my acquaintance; a cousin," he dropped his voice a little, "who lunches only a few tables away, and the man of whom I have seen most during the last ten years amidst scenes a little different from these, eh, Seaman?"

Seaman accepted the chair which the waiter had brought and sat down. The lawyer was immediately interested.

"Do I understand, then," he asked, addressing the newcomer, "that you knew Sir Everard in Africa?"

Seaman beamed. "Knew him?" he repeated, and with the first words of his speech the fact of his foreign nationality was established. "There was no one of whom I knew so much. We did business together—a great deal of business—and when we were not partners, Sir Everard generally got the best of it."

Dominey laughed. "Luck generally comes to a man either early or late in life. My luck came late. I think, Seaman, that you must have been my mascot. Nothing went wrong with me during the years that we did business together."

Seaman was a little excited. He brushed upright with the palm of his hand one of those little tufts of hair left on the side of his head, and he laid his plump fingers upon the lawyer's shoulder.

"Mr. Mangan," he said, "you listen to me. I sell this man the controlling interests in a mine, shares which I have held for four and a half years and never drew a penny dividend. I sell them to him, I say, at par. Well, I need the money and it seems to me that I had given the shares a fair chance. Within five weeks—five weeks, sir," he repeated, struggling to attune his voice to his civilised surroundings, "those shares had gone from par to fourteen and a half. To-day they stand at twenty. He gave me five thousand pounds for those shares. To-day he could walk into your stock market and sell them for one hundred thousand. That is the way money is made in Africa, Mr. Mangan, where innocents like me are to be found every day."

Dominey poured out a glass of wine and passed it to their visitor.

"Come," he said, "we all have our ups and downs. Africa owes you nothing, Seaman."

"I have done well in my small way," Seaman admitted, fingering the stem of his wineglass, "but where I have had to plod, Sir Everard here has stood and commanded fate to pour her treasures into his lap."

The lawyer was listening with a curious interest and pleasure to this half bantering conversation. He found an opportunity now to intervene.

"So you two were really friends in Africa?" he remarked, with a queer and almost inexplicable sense of relief.

"If Sir Everard permits our association to be so called," Seaman replied. "We have done business together in the great cities—in Johannesburg and Pretoria, in Kimberley and Cape Town—and we have prospected together in the wild places. We have trekked the veldt and been lost to the world for many months at a time. We have seen the real wonders of Africa together, as well as her tawdry civilisation."

"And you, too," Mr. Mangan asked, "have you retired?"

Seaman's smile was almost beatific.

"The same deal," he said, "which brought Sir Everard's

fortune to wonderful figures brought me that modest sum which I had sworn to reach before I returned to England. It is true. I have retired from money-making. It is now that I take up again my real life's work."

"If you are going to talk about your hobby," Dominey observed, "you had better order them to serve your lunch here."

"I had finished my lunch before you came in," his friend replied. "I drink another glass of wine with you, perhaps. Afterwards a liqueur — who can say? In this climate one is favoured, one can drink freely. Sir Everard and I, Mr. Mangan, have been in places where thirst is a thing to be struggled against, where for months a little weak brandy and water was our chief dissipation."

"Tell us about this hobby?" the lawyer enquired.

Dominey intervened promptly. "I protest. If he begins to talk of that, he'll be here all the afternoon."

Seaman held out his hands and rolled his head from side to side.

"But I am not so unreasonable," he objected. "Just one word — so? Very well, then," he proceeded quickly, with the air of one fearing interruption. "This must be clear to you, Mr. Mangan. I am a German by birth, naturalised in England for the sake of my business, loving Germany, grateful to England. One third of my life I have lived in Berlin, one third at Forest Hill here in London, and in the city, one third in Africa. I have watched the growth of commercial rivalries and jealousies between the two nations. There is no need for them. They might lead to worse things. I would brush them all away. My aim is to encourage a league for the promotion of more cordial social and business relations between the people of Great Britain and the people of the German Empire. There! Have I wasted much of your time? Can I not speak of my hobby without a flood of words?"

"Conciseness itself," Mangan admitted, "and I compliment you most heartily upon your scheme. If you can get the right people into it, it should prove a most valuable society."

"In Germany I have the right people. All Germans who live for their country and feel for their country loathe the thought of war. We want peace, we want friends, and, to speak as man to man," he concluded, tapping the lawyer upon the coat sleeve, "England is our best customer."

"I wish one could believe," the latter remarked, "that yours was the popular voice in your country."

Seaman rose reluctantly to his feet.

"At half-past two," he announced, glancing at his watch, "I have an appointment with a woollen manufacturer from Bradford. I hope to get him to join my council."

He bowed ceremoniously to the lawyer, nodded to Dominey with the familiarity of an old friend, and made his bustling, good-humoured way out of the room.

"A sound business man, I should think," was the former's comment. "I wish him luck with his League. You yourself, Sir Everard, will need to develop some new interests. Why not politics?"

"I really expect to find life a little difficult at first," admitted Dominey, with a shrug of his shoulders. "I have lost many of the tastes of my youth, and I am very much afraid that my friends over here will call me colonial. I can't fancy myself doing nothing down in Norfolk all the rest of my days. Perhaps I shall go into Parliament."

"You must forgive my saying," his companion declared impulsively, "that I never knew ten years make such a difference in a man in my life."

"The colonies," Dominey pronounced, "are a kill or cure sort of business. You either take your drubbing and come out a stronger man, or you go under. I had the very narrowest escape from going under myself, but I just pulled together in time. To-day I wouldn't have been without my hard times for anything in the world."

"If you will permit me," Mr. Mangan said, with an inherited pomposity, "on this our first meeting under the new conditions, I should like to offer you my hearty congratulations, not only upon what you have accomplished but upon what you have become."

"And also, I hope," Dominey rejoined, smiling a little seriously and with a curious glint in his eyes, "upon what I may yet accomplish."

The Duchess and her companion had risen to their feet, and the former, on her way out, recognising her solicitor, paused graciously.

"How do you do, Mr. Mangan?" she said. "I hope you are looking after those troublesome tenants of mine in Leicestershire?"

"We shall make our report in due course, Duchess," Mangan assured her. "Will you permit me," he added, "to bring back to your memory a relative who has just returned from abroad—Sir Everard Dominey?"

Dominey had risen to his feet a moment previously and now extended his hand. The Duchess, who was a tall, graceful woman, with masses of fair hair only faintly interspersed with grey, very fine brown eyes, the complexion of a girl, and, to quote her own confession, the manners of a kitchen maid, stared at him for a moment without any response.

"Sir Everard Dominey?" she repeated. "Everard? Ridiculous!"

Dominey's extended hand was at once withdrawn, and the tentative smile faded from his lips. The lawyer plunged into the breach.

"I can assure your Grace," he insisted earnestly, "that there is no doubt whatever about Sir Everard's identity. He only returned from Africa during the last few days."

The Duchess's incredulity remained, wholly good-natured but ministered to by her natural obstinacy.

"I simply cannot bring myself to believe it," she declared. "Come, I'll challenge you. When did we meet last?"

"At Worcester House," was the prompt reply. "I came to say good-bye to you."

The Duchess was a little staggered. Her eyes softened, a faint smile played at the corners of her lips. She was suddenly a very attractive looking woman.

"You came to say good-bye," she repeated, "and?"

"I am to take that as a challenge?" Dominey asked, standing very upright and looking her in the eyes.

"As you will."

"You were a little kinder to me," he continued, "than you are to-day. You gave me—this," he added, drawing a small picture from his pocketbook, "and you permitted—— "

"For heaven's sake, put that thing away," she cried, "and don't say another word! There's my grown-up nephew, St. Omar, paying his bill almost within earshot. Come and see me at half-past three this afternoon, and don't be a minute late. And, St. Omar," she went on, turning to the young man who stood now by her side, "this is a connection of yours—Sir Everard Dominey. He is a terrible person, but do shake hands with him and come along. I am half an hour late for my dressmaker already."

Lord St. Omar chuckled vaguely, then shook hands with his new-found relative, nodded affably to the lawyer and followed his aunt out of the room. Mangan's expression was beatific.

"Sir Everard," he exclaimed, "God bless you! If ever a woman got what she deserved! I've seen a duchess blush—first time in my life!"

CHAPTER V

Worcester House was one of those semi-palatial residences set down apparently for no reason whatever in the middle of Regent's Park. It had been acquired by a former duke at the instigation of the Regent, who was his intimate friend, and retained by later generations in mute protest against the disfiguring edifices which had made a millionaire's highway of Park Lane. Dominey, who was first scrutinised by an individual in buff waistcoat and silk hat at the porter's lodge, was interviewed by a major-domo in the great stone hall, conducted through an extraordinarily Victorian drawing-room by another myrmidon in a buff waistcoat, and finally ushered into a tiny little boudoir leading out of a larger apartment and terminating in a conservatory filled with sweet-smelling exotics. The Duchess, who was reclining in an easy-chair, held out her hand, which her visitor raised to his lips. She motioned him to a seat by her side and once more scrutinised him with unabashed intentness.

"There's something wrong about you, you know," she declared.

"That seems very unfortunate," he rejoined, "when I return to find you wholly unchanged."

"Not bad," she remarked critically. "All the same, I have changed. I am not in the least in love with you any longer."

"It was the fear of that change in you," he sighed, "which kept me for so long in the farthest corners of the world."

She looked at him with a severity which was obviously assumed.

"Look here," she said, "it is better for us to have a perfectly clear understanding upon one point. I know the exact position of your affairs, and I know, too, that the two hundred a year which your lawyer has been sending out to you came partly out of a few old trees and partly out of his own pocket. How you are going to live over here I cannot imagine, but it isn't the least use expecting

Henry to do a thing for you. The poor man has scarcely enough pocket money to pay his travelling expenses when he goes lecturing."

"Lecturing?" Dominey repeated. "What's happened to poor Henry?"

"My husband is an exceedingly conscientious man," was the dignified reply. "He goes from town to town with Lord Roberts and a secretary, lecturing on national defence."

"Dear Henry was always a little cranky, wasn't he?" Dominey observed. "Let me put your mind at rest on that other matter, though, Caroline. I can assure you that I have come back to England not to borrow money but to spend it."

His cousin shook her head mournfully. "And a few minutes ago I was nearly observing that you had lost your sense of humour!"

"I am in earnest," he persisted. "Africa has turned out to be my Eldorado. Quite unexpectedly, I must admit, I came in for a considerable sum of money towards the end of my stay there. I am paying off the mortgages at Dominey at once, and I want Henry to jot down on paper at once those few amounts he was good enough to lend me in the old days."

Caroline, Duchess of Worcester, sat perfectly still for a moment with her mouth open, a condition which was entirely natural but unbecoming.

"And you mean to tell me that you really are Everard Dominey?" she exclaimed.

"The weight of evidence is rather that way," he murmured.

He moved his chair deliberately a little nearer, took her hand and raised it to his lips. Her face was perilously near to his. She drew a little back — not too abruptly.

"My dear Everard," she whispered, "Henry is in the house! Besides — Yes, I suppose you must be Everard. Just now there was something in your eyes exactly like his. But you are so stiff. Have you been drilling out there or anything?"

He shook his head.

"One spends half one's time in the saddle."

"And you are really well off?" she asked again wonderingly.

"If I had stayed there another year," he replied, "and been

able to marry a Dutch Jewess, I should have qualified for Park Lane."

She sighed.

"It's too wonderful. Henry will love having his money back."

"And you?"

She looked positively distressed.

"You've lost all your manners," she complained. "You make love like a garden rake. You should have leaned towards me with a quiver in your voice when you said those last two words, and instead of that you look as though you were sitting at attention, with a positive glint of steel in your eyes."

"One sees a woman once in a blue moon out there," he pleaded.

She shook her head. "You've changed. It was a sixth sense with you to make love in exactly the right tone, to say exactly the right thing in the right manner."

"I shall pick it up," he declared hopefully, "with a little assistance."

She made a little grimace.

"You won't want an old woman like me to assist you, Everard. You'll have the town at your feet. You'll be able to frivol with musical comedy, flirt with our married beauties, or — I'm sorry, Everard. I forgot."

"You forgot what?" he asked steadfastly.

"I forgot the tragedy which finally drove you abroad. I forgot your marriage. Is there any change in your wife?"

"Not much, I am afraid."

"And Mr. Mangan — he thinks that you are safe over here?"

"Perfectly."

She looked at him earnestly. Perhaps she had never admitted, even to herself, how fond she had been of this scapegrace cousin.

"You'll find that no one will have a word to say against you," she told him, "now that you are wealthy and regenerate. They'll forget everything you want them to. When will you come and dine here and meet all your relatives?"

"Whenever you are kind enough to ask me," he answered. "I thought of going down to Dominey to-morrow."

She looked at him with a new thing in her eyes — something of fear, something, too, of admiration.

"But—your wife?"

"She is there, I believe," he said. "I cannot help it. I have been an exile from my home long enough."

"Don't go," she begged suddenly. "Why not be brave and have her removed. I know how tender-hearted you are, but you have your future and your career to consider. For her sake, too, you ought not to give her the opportunity——"

Dominey could never make up his mind whether the interruption which came at that moment was welcome or otherwise. Caroline suddenly broke off in her speech and glanced warningly towards the larger room. A tall, grey-haired man, dressed in old-fashioned clothes and wearing a pince-nez, had lifted the curtains. He addressed the Duchess in a thin, reedy voice.

"My dear Caroline," he began,—"ah, you must forgive me. I did not know that you were engaged. We will not stay, but I should like to present to you a young friend of mine who is going to help me at the meeting this evening."

"Do bring him in," his wife replied, her voice once more attuned to its usual drawl. "And I have a surprise for you too, Henry—a very great surprise, I think you will find it!"

Dominey rose to his feet—a tall, commanding figure—and stood waiting the approach of the newcomer. The Duke advanced, looking at him enquiringly. A young man, very obviously a soldier in mufti, was hovering in the background.

"I must plead guilty to the surprise," the Duke confessed courteously. "There is something exceedingly familiar about your face, sir, but I cannot remember having had the privilege of meeting you."

"You see," Caroline observed, "I am not the only one, Everard, who did not accept you upon a glance. This is Everard Dominey, Henry, returned from foreign exile and regenerated in every sense of the word."

"How do you do?" Dominey said, holding out his hand. "I seem to be rather a surprise to every one, but I hope you haven't quite forgotten me."

"God bless my soul!" the Duke exclaimed. "You don't mean to say that you're really Everard Dominey?"

"I am he, beyond a doubt," was the calm assurance.

"Most amazing!" the Duke declared, as he shook hands. "Most amazing! I never saw such a change in my life. Yes, yes, I see—same complexion, of course—nose and eyes—yes, yes! But you seem taller, and you carry yourself like a soldier. Dear, dear me! Africa has done wonderfully by you. Delighted, my dear Everard! Delighted!"

"You'll be more delighted still when you hear the rest of the news," his wife remarked drily. "In the meantime, do present your friend."

"Precisely so," the Duke acquiesced, turning to the young man in the background. "Most sorry, my dear Captain Bartram. The unexpected return of a connection of my wife must be my apology for this lapse of manners. Let me present you to the Duchess. Captain Bartram is just back from Germany, my dear, and is an enthusiastic supporter of our cause.—Sir Everard Dominey."

Caroline shook hands kindly with her husband's protégé, and Dominey exchanged a solemn handshake with him.

"You, too, are one of those, then, Captain Bartram, who are convinced that Germany has evil designs upon us?" the former said, smiling.

"I have just returned from Germany after twelve months' stay there," the young soldier replied. "I went with an open mind. I have come back convinced that we shall be at war with Germany within a couple of years."

The Duke nodded vigorously.

"Our young friend is right," he declared. "Three times a week for many months I have been drumming the fact into the handful of wooden-headed Englishmen who have deigned to come to our meetings. I have made myself a nuisance to the House of Lords and the Press. It is a terrible thing to realise how hard it is to make an Englishman reflect, so long as he is making money and having a good time.—You are just back from Africa, Everard?"

"Within a week, sir."

"Did you see anything of the Germans out there? Were you anywhere near their Colony?"

"I have been in touch with them for some years," Dominey replied.

"Most interesting!" his questioner exclaimed. "You may be

of service to us, Everard. You may, indeed! Now tell me, isn't it true that they have secret agents out there, trying to provoke unsettlement and disquiet amongst the Boers? Isn't it true that they apprehend a war with England before very long and are determined to stir up the Colony against us?"

"I am very sorry," Dominey replied, "but I am not a politician in any shape or form. All the Germans whom I have met out there seem a most peaceable race of men, and there doesn't seem to be the slightest discontent amongst the Boers or any one else."

The Duke's face fell. "This is very surprising."

"The only people who seem to have any cause for discontent," Dominey continued, "are the English settlers. I didn't commence to do any good myself there till a few years ago, but I have heard some queer stories about the way our own people were treated after the war."

"What you say about South Africa, Sir Everard," the young soldier remarked, "is naturally interesting, but I am bound to say that it is in direct opposition to all I have heard."

"And I," the Duke echoed fervently.

"I have lived there for the last eleven years," Dominey continued, "and although I spent the earlier part of that time trekking after big game, lately I am bound to confess that every thought and energy I possess have been centered upon money-making. For that reason, perhaps, my observations may have been at fault. I shall claim the privilege of coming to one of your first meetings, Duke, and of trying to understand this question."

His august connection blinked at him a little curiously for a moment behind his glasses.

"My dear Everard," he said, "forgive my remarking it, but I find you more changed than I could have believed possible."

"Everard is changed in more ways than one," his wife observed, with faint irony.

Dominey, who had risen to leave, bent over her hand.

"What about my dinner party, sir?" she added.

"As soon as I return from Norfolk," he replied.

"Dominey Hall will really find you?" she asked a little curiously.

"Most certainly!"

There was again that little flutter of fear in her eyes, followed by a momentary flash of admiration. Dominey shook hands gravely with his host and nodded to Bartram. The servant whom the Duchess had summoned stood holding the curtains on one side.

"I shall hope to see you again shortly, Duke," Dominey said, as he completed his leave-taking. "There is a little matter of business to be adjusted between us. You will probably hear from Mr. Mangan in a day or two."

The Duke gazed after the retreating figure of this very amazing visitor. When the curtains had fallen he turned to his wife.

"A little matter of business," he repeated. "I hope you have explained to Everard, my dear, that although, of course, we are very glad to see him back again, it is absolutely hopeless for him to look to me for any financial assistance at the present moment."

Caroline smiled.

"Everard was alluding to the money he already owes you," she explained. "He intends to repay it at once. He is also paying off the Dominey mortgages. He has apparently made a fortune in Africa."

The Duke collapsed into an easy-chair.

"Everard pay his debts?" he exclaimed. "Everard Dominey pay off the mortgages?"

"That is what I understand," his wife acquiesced.

The Duke clutched at the last refuge of a weak but obstinate man. His mouth came together like a rat-trap.

"There's something wrong about it somewhere," he declared.

CHAPTER VI

Dominey spent a very impatient hour that evening in his sitting-room at the Carlton, waiting for Seaman. It was not until nearly seven that the latter appeared.

"Are you aware," Dominey asked him, "that I am expected to call upon the Princess Eiderstrom at seven o'clock?"

"I have your word for it," Seaman replied, "but I see no tragedy in the situation. The Princess is a woman of sense and a woman of political insight. While I cannot recommend you to take her entirely into your confidence, I still think that a middle course can be judiciously pursued."

"Rubbish!" Dominey exclaimed. "As Leopold von Ragastein, the Princess has indisputable claims upon me and my liberty, claims which would altogether interfere with the career of Everard Dominey."

With methodical neatness, Seaman laid his hat, gloves and walking stick upon the sideboard. He then looked into the connecting bedroom, closed and fastened the door and extended himself in an easy-chair.

"Sit opposite to me, my friend," he said. "We will talk together."

Dominey obeyed a little sullenly. His companion, however, ignored his demeanour.

"Now, my friend," he said, beating upon the palm of one hand with the forefinger of his other, "I am a man of commerce and I do things in a business way. Let us take stock of our position. Three months ago last week, we met by appointment at a certain hotel in Cape Town."

"Only three months," Dominey muttered.

"We were unknown to one another," Seaman continued. "I had only heard of the Baron von Ragastein as a devoted German citizen and patriot, engaged in an important enterprise in East Africa by special intercession of the Kaiser, on account of a certain unfortunate happening in Hungary."

"I killed a man in a duel," Dominey said slowly, with his eyes fixed upon his companion's. "It was not an unforgivable act."

"There are duels and duels. A fight between two young men, in defence of the honour of or to gain the favour of a young lady in their own station of life, has never been against the conventions of the Court. On the other hand, to become the lover of the wife of one of the greatest nobles in Hungary, and to secure possession by killing the husband in the duel which his honour makes a necessity is looked upon very differently."

"I had no wish to kill the Prince," Dominey protested, "nor was it at my desire that we met at all. The Prince fought like a madman and slipped, after a wild lunge, on to the point of my stationary sword."

"Let that pass," Seaman said. "I am not of your order and I probably do not understand the etiquette of these matters. I simply look upon you as a culprit in the eyes of our master, and I feel that he has a right to demand from you much in the way of personal sacrifice."

"Perhaps you will tell me," Dominey demanded, "what more he would have? I have spent weary years in a godless and fever-ridden country, raising up for our arms a great troop of natives. I have undertaken other political commissions in the Colony which may bear fruit. I am to take up the work for which I was originally intended, for which I was given an English education. I am to repair to England, and, under such identity as I might assume after consultation with you at Cape Town, I am to render myself so far as possible a *persona grata* in that country. I do not wait for our meeting. I see a great chance and I make use of it. I transform myself into an English country gentleman, and I think you will admit that I have done so with great success."

"All that you say is granted," Seaman agreed. "You met me at Cape Town in your new identity, and you certainly seemed to wear it wonderfully. You have made it uncommonly expensive, but we do not grudge money."

"I could not return home to a poverty-stricken domain," Dominey pointed out. "I should have held no place whatever in English social life, and I should have received no welcome from those with whom I imagine you desire me to stand well."

"Again I make no complaints," Seaman declared. "There is no bottom to our purse, nor any stint. Neither must there be any stint to our loyalty," he added gravely.

"In this instance," Dominey protested, "it is not a matter of loyalty. Everard Dominey cannot throw himself at the feet of the Princess Eiderstrom, well-known to be one of the most passionate women in Europe, whilst her love affair with Leopold von Ragastein is still remembered. Remember that the question of our identities might crop up any day. We were friends over here in England, at school and at college, and there are many who will still remember the likeness between us. Perfectly though I may play my part, here and there there may be doubts. These will be doubts no longer if I am to be dragged at the chariot wheels of the Princess."

Seaman was silent for a moment.

"There is reason in what you say," he admitted presently. "It is for a few months only. What is your proposition?"

"That you see the Princess in my place at once," Dominey suggested eagerly. "Point out to her that for the present, for political reasons, I am and must remain Everard Dominey, to her as to the rest of the world. Let her be content with such measure of friendship and admiration as Sir Everard Dominey might reasonably offer to a beautiful woman whom he met today for the first time, and I am entirely and with all my heart at her service. But let her remember that even between us two, in the solitude of her room as in the drawing-rooms where we might meet, it can only be Everard Dominey until my mission is ended. You think, perhaps, that I lay unnecessary stress upon this. I do not. I know the Princess and I know myself."

Seaman glanced at the clock. "At what hour was your appointment?"

"It was not an appointment, it was a command," Dominey replied. "I was told to be at Belgrave Square at seven o'clock."

"I will have an understanding with the Princess," promised Seaman, as he took up his hat. "Dine with me downstairs at eight o'clock on my return."

Dominey, descending about an hour later, found his friend Seaman already established at a small, far-away table set in one of the recesses of the grill room. He was welcomed with a little wave of the hand, and cocktails were at once ordered.

"I have done your errand," Seaman announced. "Since my visit I am bound to admit that I realise a little more fully your anxiety."

"You probably had not met the Princess before?"

"I had not. I must confess that I found her a lady of somewhat overpowering temperament. I fancy, my young friend," Seaman continued, with a twitch at the corner of his lips, "that somewhere about August next year you will find your hands full."

"August next year can take care of itself," was the cool reply.

"In the meantime," Seaman continued, "the Princess understands the situation and is, I think, impressed. She will at any rate do nothing rash. You and she will meet within the course of the next few hours, but on reasonable terms. To proceed! As I drove back here after my interview with the Princess, I decided that it was time you made the acquaintance of the person who is chiefly responsible for your presence here."

"Terniloff?"

"Precisely! You have maintained, my young friend," Seaman went on after a brief pause, during which one waiter had brought their cocktails and another received their order for dinner, "a very discreet and laudable silence with regard to those further instructions which were promised to you immediately you should arrive in London. Those instructions will never be committed to writing. They are here."

Seaman touched his forehead and drained the remaining contents of his glass.

"My instructions are to trust you absolutely," Dominey observed, "and, until the greater events stir, to concentrate the greater part of my energies in leading the natural life of the man whose name and place I have taken."

"Quite so," Seaman acquiesced.

He glanced around the room for a moment or two, as though interested in the people. Satisfied at last that there was no chance of being overheard, he continued:

"The first idea you have to get out of your head, my dear friend, if it is there, is that you are a spy. You are nothing of the sort. You are not connected with our remarkably perfect system of espionage in the slightest degree. You are a free agent in all that you may choose to say or do. You can believe in Germany or fear her — whichever you like. You can join your cousin's husband in his crusade for National Service, or you can join me in my efforts to cement the bonds of friendship and affection between the citizens of the two countries. We really do not care in the least. Choose your own part. Live yourself thoroughly into the life of Sir Everard Dominey, Baronet, of Dominey Hall, Norfolk, and pursue exactly the course which you think Sir Everard himself would be likely to take."

"This," Dominey admitted, "is very broad-minded."

"It is common sense," was the prompt reply. "With all your ability, you could not in six months' time appreciably affect the position either way. Therefore, we choose to have you concentrate the whole of your energies upon one task and one task only. If there is anything of the spy about your mission here, it is not England or the English which are to engage your attention. We require you to concentrate wholly and entirely upon Terniloff."

Dominey was startled.

"Terniloff?" he repeated. "I expected to work with him, but ——"

"Empty your mind of all preconceived ideas," Seaman enjoined. "What your duties are with regard to Terniloff will grow upon you gradually as the situation develops."

"As yet," Dominey remarked, "I have not even made his acquaintance."

"I was on the point of telling you, earlier in our conversation, that I have made an appointment for you to see him at eleven o'clock to-night at the Embassy. You will go to him at that hour. Remember, you know nothing, you are waiting for instructions.

Let speech remain with him alone. Be particularly careful not to drop him a hint of your knowledge of what is coming. You will find him absolutely satisfied with the situation, absolutely content. Take care not to disturb him. He is a missioner of peace. So are you."

"I begin to understand," Dominey said thoughtfully.

"You shall understand everything when the time comes for you to take a hand," Seaman promised, "and do not in your zeal forget, my friend, that your utility to our great cause will depend largely upon your being able to establish and maintain your position as an English gentleman. So far all has gone well?"

"Perfectly, so far as I am concerned," Dominey replied. "You must remember, though, that there is your end to keep up. Berlin will be receiving frantic messages from East Africa as to my disappearance. Not even my immediate associates were in the secret."

"That is all understood," Seaman assured his companion. "A little doctor named Schmidt has spent many marks of the Government money in frantic cables. You must have endeared yourself to him."

"He was a very faithful associate."

"He has been a very troublesome friend. It seems that the natives got their stories rather mixed up concerning your namesake, who apparently died in the bush, and Schmidt continually emphasised your promise to let him hear from Cape Town. However, all this has been dealt with satisfactorily. The only real dangers are over here, and so far you seem to have encountered the principal ones."

"I have at any rate been accepted," Dominey declared, "by my nearest living relative, and incidentally I have discovered the one far-seeing person in England who knows what is in store for us."

Seaman was momentarily anxious.

"Whom do you mean?"

"The Duke of Worcester, my cousin's husband, of whom you were speaking just now."

The little man's face relaxed.

"He reminds me of the geese who saved the Capitol," he said, "a brainless man obsessed with one idea. It is queer how often these fanatics discover the truth. That reminds me," he added, taking a small memorandum book from his waistcoat pocket and glancing it through. "His Grace has a meeting to-night at the Holborn Town Hall. I shall make one of my usual interruptions."

"If he has so small a following, why don't you leave him alone?" Dominey enquired.

"There are others associated with him," was the placid reply, "who are not so insignificant. Besides, when I interrupt I advertise my own little hobby."

"These — we English are strange people," Dominey remarked, glancing around the room after a brief but thoughtful pause. "We advertise and boast about our colossal wealth, and yet we are incapable of the slightest self-sacrifice in order to preserve it. One would have imagined that our philosophers, our historians, would warn us in irresistible terms, by unanswerable scientific deduction, of what was coming."

"My compliments to your pronouns," Seaman murmured, with a little bow. *À propos* of what you were saying, you will never make an Englishman — I beg your pardon, one of your countrymen — realise anything unpleasant. He prefers to keep his head comfortably down in the sand. But to leave generalities, when do you think of going to Norfolk?"

"Within the next few days," Dominey replied.

"I shall breathe more freely when you are securely established there," his companion declared. "Great things wait upon your complete acceptance, in the country as well as in town, as Sir Everard Dominey. You are sure that you perfectly understand your position there as regards your — er — domestic affairs?"

"I understand all that is necessary," was the somewhat stiff reply.

"All that is necessary is not enough," Seaman rejoined irritably. "I thought that you had wormed the whole story out of that drunken Englishman?"

"He told me most of it. There were just one or two points which lay beyond the limits where questioning was possible."

Seaman frowned angrily.

"In other words," he complained, "you remembered that you were a gentleman and not that you were a German."

"The Englishman of a certain order," Dominey pronounced, "even though he be degenerate, has a certain obstinacy, generally connected with one particular thing, which nothing can break. We talked together on that last night until morning; we drank wine and brandy. I tore the story of my own exile from my breast and laid it bare before him. Yet I knew all the time, as I know now, that he kept something back."

There was a brief pause. During the last few minutes a certain tension had crept in between the two men. With it, their personal characteristics seemed to have become intensified. Dominey was more than ever the aristocrat; Seaman the plebeian schemer, unabashed and desperately in earnest. He leaned presently a little way across the table. His eyes had narrowed but they were as bright as steel. His teeth were more prominent than usual.

"You should have dragged it from his throat," he insisted. "It is not your duty to nurse fine personal feelings. Heart and soul you stand pledged to great things. I cannot at this moment give you any idea what you may not mean to us after the trouble has come, if you are able to play your part still in this country as Everard Dominey of Dominey Hall. I know well enough that the sense of personal honour amongst the Prussian aristocracy is the finest in the world, and yet there is not a single man of your order who should not be prepared to lie or cheat for his country's sake. You must fall into line with your fellows. Once more, it is not only your task with regard to Terniloff which makes your recognition as Everard Dominey so important to us. It is the things which are to come later.— Come, enough of this subject. I know that you understand. We grow too serious. How shall you spend your evening until eleven o'clock? Remember you did not leave England an anchorite, Sir Everard. You must have your amusements. Why not try a music hall?"

"My mind is too full of other things," Dominey objected.

"Then come with me to Holborn," the little man suggested. "It will amuse you. We will part at the door, and you shall sit at the back of the hall, out of sight. You shall hear the haunting eloquence of your cousin-in-law. You shall hear him trying to warn the men and women of England of the danger awaiting them from the great and rapacious German nation. What do you say?"

"I will come," Dominey replied in spiritless fashion. "It will be better than a music hall, at any rate. I am not at all sure, Seaman, that the hardest part of my task over here will not be this necessity for self-imposed amusements."

His companion struck the table gently but impatiently with his clenched fist.

"Man, you are young!" he exclaimed. "You are like the rest of us. You carry your life in your hands. Don't nourish past griefs. Cast the memory of them away. There's nothing which narrows a man more than morbidness. You have a past which may sometime bring the ghosts around you, but remember the sin was not wholly yours, and there is an atonement which in measured fashion you may commence whenever you please. I have said enough about that. Greatness and gaiety go hand in hand. There! You see, I was a philosopher before I became a professor of propaganda. Good! You smile. That is something gained, at any rate. Now we will take a taxicab to Holborn and I will show you something really humorous."

At the entrance to the town hall, the two men, at Seaman's instigation, parted, making their way inside by different doors. Dominey found a retired seat under a balcony, where he was unlikely to be recognised from the platform. Seaman, on the other hand, took up a more prominent position at the end of one of the front rows of benches. The meeting was by no means overcrowded, overenthusiastic, overanything. There were rows of empty benches, a good many young couples who seemed to have come in for shelter from the inclement night, a few sturdy, respectable-looking tradesmen who had come because it seemed to be the respectable thing to do, a few genuinely interested, and here and there, although they were decidedly in the minority, a sprinkling of enthusiasts. On the platform was the Duke, with civic dignitaries on either side of him; a distinguished soldier, a Member of Parliament, a half-dozen or so of nondescript residents from the neighbourhood, and Captain Bartram. The meeting was on the point of commencement as Dominey settled down in his corner.

First of all the Duke rose, and in a few hackneyed but earnest sentences introduced his young friend Captain Bartram. The latter, who sprang at once into the middle of his subject, was nervous and more than a little bitter. He explained that he had resigned his commission and was therefore free to speak his mind. He spoke of enormous military preparations in Germany and a general air of tense expectation. Against whom were these preparations? Without an earthly doubt against Germany's greatest rival, whose millions of young men, even in this hour of danger, preferred playing or watching football or cricket on Saturday afternoons to realising their duty. The conclusion of an ill-pointed but earnest speech was punctuated by the furtive entrance into the hall of a small boy selling evening newspapers, and there was a temporary diversion from any interest in the proceedings on the part of the younger portion of the audience, whilst they satisfied themselves as to the result of various Cup Ties. The Member of Parliament then descended upon them in a whirlwind of oratory and in his best House of Commons style. He spoke of black clouds and of the cold breeze that went before the coming thunderstorm. He pointed to the collapse of every great nation throughout history who had neglected the arts of self-defence. He appealed to the youth of the nation to prepare themselves to guard their womenkind, their homes, the sacred soil of their country, and at that point was interrupted by a drowsy member of the audience with stentorian lungs, who seemed just at that moment to have waked up.

"What about the Navy, guv'nor?"

The orator swept upon the interrupter in his famous platform manner. The Navy, he declared, could be trusted at all times to do its duty, but it could not fight on sea and land. Would the young man who had just interrupted do his, and enroll his name for drill and national service that evening?—and so on. The distinguished soldier, who was suffering from a cold, fired off a few husky sentences only, to the tune of rounds of applause. The proceedings were wound up by the Duke, who was obviously, with the exception of the distinguished soldier, much more in earnest than any of them, and secured upon the whole a respectful attention. He brought in a few historical allusions, pleaded for a greater spirit of earnestness and citizenship amongst the men of the country, appealed even to the women to develop their sense of responsibility, and sat down amidst a little burst of quite enthusiastic applause.—The vote of thanks to the chairman was on the point of being proposed when Mr. Seaman, standing up in his place, appealed to the chairman for permission to say a few words. The Duke, who had had some experience with Mr. Seaman before, looked at him severely, but the smile with which Mr. Seaman looked around upon the audience was so good-natured and attractive, that he had no alternative but to assent. Seaman scrambled up the steps on to the platform, coughed apologetically, bowed to the Duke, and took possession of the meeting. After a word or two of compliment to the chairman, he made his confession. He was a German citizen—he was indeed one of that bloodthirsty race. (Some laughter.) He was also, and it was his excuse for standing there, the founder and secretary of a league, doubtless well known to them, a league for promoting more friendly relations between the business men of Germany and England. Some of the remarks which he had heard that evening had pained him deeply. Business often took him to Germany, and as a German he would be doing less than his duty if he did not stand up there and tell them that the average German loved the Englishman like a brother, that the object of his life was to come into greater kinship with him, that Germany, even at that moment, was standing with hand outstretched to her relatives across the North Sea, begging for a deeper sympathy, begging for a larger understanding. (Applause from the audience, murmurs of dissent from the platform.) And as to those military preparations of which they had heard so much (with a severe glance at Captain Bartram), let them glance for one moment at the frontiers of Germany, let them realise that eastwards Germany was being continually pressed by an ancient and historic foe of enormous strength. He would not waste their time telling them of the political difficulties which Germany had had to face during the last generation. He would simply tell them this great truth,—the foe for whom Germany was obliged to make these great military preparations was Russia. If ever they were used it would be against Russia, and at Russia's instigation. — In his humble way he was striving for the betterment of relations between the dearly beloved country of his birth and the equally beloved country of his adoption. Such meetings as these, instituted, as it seemed to him, for the propagation of unfair and unjustified suspicions, were one of the greatest difficulties in his way. He could not for a moment doubt that these gentlemen upon the platform were patriots. They would prove it more profitably, both to themselves and their country, if they abandoned their present prejudiced and harmful campaign and became patrons of his Society.

Seaman's little bow to the chairman was good-humoured, tolerant, a little wistful. The Duke's few words, prefaced by an indignant protest against the intrusion of a German propagandist into an English patriotic meeting, did nothing to undo the effect produced by this undesired stranger. When the meeting broke up, it was doubtful whether a single adherent had been gained to the cause of National Service. The Duke went home full of wrath, and Seaman chuckled with genuine merriment as he stepped into the taxi which Dominey had secured, at the corner of the street.

"I promised you entertainment," he observed. "Confess that I have kept my word."

Dominey smiled enigmatically. "You certainly succeeded in making fools of a number of respectable and well-meaning men."

"The miracle of it extends further," Seaman agreed. "To-night, in its small way, is a supreme example of the transcendental follies of democracy. England is being slowly choked and strangled with too much liberty. She is like a child being overfed with jam. Imagine, in our dear country, an Englishman being allowed to mount the platform and spout, undisturbed, English propaganda in deadly opposition to German interests. The so-called liberty of the Englishman is like the cuckoo in his political nest. Countries must be governed. They cannot govern themselves. The time of war will prove all that."

"Yet in any great crisis of a nation's history," Dominey queried, "surely there is safety in a multitude of counsellors?"

"There would always be a multitude of counsellors," Seaman replied, "in Germany as in England. The trouble for this country is that they would be all expressed publicly and in the press, each view would have its adherents, and the Government be split up into factions. In Germany, the real destinies of the country are decided in secret. There are counsellors there, too, earnest and wise counsellors, but no one knows their varying views. All that one learns is the result, spoken through the lips of the Kaiser, spoken once and for all."

Dominey was showing signs of a rare interest in his companion's conversation. His eyes were bright, his usually impassive features seemed to have become more mobile and strained. He laid his hand on Seaman's arm.

"Listen," he said, "we are in London, alone in a taxicab, secure against any possible eavesdropping. You preach the advantage of our Kaiser-led country. Do you really believe that the Kaiser is the man for the task which is coming?"

Seaman's narrow eyes glittered. He looked at his companion in satisfaction. His forehead was puckered, his eternal smile gone. He was the man of intellect.

"So you are waking up from the lethargy of Africa, my friend!" he exclaimed. "You are beginning to think. As you ask me, so shall I answer. The Kaiser is a vain, bombastic dreamer, the greatest egotist who ever lived, with a diseased personality, a ceaseless craving for the limelight. But he has also the genius for government. I mean this: he is a splendid medium for the expression of the brain power of his counsellors. Their words will pass through his personality, and he will believe them his. What is more, they will sound like his. He will see himself the knight in shining armour. All Europe will bow down before this self-imagined Caesar, and no one except we who are behind will realise the ass's head. There is no one else in this world whom I have ever met so well fitted to lead our great nation on to the destiny she deserves.—And now, my friend, to-morrow, if you like, we will speak of these matters again. To-night, you have other things to think about. You are going into the great places where I never penetrate. You have an hour to change and prepare. At eleven o'clock the Prince von Terniloff will expect you."

CHAPTER VII

THERE had been a dinner party and a very small reception afterwards at the great Embassy in Carlton House Terrace. The Ambassador, Prince Terniloff, was bidding farewell to his wife's cousin, the Princess Eiderstrom, the last of his guests. She drew him on one side for a moment.

"Your Excellency," she said, "I have been hoping for a word with you all the evening."

"And I with you, dear Stephanie," he answered. "It is very early. Let us sit down for a moment."

He led her towards a settee but she shook her head.

"You have an appointment at half-past eleven," she said. "I wish you to keep it."

"You know, then?"

"I lunched to-day at the Carlton grill room. In the reception-room I came face to face with Leopold von Ragastein."

The Ambassador made no remark. It seemed to be his wish to hear first all that his companion had to say. After a moment's pause she continued:

"I spoke to him, and he denied himself. To me! I think that those were the most terrible seconds of my life. I have never suffered more. I shall never suffer so much again."

"It was most unfortunate," the Prince murmured sympathetically.

"This evening," she went on, "I received a visit from a man whom I took at first to be an insignificant member of the German bourgeoisie. I learnt something of his true position later. He came to me to explain that Leopold was engaged in this country on secret service, that he was passing under the name which he gave me, — Sir Everard Dominey, an English baronet, long lost in Africa. You know of this?"

"I know that to-night I am receiving a visit from Sir Everard Dominey."

"He is to work under your auspices?"

"By no means," the Prince rejoined warmly. "I am not favourably inclined towards this network of espionage. The school of diplomacy in which I have been brought up tries to work without such ignoble means."

"One realises that," she said. "Leopold is coming, however, to-night, to pay his respects to you."

"He is waiting for me now in my study," the Ambassador asserted.

"You will do me the service of conveying to him a message from me," she continued. "This man Seaman pointed out to me the unwisdom of any association between myself and Leopold, under present conditions. I listened to all that he had to say. I reserved my decision. I have now considered the matter. I will compromise with necessity. I will be content with the acquaintance of Sir Everard Dominey, but that I will have."

"For myself," the Ambassador reflected, "I do not even know what Von Ragastein's mission over here is, but if in Berlin they decide that, for the more complete preservation of his incognito, association between you and him is undesirable —— "

She laid her fingers upon his arm.

"Stop!" she ordered. "I am not of Berlin. I am not a German. I am not even an Austrian. I am Hungarian, and though I am willing to study your interests, I am not willing to place them before my own life. I make terms, but I do not surrender. Those terms I will discuss with Leopold. Ah, be kind to me!" she went on, with a sudden change of voice. "Since those few minutes at midday I have lived in a dream. Only one thing can quiet me. I must speak to him, I must decide with him what I will do. You will help?"

"An acquaintance between you and Sir Everard Dominey," he admitted, "is certainly a perfectly natural thing."

"Look at me," she begged.

He turned and looked into her face. Underneath her beautiful eyes were dark lines; there was something pitiful about the curve of her mouth. He remembered that although she had carried herself throughout the evening with all the dignity which was second nature to her, he had overheard more than one sympathetic comment upon her appearance.

"I can see that you are suffering," he remarked kindly.

"My eyes are hot, and inside I am on fire," she continued. "I must speak to Leopold. Freda has asked me to stay and talk to her for an hour. My car waits. Arrange that he drives me home. Oh! believe me, dear friend, I am a very human woman, and there is nothing in the world to be gained by treating me as though I were of wood or stone. To-night I can see him without observation. If you refuse, I shall take other means. I will make no promises. I will not even promise that I will not call out before him in the streets that he is a liar, that his life is a lie. I will call him Leopold von Ragastein——"

"Hush!" he begged her. "Stephanie, you are nervous. I have not yet answered your entreaty."

"You consent?"

"I consent," he promised. "After our interview, I shall bring the young man to Freda's room and present him. You will be there. He can offer you his escort."

She suddenly stooped and kissed his hand. An immense relief was in her face.

"Now I will keep you no longer. Freda is waiting for me."

The Ambassador strolled thoughtfully away into his own den at the back of the house, where Dominey was waiting for him.

"I am glad to see you," the former said, holding out his hand. "For five minutes I desire to talk to your real self. After that, for the rest of your time in England, I will respect your new identity."

Dominey bowed in silence. His host pointed to the sideboard.

"Come," he continued, "there are cigars and cigarettes at your elbow, whisky and soda on the sideboard. Make yourself at home in that chair there. Africa has really changed you very little. Do you remember our previous meeting, in Saxony?"

"I remember it perfectly, your Excellency."

"His Majesty knew how to keep Court in those days," the Ambassador went on. "One was tempted to believe oneself at an English country party. However, that much of the past. You know, of course, that I entirely disapprove of your present position here?"

"I gathered as much, your Excellency."

"We will have no reserves with one another," the Prince declared, lighting a cigar. "I know quite well that you form part of a network of espionage in this country which I consider wholly unnecessary. That is simply a question of method. I have no doubt that you are here with the same object as I am, the object which the Kaiser has declared to me with his own lips is nearest to his heart — to cement the bonds of friendship between Germany and England."

"You believe, sir, that that is possible?"

"I am convinced of it," was the earnest reply. "I do not know what the exact nature of your work over here is to be, but I am glad to have an opportunity of putting before you my convictions. I believe that in Berlin the character of some of the leading statesmen here has been misunderstood and misrepresented. I find on all sides of me an earnest and sincere desire for peace. I have convinced myself that there is not a single statesman in this country who is desirous of war with Germany."

Dominey was listening intently, with the air of one who hears unexpected things.

"But, your Excellency," he ventured, "what about the matter from our point of view? There are a great many in our country, whom you and I know of, who look forward to a war with England as inevitable. Germany must become, we all believe, the greatest empire in the world. She must climb there, as one of our friends once said, with her foot upon the neck of the British lion."

"You are out of date," the Ambassador declared earnestly. "I see now why they sent you to me. Those days have passed. There is room in the world for Great Britain and for Germany. The disintegration of Russia in the near future is a certainty. It is eastward that we must look for any great extension of territory."

"These things have been decided?"

"Absolutely! They form the soul of my mission here. My mandate is one of peace, and the more I see of English statesmen and the more I understand the British outlook, the more sanguine

I am as to the success of my efforts. This is why all this outside espionage with which Seaman is so largely concerned seems to me at times unwise and unnecessary."

"And my own mission?" Dominey enquired.

"Its nature," the Prince replied, "is not as yet divulged, but if, as I have been given to understand, it is to become closely connected with my own, then I am very sure you will presently find that its text also is Peace."

Dominey rose to his feet, prepared to take his leave.

"These matters will be solved for us," he murmured.

"There is just one word more, on a somewhat more private matter," Terniloff said in an altered tone. "The Princess Eiderstrom is upstairs."

"In this house?"

"Waiting for a word with you. Our friend Seaman has been with her this evening. I understand that she is content to subscribe to the present situation. She makes one condition, however."

"And that?"

"She insists upon it that I present Sir Everard Dominey."

The latter did not attempt to conceal his perturbation.

"I need scarcely point out to you, sir," he protested, "that any association between the Princess and myself is likely to largely increase the difficulties of my position here."

The Ambassador sighed.

"I quite appreciate that," he admitted. "Both Seaman and I have endeavoured to reason with her, but, as you are doubtless aware, the Princess is a woman of very strong will. She is also very powerfully placed here, and it is the urgent desire of the Court at Berlin to placate in every way the Hungarian nobility. You will understand, of course, that I speak from a political point of view only. I cannot ignore the fact of your unfortunate relations with the late Prince, but in considering the present position you will, I am sure, remember the greater interests."

His visitor was silent for a moment.

"You say that the Princess is waiting here?"

"She is with my wife and asks for your escort home. My wife also looks forward to the pleasure of renewing her acquaintance with you."

"I shall accept your Excellency's guidance in the matter," Dominey decided.

The Princess Terniloff was a woman of world culture, an artist, and still an extremely attractive woman. She received the visitor whom her husband brought to her in a very charming little room furnished after the style of the simplest French period, and she did her best to relieve the strain of what she understood must be a somewhat trying moment.

"We are delighted to welcome you to London, Sir Everard Dominey," she said, taking his hand, "and I hope that we shall often see you here. I want to present you to my cousin, who is interested in you, I must tell you frankly, because of your likeness to a very dear friend of hers. Stephanie, this is Sir Everard Dominey — the Princess Eiderstrom."

Stephanie, who was seated upon the couch from which her cousin had just risen, held out her hand to Dominey, who made her a very low and formal bow. Her gown was of unrelieved black. Wonderful diamonds flashed around her neck, and she wore also a tiara fashioned after the Hungarian style, a little low on her forehead. Her manner and tone still indicated some measure of rebellion against the situation.

"You have forgiven me for my insistence this morning?" she asked. "It was hard for me to believe that you were not indeed the person for whom I mistook you."

"Other people have spoken to me of the likeness," Dominey replied. "It is a matter of regret to me that I can claim to be no more than a simple Norfolk baronet."

"Without any previous experience of European Courts?"

"Without any at all."

"Your German is wonderfully pure for an untravelled man."

"Languages were the sole accomplishment I brought away from my misspent school days."

"You are not going to bury yourself in Norfolk, Sir Everard?" the Princess Terniloff enquired.

"Norfolk is very near London these days," Dominey replied, "and I have experienced more than my share of solitude during the last few years. I hope to spend a portion of my time here."

"You must dine with us one night," the Princess insisted, "and tell us about Africa. My husband would be so interested."

"You are very kind."

Stephanie rose slowly to her feet, leaned gracefully over and kissed her hostess on both cheeks, and submitted her hand to the Prince, who raised it to his lips. Then she turned to Dominey.

"Will you be so kind as to see me home?" she asked. "Afterwards, my car can take you on wherever you choose to go."

"I shall be very happy," Dominey assented.

He, too, made his farewells. A servant in the hall handed him his hat and coat, and he took his place in the car by Stephanie's side. She touched the electric switch as they glided off. The car was in darkness.

"I think," she murmured, "that I could not have borne another moment of this juggling with words. Leopold — we are alone!"

He caught the flash of her jewels, the soft brilliance of her eyes as she leaned towards him. His voice sounded, even to himself, harsh and strident.

"You mistake, Princess. My name is not Leopold. I am Everard Dominey."

"Oh, I know that you are very obstinate," she said softly, "very obstinate and very devoted to your marvellous country, but you have a soul, Leopold; you know that there are human duties as great as any your country ever imposed upon you. You know what I look for from you, what I must find from you or go down into hell, ashamed and miserable."

He felt his throat suddenly dry.

"Listen," he muttered, "until the hour strikes, I must remain to you as to the world, alone or in a crowd — Everard Dominey. There is one way and one way only of carrying through my appointed task."

She gave a little hysterical sob.

"Wait," she begged. "I will answer you in a moment. Give me your hand."

He opened the fingers which he had kept clenched together, and he felt the hot grip of her hand, holding his passionately, drawing it towards her until the fingers of her other hand, too, fell upon it. So she sat for several moments.

"Leopold," she continued presently, "I understand. You are afraid that I shall betray our love. You have reason. I am full of impulses and passion, as you know, but I have restraint. What we are to one another when we are alone, no soul in this world need know. I will be careful. I swear it. I will never even look at you as though my heart ached for your notice, when we are in the presence of other people. You shall come and see me as seldom as you wish. I will receive you alone only as often as you say. But don't treat me like this. Tell me you have come back. Throw off this hideous mask, if it be only for a moment."

He sat quite still, although her hands were tearing at his, her lips and eyes beseeching him.

"Whatever may come afterwards," he pronounced inexorably, "until the time arrives I am Everard Dominey. I cannot take advantage of your feelings for Leopold von Ragastein. He is not here. He is in Africa. Perhaps some day he will come back to you and be all that you wish."

She flung his hands away. He felt her eyes burning into his, this time with something more like furious curiosity.

"Let me look at you," she cried. "Let me be sure. Is this just some ghastly change, or are you an impostor? My heart is growing chilled. Are you the man I have waited for all these years? Are you the man to whom I have given my lips, for whose sake I offered up my reputation as a sacrifice, the man who slew my husband and left me?"

"I was exiled," he reminded her, his own voice shaking with emotion. "You know that. So far as other things are concerned, I am exiled now. I am working out my expiation."

She leaned back in her seat with an air of exhaustion. Her eyes closed. Then the car drove in through some iron gates and stopped in front of her door, which was immediately opened. A footman hurried out. She turned to Dominey.

"You will not enter," she pleaded, "for a short time?"

"If you will permit me to pay you a visit, it will give me great pleasure," he answered formally. "I will call, if I may, on my return from Norfolk."

She gave him her hand with a set smile.

"Let my people take you wherever you want to go," she invited, "and remember," she added, dropping her voice, "I do not admit defeat. This is not the last word between us."

She disappeared in some state, escorted through the great front door of one of London's few palaces by an attractive major-domo and footman in the livery of her House. Dominey drove back to the Carlton, where in the lounge he found the band playing, crowds still sitting around, amongst whom Seaman was conspicuous, in his neat dinner clothes and with his cherubic air of inviting attention from prospective new acquaintances. He greeted Dominey enthusiastically.

"Come," he exclaimed, "I am weary of solitude! I have seen scarcely a face that I recognise. My tongue is parched with inaction. I like to talk, and there has been no one to talk to. I might as well have opened up my little house in Forest Hill."

"I'll talk to you if you like," Dominey promised a little grimly, glancing at the clock and hastily ordering a whisky and soda. "I will begin by telling you this," he added, lowering his tone. "I have discovered the greatest danger I shall have to face during my enterprise."

"What is that?"

"A woman — the Princess Eiderstrom."

Seaman lit one of his inevitable cigars and threw one of his short, fat legs over the other. He gazed for a moment with an air of satisfaction at his small foot, neatly encased in court shoes.

"You surprise me," he confessed. "I have considered the matter. I cannot see any great difficulty."

"Then you must be closing your eyes to it wilfully," Dominey retorted, "or else you are wholly ignorant of the Princess's temperament and disposition."

"I believe I appreciate both," Seaman replied, "but I still do not see any peculiar difficulty in the situation. As an English nobleman you have a perfect right to enjoy the friendship of the Princess Eiderstrom."

"And I thought you were a man of sentiment!" Dominey scoffed. "I thought you understood a little of human nature. Stephanie Eiderstrom is Hungarian born and bred. Even race has never taught her self-restraint. You don't seriously suppose that after all these years, after all she has suffered — and she has suffered — she is going to be content with an emasculated form of friendship? I talk to you without reserve, Seaman. She has made it very plain to-night that she is going to be content with nothing of the sort."

"What takes place between you in private," Seaman began ——

"Rubbish!" his companion interrupted. "The Princess is an impulsive, a passionate, a distinctly primitive woman, with a good deal of the wild animal in her still. Plots or political necessities are not likely to count a snap of the fingers with her."

"But surely," Seaman protested, "she must understand that your country has claimed you for a great work?"

Dominey shook his head.

"She is not a German," he pointed out. "On the contrary, like a great many other Hungarians, I think she rather dislikes Germany and Germans. Her only concern is the personal question between us. She considers that every moment of the rest of my life should be devoted to her."

"Perhaps it is as well," Seaman remarked, "that you have arranged to go down to-morrow to Dominey. I will think out a scheme. Something must be done to pacify her."

The lights were being put out. The two men rose a little unwillingly. Dominey felt singularly indisposed for sleep, but anxious at the same time to get rid of his companion. They strolled into the darkened hall of the hotel together.

"I will deal with this matter for you as well as I can," Seaman promised. "To my mind, your greatest difficulty will be encountered to-morrow. You know what you have to deal with down at Dominey."

Dominey's face was very set and grave.

"I am prepared," he said.

Seaman still hesitated.

"Do you remember," he asked, "that when we talked over your plans at Cape Town, you showed me a picture of — of Lady Dominey?"

"I remember."

"May I have one more look at it?"

Dominey, with fingers that trembled a little, drew from the breast pocket of his coat a leather case, and from that a worn picture. The two men looked at it side by side beneath one of the electric standards which had been left burning. The face was the face of a girl, almost a child, and the great eyes seemed filled with a queer, appealing light. There was something of the same suggestion to be found in the lips, a certain helplessness, an appeal for love and protection to some stronger being.

Seaman turned away with a little grunt, and commented:

"Permitting myself to reassume for a moment or two the ordinary sentiments of an ordinary human being, I would sooner have a dozen of your Princesses to deal with than the original of that picture."

CHAPTER VIII

"YOUR ancestral home," Mr. Mangan observed, as the car turned the first bend in the grass-grown avenue and Dominey Hall came into sight. "Damned fine house, too!"

His companion made no reply. A storm had come up during the last few minutes, and, as though he felt the cold, he had dragged his hat over his eyes and turned his coat collar up to his ears. The house, with its great double front, was now clearly visible — the time-worn, Elizabethan, red brick outline that faced the park southwards, and the stone-supported, grim and weather-stained back which confronted the marshes and the sea. Mr. Mangan continued to make amiable conversation.

"We have kept the old place weathertight, somehow or other," he said, "and I don't think you'll miss the timber much. We've taken it as far as possible from the outlying woods."

"Any from the Black Wood?" Dominey asked, without turning his head.

Mr. Mangan shook his head.

"Not a stump," he replied, "and for a very excellent reason. Not one of the woodmen would ever go near the place."

"The superstition remains, then?"

"The villagers are absolutely rabid about it. There are at least a dozen who declare that they have seen the ghost of Roger Unthank, and a score or more who will swear by all that is holy that they have heard his call at night."

"Does he still select the park and the terrace outside the house for his midnight perambulations?" Dominey enquired.

The lawyer hesitated.

"The idea is, I believe," he said, "that the ghost makes his way out from the wood and sits on the terrace underneath Lady Dominey's window. All bunkum, of course, but I can assure you that every servant and caretaker we've had there has given notice within a month. That is the sole reason why I haven't ventured to recommend long ago that you should get rid of Mrs. Unthank."

"She is still in attendance upon Lady Dominey, then?"

"Simply because we couldn't get any one else to stay there," the lawyer explained, "and her ladyship positively declines to leave the Hall. Between ourselves, I think it's time a change was made. We'll have a chat after dinner, if you've no objection.—You see, we've left all the trees in the park," he went on, with an air of satisfaction. "Beautiful place, this, in the springtime. I was down last May for a night, and I never saw such buttercups in my life. The cows here were almost up to their knees in pasture, and the bluebells in the home woods were wonderful. The whole of the little painting colony down at Flankney turned themselves loose upon the place last spring."

"Some of the old wall is down, I see," Dominey remarked with a frown, as he gazed towards the enclosed kitchen garden.

Mr. Mangan was momentarily surprised.

"That wall has been down, to my knowledge, for twenty years," he reminded his companion.

Dominey nodded. "I had forgotten," he muttered.

"We wrote you, by the by," the lawyer continued, "suggesting the sale of one or two of the pictures, to form a fund for repairs, but thank goodness you didn't reply! We'll have some workpeople here as soon as you've decided what you'd like done. I'm afraid," he added, as they turned in through some iron gates and entered the last sweep in front of the house, "you won't find many familiar faces to welcome you. There's Loveybond, the gardener, whom you would scarcely remember, and Middleton, the head keeper, who has really been a godsend so far as the game is concerned. No one at all indoors, except—Mrs. Unthank."

The car drew up at that moment in front of the great porch. There was nothing in the shape of a reception. They had even to ring the bell before the door was opened by a manservant sent down a few days previously from town. In the background, wearing a brown velveteen coat, with breeches and leggings of corduroy, stood an elderly man with white side whiskers and skin as brown as a piece of parchment, leaning heavily upon a long ash stick. Half a dozen maidservants, new importations, were visible in the background, and a second man was taking possession of the luggage. Mr. Mangan took charge of the proceedings.

"Middleton," he said, resting his hand upon the old man's shoulder, "here's your master come back again. Sir Everard was very pleased to hear that you were still here; and you, Loveybond."

The old man grasped the hand which Dominey stretched out with both of his.

"I'm right glad you're back again, Squire," he said, looking at him with curious intentness, "and yet the words of welcome stick in my throat."

"Sorry you feel like that about it, Middleton," Dominey said pleasantly. "What is the trouble about my coming back, eh?"

"That's no trouble, Squire," the old man replied. "That's a joy — leastways to us. It's what it may turn out to be for you which makes one hold back like."

Dominey drew himself more than ever erect — a commanding figure in the little group.

"You will feel better about it when we have had a day or two with the pheasants, Middleton," he said reassuringly. "You have not changed much, Loveybond," he added, turning to the man who had fallen a little into the background, very stiff and uncomfortable in his Sunday clothes.

"I thankee, Squire," the latter replied a little awkwardly, with a motion of his hand towards his forehead. "I can't say the same for you, sir. Them furrin parts has filled you out and hardened you. I'll take the liberty of saying that I should never have recognised you, sir, and that's sure."

"This is Parkins," Mr. Mangan went on, pushing his way once more into the foreground, "the butler whom I engaged in London. And —— "

There was a queer and instantaneous silence. The little group of maidservants, who had been exchanging whispered confidences as to their new master's appearance, were suddenly dumb. All eyes were turned in one direction. A woman whose advent had been unperceived, but who had evidently issued from one of the recesses of the hall, stood suddenly before them all. She was as thin as a lath, dressed in severe black, with grey hair brushed back from her head and not even a white collar at her neck. Her face was long and narrow, her features curiously large, her eyes filled with anger. She spoke very slowly, but with some trace in her intonation of a north-country dialect.

"There's no place in this house for you, Everard Dominey," she said, standing in front of him as though to bar his progress. "I wrote last night to stop you, but you've shown indecent haste in coming. There's no place here for a murderer. Get back where you came from, back to your hiding."

"My good woman!" Mangan gasped. "This is really too much!"

"I've not come to bandy words with lawyers," the woman retorted. "I've come to speak to him. Can you face me, Everard Dominey, you who murdered my son and made a madwoman of your wife?"

The lawyer would have answered her, but Dominey waved him on one side.

"Mrs. Unthank," he said sternly, "return to your duties at once, and understand that this house is mine, to enter or leave when I choose."

She was speechless for a moment, amazed at the firmness of his words.

"The house may be yours, Sir Everard Dominey," she said threateningly, "but there's one part of it at least in which you won't dare to show yourself."

"You forget yourself, woman," he replied coldly. "Be so good as to return to your mistress at once, announce my coming, and say that I wait only for her permission before presenting myself in her apartments."

The woman laughed, unpleasantly, horribly. Her eyes were fixed upon Dominey curiously.

"Those are brave words," she said. "You've come back a harder man. Let me look at you."

She moved a foot or two to where the light was better. Very slowly a frown developed upon her forehead. The longer she looked, the less assured she became.

"There are things in your face I miss," she muttered.

Mr. Mangan was glad of an opportunity of asserting himself. "The fact is scarcely important, Mrs. Unthank," he said angrily. "If you will allow me to give you a word of advice, you will treat your master with the respect to which his position here entitles him."

Once more the woman blazed up.

"Respect! What respect have I for the murderer of my son? Respect! Well, if he stays here against my bidding, perhaps her ladyship will show him what respect means."

She turned around and disappeared. Every one began bustling about the luggage and talking at once. Mr. Mangan took his patron's arm and led him across the hall.

"My dear Sir Everard," he said anxiously, "I am most distressed that this should have occurred. I thought that the woman would probably be sullen, but I had no idea that she would dare to attempt such an outrageous proceeding."

"She is still, I presume, the only companion whom Lady Dominey will tolerate?" Dominey enquired with a sigh.

"I fear so," the lawyer admitted. "Nevertheless we must see Doctor Harrison in the morning. It must be understood distinctly that if she is suffered to remain, she adopts an entirely different attitude. I never heard anything so preposterous in all my life. I shall pay her a visit myself after dinner.—You will feel quite at home here in the library, Sir Everard," Mr. Mangan went on, throwing open the door of a very fine apartment on the seaward side of the house. "Grand view from these windows, especially since we've had a few of the trees cut down. I see that Parkins has set out the sherry. Cocktails, I'm afraid, are an institution you will have to inaugurate down here. You'll be grateful to me when I tell you one thing, Sir Everard. We've been hard pressed more than once, but we haven't sold a single bottle of wine out of the cellars."

Dominey accepted the glass of sherry which the lawyer had poured out but made no movement toward drinking it. He seemed during the last few minutes to have been wrapped in a brown study.

"Mangan," he asked a little abruptly, "is it the popular belief down here that I killed Roger Unthank?"

The lawyer set down the decanter and coughed.

"A plain answer," Dominey insisted.

Mr. Mangan adapted himself to the situation. He was beginning to understand his client.

"I am perfectly certain, Sir Everard," he confessed, "that there isn't a soul in these parts who isn't convinced of it. They believe that there was a fight and that you had the best of it."

"Forgive me," Dominey continued, "if I seem to ask unnecessary questions. Remember that I spent the first portion of my exile in Africa in a very determined effort to blot out the memory of everything that had happened to me earlier in life. So that is the popular belief?"

"The popular belief seems to march fairly well with the facts," Mr. Mangan declared, wielding the decanter again in view of his client's more reasonable manner. "At the time of your unfortunate visit to the Hall Miss Felbrigg was living practically alone at the Vicarage after her uncle's sudden death there, with Mrs. Unthank as housekeeper. Roger Unthank's infatuation for her was patent to the whole neighbourhood and a source of great annoyance to Miss Felbrigg. I am convinced that at no time did Lady Dominey give the young man the slightest encouragement."

"Has any one ever believed the contrary?" Dominey demanded.

"Not a soul," was the emphatic reply. "Nevertheless, when you came down, fell in love with Miss Felbrigg and carried her off, every one felt that there would be trouble."

"Roger Unthank was a lunatic," Dominey pronounced deliberately. "His behaviour from the first was the behaviour of a madman."

"The Eugene Aram type of village schoolmaster gradually drifting into positive insanity," Mangan acquiesced. "So far, every one is agreed. The mystery began when he came back from his holidays and heard the news."

"The sequel was perfectly simple," Dominey observed. "We met at the north end of the Black Wood one evening, and he attacked me like a madman. I suppose I had to some extent the best of it, but when I got back to the Hall my arm was broken, I was covered with blood, and half unconscious. By some cruel stroke of fortune, almost the first person I saw was Lady Dominey. The shock was too much for her—she fainted and——"

"And has never been quite herself since," the lawyer concluded. "Most tragic!"

"The cruel part of it was," Dominey went on, standing before the window, his hands clasped behind his back, "that my wife from that moment developed a homicidal mania against me—I, who had fought in the most absolute self-defence. That was what drove me out of the country, Mangan—not the fear of being arrested for having caused the death of Roger Unthank. I'd have stood my trial for that at any moment. It was the other thing that broke me up."

"Quite so," Mangan murmured sympathetically. "As a matter of fact, you were perfectly safe from arrest, as it happened. The body of Roger Unthank has never been found from that day to this."

"If it had——"

"You must have been charged with either murder or manslaughter."

Dominey abandoned his post at the window and raised his glass of sherry to his lips. The tragical side of these reminiscences seemed, so far as he was concerned, to have passed.

"I suppose," he remarked, "it was the disappearance of the body which has given rise to all this talk as to his spirit still inhabiting the Black Wood."

"Without a doubt," the lawyer acquiesced. "The place had a bad name already, as you know. As it is, I don't suppose there's a villager here would cross the park in that direction after dark."

Dominey glanced at his watch and led the way from the room.

"After dinner," he promised, "I'll tell you a few West African superstitions which will make our local one seem anæmic."

CHAPTER IX

"I CERTAINLY offer you my heartiest congratulations upon your cellars, Sir Everard," his guest said, as he sipped his third glass of port that evening. "This is the finest glass of Seventy I've drunk for a long time, and this new fellow I've sent you down—Parkins—tells me there's any quantity of it."

"It has had a pretty long rest," Dominey observed.

"I was looking through the cellar-book before dinner," the lawyer went on, "and I see that you still have Forty-seven and Forty-eight, and a small quantity of two older vintages. Something ought to be done about those."

"We will try one of them to-morrow night," Dominey suggested. "We might spend half an hour or so in the cellars, if we have any time to spare."

"And another half an hour," Mr. Mangan said gravely, "I should like to spend in interviewing Mrs. Unthank. Apart from any other question, I do not for one moment believe that she is the proper person to be entrusted with the care of Lady Dominey. I made up my mind to speak to you on this subject, Sir Everard, as soon as we had arrived here."

"Mrs. Unthank was old Mr. Felbrigg's housekeeper and my wife's nurse when she was a child," Dominey reminded his companion. "Whatever her faults may be, I believe she is devoted to Lady Dominey."

"She may be devoted to your wife," the lawyer admitted, "but I am convinced that she is your enemy. The situation doesn't seem to me to be consistent. Mrs. Unthank is firmly convinced that, whether in fair fight or not, you killed her son. Lady Dominey believes that, too, and it was the sight of you after the fight that sent her insane. I cannot but believe that it would be far better for Lady Dominey to have some one with her unconnected with this unfortunate chapter of your past."

"We will consult Doctor Harrison to-morrow," Dominey said. "I am very glad you came down with me, Mangan," he went on, after a minute's hesitation. "I find it very difficult to get back into the atmosphere of those days. I even find it hard sometimes," he added, with a curious little glance across the table, "to believe that I am the same man."

"Not so hard as I have done more than once," Mr. Mangan confessed.

"Tell me exactly in what respects you consider me changed?" Dominey insisted.

The lawyer hesitated.

"You seem to have lost a certain pliability, or perhaps I ought to call it looseness of disposition," he admitted. "There are many things connected with the past which I find it almost impossible to associate with you. For a trifling instance," he went on, with a slight smile, inclining his head towards his host's untasted glass. "You don't drink port like any Dominey I ever knew."

"I'm afraid that I never acquired the taste for port," Dominey observed.

The lawyer gazed at him with raised eyebrows.

"Not acquired the taste for port?" he repeated blankly.

"I should have said reacquired," Dominey hastened to explain. "You see, in the bush we drank a simply frightful amount of spirits, and that vitiates the taste for all wine."

The lawyer glanced enviously at his host's fine bronzed complexion and clear eyes.

"You haven't the appearance of ever having drunk anything, Sir Everard," he observed frankly. "One finds it hard to believe the stories that were going about ten or fifteen years ago."

"The Dominey constitution, I suppose!"

The new butler entered the room noiselessly and came to his master's chair.

"I have served coffee in the library, sir," he announced. "Mr. Middleton, the gamekeeper, has just called, and asks if he could have a word with you before he goes to bed to-night, sir. He seems in a very nervous and uneasy state."

"He can come to the library at once," Dominey directed; "that is, if you are ready for your coffee, Mangan."

"Indeed I am," the lawyer assented, rising. "A great treat, that wine. One thing the London restaurants can't give us. Port should never be drunk away from the place where it was laid down."

The two men made their way across the very fine hall, the walls of which had suffered a little through lack of heating, into the library, and seated themselves in easy-chairs before the blazing log fire. Parkins silently served them with coffee and brandy. He had scarcely left the room before there was a timid knock and Middleton made his somewhat hesitating entrance.

"Come in and close the door," Dominey directed. "What is it, Middleton? Parkins says you wish to speak to me."

The man came hesitatingly forward. He was obviously distressed and uneasy, and found speech difficult. His face glistened with the rain which had found its way, too, in long streaks down his velveteen coat. His white hair was wind-tossed and disarranged.

"Bad night," Dominey remarked.

"It's to save its being a worse one that I'm here, Squire," the old man replied hoarsely. "I've come to ask you a favour and to beg you to grant it for your own sake. You'll not sleep in the oak room to-night?"

"And why not?" Dominey asked.

"It's next her ladyship's."

"Well?"

The old man was obviously perturbed, but his master, as though of a purpose, refused to help him. He glanced at Mangan and mumbled to himself.

"Say exactly what you wish to, Middleton," Dominey invited. "Mr. Mangan and his father and grandfather have been solicitors to the estate for a great many years. They know all our family history."

"I can't get rightly into touch with you, Squire, and that's a fact," Middleton went on despairingly. "The shape of you seems larger and your voice harder. I don't seem to be so near to you as I'd wished, to say what's in my heart."

"I have had a rough time, Middleton," Dominey reminded him. "No wonder I have changed! Never mind, speak to me just as man to man."

"It was I who first met you, Squire," the old man went on, "when you tottered home that night across the park, with your arm hanging helplessly by your side, and the blood streaming down your face and clothes, and the red light in your eyes—murderous fire, they called it. I heard her ladyship go into hysterics. I saw her laugh and sob like a maniac, and, God help us! that's what she's been ever since."

The two men were silent. Middleton had raised his voice, speaking with fierce excitement. It was obvious that he had only paused for breath. He had more to say.

"I was by your side, Squire," he went on, "when her ladyship caught up the knife and ran at you, and, as you well know, it was I, seizing her from behind, that saved a double tragedy that night, and it was I who went for the doctor the next morning, when she'd stolen into your room in the night and missed your throat by a bare inch. I heard her call to you, heard her threat. It was a madwoman's threat, Squire, but her ladyship is a madwoman at this moment, and with a knife in her hand you'll never be safe in this house."

"We must see," Dominey said quietly, "that she is not allowed to get possession of any weapon."

"Aye! Make sure of that," Middleton scoffed, "with Mother Unthank by her side! Her ladyship's mad because of the horror of that night, but Mother Unthank is mad with hate, and there isn't a week passes," the old man went on, his voice dropping lower and his eyes burning, "that Roger Unthank's spirit doesn't come and howl for your blood beneath their window. If you stay here this night, Squire, come over and sleep in the little room they've got ready for you on the other side of the house."

Mr. Mangan had lost his smooth, after-dinner appearance. His face was distinctly pale, his smoothly brushed hair was rumpled, and his coffee was growing cold. This was a very different thing from the vague letters and rumours which had reached him from time to time and which he had put out of his mind with all the contempt of the materialist.

"It is very good of you to warn me, Middleton," Dominey said, "but I can lock my door, can I not?"

"Lock the door of the oak room!" was the scornful reply. "And what good would that do? You know well enough that the wall's double on three sides, and there are more secret entrances than even I know of. The oak room's not for you this night, Squire. It's hoping to get you there that's keeping them quiet."

"Tell us what you meant, Middleton," the lawyer asked, with ill-assumed indifference, "when you spoke of the howling of Roger Unthank's spirit?"

The old man turned patiently around.

"Just that, sir," he replied. "It's round the house most weeks. Except for me odd nights, and Mrs. Unthank, there's been scarcely a servant would sleep in the Hall for years. Some of the maids they do come up from the village, but back they go before nightfall, and until morning there isn't a living soul would cross the park — no, not for a hundred pounds."

"A howl, you call it?" Mr. Mangan observed.

"That's mostly like a dog what's hurt itself," Middleton explained equably, "like a dog, that is, with a touch of the human in its throat, as we've all heard in our time, sir. You'll hear it yourself, sir, maybe to-night or to-morrow night."

"You've heard it then, Middleton?" his master asked.

"Why, surely, sir," the old man replied in surprise. "Most weeks for the last ten years."

"Haven't you ever got up and gone out to see what it was?"

The old man shook his head.

"But I knew right well what that was, sir," he said, "and I'm not one for looking on spirits. Spirits there are that walk this world, as we well know, and the spirit of Roger Unthank walks from between the Black Wood and these windows, come every week of the year. But I'm not for looking at him. There's evil comes of that. I turn over in my bed, and I stop my ears, but I've never yet raised a blind."

"Tell me, Middleton," Dominey asked, "is Lady Dominey terrified at these — er — visitations?"

"That I can't rightly say, sir. Her ladyship's always sweet and gentle, with kind words on her lips for every one, but there's the terror there in her eyes that was lit that night when you staggered into the hall, Squire, and I've never seen it properly quenched yet, so to speak. She carries fear with her, but whether it's the fear of seeing you again, or the fear of Roger Unthank's spirit, I could not tell."

Dominey seemed suddenly to become possessed of a strange desire to thrust the whole subject away. He dismissed the old man kindly but a little abruptly, accompanying him to the corridor which led to the servants' quarters and talking all the time about the pheasants. When he returned, he found that his guest had emptied his second glass of brandy and was surreptitiously mopping his forehead.

"That," the latter remarked, "is the class of old retainer who lives too long. If I were a Dominey of the Middle Ages, I think a stone around his neck and the deepest well would be the sensible way of dealing with him. He made me feel positively uncomfortable."

"I noticed it," Dominey remarked, with a faint smile. "I'm not going to pretend that it was a pleasant conversation myself."

"I've heard some ghost stories," Mangan went on, "but a spook that comes and howls once a week for ten years takes some beating."

Dominey poured himself out a glass of brandy with a steady hand.

"You've been neglecting things here, Mangan," he complained. "You ought to have come down and exorcised that ghost. We shall have those smart maidservants of yours off to-morrow, I suppose, unless you and I can get a little ghost-laying in first."

Mr. Mangan began to feel more comfortable. The brandy and the warmth of the burning logs were creeping into his system.

"By the by, Sir Everard," he enquired, a little later on, "where are you going to sleep to-night?"

Dominey stretched himself out composedly.

"There is obviously only one place for me," he replied. "I can't disappoint any one. I shall sleep in the oak room."

CHAPTER X

For the first few tangled moments of nightmare, slowly develop ing into a live horror, Dominey fancied himself back in Africa, with the hand of an enemy upon his throat. Then a rush of awakened memories — the silence of the great house, the mysterious rustling of the heavy hangings around the black oak fourposter on which he lay, the faint pricking of something deadly at his throat — these things rolled back the curtain of unreality, brought him acute and painful consciousness of a situation almost appalling. He opened his eyes, and although a brave and callous man he lay still, paralysed with the fear which forbids motion. The dim light of a candle, recently lit, flashed upon thc bodkin-like dagger held at his throat. He gazed at the thin line of gleaming steel, fascinated. Already his skin had been broken, a few drops of blood were upon the collar of his pyjamas. The hand which held that deadly, assailing weapon — small, slim, very feminine, curving from somewhere behind the bed curtain — belonged to some unseen person. He tried to shrink farther back upon the pillow. The hand followed him, displaying glimpses now of a soft, white-sleeved arm. He lay quite still, the muscles of his right arm growing tenser as he prepared for a snatch at those cruel fingers. Then a voice came, — a slow, feminine and rather wonderful voice.

"If you move," it said, "you will die. Remain quite still."

Dominey was fully conscious now, his brain at work, calculating his chances with all the cunning of the trained hunter who seeks to avoid death. Reluctantly he was compelled to realise that no movement of his could be quick enough to prevent the driving of that thin stiletto into his throat, if his hidden assailant should keep her word. So he lay still.

"Why do you want to kill me?" he asked, a little tensely.

There was no reply, yet somehow he knew that he was being

watched. Ever so slightly those curtains around which the arm had come, were being parted. Through the chink some one was looking at him. The thought came that he might call out for help, and once more his unseen enemy read his thought.

"You must be very quiet," the voice said, — that voice which it was difficult for him to believe was not the voice of a child. "If you even speak above a whisper, it will be the end. I wish to look at you."

A little wider the crack opened, and then he began to feel hope. The hand which held the stiletto was shaking, he heard something which sounded like quick breathing from behind the curtains — the breathing of a woman astonished or terrified — and then, so suddenly that for several seconds he could not move or take advantage of the circumstance, the hand with its cruel weapon was withdrawn around the curtain and a woman began to laugh, softly at first, and then with a little hysterical sob thrusting its way through that incongruous note of mirth.

He lay upon the bed as though mesmerised, finding at his first effort that his limbs refused their office, as might the limbs of one lying under the thrall of a nightmare. The laugh died away, there was a sound like a scraping upon the wall, the candle was suddenly blown out. Then his nerve began to return and with it his control over his limbs. He crawled to the side of the bed remote from the curtains, stole to the little table on which he had left his revolver and an electric torch, snatched at them, and, with the former in his right hand, flashed a little orb of light into the shadows of the great apartment. Once more something like terror seized him. The figure which had been standing by the side of his bed had vanished. There was no hiding place in view. Every inch of the room was lit up by the powerful torch he carried, and, save for himself, the room was empty. The first moment of realisation was chill and unnerving. Then the slight smarting of the wound at his throat became convincing proof to him that there was nothing supernatural about this visit. He lit up half-a-dozen of the candles distributed about the place and laid down his torch. He was ashamed to find that his forehead was dripping with perspiration.

"One of the secret passages, of course," he muttered to himself, stooping for a moment to examine the locked, folding doors which separated his room from the adjoining one. "Perhaps, when one reflects, I have run unnecessary risks."

Dominey was standing at the window, looking out at the tumbled grey waters of the North Sea, when Parkins brought him hot water and tea in the morning. He thrust his feet into slippers and held out his arms for a dressing-gown.

"Find out where the nearest bathroom is, Parkins," he ordered, "and prepare it. I have quite forgotten my way about here."

"Very good, sir."

The man was motionless for a moment, staring at the blood on his master's pyjamas. Dominey glanced down at it and turned the dressing-gown up to his throat.

"I had a slight accident this morning," he remarked carelessly. "Any ghost alarms last night?"

"None that I heard of, sir," the man replied. "I am afraid we should have difficulty in keeping the young women from London, if they heard what I heard the night of my arrival."

"Very terrible, was it?" Dominey asked with a smile.

Parkins' expression remained immovable. There was in his tone, however, a mute protest against his master's levity.

"The cries were the most terrible I have ever heard, sir," he said. "I am not a nervous person, but I found them most disturbing."

"Human or animal?"

"A mixture of both, I should say, sir."

"You should camp out for the night on the skirts of an African forest," Dominey remarked. "There you get a whole orchestra of wild animals, every one of them trying to freeze your blood up."

"I was out in South Africa during the Boer War, sir," Parkins replied, "and I went big game hunting with my master afterwards. I do not think that any animal was ever born in Africa with so terrifying a cry as we heard the night before last."

"We must look into the matter," Dominey muttered.

"I have already prepared a bath, sir, at the end of the corridor," the man announced. "If you will allow me, I will show you the way."

Dominey, when he descended about an hour later, found his guest awaiting him in a smaller dining-room, which looked out eastwards towards the sea, a lofty apartment with great windows and with an air of faded splendour which came from the ill-cared-for tapestries, hanging in places from the wall. Mr. Mangan had, contrary to his expectations, slept well and was in excellent spirits. The row of silver dishes upon the sideboard inspired him with an added cheerfulness.

"So there were no ghosts walking last night, eh?" he remarked, as he took his place at the table. "Wonderful thing this absolute quiet is after London. Give you my word, I never heard a sound from the moment my head touched the pillow until I woke a short while ago."

Dominey returned from the sideboard, carrying also a well-filled plate.

"I had a pretty useful night's rest myself," he observed.

Mangan raised his eyeglass and gazed at his host's throat.

"Cut yourself, eh?" he queried.

"Razor slipped," Dominey told him. "You get out of the use of those things in Africa."

"You've managed to give yourself a nasty gash," Mr. Mangan observed curiously.

"Parkins is going to send up for a new set of safety razors for me," Dominey announced. "About our plans for the day,—I've ordered the car for two-thirty this afternoon, if that suits you. We can look around the place quietly this morning. Mr. Johnson is sleeping over at a farmhouse near here. We shall pick him up en route. And I have told Lees, the bailiff, to come with us too."

Mr. Mangan nodded his approval.

"Upon my word," he confessed, "it will be a joy to me to go and see some of these fellows without having to put 'em off about repairs and that sort of thing. Johnson has had the worst of it, poor chap, but there are one or two of them took it into their heads to come up to London and worry me at the office."

"I intend that there shall be no more dissatisfaction amongst my tenants."

Mr. Mangan set off for another prowl towards the sideboard.

"Satisfied tenants you never will get in Norfolk," he declared.

"I must admit, though, that some of them have had cause to grumble lately. There's a fellow round by Wells who farms nearly eight hundred acres——"

He broke off in his speech. There was a knock at the door, not an ordinary knock at all, but a measured, deliberate tapping, three times repeated.

"Come in," Dominey called out.

Mrs. Unthank entered, severer, more unattractive than ever in the hard morning light. She came to the end of the table, facing the place where Dominey was seated.

"Good morning, Mrs. Unthank," he said.

She ignored his greeting.

"I am the bearer of a message," she announced.

"Pray deliver it," Dominey replied.

"Her ladyship would be glad for you to visit her in her apartment at once."

Dominey leaned back in his chair. His eyes were fixed upon the face of the woman whose antagonism to himself was so apparent. She stood in the path of a long gleam of morning sunlight. The wrinkles in her face, her hard mouth, her cold, steely eyes were all clearly revealed.

"I am not at all sure," he said, with a purpose in his words, "that any further meeting between Lady Dominey and myself is at present desirable."

If he had thought to disturb this messenger by his suggestion, he was disappointed.

"Her ladyship desires me to assure you," she added, with a note of contempt in her tone, "that you need be under no apprehension."

Dominey admitted defeat and poured himself out some more coffee. Neither of the two noticed that his fingers were trembling.

"Her ladyship is very considerate," he said. "Kindly say that I shall follow you in a few minutes."

Dominey, following within a very few minutes of his summons, was ushered into an apartment large and sombrely elegant, an apartment of faded white and gold walls, of chandeliers glittering with lustres, of Louis Quinze furniture, shabby but priceless. To his surprise, although he scarcely noticed it at the time, Mrs.

Unthank promptly disappeared. He was from the first left alone with the woman whom he had come to visit.

She was sitting up on her couch and watching his approach. A woman? Surely only a child, with pale cheeks, large, anxious eyes, and masses of brown hair brushed back from her forehead. After all, was he indeed a strong man, vowed to great things? There was a queer feeling in his throat, almost a mist before his eyes. She seemed so fragile, so utterly, sweetly pathetic. And all the time there was the strange light, or was it want of light, in those haunting eyes. His speech of greeting was never spoken.

"So you have come to see me, Everard," she said, in a broken tone. "You are very brave."

He possessed himself of her hand, the hand which a few hours ago had held a dagger to his throat, and kissed the waxen-like fingers. It fell to her side like a lifeless thing. Then she raised it and began rubbing softly at the place where his lips had fallen.

"I have come to see you at your bidding," he replied, "and for my pleasure."

"Pleasure!" she murmured, with a ghastly little smile. "You have learnt to control your words, Everard. You have slept here and you live. I have broken my word. I wonder why?"

"Because," he pleaded, "I have not deserved that you should seek my life."

"That sounds strangely," she reflected. "Doesn't it say somewhere in the Bible—'A life for a life'? You killed Roger Unthank."

"I have killed other men since in self-defence," Dominey told her. "Sometimes it comes to a man that he must slay or be slain. It was Roger Unthank——"

"I shall not talk about him any longer," she decided quite calmly. "The night before last, his spirit was calling to me below my window. He wants me to go down into Hell and live with him. The very thought is horrible."

"Come," Dominey said, "we will speak of other things. You must tell me what presents I can buy you. I have come back from Africa rich."

"Presents?"

For a single wonderful moment, hers was the face of a child who has been offered toys. Her smile of anticipation was delightful, her eyes had lost that strange vacancy. Then, before he could say another word, it all came back again.

"Listen to me," she said. "This is important. I have sent for you because I do not understand why, quite suddenly last night, after I had made up my mind, I lost the desire to kill you. It is gone now. I am not sure about myself any longer. Draw your chair nearer to mine. Or no, come to my side, here at the other end of the sofa."

She moved her skirts to make room for him. When he sat down, he felt a strange trembling through all his limbs.

"Perhaps," she went on, "I shall break my oath. Indeed, I have already broken it. Let me look at you, my husband. It is a strange thing to own after all these years — a husband."

Dominey felt as though he were breathing an atmosphere of turgid and poisoned sweetness. There was a flavour of unreality about the whole situation, — the room, this child woman, her beauty, her deliberate, halting speech and the strange things she said.

"You find me changed?" he asked.

"You are very wonderfully changed. You look stronger, you are perhaps better-looking, yet there is something gone from your face which I thought one never lost."

"You," he said cautiously, "are more beautiful than ever, Rosamund."

She laughed a little drearily.

"Of what use has my beauty been to me, Everard, since you came to my little cottage and loved me and made me love you, and took me away from Dour Roger? Do you remember the school children used to call him Dour Roger? — But that does not matter. Do you know, Everard, that since you left me my feet have not passed outside these gardens?"

"That can be altered when you wish," he said quickly. "You can visit where you will. You can have a motor-car, even a house in town. I shall bring some wonderful doctors here, and they will make you quite strong again."

Her large eyes were lifted almost piteously to his.

"But how can I leave here?" she asked plaintively. "Every week, sometimes oftener, he calls to me. If I went away, his spirit would break loose and follow me. I must be here to wave my hand; then he goes away."

Dominey was conscious once more of that strange and most unexpected fit of emotion. He was unrecognisable even to himself. Never before in his life had his heart beaten as it was beating now. His eyes, too, were hot. He had travelled around the world in search of new things, only to find them in this strange, faded chamber, side by side with this suffering woman. Nevertheless, he said quietly:

"We must send you some place where the people are kinder and where life is pleasanter. Perhaps you love music and to see beautiful pictures. I think that we must try and keep you from thinking."

She sighed in a perplexed fashion.

"I wish that I could get it out of my blood that I want to kill you. Then you could take me right away. Other married people have lived together and hated each other. Why shouldn't we? We may forget even to hate."

Dominey staggered to his feet, walked to a window, threw it open and leaned out for a moment. Then he closed it and came back. This new element in the situation had been a shock to him. All the time she was watching him composedly.

"Well?" she asked, with a strange little smile. "What do you say? Would you like to hold as a wife's the hand which frightened you so last night?"

She held it out to him, soft and warm. Her fingers even returned the pressure of his. She looked at him pleasantly, and once more he felt like a man who has wandered into a strange country and has lost his bearings.

"I want you so much to be happy," he said hoarsely, "but you are not strong yet, Rosamund. We cannot decide anything in a hurry."

"How surprised you are to find that I am willing to be nice to you!" she murmured. "But why not? You cannot know why

I have so suddenly changed my mind about you — and I have changed it. I have seen the truth these few minutes. There is a reason, Everard, why I should not kill you."

"What is it?" he demanded.

She shook her head with all the joy of a child who keeps a secret.

"You are clever," she said. "I will leave you to find it out. I am excited now, and I want you to go away for a little time. Please send Mrs. Unthank to me."

The prospect of release was a strange relief, mingled still more strangely with regret. He lingered over her hand.

"If you walk in your sleep to-night, then," he begged, "you will leave your dagger behind?"

"I have told you," she answered, as though surprised, "that I have abandoned my intention. I shall not kill you. Even though I may walk in my sleep — and sometimes the nights are so long — it will not be your death I seek."

CHAPTER XI

DOMINEY left the room like a man in a dream, descended the stairs to his own part of the house, caught up a hat and stick and strode out into the sea mist which was fast enveloping the gardens. There was all the chill of the North Pole in that ice-cold cloud of vapour, but nevertheless his forehead remained hot, his pulses burning. He passed out of the postern gate which led from the walled garden on to a broad marsh, with dikes running here and there, and lapping tongues of sea water creeping in with the tide. He made his way seaward with uncertain steps until he reached a rough and stony road; here he hesitated for a moment, looking about him, and then turned back at right angles. Soon he came to a little village, a village of ancient cottages, with seasoned, red-brick tiles, trim little patches of garden, a church embowered with tall elm trees, a triangular green at the cross-roads. On one side a low, thatched building,—the Dominey Arms; on another, an ancient, square, stone house, on which was a brass plate. He went over and read the name, rang the bell, and asked the trim maidservant who answered it, for the doctor. Presently, a man of youthful middle-age presented himself in the surgery and bowed. Dominey was for a moment at a loss.

"I came to see Doctor Harrison," he ventured.

"Doctor Harrison retired from practice some years ago," was the courteous reply. "I am his nephew. My name is Stillwell."

"I understood that Doctor Harrison was still in the neighbourhood," Dominey said. "My name is Dominey—Sir Everard Dominey."

"I guessed as much," the other replied. "My uncle lives with me here, and to tell you the truth he was hoping that you would come and see him. He retains one patient only," Doctor Stillwell added, in a graver tone. "You can imagine who that would be."

His caller bowed. "Lady Dominey, I presume."

The young doctor opened the door and motioned to his guest to precede him.

"My uncle has his own little apartment on the other side of the house," he said. "You must let me take you to him."

They moved across the pleasant white stone hall into a small apartment with French windows leading out to a flagged terrace and tennis lawn. An elderly man, broad-shouldered, with weather-beaten face, grey hair, and of somewhat serious aspect, looked around from the window before which he was standing examining a case of fishing flies.

"Uncle, I have brought an old friend in to see you," his nephew announced.

The doctor glanced expectantly at Dominey, half moved forward as though to greet him, then checked himself and shook his head doubtfully.

"You certainly remind me very much of an old friend, sir," he said, "but I can see now that you are not he. I do not believe that I have ever seen you before in my life."

There was a moment's somewhat tense silence. Then Dominey advanced a little stiffly and held out his hand.

"Come, Doctor," he said, "I can scarcely have changed as much as all that. Even these years of strenuous life—— "

"You mean to tell me that I am speaking to Everard Dominey?" the doctor interposed.

"Without a doubt!"

The doctor shook hands coolly. His was certainly not the enthusiastic welcome of an old family attendant to the representative of a great family.

"I should certainly never have recognised you," he confessed.

"My presence here is nevertheless indisputable," Dominey continued. "Still attracted by your old pastime, I see, Doctor?"

"I have only taken up fly fishing," the other replied drily, "since I gave up shooting."

There was another somewhat awkward pause, which the younger man endeavoured to bridge over.

"Fishing, shooting, golf," he said; "I really don't know what we poor medical practitioners would do in the country without sport."

"I shall remind you of that later," Dominey observed. "I am told that the shooting is one of the only glories which has not passed away from Dominey."

"I shall look forward to the reminder," was the prompt response.

His uncle, who had been bending once more over the case of flies, turned abruptly around.

"Arthur," he said, addressing his nephew, "you had better start on your round. I dare say Sir Everard would like to speak to me privately."

"I wish to speak to you certainly," Dominey admitted, "but only professionally. There is no necessity —— "

"I am late already, if you will excuse me," Doctor Stillwell interrupted. "I will be getting on. You must excuse my uncle, Sir Everard," he added in a lower tone, drawing him a little towards the door, "if his manners are a little gruff. He is devoted to Lady Dominey, and I sometimes think that he broods over her case too much."

Dominey nodded and turned back into the room to find the doctor, his hands in his old-fashioned breeches pockets, eying him steadfastly.

"I find it very hard to believe," he said a little curtly, "that you are really Everard Dominey."

"I am afraid you will have to accept me as a fact, nevertheless."

"Your present appearance," the old man continued, eying him appraisingly, "does not in any way bear out the description I had of you some years ago. I was told that you had become a broken-down drunkard."

"The world is full of liars," Dominey said equably. "You appear to have met with one, at least."

"You have not even," the doctor persisted, "the appearance of a man who has been used to excesses of any sort."

"Good old stock, ours," his visitor observed carelessly. "Plenty of two-bottle men behind my generation."

"You have also gained courage since the days when you fled from England. You slept at the Hall last night?

"Where else? I also, if you want to know, occupied my own

bedchamber — with results," Dominey added, throwing his head a little back, to display the scar on his throat, "altogether insignificant."

"That's just your luck," the doctor declared. "You've no right to have gone there without seeing me; no right, after all that has passed, to have even approached your wife."

"You seem rather a martinet as regards my domestic affairs," Dominey observed.

"That's because I know your history," was the blunt reply.

Uninvited, Dominey seated himself in an easy-chair.

"You were never my friend, Doctor," he said. "Let me suggest that we conduct this conversation on a purely professional basis."

"I was never your friend," came the retort, "because I have known you always as a selfish brute; because you were married to the sweetest woman on God's earth, gave up none of your bad habits, frightened her into insanity by reeling home with another man's blood on your hands, and then stayed away for over ten years instead of making an effort to repair the mischief you had done."

"This," observed Dominey, "is history, dished up in a somewhat partial fashion. I repeat my suggestion that we confine our conversation to the professional."

"This is my house," the other rejoined, "and you came to see me. I shall say exactly what I like to you, and if you don't like it you can get out. If it weren't for Lady Dominey's sake, you shouldn't have passed this threshold."

"Then for her sake," Dominey suggested in a softer tone, "can't you forget how thoroughly you disapprove of me? I am here now with only one object: I want you to point out to me any way in which we can work together for the improvement of my wife's health."

"There can be no question of a partnership between us."

"You refuse to help?"

"My help isn't worth a snap of the fingers. I have done all I can for her physically. She is a perfectly sound woman. The rest depends upon you, and you alone, and I am not very hopeful about it."

"Upon me?" Dominey repeated, a little taken aback.

"Fidelity," the doctor grunted, "is second nature with all good women. Lady Dominey is a good woman, and she is no exception to the rule. Her brain is starved because her heart is aching for love. If she could believe in your repentance and reform, if any atonement for the past were possible and were generously offered, I cannot tell what the result might be. They tell me that you are a rich man now, although heaven knows, when one considers what a lazy, selfish fellow you were, that sounds like a miracle. You could have the great specialists down. They couldn't help, but it might salve your conscience to pay them a few hundred guineas."

"Would you meet them?" Dominey asked anxiously. "Tell me whom to send for?"

"Pooh! Those days are finished with me," was the curt reply. "I would meet none of them. I am a doctor no longer. I have become a villager. I go to see Lady Dominey as an old friend."

"Give me your advice," Dominey begged. "Is it of any use sending for specialists?"

"Just for the present, none at all."

"And what about that horrible woman, Mrs. Unthank?"

"Part of your task, if you are really going to take it up. She stands between your wife and the sun."

"Then why have you suffered her to remain there all those years?" Dominey demanded.

"For one thing, because there has been no one to replace her," the doctor replied, "and for another, because Lady Dominey, believing that you slew her son, has some fantastic idea of giving her a home and shelter as a kind of expiation."

"You think there is no affection between the two?" Dominey asked.

"Not a scrap," was the blunt reply, "except that Lady Dominey is of so sweet and gentle a nature——"

The doctor paused abruptly. His visitor's fingers had strayed across his throat.

"That's a different matter," the former continued fiercely. "That's just where the weak spot in her brain remains. If you ask me, I believe it's pandered to by Mrs. Unthank. Come to think of it," he went on, "the Domineys were never cowards.

If you get your courage back, send Mrs. Unthank away, sleep with your doors wide open. If a single night passes without Lady Dominey coming to your room with a knife in her hand, she will be cured in time of that mania at any rate. Dare you do that?"

Dominey's hesitation was palpable,—also his agitation. The doctor grinned contemptuously.

"Still afraid!" he scoffed.

"Not in the way you imagine," his visitor replied. "My wife has already promised to make no further attempt upon my life."

"Well, you can cure her if you want to," the doctor declared, "and if you do, you will have the sweetest companion for life any man could have. But you'll have to give up the idea of town houses and racing and yachting, and grouse moors in Scotland, and all those sort of things I suppose you've been looking forward to. You'll have for some time, at any rate, to give every moment of your time to your wife."

Dominey moved uneasily in his chair.

"For the next few months," he said, "that would be impossible."

"Impossible!"

The doctor repeated the word, seemed to roll it round in his mouth with a sort of wondering scorn.

"I am not quite the idler I used to be," Dominey explained, frowning. "Nowadays, you cannot make money without assuming responsibilities. I am clearing off the whole of the mortgages upon the Dominey estates within the next few months."

"How you spend your time is your affair, not mine," the doctor muttered. "All that I say about the matter is that your wife's cure, if ever it comes to pass, is in your hands. And now—come over to me here, in the light of this window. I want to look at you."

Dominey obeyed with a little shrug of the shoulders. There was no sunshine, but the white north light was in its way searching. It showed the sprinkling of grey in his ruddy-brown hair, the suspicion of it in his closely trimmed moustache, but it could find no weak spot in his steady eyes, in the tan of his hard, manly complexion, or even in the set of his somewhat arrogant lips. The old doctor took up his box of flies again and jerked his head towards the door.

"You are a miracle," he said, "and I hate miracles. I'll come and see Lady Dominey in a day or so."

CHAPTER XII

Dominey spent a curiously placid, and, to those with whom he was brought into contact, an entirely satisfactory afternoon. With Mr. Mangan by his side, murmuring amiable platitudes, and Mr. Johnson, his agent, opposite, revelling in the unusual situation of a satisfied landlord and delighted tenants, he made practically the entire round of the Dominey estates. They reached home late, but Dominey, although he seemed to be living in another world, was not neglectful of the claims of hospitality. Probably for the first time in their lives, Mr. Johnson and Lees, the bailiff, watched the opening of a magnum of champagne. Mr. Johnson cleared his throat as he raised his glass.

"It isn't only on my own account, Sir Everard," he said, "that I drink your hearty good health. I have your tenants too in my mind. They've had a rough time, some of them, and they've stood it like white men. So here's from them and me to you, sir, and may we see plenty of you in these parts."

Mr. Lees associated himself with these sentiments, and the glasses were speedily emptied and filled again.

"I suppose you know, Sir Everard," the agent observed, "that what you've promised to do to-day will cost a matter of ten to fifteen thousand pounds."

Dominey nodded.

"Before I go to bed to-night," he said, "I shall send a cheque for twenty thousand pounds to the estate account at your bank at Wells. The money is there waiting, put aside for just that one purpose and — well, you may just as well have it."

Agent and bailiff leaned back in the tonneau of their motor-car, half an hour later, with immense cigars in their mouths and a pleasant, rippling warmth in their veins. They had the sense of having drifted into fairyland. Their philosophy, however, met the situation.

"It's a fair miracle," Mr. Lees declared.

"A modern romance," Mr. Johnson, who read novels, murmured. "Hello, here's a visitor for the Hall," he added, as a car swept by them.

"Comfortable-looking gent, too," Mr. Lees remarked.

The "comfortable-looking gent" was Otto Seaman, who presented himself at the Hall with a small dressing-bag and a great many apologies.

"Found myself in Norwich, Sir Everard," he explained. "I have done business there all my life, and one of my customers needed looking after. I finished early, and when I found that I was only thirty miles off you, I couldn't resist having a run across. If it is in any way inconvenient to put me up for the night, say so ——"

"My dear fellow!" Dominey interrupted. "There are a score of rooms ready. All that we need is to light a fire, and an old-fashioned bed-warmer will do the rest. You remember Mr. Mangan?"

The two men shook hands, and Seaman accepted a little refreshment after his drive. He lingered behind for a moment after the dressing bell had rung.

"What time is that fellow going?" he asked.

"Nine o'clock to-morrow morning," Dominey replied.

"Not a word until then," Seaman whispered back. "I must not seem to be hanging after you too much — I really did not want to come — but the matter is urgent."

"We can send Mangan to bed early," Dominey suggested.

"I am the early bird myself," was the weary reply. "I was up all last night. To-morrow morning will do."

Dinner that night was a pleasant and social meal. Mr. Mangan especially was uplifted. Everything to do with the Domineys for the last fifteen years had reeked of poverty. He had really had a hard struggle to make both ends meet. There had been disagreeable interviews with angry tenants, formal interviews with dissatisfied mortgagees, and remarkably little profit at the end of the year to set against these disagreeable episodes. The new situation was almost beatific. The concluding touch, perhaps, was in Parkins' congratulatory whisper as he set a couple of decanters upon the table.

"I have found a bin of Cockburn's *fifty-one,* sir," he announced, including the lawyer in his confidential whisper. "I thought you might like to try a couple of bottles, as Mr. Mangan seems rather a connoisseur, sir. The corks appear to be in excellent condition."

"After this," Mr. Mangan sighed, "it will be hard to get back to the austere life of a Pall Mall club!"

Seaman, very early in the evening, pleaded an extraordinary sleepiness and retired, leaving his host and Mangan alone over the port. Dominey, although an attentive host, seemed still a little abstracted. Even Mr. Mangan, who was not an observant man, was conscious that a certain hardness, almost arrogance of speech and manner, seemed temporarily to have left his patron.

"I can't tell you, Sir Everard," he said, as he sipped his first glass of wine, "what a pleasure it is to me to see, as it were, this recrudescence of an old family. If I might be allowed to say so, there's only one thing necessary to round the whole business off, as it were."

"And that?" Dominey asked unthinkingly.

"The return of Lady Dominey to health. I was one of the few, you may remember, privileged to make her acquaintance at the time of your marriage."

"I paid a visit this morning," Dominey said, "to the doctor who has been in attendance upon her since her marriage. He agrees with me that there is no reason why Lady Dominey should not, in course of time, be restored to perfect health."

"I take the liberty of finishing my glass to that hope, Sir Everard," the lawyer murmured.

Both glasses were set down empty, only the stem of Dominey's was snapped in two. Mr. Mangan expressed his polite regrets.

"This old glass," he murmured, looking at his own admiringly, "becomes very fragile."

Dominey did not answer. His brain had served him a strange trick. In the shadows of the room he had fancied that he could see Stephanie Eiderstrom holding out her arms, calling to him to fulfil the pledges of long ago, and behind her——

"Have you ever been in love, Mangan?" Dominey asked his companion.

"I, sir? Well, I'm not sure," the man of the world replied, a little startled by the abruptness of the question. "It's an old-fashioned way of looking at things now, isn't it?"

Dominey relapsed into thoughtfulness.

"I suppose so," he admitted.

That night a storm rolled up from somewhere across that grey waste of waters, a storm heralded by a wind which came booming over the marshes, shaking the latticed windows of Dominey Place, shrieking and wailing amongst its chimneys and around its many corners. Black clouds leaned over the land, and drenching streams of rain dashed against the loose-framed sashes of the windows. Dominey lit the tall candles in his bedroom, fastened a dressing-gown around him, threw himself into an easy-chair, and, fixing an electric reading lamp by his side, tried to read. Very soon the book slipped from his fingers. He became suddenly tense and watchful. His eyes counted one by one the panels in the wall by the left-hand side of the bed. The familiar click was twice repeated. For a moment a dark space appeared. Then a woman, stooping low, glided into the room. She came slowly towards him, drawn like a moth towards that semicircle of candle. Her hair hung down her back like a girl's, and the white dressing-gown which floated diaphanously about her was unexpectedly reminiscent of Bond Street.

"You are not afraid?" she asked anxiously. "See, I have nothing in my hands. I almost think that the desire has gone. You remember the little stiletto I had last night? To-day I threw it into the well. Mrs. Unthank was very angry with me."

"I am not afraid," he assured her, "but——"

"Ah, but you will not scold me?" she begged. "It is the storm which terrifies me."

He drew a low chair for her into the little circle of light and arranged some cushions. As she sank into it, she suddenly looked up at him and smiled, a smile of rare and wonderful beauty. Dominey felt for a moment something like the stab of a knife at his heart.

"Sit here and rest," he invited. "There is nothing to fear."

"In my heart I know that," she answered simply. "These storms are part of our lives. They come with birth, and they shake the world when death seizes us. One should not be afraid, but I have been so ill, Everard. Shall I call you Everard still?"

"Why not?" he asked.

"Because you are not like Everard to me any more," she told him, "because something has gone from you, and something has come to you. You are not the same man. What is it? Had you troubles in Africa? Did you learn what life was like out there?"

He sat looking at her for a moment, leaning back in his chair, which he had pushed a few feet into the shadows. Her hair was glossy and splendid, and against it her skin seemed whiter and more delicate than ever. Her eyes were lustrous but plaintive, and with something of the child's fear of harm in them. She looked very young and very fragile to have been swayed through the years by an evil passion.

"I learnt many things there, Rosamund," he told her quietly. "I learnt a little of the difference between right doing and wrong-doing. I learned, too, that all the passions of life burn themselves out, save one alone."

She twisted the girdle of her dressing-gown in her fingers for a moment. His last speech seemed to have been outside the orbit of her comprehension or interest.

"You need not be afraid of me any more, Everard," she said, a little pathetically.

"I have no fear of you," he answered.

"Then why don't you bring your chair forward and come and sit a little nearer to me?" she asked, raising her eyes. "Do you hear the wind, how it shrieks at us? Oh, I am afraid!"

He moved forward to her side, and took her hand gently in his. Her fingers responded at once to his pressure. When he spoke, he scarcely recognised his own voice. It seemed to him thick and choked.

"The wind shall not hurt you, or anything else," he promised.

"I have come back to take care of you."

She sighed, smiled like a tired child, and her eyes closed as her head fell farther back amongst the cushions.

"Stay just like that, please," she begged. "Something quite new is coming to me. I am resting. It is the sweetest rest I ever felt. Don't move, Everard. Let my fingers stay in yours — so."

The candles burned down in their sockets, the wind rose to greater furies, and died away only as the dawn broke through the storm clouds. A pale light stole into the room. Still the woman slept, and still her fingers seemed to keep their clutch upon his hand. Her breathing was all the time soft and regular. Her silky black eyelashes lay motionless upon her pale cheeks. Her mouth — a very perfectly shaped mouth — rested in quiet lines. Somehow he realised that about this slumber there was a new thing. With hot eyes and aching limbs he sat through the night. Dream after dream rose up and passed away before that little background of tapestried wall. When she opened her eyes and looked at him, the same smile parted her lips as the smile which had come there when she had passed away to sleep.

"I am so rested," she murmured. "I feel so well. I have had dreams, beautiful dreams."

The fire had burned out, and the room was chilly.

"You must go back to your own room now," he said.

Very slowly her fingers relaxed. She held out her arms.

"Carry me," she begged. "I am only half awake. I want to sleep again."

He lifted her up. Her fingers closed around his neck, her head fell back with a little sigh of content. He tried the folding doors, and, finding some difficulty in opening them, carried her out into the corridor, into her own room, and laid her upon the untouched bed.

"You are comfortable?" he asked.

"Quite," she murmured drowsily. "Kiss me, Everard."

Her hands drew his face down. His lips rested upon her forehead. Then he drew the bedclothes over her and fled.

CHAPTER XIII

There was a cloud on Seaman's good-humoured face as, muffled up in their overcoats, he and his host walked up and down the terrace the next morning, after the departure of Mr. Mangan. He disclosed his mind a little abruptly.

"In a few minutes," he said, "I shall come to the great purpose of my visit. I have great and wonderful news for you. But it will keep."

"The time for action has arrived?" Dominey asked curiously. "I hope you will remember that as yet I am scarcely established here."

"It is with regard to your establishment here," Seaman explained drily, "that I desire to say a word. We have seen much of one another since we met in Cape Town. The passion and purpose of my life you have been able to judge. Of those interludes which are necessary to a human being, unless his system is to fall to pieces as dry dust, you have also seen something. I trust you will not misunderstand me when I say that apart from the necessities of my work, I am a man of sentiment."

"I am prepared to admit it," Dominey murmured a little idly.

"You have undertaken a great enterprise. It was, without a doubt, a miraculous piece of fortune which brought the Englishman, Dominey, to your camp just at the moment when you received your orders from headquarters. Your self-conceived plan has met with every encouragement from us. You will be placed in a unique position to achieve your final purpose. Now mark my words and do not misunderstand me. The very keynote of our progress is ruthlessness. To take even a single step forward towards the achievement of that purpose is worth the sacrifice of all the scruples and delicacies conceivable. But when a certain course of action is without profit to our purpose, I see ugliness in it. It distresses me."

"What the devil do you mean?" Dominey demanded.

"I sleep with one ear open," Seaman replied.

"Well?"

"I saw you leave your room early this morning," Seaman continued, "carrying Lady Dominey in your arms."

There were little streaks of pallor underneath the tan in Dominey's face. His eyes were like glittering metal. It was only when he had breathed once or twice quickly that he could command his voice.

"What concern is this of yours?" he demanded.

Seaman gripped his companion's arm.

"Look here," he said, "we are too closely allied for bluff. I am here to help you fill the shoes of another man, so far as regards his estates, his position, and character, which, by the by, you are rehabilitating. I will go further. I will admit that it is not my concern to interfere in any ordinary amour you might undertake, but—I shall tell you this, my friend, to your face—that to deceive a lady of weak intellect, however beautiful, to make use of your position as her supposed husband, is not, save in the vital interests of his country, the action of a Prussian nobleman."

Dominey's passion seemed to have burned itself out without expression. He showed not the slightest resentment at his companion's words.

"Have no fear, Seaman," he enjoined him. "The situation is delicate, but I can deal with it as a man of honour."

"You relieve me," Seaman confessed. "You must admit that the spectacle of last night was calculated to inspire me with uneasiness."

"I respect you for your plain words," Dominey declared. "The fact is, that Lady Dominey was frightened of the storm last night and found her way into my room. You may be sure that I treated her with all the respect and sympathy which our positions demanded."

"Lady Dominey," Seaman remarked meditatively, "seems to be curiously falsifying certain predictions."

"In what way?"

"The common impression in the neighbourhood here is that

she is a maniac chiefly upon one subject—her detestation of you. She has been known to take an oath that you should die if you slept in this house again. You naturally, being a brave man, ignored all this, yet in the morning after your first night here there was blood upon your night clothes."

Dominey's eyebrows were slowly raised.

"You are well served here," he observed, with involuntary sarcasm.

"That, for your own sake as well as ours, is necessary," was the terse reply. "To continue, people of unsound mind are remarkably tenacious of their ideas. There was certainly nothing of the murderess in her demeanour towards you last night. Cannot you see that a too friendly attitude on her part might become fatal to our schemes?"

"In what way?"

"If ever your identity is doubted," Seaman explained, "the probability of which is, I must confess, becoming less every day, the fact that Lady Dominey seems to have so soon forgotten all her enmity towards you would be strong presumptive evidence that you are not the man you claim to be."

"Ingenious," Dominey assented, "and very possible. All this time, however, we speak on what you yourself admit to be a side issue."

"You are right," Seaman confessed. "Very well, then, listen. A great moment has arrived for you, my friend."

"Explain, if you please."

"I shall do so. You have seen proof, during the last few days, that you have an organisation behind you to whom money is dross. It is the same in diplomacy as in war. Germany will pay the price for what she intends to achieve. Ninety thousand pounds was yesterday passed to the credit of your account for the extinction of certain mortgages. In a few months' or a few years' time, some distant Dominey will benefit to that extent. We cannot recover the money. It is just an item in our day by day expenses."

"It was certainly a magnificent way of establishing me," Dominey admitted.

"Magnificent, but safest in the long run," Seaman declared.

"If you had returned a poor man, everybody's hand would have been against you; suspicions, now absolutely unkindled, might have been formed; and, more important, perhaps, than either, you would not have been able to take your place in Society, which is absolutely necessary for the furtherance of our scheme."

"Is it not almost time," Dominey enquired, "that the way was made a little clearer for me?"

"That would have been my task this morning," Seaman replied, "but for the news I bring. In passing, however, let me promise you this. You will never be asked to stoop to the crooked ways of the ordinary spy. We want you for a different purpose."

"And the news?"

"What must be the greatest desire in your heart," Seaman said solemnly, "is to be granted. The Kaiser has expressed a desire to see you, to give you his instructions in person."

Dominey stopped short upon the terrace. He withdrew his arm from his companion's and stared at him blankly.

"The Kaiser?" he exclaimed. "You mean that I am to go to Germany?"

"We shall start at once," Seaman replied. "Personally, I do not consider the proceeding discreet or necessary. It has been decided upon, however, without consulting me."

"I consider it suicidal," Dominey protested. "What explanation can I possibly make for going to Germany, of all countries in the world, before I have had time to settle down here?"

"That of itself will not be difficult," his companion pointed out. "Many of the mines in which a share has been bought in your name are being run with German capital. It is easy to imagine that a crisis has arisen in the management of one of them. We require the votes of our fellow shareholders. You need not trouble your head about that. And think of the wonder of it! If only for a single day your sentence of banishment is lifted. You will breathe the air of the Fatherland once more."

"It will be wonderful," Dominey muttered.

"It will be for you," Seaman promised, "a breath of the things that are to come. And now, action. How I love action! That time-table, my friend, and your chauffeur."

It was arranged that the two men should leave during the

morning for Norwich by motor-car and thence to Harwich. Dominey, having changed into travelling clothes, sent a messenger for Mrs. Unthank, who came to him presently in his study. He held out a chair to her, which she declined, however, to take.

"Mrs. Unthank," he said, "I should like to know why you have been content to remain my wife's attendant for the last ten years?"

Mrs. Unthank was startled by the suddenness of the attack.

"Lady Dominey has needed me," she answered, after a moment's pause.

"Do you consider," he asked, "that you have been the best possible companion for her?"

"She has never been willing to accept any other," the woman replied.

"Are you very devoted to my wife?" he enquired.

Mrs. Unthank, grim and fierce though she was and appeared to be, was obviously disconcerted by Dominey's line of questions.

"If I weren't," she demanded, "should I have been here all these years?"

"I scarcely see," he continued, "what particular claim my wife has had upon you. I understand, moreover, that you are one of those who firmly believe that I killed your son. Is this attendance upon my wife a Christian act, then — the returning of good for evil?"

"Exactly what do you want to say to me, Sir Everard?" she asked harshly.

"I wish to say this," Dominey replied, "that I am determined to bring about my wife's restoration to health. For that reason I am going to have specialists down here, and above all things to change for a time her place of residence. My own feeling is that she will stand a much better chance of recovery without your attendance."

"You would dare to send me away?" the woman demanded.

"That is my intention," Dominey confessed. "I have not spoken to Lady Dominey yet, but I hope that very soon my influence over her will be such that she will be content to obey my wishes. I look upon your future from the financial point of view, as my care. I shall settle upon you the sum of three hundred pounds a year."

The woman showed her first sign of weakness. She began to shake. There was a curious look of fear in her eyes.

"I can't leave this place, Sir Everard," she cried. "I must stay here!"

"Why?" he demanded.

"Lady Dominey couldn't do without me," she answered sullenly.

"That," he replied, "is for her to decide. Personally, from enquiries I have made, I believe that you have encouraged in her that ridiculous superstition about the ghost of your son. I also believe that you have kept alive in her that spirit of unreasonable hatred which she has felt towards me."

"Unreasonable, you call it?" the woman almost shouted. "You, who came home to her with the blood on your hands of the man whom, if only you had kept away, she might one day have loved? Unreasonable, you call it?"

"I have finished what I had to say, Mrs. Unthank," Dominey declared. "I am compelled by important business to leave here for two or three days. On my return I shall embark upon the changes with which I have acquainted you. In the meantime," he added, watching a curious change in the woman's expression, "I have written this morning to Doctor Harrison, asking him to come up this afternoon and to keep Lady Dominey under his personal observation until my return."

She stood quite still, looking at him. Then she came a little nearer and leaned forward, as though studying his face.

"Eleven years," she muttered, "do change many men, but I never knew a man made out of a weakling."

"I have nothing more to say to you," Dominey replied, "except to let you know that I am coming to see my wife in the space of a few minutes."

The motor-horn was already sounding below when Dominey was admitted to his wife's apartment. She was dressed in a loose gown of a warm crimson colour, and she had the air of one awaiting his arrival expectantly. The passion of hatred seemed to have passed from her pale face and from the depths of her strangely soft eyes. She held out her hands towards him. Her brows were a little puckered. The disappointment of a child lurked in her manner.

"You are going away?" she murmured.

"In a very few moments," he told her. "I have been waiting to see you for an hour."

She made a grimace.

"It was Mrs. Unthank. I think that she hid my things on purpose. I was so anxious to see you."

"I want to talk to you about Mrs. Unthank," he said. "Should you be very unhappy if I sent her away and found some one younger and kinder to be your companion?"

The idea seemed to be outside the bounds of her comprehension.

"Mrs. Unthank would never go," she declared. "She stays here to listen to the voice. All night long sometimes she waits and listens, and it doesn't come. Then she hears it, and she is rested."

"And you?" he asked.

"I am afraid," she confessed. "But then, you see, I am not very strong."

"You are not fond of Mrs. Unthank?" he enquired anxiously.

"I don't think so," she answered, in a perplexed tone. "I think I am very much afraid of her. But it is no use, Everard! She would never go away."

"When I return," Dominey said, "we shall see."

She took his arm and linked her hands through it.

"I am so sorry that you are going," she murmured. "I hope you will soon come back. Will you come back—my husband?"

Dominey's nails cut into the flesh of his clenched hands.

"I will come back within three days," he promised.

"Do you know," she went on confidentially, "something has come into my mind lately. I spoke about it yesterday, but I did not tell you what it was. You need never be afraid of me any more. I understand."

"What do you understand?" he demanded huskily.

"The knowledge must have come to me," she went on, dropping her voice a little and whispering almost in his ear, "at the very moment when my dagger rested upon your throat, when I suddenly felt the desire to kill die away. You are very like him sometimes, but you are not Everard. You are not my husband at all. You are another man."

Dominey gave a little gasp. They both turned towards the door. Mrs. Unthank was standing there, her gaunt, hard face lit up with a gleam of something which was like triumph, her eyes glittering. Her lips, as though involuntarily, repeated her mistress' last words.

"Another man!"

CHAPTER XIV

THERE were times during their rapid journey when Seaman, studying his companion, became thoughtful. Dominey seemed, indeed, to have passed beyond the boundaries of any ordinary reserve, to have become like a man immeshed in the toils of a past so absorbing that he moved as though in a dream, speaking only when necessary and comporting himself generally like one to whom all externals have lost significance. As they embarked upon the final stage of their travels, Seaman leaned forward in his seat in the sombrely upholstered, overheated compartment.

"Your home-coming seems to depress you, Von Ragastein," he said.

"It was not my intention," Dominey replied, "to set foot in Germany again for many years."

"The past still bites, eh?"

"Always."

The train sped on through long chains of vineyard-covered hills, out into a stretch of flat country, into forests of pines, in the midst of which were great cleared spaces, where, notwithstanding the closely drawn windows, the resinous odour from the fallen trunks seemed to permeate the compartment. Presently they slackened speed. Seaman glanced at his watch and rose.

"Prepare yourself, my friend," he said. "We descend in a few minutes."

Dominey glanced out of the window.

"But where are we?" he enquired.

"Within five minutes of our destination."

"But there is not a house in sight," Dominey remarked wonderingly.

"You will be received on board His Majesty's private train," Seaman announced. "The Kaiser, with his staff, is making one of his military tours. We are honoured by being permitted to travel back with him as far as the Belgian frontier."

They had come to a standstill now. A bearded and uniformed official threw open the door of their compartment, and they stepped on to the narrow wooden platform of a small station which seemed to have been recently built of fresh pine planks. The train, immediately they had alighted, passed on. Their journey was over.

A brief conversation was carried on between Seaman and the official, during which Dominey took curious note of his surroundings. Around the station, half hidden in some places by the trees and shrubs, was drawn a complete cordon of soldiers, who seemed to have recently disembarked from a military train which stood upon a siding. In the middle of it was a solitary saloon carriage, painted black, with much gold ornamentation, and having emblazoned upon the central panel the royal arms of Germany. Seaman, when he had finished his conversation, took Dominey by the arm and led him across the line towards it. An officer received them at the steps and bowed punctiliously to Dominey, at whom he gazed with much interest.

"His Majesty will receive you at once," he announced. "Follow me."

They boarded the train and passed along a richly carpeted corridor. Their guide paused and pointed to a small retiring-room, where several men were seated.

"Herr Seaman will find friends there," he said. "His Imperial Majesty will receive him for a few minutes later. The Baron von Ragastein will come this way."

Dominey was ushered now into the main saloon. His guide motioned him to remain near the entrance, and, himself advancing a few paces, stood at the salute before a seated figure who was bending over a map, which a stern-faced man in the uniform of a general had unrolled before him. The Kaiser glanced up at the sound of footsteps and whispered something in the general's ear. The latter clicked his heels together and retired. The Kaiser beckoned Dominey to advance.

"The Baron von Ragastein, your Majesty," the young officer murmured.

Dominey stood at attention for a moment and bowed a little awkwardly. The Kaiser smiled.

"It pleases me," he said, "to see a German officer ill at ease without his uniform. Count, you will leave us. Baron von Ragastein, be seated."

"Sir Everard Dominey, at your service, Majesty," Dominey replied, as he took the chair to which his august host pointed.

"Thorough in all things, I see," the latter observed. "Sit there and be at your ease. Good reports have reached me of your work in Africa."

"I did my best to execute your Majesty's will," Dominey ventured.

"You did so well," the Kaiser pronounced, "that my counsellors were unanimous in advising your withdrawal to what will shortly become the great centre of interest. From the moment of receiving our commands you appear to have displayed initiative. I gather that your personation of this English baronet has been successfully carried through?"

"Up to the present, your Majesty."

"Important though your work in Africa was," the Kaiser continued, "your present task is a far greater one. I wish to speak to you for these few minutes without reserve. First, though, drink a toast with me."

From a mahogany stand at his elbow, the Kaiser drew out a long-necked bottle of Moselle, filled two very beautiful glasses, passed one to his companion and raised the other.

"To the Fatherland!" he said.

"To the Fatherland!" Dominey repeated.

They set down their glasses, empty. The Kaiser threw back the grey military cloak which he was wearing, displaying a long row of medals and decorations. His fingers still toyed with the stem of his wineglass. He seemed for a moment to lose himself in thought. His hard and somewhat cruel mouth was tightly closed; there was a slight frown upon his forehead. He was sitting upright, taking no advantage of the cushioned back of his easy-chair, his eyes a little screwed up, the frown deepening. For quite five minutes there was complete silence. One might have gathered that, turning aside from great matters, he had been devoting himself entirely to the scheme in which Dominey was concerned.

"Von Ragastein," he said at last, "I have sent for you to have a few words concerning your habitation in England. I wish you to receive your impressions of your mission from my own lips."

"Your Majesty does me great honour," Dominey murmured.

"I wish you to consider yourself," the Kaiser continued, "as entirely removed from the limits, the authority and the duties of my espionage system. From you I look for other things. I desire you to enter into the spirit of your assumed position. As a typical English country gentleman I desire you to study the labour question, the Irish question, the progress of this National Service scheme, and other social movements of which you will receive notice in due time. I desire a list compiled of those writers who, in the Reviews, or by means of fiction, are encouraging the suspicions which I am inclined to fancy England has begun to entertain towards the Fatherland. These things are all on the fringe of your real mission. That, I believe, our admirable friend Seaman has already confided to you. It is to seek the friendship, if possible the intimacy, of Prince Terniloff."

The Kaiser paused, and once more his eyes wandered to the landscape which rolled away from the plate-glass windows of the car. They were certainly not the eyes of a dreamer, and yet in those moments they seemed filled with brooding pictures.

"The Prince has already received me graciously," Dominey confided.

"Terniloff is the dove of peace," the Kaiser pronounced. "He carries the sprig of olive in his mouth. My statesmen and counsellors would have sent to London an ambassador with sterner qualities. I preferred not. Terniloff is the man to gull fools, because he is a fool himself. He is a fit ambassador for a country which has not the wit to arm itself on land as well as by sea, when it sees a nation, mightier, more cultured, more splendidly led than its own, creeping closer every day."

"The English appear to put their whole trust in their navy, your Majesty," Dominey observed tentatively.

The eyes of his companion flashed. His lips curled contemptuously.

"Fools!" he exclaimed. "Of what use will their navy be when my sword is once drawn, when I hold the coast towns of Calais and Boulogne, when my cannon command the Straits of Dover! The days of insular nations are passed, passed as surely as the days of England's arrogant supremacy upon the seas."

The Kaiser refilled his glass and Dominey's.

"In some months' time, Von Ragastein," he continued, "you will understand why you have been enjoined to become the friend and companion of Terniloff. You will understand your mission a little more clearly than you do now. Its exact nature waits upon developments. You can at all times trust Seaman."

Dominey bowed and remained silent. His companion continued after another brief spell of silent brooding.

"Von Ragastein," he said, "my decree of banishment against you was a just one. The morals of my people are as sacred to me as my oath to win for them a mightier empire. You first of all betrayed the wife of one of the most influential noblemen of a State allied to my own, and then, in the duel that followed, you slew him."

"It was an accident, your Majesty," Dominey pleaded. "I had no intention of even wounding the Prince."

The Kaiser frowned. All manner of excuses were loathsome to him.

"The accident should have happened the other way," he rejoined sharply. "I should have lost a valuable servant, but it was your life which was forfeit, and not his. Still, they tell me that your work in Africa was well and thoroughly done. I give you this one great chance of rehabilitation. If your work in England commends itself to me, the sentence of exile under which you suffer shall be rescinded."

"Your Majesty is too good," Dominey murmured. "The work, for its own sake, will command my every effort, even without the hope of reward."

"That," the Kaiser said, "is well spoken. It is the spirit, I believe, with which every son of my Empire regards the future. I think that they, too, more especially those who surround my person, have felt something of that divine message which has come to me. For many years I have, for the sake of my people, willed peace. Now that the time draws near when Heaven has shown me another duty, I have no fear but that every loyal German will bow his head before the lightnings which will play around my sword and share with me the iron will to wield it. Your audience is finished, Baron von Ragastein. You will take your place with the gentlemen of my suite in the retiring-room. We shall proceed within a few minutes and leave you at the Belgian frontier."

Dominey rose, bowed stiffly and backed down the carpeted way. The Kaiser was already bending once more over the map. Seaman, who was waiting outside the door of the anteroom, called him in and introduced him to several members of the suite. One, a young man with a fixed monocle, scars upon his face, and a queer, puppet-like carriage, looked at him a little strangely.

"We met some years ago in Munich, Baron," he remarked.

"I acknowledge no former meetings with any one in this country," Dominey replied stiffly. "I obey the orders of my Imperial master when I wipe from my mind every episode or reminiscence of my former days."

The young man's face cleared, and Seaman, by his side, who had knitted his brows thoughtfully, nodded understandingly.

"You are certainly a great actor, Baron," he declared. "Even your German has become a little English. Sit down and join us in a glass of beer. Luncheon will be served to us here in a few minutes. You will not be recalled to the Presence until we set you down."

Dominey bowed stiffly and took his place with the others. The train had already started. Dominey gazed thoughtfully out of the window. Seaman, who was waiting about for his audience, patted him on the arm.

"Dear friend," he said, "I sympathise with you. You sorrow because your back is now to Berlin. Still, remember this, that the day is not far off when the sentence of exile against you will be annulled. You will have expiated that crime which, believe me, although I do not venture to claim a place amongst them, none of your friends and equals have ever regarded in the same light as His Imperial Majesty."

A smiling steward, in black livery with white facings, made his appearance and served them with beer in tall glasses. The senior officer there, who had now seated himself opposite to Dominey, raised his glass and bowed.

"To the Baron von Ragastein," he said, "whose acquaintance I regret not having made before to-day. May we soon welcome him back, a brother in arms, a companion in great deeds! Hoch!"

CHAPTER XV

Sir Everard Dominey, Baronet, the latest and most popular recruit to Norfolk sporting society, stood one afternoon, some months after his return from Germany, at the corner of the long wood which stretched from the ridge of hills behind almost to the kitchen gardens of the Hall. At a reasonable distance on his left, four other guns were posted. On one side of him stood Middleton, leaning on his ash stick and listening to the approach of the beaters; on the other, Seaman, curiously out of place in his dark grey suit and bowler hat. The old keeper, whom time seemed to have cured of all his apprehensions, was softly garrulous and very happy.

"That do seem right to have a Squire Dominey at this corner," he observed, watching a high cock pheasant come crashing down over their heads. "I mind when the Squire, your father, sir, gave up this corner one day to Lord Wendermere, whom folks called one of the finest pheasant shots in England, and though they streamed over his head like starlings, he'd nowt but a few cripples to show for his morning's work."

"Come out with a bit of a twist from the left, don't they?" Dominey remarked, repeating his late exploit.

"They do that, sir," the old man assented, "and no one but a Dominey seems to have learnt the knack of dealing with them proper. That foreign Prince, so they say, is well on to his birds, but I wouldn't trust him at this corner."

The old man moved off a few paces to some higher ground, to watch the progress of the beaters through the wood. Seaman turned to his companion and there was a note of genuine admiration in his tone.

"My friend," he declared, "you are a miracle. You seem to have developed the Dominey touch even in killing pheasants."

"You must remember that I have shot higher ones in Hungary," was the easy reply.

"I am not a sportsman," Seaman admitted. "I do not understand sport. But I do know this: there is an old man who has lived on this land since the day of his birth, who has watched you shoot, reverently, and finds even the way you hold your gun familiar."

"That twist of the birds," Dominey explained, "is simply a local superstition. The wood ends on the slant, and they seem to be flying more to the left than they really are."

Seaman gazed steadfastly for a moment along the side of the wood.

"Her Grace is coming," he said. "She seems to share the Duke's dislike of me, and she is too great a lady to conceal her feelings. Just one word before I go. The Princess Eiderstrom arrives this afternoon."

Dominey frowned, then, warned by the keeper's shout, turned around and killed a hare.

"My friend," he said, with a certain note of challenge in his tone, "I am not certain that you have told me all that you know concerning the Princess's visit."

Seaman was thoughtful for a brief space of time.

"You are right," he admitted, "I have not. It is a fault which I will repair presently."

He strolled away to the next stand, where Mr. Mangan was displaying an altogether different standard of proficiency. The Duchess came up to Dominey a few minutes later.

"I told Henry I shouldn't stop with him another moment," she declared. "He has fired off about forty cartridges and wounded one hare."

"Henry is not keen," Dominey remarked, "although I think you are a little hard on him, are you not? I saw him bring down a nice cock just now. So far as regards the birds, it really does not matter. They are all going home."

The Duchess was very smartly tailored in clothes of brown heather mixture. She wore thick shoes and gaiters and a small hat. She was looking very well but a little annoyed.

"I hear," she said, "that Stephanie is coming to-day."

Dominey nodded, and seemed for a moment intent on watching the flight of a pigeon which kept tantalisingly out of range.

"She is coming down for a few days," he assented. "I am afraid that she will be bored to death."

"Where did you become so friendly with her?" his cousin asked curiously.

"The first time we ever met," Dominey replied, "was in the Carlton grill room, a few days after I landed in England. She mistook me for some one else, and we parted with the usual apologies. I met her the same night at Carlton House Terrace — she is related to the Terniloffs — and we came across one another pretty often after that, during the short time I was in town."

"Yes," the Duchess murmured meditatively. "That is another of the little surprises you seem to have all ready dished up for us. How on earth did you become so friendly with the German Ambassador?"

Dominey smiled tolerantly.

"Really," he replied, "there is not anything so very extraordinary about it, is there? Mr. Seaman, my partner in one or two mining enterprises, took me to call upon him. He is very interested in East Africa, politically and and as a sportsman. Our conversations seemed to interest him and led to a certain intimacy, — of which I may say that I am proud. I have the greatest respect and liking for the Prince."

"So have I," Caroline agreed. "I think he's charming. Henry declares that he must be either a fool or a knave."

"Henry is blinded by prejudice," Dominey declared a little impatiently. "He cannot imagine a German who feasts with any one else but the devil."

"Don't get annoyed, dear," she begged, resting her fingers for a moment upon his coat sleeve. "I admire the Prince immensely. He is absolutely the only German I ever met whom one felt instinctively to be a gentleman. — Now what are you smiling at?"

Dominey turned a perfectly serious face towards her. "Not guilty," he pleaded.

"I saw you smile."

"It was just a quaint thought. You are rather sweeping, are you not, Caroline?"

"I'm generally right," she declared.— "To return to the subject of Stephanie."

"Well?"

"Do you know whom she mistook you for in the Carlton grill room?"

"Tell me?" he answered evasively.

"She mistook you for a Baron Leopold von Ragastein," Caroline continued drily. "Von Ragastein was her lover in Hungary. He fought a duel with her husband and killed him. The Kaiser was furious and banished him to East Africa."

Dominey picked up his shooting-stick and handed his gun to Middleton. The beaters were through the wood.

"Yes, I remember now," he said. "She addressed me as Leopold."

"I still don't see why it was necessary to invite her here," his companion observed a little petulantly. "She may—call you Leopold again!"

"If she does, I shall be deaf," Dominey promised. "But seriously, she is a cousin of the Princess Terniloff, and the two women are devoted to one another. The Princess hates shooting parties, so I thought they could entertain one another."

"Bosh! Stephanie will monopolise you all the time! That's what she's coming for."

"You are not suggesting that she intends seriously to put me in the place of my double?" Dominey asked, with mock alarm.

"Oh, I shouldn't wonder! And she's an extraordinarily attractive woman. I'm full of complaints, Everard. There's that other horrible little man, Seaman. You know that the very sight of him makes Henry furious. I am quite sure that he never expected to sit down at the same table with him."

"I am really sorry about that," Dominey assured her, "but you see His Excellency takes a great interest in him on account of this Friendship League, of which Seaman is secretary, and he particularly asked to have him here."

"Well, you must admit that the situation is a little awkward for Henry," she complained. "Next to Lord Roberts, Henry is practically the leader of the National Service movement here; he hates Germany and distrusts every German he ever met, and in a small house party like this we meet the German Ambassador and a man who is working hard to lull to sleep the very sentiments which Henry is endeavouring to arouse."

"It sounds very pathetic," Dominey admitted, with a smile, "but even Henry likes Terniloff, and after all it is stimulating to meet one's opponents sometimes."

"Of course he likes Terniloff," Caroline assented, "but he hates the things he stands for. However, I'd have forgiven you everything if only Stephanie weren't coming. That woman is really beginning to irritate me. She always seems to be making mysterious references to some sentimental past in which you both are concerned, and for which there can be no foundation at all except your supposed likeness to her exiled lover. Why, you never met her until that day at the Carlton!"

"She was a complete stranger to me," Dominey asserted.

"Then all I can say is that you have been unusually rapid if you've managed to create a past in something under three months!" Caroline pronounced suspiciously. "I call her coming here a most bare-faced proceeding, especially as this is practically a bachelor establishment."

They had arrived at the next stand, and conversation was temporarily suspended. A flight of wild ducks were put out from a pool in the wood, and for a few minutes every one was busy. Middleton watched his master with unabated approval.

"You're most as good as the old Squire with them high ducks, Sir Everard," he said. "That's true very few can touch 'em when they're coming out nigh to the pheasants. They can't believe in the speed of 'em."

"Do you think Sir Everard shoots as well as he did before he went to Africa?" Caroline asked.

Middleton touched his hat and turned to Seaman, who was standing in the background.

"Better, your Grace," he answered, "as I was saying to this gentleman here, early this morning. He's cooler like and swings more level. I'd have known his touch on a gun anywhere, though."

There was a glint of admiration in Seaman's eyes. The beaters came through the wood, and the little party of guns gossiped together while the game was collected. Terniloff, his usual pallor chased away by the bracing wind and the pleasure of the sport, was affable and even loquacious. He had great estates of his own in Saxony and was explaining to the Duke his manner of shooting them. Middleton glanced at his horn-rimmed watch.

"There's another hour's good light, sir," he said. "Would you care about a partridge drive, or should we go through the home copse?"

"If I might make a suggestion," Terniloff observed diffidently, "most of the pheasants went into that gloomy-looking wood just across the marshes."

There was a moment's rather curious silence. Dominey had turned and was looking towards the wood in question, as though fascinated by its almost sinister-like blackness and density. Middleton had dropped some game he was carrying and was muttering to himself.

"We call that the Black Wood," Dominey said calmly, "and I am rather afraid that the pheasants who find their way there claim sanctuary. What do you think, Middleton?"

The old man turned his head slowly and looked at his master. Somehow or other, every scrap of colour seemed to have faded out of his bronzed face. His eyes were filled with that vague horror of the supernatural common amongst the peasant folk of various localities. His voice shook. The old fear was back again.

"You wouldn't put the beaters in there, Squire?" he faltered; "not that there's one of them would go."

"Have we stumbled up against a local superstition?" the Duke enquired.

"That's not altogether local, your Grace," Middleton replied, "as the Squire himself will tell you. I doubt whether there's a beater in all Norfolk would go through the Black Wood, if you paid him red gold for it.— Here, you lads."

He turned to the beaters, who were standing waiting for instructions a few yards away. There were a dozen of them, stalwart men for the most part, clad in rough smocks and breeches and carrying thick sticks.

"There's one of the gentlemen here," Middleton announced, addressing them, "who wants to know if you'd go through the Black Wood of Dominey for a sovereign apiece, eh? — Watch their faces, your Grace. — Now then, lads?"

There was no possibility of any mistake. The very suggestion seemed to have taken the healthy sunburn from their cheeks. They fumbled with their sticks uneasily. One of them touched his hat and spoke to Dominey.

"I'm one as 'as seen it, sir, as well as heard," he said. "I'd sooner give up my farm than go nigh the place."

Caroline suddenly passed her arm through Dominey's. There was a note of distress in her tone.

"Henry, you're an idot!" she exclaimed. "It was my fault, Everard. I'm so sorry. Just for one moment I had forgotten. I ought to have stopped Henry at once. The poor man has no memory."

Dominey's arm responded for a moment to the pressure of her fingers. Then he turned to the beaters.

"Well, no one is going to ask you to go to the Black Wood," he promised. "Get round to the back of Hunt's stubbles, and bring them into the roots and then over into the park. We will line the park fence. How is that, Middleton, eh?"

The keeper touched his hat and stepped briskly off.

"I'll just have a walk with them myself, sir," he said. "Them birds do break at Fuller's corner. I'll see if I can flank them. You'll know where to put the guns, Squire."

Dominey nodded. One and all the beaters were walking with most unaccustomed speed towards their destination. Their backs were towards the Black Wood. Terniloff came up to his host.

"Have I, by chance, been terribly tactless?" he asked.

Dominey shook his head.

"You asked a perfectly natural question, Prince," he replied. "There is no reason why you should not know the truth. Near that wood occurred the tragedy which drove me from England for so many years."

"I am deeply grieved," the Prince began ——

"It is false sentiment to avoid allusions to it," Dominey interrupted. "I was attacked there one night by a man who had some cause for offence against me. We fought, and I reached home in a somewhat alarming state. My condition terrified my wife so much that she has been an invalid ever since. But here is the point which has given birth to all these superstitions, and which made me for many years a suspected person. The man with whom I fought has never been seen since."

Terniloff was at once too fascinated by the story and puzzled by his host's manner of telling it to maintain his apologetic attitude.

"Never seen since!" he repeated.

"My own memory as to the end of our fight is uncertain," Dominey continued. "My impression is that I left my assailant unconscious upon the ground."

"Then it is his ghost, I imagine, who haunts the Black Wood?"

Dominey shook himself as one who would get rid of an unwholesome thought.

"The wood itself, Prince," he explained, as they walked along, "is a noisome place. There are quagmires even in the middle of it, where a man may sink in and be never heard of again. Every sort of vermin abounds there, every unclean insect and bird are to be found in the thickets. I suppose the character of the place has encouraged the local superstition in which every one of those men firmly believes."

"They absolutely believe the place to be haunted, then?"

"The superstition goes further," Dominey continued. "Our locals say that somewhere in the heart of the wood, where I believe that no human being for many years has dared to penetrate, there is living in the spiritual sense some sort of a demon who comes out only at night and howls underneath my windows."

"Has any one ever seen it?"

"One or two of the villagers; to the best of my belief, no one else," Dominey replied.

Terniloff seemed on the point of asking more questions, but the Duke touched him on the arm and drew him on one side, as though to call his attention to the sea fogs which were rolling up from the marshes.

"Prince," he whispered, "the details of that story are inextricably mixed up with the insanity of Lady Dominey. I am sure you understand."

The Prince, a diplomatist to his fingertips, appeared shocked, although a furtive smile still lingered upon his lips.

"I regret my *faux pas* most deeply," he murmured. "Sir Everard," he went on, "you promised to tell me of some of your days with a shotgun in South Africa. Isn't there a bird there which corresponds with your partridges?"

Dominey smiled.

"If you can kill the partridges which Middleton is going to send over in the next ten minutes," he said, "you could shoot anything of the sort that comes along in East Africa, with a catapult. If you will stand just a few paces there to the left, Henry, Terniloff by the gate, Stillwell up by the left-hand corner, Mangan next, Eddy next, and I shall be just beyond towards the oak clump. Will you walk with me, Caroline?"

His cousin took his arm as they walked off and pressed it.

"Everard, I congratulate you," she said. "You have conquered your nerve absolutely. You did a simple and a fine thing to tell the whole story. Why, you were almost matter-of-fact. I could even have imagined you were telling it about some one else."

Her host smiled enigmatically.

"Curious that it should have struck you like that," he remarked. 'Do you know, when I was telling it I had the same feeling.— Do you mind crouching down a little now? I am going to blow the whistle."

CHAPTER XVI

Even in the great dining-room of Dominey Hall, the mahogany table which was its great glory was stretched that evening to its extreme capacity. Besides the house party, which included the Right Honourable Gerald Watson, a recently appointed Cabinet Minister, there were several guests from the neighbourhood — the Lord Lieutenant of the County and other notabilities. Caroline, with the Lord Lieutenant on one side of her and Terniloff on the other, played the part of hostess adequately but without enthusiasm. Her eyes seldom left for long the other end of the table, where Stephanie, at Dominey's left hand, with her crown of exquisitely coiffured red-gold hair, her marvellous jewellery, her languorous grace of manner, seemed more like one of the beauties of an ancient Venetian Court than a modern Hungarian Princess gowned in the Rue de la Paix. Conversation remained chiefly local and concerned the day's sport and kindred topics. It was not until towards the close of the meal that the Duke succeeded in launching his favourite bubble.

"I trust, Everard," he said, raising his voice a little as he turned towards his host, "that you make a point of inculcating the principles of National Service into your tenantry here."

Dominey's reply was a little dubious.

"I am afraid they do not take to the idea very kindly in this part of the world," he confessed. "Purely agricultural districts are always a little difficult."

"It is your duty as a landowner," the Duke insisted, "to alter their point of view. There is not the slightest doubt," he added, looking belligerently over the top of his *pince nez* at Seaman, who was seated at the opposite side of the table, "that before long we shall find ourselves — and in a shocking state of unpreparedness, mind you — at war with Germany."

Lady Maddeley, the wife of the Lord Lieutenant, who sat at his side, seemed a little startled. She was probably one of the only people present who was not aware of the Duke's foible.

"Do you really think so?" she asked. "The Germans seem such civilised people, so peaceful and domestic in their home life, and that sort of thing."

The Duke groaned. He glanced down the table to be sure that Prince Terniloff was out of hearing.

"My dear Lady Maddeley," he declared, "Germany is not governed like England. When the war comes, the people will have had nothing to do with it. A great many of them will be just as surprised as you will be, but they will fight all the same."

Seaman, who had kept silence during the last few moments with great difficulty, now took up the Duke's challenge.

"Permit me to assure you, madam," he said, bowing across the table, "that the war with Germany of which the Duke is so afraid will never come. I speak with some amount of knowledge because I am a German by birth, although naturalised in this country. I have as many and as dear friends in Berlin as in London, and with the exception of my recent absence in Africa, where I had the pleasure to meet our host, I spent a great part of my time going back and forth between the two capitals. I have also the honour to be the secretary of a society for the promotion of a better understanding between the citizens of Germany and England."

"Rubbish!" the Duke exclaimed. "The Germans don't want a better understanding. They only want to fool us into believing that they do."

Seaman looked a little pained. He stuck to his guns, however.

"His Grace and I," he observed, "are old opponents on this subject."

"We are indeed," the Duke agreed. "You may be an honest man, Mr. Seaman, but you are a very ignorant one upon this particular topic."

"You are probably both right in your way," Dominey intervened, very much in the manner of a well-bred host making his usual effort to smooth over two widely divergent points of view. "There is no doubt a war party in Germany and a peace party, statesmen who place economic progress first, and others who are tainted with a purely military lust for conquest. In this country it is very hard for us to strike a balance between the two."

Seaman beamed his thanks upon his host.

"I have friends," he said impressively, "in the very highest circles of Germany, who are continually encouraging my work here, and I have received the benediction of the Kaiser himself upon my efforts to promote a better feeling in this country. And if you will forgive my saying so, Duke, it is such ill-advised and ill-founded statements as you are constantly making about my country which is the only bar to a better understanding between us."

"I have my views," the Duke snapped, "and they have become convictions. I shall continue to express them at all times and with all the eloquence at my command."

The Ambassador, to whom portions of this conversation had now become audible, leaned a little forward in his place.

"Let me speak first as a private individual," he begged, "and express my well-studied opinion that war between our two countries would be simply race suicide, an indescribable and an abominable crime. Then I will remember what I represent over here, and I will venture to add in my ambassadorial capacity that I come with an absolute and heartfelt mandate of peace. My task over here is to secure and ensure it."

Caroline flashed a warning glance at her husband.

"How nice of you to be so frank, Prince!" she said. "The Duke sometimes forgets, in the pursuit of his hobby, that a private dinner table is not a platform. I insist upon it that we discuss something of more genuine interest."

"There isn't a more vital subject in the world," the Duke declared, resigning himself, however, to silence.

"We will speak," the Ambassador suggested, "of the way in which our host brought down those tall pheasants."

"You will tell me, perhaps," Seaman suggested to the lady on his right, "how you English women have been able to secure for yourselves so much more liberty than our German wives enjoy?"

"Later on," Stephanie whispered to her host, with a little tremble in her voice, "I have a surprise for you."

After dinner, Dominey's guests passed naturally enough to the relaxations which each preferred. There were two bridge tables, Terniloff and the Cabinet Minister played billiards, and Seaman, with a touch which amazed every one, drew strange music from the yellow keys of the old-fashioned grand piano in the drawing-room. Stephanie and her host made a slow progress through the hall and picture gallery. For some time their conversation was engaged solely with the objects to which Dominey drew his companion's attention. When they had passed out of possible hearing, however, of any of the other guests, Stephanie's fingers tightened upon her companion's arm.

"I wish to speak to you alone," she said, "without the possibility of any one overhearing."

Dominey hesitated and looked behind.

"Your guests are well occupied," she continued a little impatiently, "and in any case I am one of them. I claim your attention."

Dominey threw open the door of the library and turned on a couple of the electric lights. She made her way to the great open fireplace, on which a log was burning, looked down into the shadows of the room and back again into her host's face.

"For one moment," she begged, "turn on all the lights. I wish to be sure that we are alone."

Dominey did as he was bidden. The furthermost corners of the room, with its many wings of book-filled shelves, were illuminated. She nodded.

"Now turn them all out again except this one," she directed, "and wheel me up an easy-chair.—No, I choose this settee. Please seat yourself by my side."

"Is this going to be serious?" he asked, with some slight disquietude.

"Serious but wonderful," she murmured, lifting her eyes to his. "Will you please listen to me, Leopold?"

She was half curled up in a corner of the settee, her head resting slightly upon her long fingers, her brown eyes steadily fixed upon her companion. There was an atmosphere about her of serious yet of tender things. Dominey's face seemed to fall into more rigid lines as he realised the appeal of her eyes.

"Leopold," she began, "I left this country a few weeks ago, feeling that you were a brute, determined never to see you again, half inclined to expose you before I went as an impostor and a charlatan. Germany means little to me, and a patriotism which took no account of human obligations left me absolutely unresponsive. I meant to go home and never to return to London. My heart was bruised, and I was very unhappy."

She paused, but her companion made no sign. She paused for so long, however, that speech became necessary.

"You are speaking, Princess," he said calmly, "to one who is not present. My name is no longer Leopold."

She laughed at him with a curious mixture of tenderness and bitterness.

"My friend," she continued, "I am terrified to think, besides your name, how much of humanity you have lost in your new identity. To proceed, it suited my convenience to remain for a few days in Berlin, and I was therefore compelled to present myself at Potsdam. There I received a great surprise. Wilhelm spoke to me of you, and though, alas! my heart is still bruised, he helped me to understand."

"Is this wise?" he asked a little desperately.

She ignored his words.

"I was taken back into favour at Court," she went on. "For that I owe to you my thanks. Wilhelm was much impressed by your recent visit to him, and by the way in which you have established yourself here. He spoke also with warm commendation of your labours in Africa, which he seemed to appreciate all the more as you were sent there an exile. He asked me, Leopold," she added, dropping her voice a little, "if my feeling towards you remained unchanged."

Dominey's face remained unrelaxed. Persistently he refused the challenge of her eyes.

"I told him the truth," she proceeded. "I told him how it all began, and how it must last with me—to the end. We spoke even of the duel. I told him what both your seconds had explained to me, — that turn of the wrist, Conrad's wild lunge, how he literally threw himself upon the point of your sword. Wilhelm understands and forgives, and he has sent you this letter."

She drew a small grey envelope from her pocket. On the seal were the Imperial Hohenzollern arms. She passed it to him.

"Leopold," she whispered, "please read that."

He shook his head, although he accepted the letter with reluctant fingers.

"Leopold again," he muttered. "It is not for me."

"Read the superscription," she directed.

He obeyed her. It was addressed in a strange, straggling handwriting to *Sir Everard Dominey, Baronet.* He broke the seal unwillingly and drew out the letter. It was dated barely a fortnight back. There was neither beginning nor ending; just a couple of sentences scrawled across the thick notepaper:

> "It is my will that you offer your hand in marriage to the Princess Stephanie of Eiderstrom. Your union shall be blessed by the Church and approved by my Court.
>
> WILHELM."

Dominey sat as a man enthralled with silence. She watched him.

"Not on your knees yet?" she asked, with faint but somewhat resentful irony. "Can it be, Leopold, that you have lost your love for me? You have changed so much and in so many ways. Has the love gone?"

Even to himself his voice sounded harsh and unnatural, his words instinct with the graceless cruelty of a clown.

"This is not practical," he declared. "Think! I am as I have been addressed here, and as I must remain yet for months to come — Everard Dominey, an Englishman and the owner of this house — the husband of Lady Dominey."

"Where is your reputed wife?" Stephanie demanded, frowning.

"In the nursing home where she has been for the last few months," he replied. "She has already practically recovered. She cannot remain there much longer."

"You must insist upon it that she does."

"I ask you to consider the suspicions which would be excited by such a course," Dominey pleaded earnestly, "and further, can you explain to me in what way I, having already, according to the belief of everybody, another wife living, can take advantage of this mandate?"

She looked at him wonderingly.

"You make difficulties? You sit there like the cold Englishman whose place you are taking, you whose tears have fallen before now upon my hand, whose lips——"

"You speak of one who is dead," Dominey interrupted, "dead until the coming of great events may bring him to life again. Until that time your lover must be dumb."

Then her anger blazed out. She spoke incoherently, passionately, dragged his face down to hers and clenched her fist the next moment as though she would have struck it. She broke down with a storm of tears.

"Not so hard—not so hard, Leopold!" she implored. "Oh! yours is a great task, and you must carry it through to the end, but we have his permission—there can be found a way—we could be married secretly. At least your lips—your arms! My heart is starved, Leopold."

He rose to his feet. Her arms were still twined about his neck, her lips hungry for his kisses, her eyes shining up into his.

"Have pity on me, Stephanie," he begged. "Until our time has come there is dishonour even in a single kiss. Wait for the day, the day you know of."

She unwound her arms and shivered slightly. Her hurt eyes regarded him wonderingly.

"Leopold," she faltered, "what has changed you like this? What has dried up all the passion in you? You are a different man. Let me look at you."

She caught him by the shoulders, dragged him underneath the electric globe, and stood there gazing into his face. The great log upon the hearth was spluttering and fizzing. Through the closed door came the faint wave of conversation and laughter from outside. Her breathing was uneven, her eyes were seeking to rend the mask from his face.

"Can you have learnt to care for any one else?" she muttered. "There were no women in Africa. This Rosamund Dominey, your reputed wife—they tell me that she is beautiful, that you have been kindness itself to her, that her health has improved since your coming, that she adores you. You wouldn't dare——"

"No," he interrupted, "I should not dare."

"Then what are you looking at?" she demanded. "Tell me that?"

His eyes were following the shadowed picture which had passed out of the room. He saw once more the slight, girlish form, the love-seeking light in those pleading dark eyes, the tremulous lips, the whole sweet appeal for safety from a frightened child to him, the strong man. He felt the clinging touch of those soft fingers laid upon his, the sweetness of those marvellously awakened emotions, so cruelly and drearily stifled through a cycle of years. The woman's passion by his side seemed suddenly tawdry and unreal, the seeking of her lips for his something horrible. His back was towards the door, and it was her cry of angry dismay which first apprised him of a welcome intruder. He swung around to find Seaman standing upon the threshold—Seaman to him a very angel of deliverance.

"I am indeed sorry to intrude, Sir Everard," the newcomer declared, with a shade of genuine concern on his round, good-humoured face. "Something has happened which I thought you ought to know at once. Can you spare me a moment?"

The Princess swept past them without a word of farewell or a backward glance. She had the carriage and the air of an insulted queen. A shade of deeper trouble came into Seaman's face as he stepped respectfully on one side.

"What is it that has happened?" Dominey demanded.

"Lady Dominey has returned," was the quiet reply.

CHAPTER XVII

IT SEEMED to Dominey that he had never seen anything more pathetic than that eager glance, half of hope, half of apprehension, flashed upon him from the strange, tired eyes of the woman who was standing before the log fire in a little recess of the main hall. By her side stood a pleasant, friendly looking person in the uniform of a nurse; a yard or two behind, a maid carrying a jewel case. Rosamund, who had thrown back her veil, had been standing with her foot upon the fender. Her whole expression changed as Dominey came hastily towards her with outstretched hands.

"My dear child," he exclaimed, "welcome home!"

"Welcome?" she repeated, with a little glad catch in her throat. "You mean it?"

With a self-control of which he gave no sign, he touched the lips which were raised so eagerly to his as tenderly and reverently as though this were some strange child committed to his care.

"Of course I mean it," he answered heartily. "But what possessed you to come without giving us notice? How was this, nurse?"

"Her ladyship has had no sleep for two nights," the latter replied. "She has been so much better that we dreaded the thought of a relapse, so Mrs. Coulson, our matron, thought it best to let her have her own way about coming. Instead of telegraphing to you, unfortunately, we telegraphed to Doctor Harrison, and I believe he is away."

"Is it very wrong of me?" Rosamund asked, clinging to Dominey's arm. "I had a sudden feeling that I must get back here. I wanted to see you again. Every one has been so sweet and kind at Falmouth, especially Nurse Alice here, but they weren't quite the same thing. You are not angry? These people who are staying here will not mind?"

"Of course not," he assured her cheerfully. "They will be your guests. To-morrow you must make friends with them all."

"There was a very beautiful woman," she said timidly, "with red hair, who passed by just now. She looked very angry. That was not because I have come?"

"Why should it be?" he answered. "You have a right here—a better right than any one."

She drew a long sigh of contentment.

"Oh, but this is wonderful!" she cried. "And you, dear—I shall call you Everard, mayn't I?—you look just as I hoped you might. Will you take me upstairs, please? Nurse, you can follow us."

She leaned heavily on his arm and even loitered on the way, but her steps grew lighter as they approached her own apartment. Finally, as they reached the corridor, she broke away from him and tripped on with the gaiety almost of a child to the door of her room. Then came a little cry of disappointment as she flung open the door. Several maids were there, busy with a refractory fire and removing the covers from the furniture, but the room was half full of smoke and entirely unprepared.

"Oh, how miserable!" she exclaimed. "Everard, what shall I do?"

He threw open the door of his own apartment. A bright fire was burning in the grate, the room was warm and comfortable. She threw herself with a little cry of delight into the huge Chesterfield drawn up to the edge of the hearthrug.

"I can stay here, Everard, can't I, until you come up to bed?" she pleaded. "And then you can sit and talk to me, and tell me who is here and all about the people. You have no idea how much better I am. All my music has come back to me, and they say that I play bridge ever so well. I shall love to help you entertain."

The maid was slowly unfastening her mistress's boots. Rosamund held up her foot for him to feel.

"See how cold I am!" she complained. "Please rub it. I am going to have some supper up here with nurse. Will one of you maids please go down and see about it? What a lot of nice new things you have, Everard!" she added, looking around. "And that picture of me from the drawing-room, on the table!" she cried, her eyes suddenly soft with joy. "You dear thing! What made you bring that up?"

"I wanted to have it here," he told her.

"I'm not so nice as that now," she sighed, a little wistfully.

"Do not believe it," he answered. "You have not changed in the least. You will be better-looking still when you have been here for a few months."

She looked at him almost shyly—tenderly, yet still with that gleam of aloofness in her eyes.

"I think," she murmured, "I shall be just what you want me to be. I think you could make me just what you want. Be very kind to me, please," she begged, stretching her arms out to him. "I suppose it is because I have been ill so long, but I feel so helpless, and I love your strength and I want you to take care of me. Your own hands are quite cold," she added anxiously. "You look pale, too. You're not ill, Everard?"

"I am very well," he assured her, struggling to keep his voice steady. "Forgive me now, won't you, if I hurry away. There are guests here—rather important guests. To-morrow you must come and see them all."

"And help you?"

"And help me."

Dominey made his escape and went reeling down the corridor. At the top of the great quadrangular landing he stopped and stood with half-closed eyes for several moments. From downstairs he could hear the sound of pleasantly raised voices, the music of a piano in the distance, the click of billiard balls. He waited until he had regained his self-possession. Then, as he was on the point of descending, he saw Seaman mounting the stairs. At a gesture he waited for him, waited until he came, and, taking him by the arm, led him to a great settee in a dark corner. Seaman had lost his usual blitheness. The good-humoured smile played no longer about his lips.

"Where is Lady Dominey?" he asked.

"In my room, waiting until her own is prepared."

Seaman's manner was unusually grave.

"My friend," he said, "you know very well that when we walk in the great paths of life I am unscrupulous. In those other hours, alas! I have a weakness.—I love women."

"Well?" Dominey muttered.

"I will admit," the other continued, "that you are placed in a delicate and trying position. Lady Dominey seems disposed to offer to you the affection which, notwithstanding their troubles together, she doubtless felt for her husband. I risk your anger, my friend, but I warn you to be very careful how you encourage her."

A light flashed in Dominey's eyes. For the moment angry words seemed to tremble upon his lips. Seaman's manner, however, was very gentle. He courted no offence.

"If you were to take advantage of your position with—with any other, I would shrug my shoulders and stand on one side, but this mad Englishman's wife, or rather his widow, has been mentally ill. She is still weak-minded, just as she is tender-hearted. I watched her as she passed through the hall with you just now. She turns to you for love as a flower to the sun after a long spell of cold, wet weather. Von Ragastein, you are a man of honour. You must find means to deal with this situation, however difficult it may become."

Dominey had recovered from his first wave of weakness. His companion's words excited no sentiment of anger. He was conscious even of regarding him with a greater feeling of kindness than ever before.

"My friend," he said, "you have shown me that you are conscious of one dilemma in which I find myself placed, and which I must confess is exercising me to the utmost. Let me now advise you of another. The Princess Eiderstrom has brought me an autograph letter from the Kaiser, commanding me to marry her."

"The situation," Seaman declared grimly, "but for its serious side, would provide all the elements for a Palais Royal farce. For the present, however, you have duties below. I have said the words which were thumping against the walls of my heart."

Their descent was opportune. Some of the local guests were preparing to make their departure, and Dominey was in time to receive their adieux. They all left messages for Lady Dominey, spoke of a speedy visit to her, and expressed themselves as delighted to hear of her return and recovery. As the last car rolled away, Caroline took her host's arm and led him to a chimney seat by the huge log fire in the inner hall.

"My dear Everard," she said, "you really are a very terrible person."

"Exactly why?" he demanded.

"Your devotion to my sex," she continued, "is flattering but far too catholic. Your return to England appears to have done what we understood to be impossible—restored your wife's reason. A fiery-headed Hungarian Princess has pursued you down here, and has now gone to her room in a tantrum because you left her side for a few minutes to welcome your wife. And there remains our own sentimental little flirtation, a broken and, alas, a discarded thing! There is no doubt whatever, Everard, that you are a very bad lot."

"You are distressing me terribly," Dominey confessed, "but all the same, after a somewhat agitated evening I must admit that I find it pleasant to talk with some one who is not wielding the lightnings. May I have a whisky and soda?"

"Bring me one, too, please," Caroline begged. "I fear that it will seriously impair the note which I had intended to strike in our conversation, but I am thirsty. And a handful of those Turkish cigarettes, too. You can devote yourself to me with a perfectly clear conscience. Your most distinguished guest has found a task after his own heart. He has got Henry in a corner of the billiard-room and is trying to convince him of what I am sure the dear man really believes himself—that Germany's intentions towards England are of a particularly dovelike nature. Your Right Honourable guest has gone to bed, and Eddy Pelham is playing billiards with Mr. Mangan. Every one is happy. You can devote yourself to soothing my wounded vanity, to say nothing of my broken heart."

"Always gibing at me," Dominey grumbled.

"Not always," she answered quietly, raising her eyes for a moment. "There was a time, Everard, before that terrible tragedy—the last time you stayed at Dunratter—when I didn't gibe."

"When, on the contrary, you were sweetness itself," he reflected.

She sighed reminiscently.

"That was a wonderful month," she murmured. "I think it was then for the first time that I saw traces of something in you which I suppose accounts for your being what you are to-day."

"You think that I have changed, then?"

She looked him in the eyes.

"I sometimes find it difficult to believe," she admitted, "that you are the same man."

He turned away to reach for his whisky and soda.

"As a matter of curiosity," he asked, "why?"

"To begin with, then," she commented, "you have become almost a precisian in your speech. You used to be rather slangy at times."

"What else?"

"You used always to clip your final g's."

"Shocking habit," he murmured. "I cured myself of that by reading aloud in the bush.—Go on, please?"

"You carry yourself so much more stiffly. Sometimes you have the air of being surprised that you are not in uniform."

"Trifles, all these things," he declared. "Now for something serious?"

"The serious things are pretty good," she admitted. "You used to drink whiskys and sodas at all hours of the day, and quite as much wine as was good for you at dinner time. Now, although you are a wonderful host, you scarcely take anything yourself."

"You should see me at the port," he told her, "when you ladies are well out of the way! Some more of the good, please?"

"All your best qualities seem to have come to the surface," she went on, "and I think that the way you have come back and faced it all is simply wonderful. Tell me, if that man's body should be discovered after all these years, would you be charged with manslaughter?"

He shook his head. "I do not think so, Caroline."

"Everard."

"Well?"

"Did you kill Roger Unthank?"

A portion of the burning log fell on to the hearth. Then there was silence. They heard the click of the billiard balls in the adjoining room. Dominey leaned forward and with a pair of small tongs replaced the burning wood upon the fire. Suddenly he felt his hands clasped by his companion's.

"Everard dear," she said, "I am so sorry. You came to me a little tired to-night, didn't you? I think that you needed sympathy, and here I am asking you once more that horrible question. Forget it, please. Talk to me like your old dear self. Tell me about Rosamund's return? Is she really recovered, do you think?"

"I saw her only for a few minutes," Dominey replied, "but she seemed to me absolutely better. I must say that the weekly reports I have received from the nursing home quite prepared me for a great improvement. She is very frail, and her eyes still have that restless look, but she talks quite coherently."

"What about that horrible woman?"

"I have pensioned Mrs. Unthank. To my surprise I hear that she is still living in the village."

"And your ghost?"

"Not a single howl all the time that Rosamund has been away."

"There is one thing more," Caroline began hesitatingly.

That one thing lacked forever the clothing of words. There came a curious, almost dramatic interruption. Through the silence of the hall there pealed the summons of the great bell which hung over the front door. Dominey glanced at the clock in amazement.

"Midnight!" he exclaimed. "Who on earth can be coming here at this time of night!"

Instinctively they both rose to their feet. A manservant had turned the great key, drawn the bolts, and opened the door with difficulty. Little flakes of snow and a gust of icy wind swept into the hall, and following them the figure of a man, white from head to foot, his hair tossed with the wind, almost unrecognisable after his struggle.

"Why, Doctor Harrison!" Dominey cried, taking a quick step forward. "What brings you here at this time of night!"

The doctor leaned upon his stick for a moment. He was out of breath, and the melting snow was pouring from his clothes on to the oak floor. They relieved him of his coat and dragged him towards the fire.

"I must apologise for disturbing you at such an hour," he said, as he took the tumbler which Dominey pressed into his hand. "I have only just received Lady Dominey's telegram. I had to see you — at once."

CHAPTER XVIII

THE doctor, with his usual bluntness, did not hesitate to make it known that this unusual visit was of a private nature. Caroline promptly withdrew, and the two men were left alone in the great hall. The lights in the billiard-room and drawing-room were extinguished. Every one in the house except a few servants had retired.

"Sir Everard," the doctor began, "this return of Lady Dominey's has taken me altogether by surprise. I had intended to-morrow morning to discuss the situation with you."

"I am most anxious to hear your report," Dominey said.

"My report is good," was the confident answer. "Although I would not have allowed her to have left the nursing home so suddenly had I known, there was nothing to keep her there. Lady Dominey, except for one hallucination, is in perfect health, mentally and physically."

"And this one hallucination?"

"That you are not her husband."

Dominey was silent for a moment. Then he laughed a little unnaturally.

"Can a person be perfectly sane," he asked, "and yet be subject to an hallucination which must make the whole of her surroundings seem unreal?"

"Lady Dominey is perfectly sane," the doctor answered bluntly, "and as for that hallucination, it is up to you to dispel it."

"Perhaps you can give me some advice?" Dominey suggested.

"I can, and I am going to be perfectly frank with you," the doctor replied. "To begin with then, there are certain obvious changes in you which might well minister to Lady Dominey's hallucination. For instance, you have been in England now some eight months, during which time you have revealed an entirely new personality. You seem to have got rid of every one of your bad habits, you drink moderately, as a gentleman should, you have subdued your violent temper, and you have collected around you, where your personality could be the only inducement, friends of distinction and interest. This is not at all what one expected from the Everard Dominey who scuttled out of England a dozen years ago."

"You are excusing my wife," Dominey remarked.

"She needs no excuses," was the brusque reply. "She has been a long-enduring and faithful woman, suffering from a cruel illness, brought on, to take the kindest view of it, through your clumsiness and lack of discretion. Like all good women, forgiveness is second nature to her. It has now become her wish to take her proper place in life."

"But if her hallucination continues," Dominey asked, "if she seriously doubts that I am indeed her husband, how can she do that?"

"That is the problem you and I have to face," the doctor said sternly. "The fact that your wife has been willing to return here to you, whilst still subject to that hallucination, is a view of the matter which I can neither discuss nor understand. I am here to-night, though, to lay a charge upon you. You have to remember that your wife needs still one step towards a perfect recovery, and until that step has been surmounted you have a very difficult but imperative task."

Dominey set his teeth for a moment. He felt the doctor's keen grey eyes glowering from under his shaggy eyebrows as he leaned forward, his hands upon his knees.

"You mean," Dominey suggested quietly, "that until that hallucination has passed we must remain upon the same terms as we have done since my arrival home."

"You've got it," the doctor assented. "It's a tangled-up position, but we've got to deal with it — or rather you have. I can assure you," he went on, "that all her other delusions have gone. She speaks of the ghost of Roger Unthank, of the cries at night, of his mysterious death, as parts of a painful past. She is quite conscious of her several attempts upon your life and bitterly regrets them. Now we come to the real danger. She appears to be possessed of a passionate devotion towards you, whilst still believing that you are not her husband."

Dominey pushed his chair back from the fire as though he felt the heat. His eyes seemed glued upon the doctor's.

"I do not pretend," the latter continued gravely, "to account for that, but it is my duty to warn you, Sir Everard, that that devotion may lead her to great lengths. Lady Dominey is naturally of an exceedingly affectionate disposition, and this return to a stronger condition of physical health and a fuller share of human feelings has probably reawakened all those tendencies which her growing fondness for you and your position as her reputed husband make perfectly natural. I warn you, Sir Everard, that you may find your position an exceedingly difficult one, but, difficult though it may be, there is a plain duty before you. Keep and encourage your wife's affection if you can, but let it be a charge upon you that whilst the hallucination remains that affection must never pass certain bounds. Lady Dominey is a good and sweet woman. If she woke up one morning with that hallucination still in her mind, and any sense of guilt on her conscience, all our labours for these last months might well be wasted, and she herself might very possibly end her days in a madhouse."

"Doctor," Dominey said firmly. "I appreciate every word you say. You can rely upon me."

The doctor looked at him.

"I believe I can," he admitted, with a sigh of relief. "I am glad of it."

"There is just one more phase of the position," Dominey went on, after a pause. "Supposing this hallucination of hers should pass? Supposing she should suddenly become convinced that I am her husband?"

"In that case," the doctor replied earnestly, "the position would be exactly reversed, and it would be just as important for you not to check the affection which she might offer to you as it would be in the other case for you to accept it. The moment she realises, with her present predispositions, that you really are her lawful husband, that moment will be the beginning of a new life for her."

Somehow they both seemed to feel that the last words had been spoken. After a brief pause, the doctor helped himself to a farewell drink, filled his pipe and stood up. The car which Dominey had ordered from the garage was already standing at the door. It was curious how both of them seemed disinclined to refer again even indirectly to the subject which they had been discussing.

"Very good of you to send me back," the doctor said gruffly. "I started out all right, but it was a drear walk across the marshes."

"I am very grateful to you for coming," Dominey replied, with obvious sincerity. "You will come and have a look at the patient in a day or two?"

"I'll stroll across as soon as you've got rid of some of this houseful," the doctor promised. "Good night!"

The two men parted, and curiously enough Dominey was conscious that with those few awkward words of farewell some part of the latent antagonism between them had been buried. Left to himself, he wandered for some moments up and down the great, dimly lit hall. A strange restlessness seemed to have fastened itself upon him. He stood for a time by the dying fire, watching the grey ashes, stirred uneasily by the wind which howled down the chimney. Then he strolled to a different part of the hall, and one by one he turned on, by means of the electric switches, the newly installed lights which hung above the sombre oil pictures upon the wall. He looked into the faces of some of these dead Domineys, trying to recall what he had heard of their history, and dwelling longest upon a gallant of the Stuart epoch, whose misdeeds had supplied material for every intimate chronicler of those days. When at last the sight of a sleepy manservant hovering in the background forced his steps upstairs, he still lingered for a few moments in the corridor and turned the handle of his bedroom door with almost reluctant fingers. His heart gave a great jump as he realised that there was some one there. He stood for a moment upon the threshold, then laughed shortly to himself at his foolish imagining. It was his servant who was patiently awaiting his arrival.

"You can go to bed, Dickens," he directed. "I shall not want you again to-night. We shoot in the morning."

The man silently took his leave, and Dominey commenced his

preparations for bed. He was in no humour for sleep, however, and, still attired in his shirt and trousers, he wrapped a dressing-gown around him, drew a reading lamp to his side, and threw himself into an easy-chair, a book in his hand. It was some time before he realised that the volume was upside down, and even when he had righted it, the words he saw had no meaning for him. All the time a queer procession of women's faces was passing before his eyes — Caroline, with her half-flirtatious, wholly sentimental *bon camaraderie;* Stephanie, with her voluptuous figure and passion-lit eyes; and then, blotting the others utterly out of his thoughts and memory, Rosamund, with all the sweetness of life shining out of her eager face. He saw her as she had come to him last, with that little unspoken cry upon her tremulous lips, and the haunting appeal in her soft eyes. All other memories faded away. They were as though they had never been. Those dreary years of exile in Africa, the day by day tension of his precarious life, were absolutely forgotten. His heart was calling all the time for an unknown boon. He felt himself immeshed in a world of cobwebs, of weakness more potent than all his boasted strength. Then he suddenly felt that the madness which he had begun to fear had really come. It was the thing for which he longed yet dreaded most — the faint click, the soft withdrawal of the panel, actually pushed back by a pair of white hands. Rosamund herself was there. Her eyes shone at him, mystically, wonderfully. Her lips were parted in a delightful smile, a smile in which there was a spice of girlish mischief. She turned for a moment to close the panel. Then she came towards him with her finger upraised.

"I cannot sleep," she said softly. "Do you mind my coming for a few minutes?"

"Of course not," he answered. "Come and sit down."

She curled up in his easy-chair.

"Just for a moment," she murmured contentedly. "Give me your hands, dear. But how cold! You must come nearer to the fire yourself."

He sat on the arm of her chair, and she stroked his head with her hands.

"You were not afraid, then," she asked, "when you saw me come through the panel?"

"I should never be afraid of any harm that you might bring me, dear," he assured her.

"Because all that foolishness is really gone," she continued eagerly. "I know that whatever happened to poor Roger, it was not you who killed him. Even if I heard his ghost calling again to-night, I should have no fear. I can't think why I ever wanted to hurt you, Everard. I am sure that I always loved you."

His arm went very softly around her. She responded to his embrace without hesitation. Her cheek rested upon his shoulder, he felt the warmth of her arm through her white, fur-lined dressing-gown.

"Why do you doubt any longer then," he asked hoarsely, "that I am your husband?"

She sighed.

"Ah, but I know you are not," she answered. "Is it wrong of me to feel what I do for you, I wonder? You are so like yet so unlike him. He is dead. He died in Africa. Isn't it strange that I should know it? But I do!"

"But who am I then?" he whispered.

She looked at him pitifully.

"I do not know," she confessed, "but you are kind to me, and when I feel you are near I am happy. It is because I wanted to see you that I would not stay any longer at the nursing home. That must mean that I am very fond of you."

"You are not afraid," he asked "to be here alone with me?"

She put her other arm around his neck and drew his face down.

"I am not afraid," she assured him. "I am happy.—But, dear, what is the matter? A moment ago you were cold. Now your head is wet, your hands are burning. Are you not happy because I am here?"

Her lips were seeking his. His own touched them for a moment. Then he kissed her on both cheeks. She made a little grimace.

"I am afraid," she said, "that you are not really fond of me."

"Can't you believe," he asked hoarsely, "that I am really

Everard — your husband? Look at me. Can't you feel that you have loved me before?"

She shook her head a little sadly.

"No, you are not Everard," she sighed; "but," she added, her eyes lighting up, "you bring me love and happiness and life, and —— "

A few seconds before, Dominey felt from his soul that he would have welcomed an earthquake, a thunderbolt, the crumbling of the floor beneath his feet to have been spared the torture of her sweet importunities. Yet nothing so horrible as this interruption which really came could ever have presented itself before his mind. Half in his arms, with her head thrown back, listening — he, too, horrified, convulsed for a moment even with real physical fear — they heard the silence of the night broken by that one awful cry, the cry of a man's soul in torment, imprisoned in the jaws of a beast. They listened to it together until its echoes died away. Then what was, perhaps, the most astonishing thing of all, she nodded her head slowly, unperturbed, unterrified.

"You see," she said, "I must go back. He will not let me stay here. He must think that you are Everard. It is only I who know that you are not."

She slipped from the chair, kissed him, and, walking quite firmly across the floor, touched the spring and passed through the panel. Even then she turned around and waved a little good-bye to him. There was no sign of fear in her face; only a little dumb disappointment. The panel glided to and shut out the vision of her. Dominey held his head like a man who fears madness.

CHAPTER XIX

DAWN the next morning was heralded by only a thin line of red parting the masses of black-grey snow clouds which still hung low down in the east. The wind had dropped, and there was something ghostly about the still twilight as Dominey issued from the back regions and made his way through the untrodden snow round to the side of the house underneath Rosamund's window. A little exclamation broke from his lips as he stood there. From the terraced walk, down the steps, and straight across the park to the corner of the Black Wood, were fresh tracks. The cry had been no fantasy. Somebody or something had passed from the Black Wood and back again to this spot in the night.

Dominey, curiously excited by his discovery, examined the footmarks eagerly, then followed them to the corner of the wood. Here and there they puzzled him. They were neither like human footsteps or the track of any known animal. At the edge of the wood they seemed to vanish into the heart of a great mass of brambles, from which here and there the snow had been shaken off. There was no sign of any pathway; if ever there had been one, neglect of years had obliterated it. Bracken, brambles, shrubs and bushes had grown up and degenerated, only to be succeeded by a ranker and more dense form of undergrowth. Many of the trees, although they were still plentiful, had been blown down and left to rot on the ground. The place was silent except for the slow drip of falling snow from the drooping leaves. He took one more cautious step forward and found himself slowly sinking. Black mud was oozing up through the snow where he had set his feet. He was just able to scramble back. Picking his way with great caution, he commenced a leisurely perambulation of the whole of the outside of the wood.

Heggs, the junior keeper, an hour or so later, went over the gun rack once more, tapped the empty cases, and turned towards Middleton, who was sitting in a chair before the fire, smoking his pipe.

"I can't find master's number two gun, Mr. Middleton," he announced. "That's missing."

"Look again, lad," the old keeper directed, removing the pipe from his mouth. "The master was shooting with it yesterday. Look amongst those loose 'uns at the far end of the rack. It must be somewhere there."

"Well, that it isn't," the young man replied obstinately.

The door of the room was suddenly opened, and Dominey entered with the missing gun under his arm. Middleton rose to his feet at once and laid down his pipe. Surprise kept him temporarily silent.

"I want you to come this way with me for a moment," his master ordered.

The keeper took up his hat and stick and followed. Dominey led him to where the tracks had halted on the gravel outside Rosamund's window and pointed across to the Black Wood.

"What do you make of those?" he enquired.

Middleton did not hesitate. He shook his head gravely.

"Was anything heerd last night, sir?"

"There was an infernal yell underneath this window."

"That was the spirit of Roger Unthank, for sure," Middleton pronounced, with a little shudder. "When he do come out of that wood, he do call."

"Spirits," his master pointed out, "do not leave tracks like that behind."

Middleton considered the matter.

"They do say hereabout," he confided, "that the spirit of Roger Unthank have been taken possession of by some sort of great animal, and that it do come here now and then to be fed."

"By whom?" Dominey enquired patiently.

"Why, by Mrs. Unthank."

"Mrs. Unthank has not been in this house for many months. From the day she left until last night, so far as I can gather, nothing has been heard of this ghost, or beast, or whatever it is."

"That do seem queer, surely," Middleton admitted.

Dominey followed the tracks with his eyes to the wood and back again.

"Middleton," he said, "I am learning something about spirits. It seems that they not only make tracks, but they require feeding. Perhaps if that is so they can feel a charge of shot inside them."

The old man seemed for a moment to stiffen with slow horror.

"You wouldn't shoot at it, Squire?" he gasped.

"I should have done so this morning if I had had a chance," Dominey replied. "When the weather is a little drier, I am going to make my way into that wood, Middleton, with a rifle under my arm."

"Then as God's above, you'll never come out, Squire!" was the solemn reply.

"We will see," Dominey muttered. "I have hacked my way through some queer country in Africa."

"There's nowt like this wood in the world, sir," the old man asserted doggedly. "The bottom's rotten from end to end and the top's all poisonous. The birds die there on the trees. It's chock-ful of reptiles and unclean things, with green and purple fungi, two feet high, with poison in the very sniff of them. The man who enters that wood goes to his grave."

"Nevertheless," Dominey said firmly, "within a very short time I am going to solve the mystery of this nocturnal visitor."

They returned to the house, side by side. Just before they entered, Dominey turned to his companion.

"Middleton," he said, "you keep up the good old customs, I suppose, and spend half an hour at the 'Dominey Arms' now and then?"

"Most every night of my life, sir," the old man replied, "from eight till nine. I'm a man of regular habits, and that do seem right to me that with the work done right and proper a man should have his relaxation."

"That is right, John," Dominey assented. "Next time you are there, don't forget to mention that I am going to have that wood looked through. I should like it to get about, you understand?"

"That'll fair flummox the folk," was the doubtful reply, "but I'll let 'em know, Squire. There'll be a rare bit of talk, I can promise you that."

Dominey handed over his gun, went to his room, bathed and changed, and descended for breakfast. There was a sudden hush as he entered, which he very well understood. Every one began to talk about the prospect of the day's sport. Dominey helped himself from the sideboard and took his place at the table.

"I hope," he said, "that our very latest thing in ghosts did not disturb anybody."

"We all seem to have heard the same thing," the Cabinet Minister observed, with interest,—"a most appalling and unearthly cry. I have lately joined every society connected with spooks and find them a fascinating study."

"If you want to investigate," Dominey observed, as he helped himself to coffee, "you can bring out a revolver and prowl about with me one night. From the time when I was a kid, before I went to Eton, up till when I left here for Africa, we had a series of highly respectable and well-behaved ghosts, who were a credit to the family and of whom we were somewhat proud. This latest spook, however, is something quite outside the pale."

"Has he a history?" Mr. Watson asked, with interest.

"I am informed," Dominey replied, "that he is the spirit of a schoolmaster who once lived here, and for whose departure from the world I am supposed to be responsible. Such a spook is neither a credit nor a comfort to the family."

Their host spoke with such an absolute absence of emotion that every one was conscious of a curious reluctance to abandon a subject full of such fascinating possibilities. Terniloff was the only one, however, who made a suggestion.

"We might have a battue in the wood," he proposed.

"I am not sure," Dominey told them, "that the character of the wood is not more interesting than the ghost who is supposed to dwell in it. You remember how terrified the beaters were yesterday at the bare suggestion of entering it? For generations it has been held unclean. It is certainly most unsafe. I went in over my knees on the outskirts of it this morning.—Shall we say half-past ten in the gun room?"

Seaman followed his host out of the room.

"My friend," he said, "you must not allow these local circumstances to occupy too large a share of your thoughts. It is true that these are the days of your relaxation. Still, there is the Princess for you to think of. After all, she has us in her power. The merest whisper in Downing Street, and behold, catastrophe!"

Dominey took his friend's arm.

"Look here, Seaman," he rejoined, "it's easy enough to say there is the Princess to be considered, but will you kindly tell me what on earth more I can do to make her see the position? Necessity demands that I should be on the best of terms with Lady Dominey and that I should not make myself in any way conspicuous with the Princess."

"I am not sure," Seaman reflected, "that the terms you are on with Lady Dominey matter very much to any one. So far as regards the Princess, she is an impulsive and passionate person, but she is also *grande dame* and a diplomatist. I see no reason why you should not marry her secretly in London, in the name of Everard Dominey, and have the ceremony repeated under your rightful name later on."

They had paused to help themselves to cigarettes, which were displayed with a cabinet of cigars on a round table in the hall. Dominey waited for a moment before he answered.

"Has the Princess confided to you that that is her wish?" he asked.

"Something of the sort," Seaman acknowledged. "She wishes the suggestion, however, to come from you."

"And your advice?"

Seaman blew out a little cloud of cigar smoke.

"My friend," he confessed, "I am a little afraid of the Princess. I ask you no questions as to your own feelings with regard to her. I take it for granted that as a man of honour it will be your duty to offer her your hand in marriage, sooner or later. I see no harm in anticipating a few months, if by that means we can pacify her. Terniloff would arrange it at the Embassy. He is devoted to her, and it will strengthen your position with him."

Dominey turned away towards the stairs.

"We will discuss this again before we leave," he said gloomily.

Dominey was admitted at once by her maid into his wife's

sitting-room. Rosamund, in a charming morning robe of pale blue lined with grey fur, had just finished breakfast. She held out her hands to him with a delighted little cry of welcome.

"How nice of you to come, Everard!" she exclaimed. "I was hoping I should see you for a moment before you went off."

He raised her fingers to his lips and sat down by her side. She seemed entirely delighted by his presence, and he felt instinctively that she was quite unaffected by the event of the night before.

"You slept well?" he enquired.

"Perfectly," she answered.

He tackled the subject bravely, as he had made up his mind to on every opportunity.

"You do not lie awake thinking of our nocturnal visitor, then?"

"Not for one moment. You see," she went on conversationally, "if you were really Everard, then I might be frightened, for some way or other I feel that if Everard comes here, the spirit of Roger Unthank will do him some sort of mischief."

"Why?" he asked.

"You don't know about these things, of course," she went on, "but Roger Unthank was in love with me, although I had scarcely ever spoken to him, before I married Everard. I think I told you that much yesterday, didn't I? After I was married, the poor man nearly went out of his mind. He gave up his work and used to haunt the park here. One evening Everard caught him and they fought, and Roger Unthank was never seen again. I think that any one around here would tell you," she went on, dropping her voice a little, "that Everard killed Roger and threw him into one of those swampy places near the Black Wood, where a body sinks and sinks and nothing is ever seen of it again."

"I do not believe he did anything of the sort," Dominey declared.

"Oh, I don't know," she replied doubtfully. "Everard had a terrible temper, and that night he came home covered with blood, looking — awful! It was the night when I was taken ill."

"Well, no more tragedies," he insisted. "I have come up to remind you that we have guests here. When are you coming down to see them?"

She laughed like a child.

"You say 'we' just as though you were really my husband," she declared.

"You must not tell any one else of your fancy," he warned her.

She acquiesced at once.

"Oh, I quite understand," she assured him. "I shall be very, very careful. And, Everard, you have such clever guests, not at all the sort of people my Everard would have had here, and I have been out of the world for so long, that I am afraid I sha'n't be able to talk to them. Nurse Alice is tremendously impressed. I am sure I should be terrified to sit at the end of the table, and Caroline will hate not being hostess any longer. Let me come down at tea-time and after dinner, and slip into things gradually. You can easily say that I am still an invalid, though of course I'm not at all."

"You shall do exactly as you choose," he promised as he took his leave.

So when the shooting party tramped into the hall that afternoon, a little weary, but flushed with exercise and the pleasure of the day's sport, they found, seated in a corner of the room, behind the great round table upon which tea was set out, a rather pale but extraordinarily childlike and fascinating woman, with large, sweet eyes which seemed to be begging for their protection and sympathy as she rose hesitatingly to her feet. Dominey was by her side in a moment, and his first few words of introduction brought every one around her. She said very little, but what she said was delightfully natural and gracious.

"It has been so kind of you," she said to Caroline, "to help my husband entertain his guests. I am very much better, but I have been ill for so long that I have forgotten a great many things, and I should be a very poor hostess. But I want to make tea for you, please, and I want you all to tell me how many pheasants you have shot."

Terniloff seated himself on the settee by her side.

"I am going to help you in this complicated task," he declared. "I am sure those sugar tongs are too heavy for you to wield alone."

She laughed at him gaily.

"But I am not really delicate at all," she assured him. "I have had a very bad illness, but I am quite strong again."

"Then I will find some other excuse for sitting here," he said. "I will tell you all about the high pheasants your husband killed, and about the woodcock he brought down after we had all missed it."

"I shall love to hear about that," she assented. "How much sugar, please, and will you pass those hot muffins to the Princess? And please touch that bell. I shall want more hot water. I expect you are all very thirsty. I am so glad to be here with you."

CHAPTER XX

Arm in arm, Prince Terniloff and his host climbed the snow-covered slope at the back of a long fir plantation, towards the little beflagged sticks which indicated their stand. There was not a human being in sight, for the rest of the guns had chosen a steeper but somewhat less circuitous route.

"Von Ragastein," the Ambassador said, "I am going to give myself the luxury of calling you by your name. You know my one weakness, a weakness which in my younger days very nearly drove me out of diplomacy. I detest espionage in every shape and form, even where it is necessary. So far as you are concerned, my young friend," he went on, "I think your position ridiculous. I have sent a private despatch to Potsdam, in which I have expressed that opinion."

"So far," Dominey remarked, "I have not been overworked."

"My dear young friend," the Prince continued, "you have not been overworked because there has been no legitimate work for you to do. There will be none. There could be no possible advantage accruing from your labours here to compensate for the very bad effect which the discovery of your true name and position would have in the English Cabinet."

"I must ask you to remember," Dominey begged, "that I am here as a blind servant of the Fatherland. I simply obey orders."

"I will grant that freely," the Prince consented. "But to continue. I am now at the end of my first year in this country. I feel able to congratulate myself upon a certain measure of success. From that part of the Cabinet with whom I have had to do, I have received nothing but encouragement in my efforts to promote a better understanding between our two countries."

"The sky certainly seems clear enough just now," agreed Dominey.

"I have convinced myself," the Prince said emphatically, "that there is a genuine and solid desire for peace with Germany existing in Downing Street. In every argument I have had, in every concession I have asked for, I have been met with a sincere desire to foster the growing friendship between our countries. I am proud of my work here, Von Ragastein. I believe that I have brought Germany and England nearer together than they have been since the days of the Boer War."

"You are sure, sir," Dominey asked, "that you are not confusing personal popularity with national sentiment?"

"I am sure of it," the Ambassador answered gravely. "Such popularity as I may have achieved here has been due to an appreciation of the more healthy state of world politics now existing. It has been my great pleasure to trace the result of my work in a manuscript of memoirs, which some day, when peace is firmly established between our two countries, I shall cause to be published. I have put on record there evidences of the really genuine sentiment in favour of peace which I have found amongst the present Cabinet."

"I should esteem it an immense privilege," Dominey said, "to be given a private reading of these memoirs."

"That may be arranged," was the suave reply. "In the meantime, Von Ragastein, I want you to reconsider your position here."

"My position is not voluntary," Dominey repeated. "I am acting under orders."

"Precisely," the other acquiesced, "but matters have changed very much during the last six months. Even at the risk of offending France, England is showing wonderful pliability with regard to our claims in Morocco. Every prospect of disagreement between our two countries upon any vital matter has now disappeared."

"Unless," Dominey said thoughtfully, "the desire for war should come, not from Downing Street but from Potsdam."

"We serve an honourable master," Terniloff declared sternly, "and he has shown me his mind. His will is for peace, and for the great triumphs to which our country is already entitled by reason of her supremacy in industry, in commerce, in character and in genius. These are the weapons which will make Germany the greatest Power in the world. No empire has ever hewn its way to permanent glory by the sword alone. We have reached our stations, I see. Come to me after this drive is finished, my host. All that I have said so far has been by way of prelude."

The weather had turned drier, the snow was crisp, and a little party of women from the Hall reached the guns before the beaters were through the wood. Caroline and Stephanie both took their places by Dominey's side. The former, however, after a few minutes passed on to Terniloff's stand. Stephanie and Dominey were alone for the first time since their stormy interview in the library.

"Has Maurice been talking to you?" she asked a little abruptly.

"His Excellency and I are, to tell you the truth," Dominey confessed, "in the midst of a most interesting conversation."

"Has he spoken to you about me?"

"Your name has not yet been mentioned."

She made a little grimace. In her wonderful furs and Russian turban hat she made rather a striking picture against the background of snow.

"An interesting conversation in which my name has not been mentioned!" she repeated satirically.

"I think you were coming into it before very long," Dominey assured her. "His Excellency warned me that all he had said so far was merely the prelude to a matter of larger importance."

Stephanie smiled.

"Dear Maurice is so diplomatic," she murmured. "I am perfectly certain he is going to begin by remonstrating with you for your shocking treatment of me."

Their conversation was interrupted for a few minutes by the sport. Dominey called the faithful Middleton to his side for a further supply of cartridges. Stephanie bided her time, which came when the beaters at last emerged from the wood.

"Shocking," Stephanie repeated, reverting to their conversation, "is the mildest word in my vocabulary which I can apply to your treatment of me. Honestly, Leopold, I feel bruised all over inside. My pride is humbled."

"It is because you look at the matter only from a feminine point of view," Dominey persisted.

"And you,"she answered in a low tone, "once the fondest and the most passionate of lovers, only from a political one. You think a great deal of your country, Leopold. Have I no claims upon you?"

"Upon Everard Dominey, none," he insisted. "When the time comes, and Leopold von Ragastein can claim all that is his right, believe me, you will have no cause to complain of coldness or dilatoriness. He will have only one thought, only one hope—to end the torture of these years of separation as speedily as may be."

The strained look passed from her face. Her tone became more natural.

"But, dear," she pleaded, "there is no need to wait. Your Sovereign gives you permission. Your political chief will more than endorse it."

"I am on the spot," Dominey replied, "and believe me I know what is safest and best. I cannot live as two men and keep my face steadfast to the world. The Prince, however, has not spoken to me yet. I will hear what he has to say."

Stephanie turned a little haughtily away.

"You are putting me in the position of a suppliant!" she exclaimed. "To-night we must have an understanding."

The little party moved on all together to another cover. Rosamund had joined them and hung on to Dominey's arm with delight. The brisk walk across the park had brought colour to her cheeks. She walked with all the free and vigorous grace of a healthy woman. Dominey found himself watching her, as she deserted him a little later on to stand by Terniloff's side, with a little thrill of tangled emotions. He felt a touch on his arm. Stephanie, who was passing with another of the guns, paused to whisper in his ear:

"There might be a greater danger—one that has evaded even your cautious mind—in overplaying your part!"

Dominey was taken possession of by Caroline on their walk to the next stand. She planted herself on a shooting stick by his side and commenced to take him roundly to task.

"My dear Everard," she said, "you are one of the most wonderful examples of the reformed rake I ever met! You have even acquired respectability. For heaven's sake, don't disappoint us all!"

"I seem to be rather good at that," Dominey observed a little drearily.

"Well, you are the master of your own actions, are you not?" she asked. "What I want to say in plain words is, don't go and make a fool of yourself with Stephanie."

"I have not the least intention of doing anything of the sort."

"Well, she has! Mark my words, Everard, I know that woman. She is clever and brilliant and anything else you like, but for some reason or other she has set her mind upon you. She looks at dear little Rosamund as though she hadn't a right to exist. Don't look so sorry for yourself. You must have encouraged her."

Dominey was silent. Fortunately, the exigencies of the next few minutes demanded it. His cousin waited patiently until there came a pause in the shooting.

"Now let me hear what you have to say for yourself, sir? So far as I can see, you've been quite sweet to your wife, and she adores you. If you want to have an affair with the Princess, don't begin it here. You'll have your wife ill again if you make her jealous."

"My dear Caroline, there will be no affair between Stephanie and me. Of that you may rest assured."

"You mean to say that this is altogether on her side, then?" Caroline persisted.

"You exaggerate her demeanour," he replied, "but even if what you suggest were true——"

"Oh, I don't want a lot of protestations!" she interrupted. "I am not saying that you encourage her much, because I don't believe you do. All I want to point out is that, having really brought your wife back almost to health, you must be extraordinarily and wonderfully careful. If you want to talk nonsense with Stephanie, do it in Belgrave Square."

Dominey was watching the gyrations of a falling pheasant. His left hand was stretched out towards the cartridge bag which Caroline was holding. He clasped her fingers for a moment before he helped himself.

"You are rather a dear," he said. "I would not do anything to hurt Rosamund for the world."

"If you can't get rid of your old tricks altogether and must flirt," she remarked, "well, I'm always somewhere about. Rosamund wouldn't mind me, because there are a few grey hairs in my sandy ones.—And here comes your man across the park—looks as though he had a message for you. So long as nothing has happened to your cook, I feel that I could face ill tidings with composure."

Dominey found himself watching with fixed eyes the approach of his rather sad-faced manservant through the snow. Parkins was not dressed for such an enterprise, nor did he seem in any way to relish it. His was the stern march of duty, and, curiously enough, Dominey felt from the moment he caught sight of him that he was in some respects a messenger of Fate. Yet the message which he delivered, when at last he reached his master's side, was in no way alarming.

"A person of the name of Miller has arrived here, sir," he announced, "from Norwich. He is, I understand, a foreigner of some sort, who has recently landed in this country. I found it a little difficult to understand him, but her Highness's maid conversed with him in German, and I understand that he either is or brings you a message from a certain Doctor Schmidt, with whom you were acquainted in Africa."

The warning whistle blew at that moment, and Dominey swung round and stood at attention. His behaviour was perfectly normal. He let a hen pheasant pass over his head, and brought down a cock from very nearly the limit distance. He reloaded before he turned to Parkins.

"Is this person in a hurry?" he said.

"By no means, sir," the man replied. "I told him that you would not be back until three or four o'clock, and he is quite content to wait."

Dominey nodded.

"Look after him yourself then, Parkins," he directed. "We shall not be shooting late to-day. Very likely I will send Mr. Seaman back to talk to him."

The man raised his hat respectfully and turned back towards the house. Caroline was watching her companion curiously.

"Do you find many of your acquaintances in Africa look you up, Everard?" she asked.

"Except for Seaman," Dominey replied, looking through the barrels of his gun, "who really does not count because we crossed together, this is my first visitor from the land of fortune. I expect there will be plenty of them by and by, though. Colonials have a wonderful habit of sticking to one another."

CHAPTER XXI

THERE was nothing in the least alarming about the appearance of Mr. Ludwig Miller. He had been exceedingly well entertained in the butler's private sitting-room and had the air of having done full justice to the hospitality which had been offered him. He rose to his feet at Dominey's entrance and stood at attention. But for some slight indications of military training, he would have passed anywhere as a highly respectable retired tradesman.

"Sir Everard Dominey?" he enquired.

Dominey nodded assent. "That is my name. Have I seen you before?"

The man shook his head. "I am a cousin of Doctor Schmidt. I arrived in the Colony from Rhodesia, after your Excellency had left."

"And how is the doctor?"

"My cousin is, as always, busy but in excellent health," was the reply. "He sends his respectful compliments and his good wishes. Also this letter."

With a little flourish the man produced an envelope inscribed

To Sir Everard Dominey, Baronet,
Dominey Hall,
In the County of Norfolk,
England.

Dominey broke the seal just as Seaman entered.

"A messenger here from Doctor Schmidt, an acquaintance of mine in East Africa," he announced. "Mr. Seaman came home from South Africa with me," he explained to his visitor.

The two men looked steadily into each other's eyes. Dominey watched them, fascinated. Neither betrayed himself by even the fall of an eyelid. Yet Dominey, his perceptive powers at their very keenest in this moment which instinct told him was one of crisis, felt the unspoken, unbetokened recognition which passed between them. Some commonplace remark was uttered and responded to. Dominey read the few lines which seemed to take him back for a moment to another world:

> "Honoured and Honourable Sir,
>
> "I send you my heartiest and most respectful greeting. Of the progress of all matters here you will learn from another source.
>
> "I recommend to your notice and kindness my cousin, the bearer of this letter — Mr. Ludwig Miller. He will lay before you certain circumstances of which it is advisable for you to have knowledge. You may speak freely with him. He is in all respects to be trusted.
>
> (Signed) "KARL SCHMIDT."

"Your cousin is a little mysterious," Dominey remarked, as he passed the letter to Seaman. "Come, what about these circumstances?"

Ludwig Miller looked around the little room and then at Seaman. Dominey affected to misunderstand his hesitation.

"Our friend here knows everything," he declared. "You can speak to him as to myself."

The man began as one who has a story to tell.

"My errand here is to warn you," he said, "that the Englishman whom you left for dead at Big Bend, on the banks of the Blue River, has been heard of in another part of Africa."

Dominey shook his head incredulously. "I hope you have not come all this way to tell me that! The man was dead."

"My cousin himself," Miller continued, "was hard to convince. The man left his encampment with whisky enough to kill him, thirst enough to drink it all, and no food."

"So I found him," Dominey assented, "deserted by his boys and raving. To silence him forever was a child's task."

"The task, however, was unperformed," the other persisted.

"From three places in the Colony he has been heard of, struggling to make his way to the coast."

"Does he call himself by his own name?" Dominey asked.

"He does not," Miller admitted. "My cousin, however, desired me to point out to you the fact that in any case he would probably be shy of doing so. He is behaving in an absurd manner; he is in a very weakly state; and without a doubt he is to some degree insane. Nevertheless, the fact remains that he is in the Colony, or was three months ago, and that if he succeeds in reaching the coast you may at any time be surprised by a visit from him here. I am sent to warn you in order that you may take what steps may be necessary and not be placed at a disadvantage if he should appear."

"This is queer news you have brought us, Miller," Seaman said thoughtfully.

"It is news which greatly disturbed Doctor Schmidt," the man replied. "He has had the natives up one after the other for cross-examination. Nothing can shake their story."

"If we believed it," Seaman continued, "this other European, if he had business in this direction, might walk in here at any moment."

"It was to warn you of that possibility that I am here."

"How much do you know personally," Seaman asked, "of the existent circumstances?"

The man shook his head vaguely.

"I know nothing," he admitted. "I went out to East Africa some years ago, and I have been a trader in Mozambique in a small way. I supplied outfits for officers and hospitals and sportsmen. Now and then I have to return to Europe to buy fresh stock. Doctor Schmidt knew that, and he came to see me just before I sailed. He first thought of writing a very long letter. Afterwards he changed his mind. He wrote only those few lines I brought, but he told me those other things."

"You have remembered all that he told you?" Dominey asked.

"I can think of nothing else," was the reply, after a moment's pause. "The whole affair has been a great worry to Doctor Schmidt. There are things connected with it which he has never understood, things connected with it which he has always found mysterious."

"Hence your presence here, Johann Wolff, eh?" Seaman asked, in an altered tone.

The visitor's expression remained unchanged except for the faint surprise which shone out of his blue eyes.

"Johann Wolff," he repeated. "That is not my name. I am Ludwig Miller, and I know nothing of this matter beyond what I have told you. I am just a messenger."

"Once in Vienna and twice in Cracow, my friend, we have met," Seaman reminded him softly but very insistently.

The other shook his head gently. "A mistake. I have been in Vienna once, many years ago, but Cracow never."

"You have no idea with whom you are talking?"

"Herr Seaman was the name, I understood."

"It is a very good name," Seaman scoffed. "Look here and think."

He undid his coat and waistcoat and displayed a plain vest of chamois leather. Attached to the left-hand side of it was a bronze decoration, with lettering and a number. Miller stared at it blankly and shook his head.

"Information Department, Bureau Twelve, password—'The Day is coming,'" Seaman continued, dropping his voice.

His listener shook his head and smiled with the puzzled ignorance of a child.

"The gentleman mistakes me for some one else," he replied. "I know nothing of these things."

Seaman sat and studied this obstinate visitor for several minutes without speaking, his finger tips pressed together, his eyebrows gently contracted. His vis-à-vis endured this scrutiny without flinching, calm, phlegmatic, the very prototype of the bourgeois German of the tradesman class.

"Do you propose," Dominey enquired, "to stay in these parts long?"

"One or two days—a week, perhaps," was the indifferent answer. "I have a cousin in Norwich who makes toys. I love the English country. I spend my holiday here, perhaps."

"Just so," Seaman muttered grimly. "The English country under a foot of snow! So you have nothing more to say to me, Johann Wolff?"

"I have executed my mission to his Excellency," was the apologetic reply. "I am sorry to have caused displeasure to you, Herr Seaman."

The latter rose to his feet. Dominey had already turned towards the door.

"You will spend the night here, of course, Mr. Miller?" he invited. "I dare say Mr. Seaman would like to have another talk with you in the morning."

"I shall gladly spend the night here, your Excellency," was the polite reply. "I do not think that I have anything to say, however, which would interest your friend."

"You are making a great mistake, Wolff," Seaman declared angrily. "I am your superior in the Service, and your attitude towards me is indefensible."

"If the gentleman would only believe," the culprit begged, "that he is mistaking me for some one else!"

There was trouble in Seaman's face as the two men made their way to the front of the house and trouble in his tone as he answered his companion's query.

"What do you think of that fellow and his visit?"

"I do not know yet what to think, but there is a great deal that I know," Seaman replied gravely. "The man is a spy, a favourite in the Wilhelmstrasse and only made use of on important occasions. His name is Wolff—Johann Wolff."

"And this story of his?"

"You ought to be the best judge of that."

"I am," Dominey assented confidently. "Without the shadow of a doubt I threw the body of the man I killed into the Blue River and watched it sink."

"Then the story is a fake," Seaman decided. "For some reason or other we have come under the suspicion of our own secret service."

Seaman, as they emerged into the hall, was summoned imperiously to her side by the Princess Eiderstrom. Dominey disappeared for a moment and returned presently, having discarded some of his soaked shooting garments. He was followed by his valet, bearing a note upon a silver tray.

"From the person in Mr. Parkins' room—to Mr. Seaman, sir," the man announced, in a low tone.

Dominey took it from the salver with a little nod. Then he turned to where the youngest and most frivolous of his guests was in the act of rising from the tea table.

"A game of pills, Eddy," he proposed. "They tell me that pool is one of your great accomplishments."

"I'm pretty useful," the young man confessed, with a satisfied chuckle. "Give you a black at snooker, what?"

Dominey took his arm and led him into the billiard-room. "You will give me nothing, young fellow," he replied. "Set them up, and I will show you how I made a living for two months at Johannesberg!"

CHAPTER XXII

THE evening at Dominey Hall was practically a repetition of the previous one, with a different set of guests from the outer world. After dinner, Dominey was absent for a few minutes and returned with Rosamund upon his arm. She received the congratulations of her neighbours charmingly, and a little court soon gathered around her. Doctor Harrison, who had been dining, remained upon its outskirts, listening to her light-hearted and at times almost brilliant chatter with grave and watchful interest. Dominey, satisfied that she was being entertained, obeyed Terniloff's gestured behest and strolled with him to a distant corner of the hall.

"Let me now, my dear host," the Prince began, with some eagerness in his tone, "continue and, I trust, conclude the conversation to which all that I said this morning was merely the prelude."

"I am entirely at your service," murmured his host.

"I have tried to make you understand that from my own point of view — and I am in a position to know something — the fear of war between this country and our own has passed. England is willing to make all reasonable sacrifices to ensure peace. She wants peace, she intends peace, therefore there will be peace. Therefore, I maintain, my young friend, it is better for you to disappear at once from this false position."

"I am scarcely my own master," Dominey replied. "You yourself must know that. I am here as a servant under orders."

"Join your protest with mine," the Prince suggested. "I will make a report directly I get back to London. To my mind, the matter is urgent. If anything should lead to the discovery of your false position in this country, the friendship between us which has become a real pleasure to me must seriously undermine my own position."

Dominey had risen to his feet and was standing on the hearth-rug, in front of a fire of blazing logs. The Ambassador was sitting with crossed legs in a comfortable easy-chair, smoking one of the long, thin cigars which were his particular fancy.

"Your Excellency," Dominey said, "there is just one fallacy in all that you have said."

"A fallacy?"

"You have come to the absolute conclusion," Dominey continued, "that because England wants peace there will be peace. I am of Seaman's mind. I believe in the ultimate power of the military party of Germany. I believe that in time they will thrust their will upon the Kaiser, if he is not at the present moment secretly in league with them. Therefore, I believe that there will be war."

"If I shared that belief with you, my friend," the Ambassador said quietly, "I should consider my position here one of dishonour. My mandate is for peace, and my charge is from the Kaiser's lips."

Stephanie, with the air of one a little weary of the conversation, broke away from a distant group and came towards them. Her beautiful eyes seemed tired, she moved listlessly, and she even spoke with less than her usual assurance.

"Am I disturbing a serious conversation?" she asked. "Send me away if I am."

"His Excellency and I," Dominey observed, "have reached a cul-de-sac in our argument, — the blank wall of good-natured but fundamental disagreement."

"Then I shall claim you for a while," Stephanie declared, taking Dominey's arm. "Lady Dominey has attracted all the men to her circle, and I am lonely."

The Prince bowed.

"I deny the cul-de-sac," he said, "but I yield our host! I shall seek my opponent at billiards."

He turned away and Stephanie sank into his vacant place.

"So you and my cousin," she remarked, as she made room for Dominey to sit by her side, "have come to a disagreement."

"Not an unfriendly one," her host assured her.

"That I am sure of. Maurice seems, indeed, to have taken a

wonderful liking to you. I cannot remember that you ever met before, except for that day or two in Saxony?"

"That is so. The first time I exchanged any intimate conversation with the Prince was in London. I have the utmost respect and regard for him, but I cannot help feeling that the pleasant intimacy to which he has admitted me is to a large extent owing to the desire of our friends in Berlin. So far as I am concerned, I have never met any one, of any nation, whose character I admire more."

"Maurice lives his life loftily. He is one of the few great aristocrats I have met who carries his nobility of birth into his simplest thought and action. There is just one thing," she added, "which would break his heart."

"And that?"

"The subject upon which you two disagree—a war between Germany and this country."

"The Prince is an idealist," Dominey said. "Sometimes I wonder why he was sent here, why they did not send some one of a more intriguing character."

She shrugged her shoulders.

"You agree with that great Frenchman," she observed, "that no ambassador can remain a gentleman—politically."

"Well, I have never been a diplomat, so I cannot say," Dominey replied.

"You have many qualifications, I should think," she observed cuttingly.

"Such as?"

"You are absolutely callous, absolutely without heart or sympathy where your work is concerned."

"I do not admit it," he protested.

"I go back to London to-morrow," she continued, "a very miserable and unhappy woman. I take with me the letter which should have brought me happiness. The love for which I have sacrificed my life has failed me. Not even the whip of a royal command, not even all that I have to offer, can give me even five seconds of happiness."

"All that I have pleaded for," Dominey reminded her earnestly, "is delay."

"And what delay do you think," she asked, with a sudden note of passion in her tone, "would the Leopold von Ragastein of six years ago have pleaded for? Delay! He found words then which would have melted an iceberg. He found words the memory of which comes to me sometimes in the night and which mocks me. He had no country then save the paradise where lovers walk, no rule but a queen, and I was she. And now——"

Dominey felt a strange pang of distress. She saw the unusual softening in his face, and her eyes lit up.

"Just for a moment," she broke off, "you were like Leopold. As a rule, you know, you are not like him. I think that you left him somewhere in Africa and came home in his likeness."

"Believe that for a little time," Dominey begged earnestly.

"What if it were true?" she asked abruptly. "There are times when I do not recognise you. There are words Leopold used to use which I have never heard from your lips. Is not West Africa the sorcerer's paradise? Perhaps you are an impostor, and the man I love is there still, in trouble—perhaps ill. You play the part of Everard Dominey like a very king of actors. Perhaps before you came here you played the part of Leopold. You are not my Leopold. Love cannot die as you would have me believe."

"Now," he said coolly, "you are coming round to my way of thinking. I have been assuring you, from the very first moment we met at the Carlton, that I was not your Leopold—that I was Everard Dominey."

"I shall put you to the test," she exclaimed suddenly, rising to her feet. "Your arm, if you please."

She led him across the hall to where little groups of people were gossiping, playing bridge, and Seaman, the centre of a little group of gullible amateur speculators, was lecturing on mines. They stopped to say a word or two here and there, but Stephanie's fingers never left her companion's arm. They passed down a corridor hung with a collection of wonderful sporting prints in which she affected some interest, into a small gallery which led into the ballroom. Here they were alone. She laid her hands upon his shoulders and looked up into his eyes. Her lips drew nearer to his.

"Kiss me—upon the lips, Leopold," she ordered.

"There is no Leopold here," he replied; "you yourself have said it."

She came a little nearer. "Upon the lips," she whispered.

He held her, stooped down, and their lips met. Then she stood apart from him. Her eyes were for a moment closed, her hands were extended as though to prevent any chance of his approaching her again.

"Now I know the truth," she muttered.

Dominey found an opportunity to draw Seaman away from his little group of investment-seeking friends.

"My friend," he said, "trouble grows."

"Anything more from Schmidt's supposed emissary?" Seaman asked quickly.

"No. I am going to keep away from him this evening, and I advise you to do the same. The trouble is with the Princess."

"With the Princess," declared Seaman. "I think you have blundered. I quite appreciate your general principles of behaving internally and externally as though you were the person whom you pretend to be. It is the very essence of all successful espionage. But you should know when to make exceptions. I see grave objections myself to your obeying the Kaiser's behest. On the other hand, I see no objection whatever to your treating the Princess in a more human manner, to your visiting her in London, and giving her more ardent proofs of your continued affection."

"If I once begin ——"

"Look here," Seaman interrupted, "the Princess is a woman of the world. She knows what she is doing, and there is a definite tie between you. I tell you frankly that I could not bear to see you playing the idiot for a moment with Lady Dominey, but with the Princess, scruples don't enter into the question at all. You should by no means make an enemy of her."

"Well, I have done it," Dominey acknowledged. "She has gone off to bed now, and she is leaving early to-morrow morning. She thinks I have borrowed some West African magic, that I have left her lover's soul out there and come home in his body."

"Well, if she does," Seaman declared, "you are out of your troubles."

"Am I!" Dominey replied gloomily. "First of all, she may do a lot of mischief before she goes. And then, supposing by any thousand to one chance the story of this cousin of Schmidt's should be true, and she should find Dominey out there, still alive? The Princess is not of German birth, you know. She cares nothing for Germany's future. As a matter of fact, I think, like a great many Hungarians, she prefers England. They say that an Englishman has as many lives as a cat. Supposing that chap Dominey did come to life again and she brings him home? You say yourself that you do not mean to make much use of me until after the war has started. In the parlance of this country of idioms, that will rather upset the apple cart, will it not?"

"Has the Princess a suite of rooms here?" Seaman enquired.

"Over in the west wing. Good idea! You go and see what you can do with her. She will not think of going to bed at this time of night."

Seaman nodded.

"Leave it to me," he directed. "You go out and play the host."

Dominey played the host first and then the husband. Rosamund welcomed him with a little cry of pleasure.

"I have been enjoying myself so much, Everard!" she exclaimed. "Everybody has been so kind, and Mr. Mangan has taught me a new Patience."

"And now, I think," Doctor Harrison intervened a little gruffly, "It's time to knock off for the evening."

She turned very sweetly to Everard.

"Will you take me upstairs?" she begged. "I have been hoping so much that you would come before Doctor Harrison sent me off."

"I should have been very disappointed if I had been too late," Dominey assured her. "Now say good night to everybody."

"Why, you talk to me as though I were a child," she laughed. "Well, good-bye, everybody, then. You see, my stern husband is taking me off. When are you coming to see me, Doctor Harrison?"

"Nothing to see you for," was the gruff reply. "You are as well as any woman here."

"Just a little unsympathetic, isn't he?" she complained to Dominey. "Please take me through the hall, so that I can say good-bye to every one else. Is the Princess Eiderstrom there?"

"I am afraid that she has gone to bed," Dominey answered, as they passed out of the room. "She said something about a headache."

"She is very beautiful," Rosamund said wistfully. "I wish she looked as though she liked me a little more. Is she very fond of you, Everard?"

"I think that I am rather in her bad books just at present," Dominey confessed.

"I wonder! I am very observant, and I have seen her looking at you sometimes— Of course," Rosamund went on, "as I am not really your wife and you are not really my husband, it is very stupid of me to feel jealous, isn't it, Everard?"

"Not a bit," he answered. "If I am not your husband, I will not be anybody else's."

"I love you to say that," she admitted, with a little sigh, "but it seems wrong somewhere. Look how cross the Duchess looks! Some one must have played the wrong card."

Rosamund's farewells were not easily made; Terniloff especially seemed reluctant to let her go. She excused herself gracefully, however, promising to sit up a little later the next evening. Dominey led the way upstairs, curiously gratified at her lingering progress. He took her to the door of her room and looked in. The nurse was sitting in an easy-chair, reading, and the maid was sewing in the background.

"Well, you look very comfortable here," he declared cheerfully. "Pray do not move, nurse."

Rosamund held his hands, as though reluctant to let him go. Then she drew his face down and kissed him.

"Yes," she said a little plaintively, "it's very comfortable.—Everard?"

"Yes, dear?"

She drew his head down and whispered in his ear.

"May I come in and say good night for two minutes?"

He smiled—a wonderfully kind smile—but shook his head. "Not to-night, dear," he replied. "The Prince loves to sit up late, and I shall be downstairs with him. Besides, that bully of a doctor of yours insists upon ten hours' sleep."

She sighed like a disappointed child.

"Very well." She paused for a moment to listen. "Wasn't that a car?" she asked.

"Some of our guests going early, I dare say," he replied, as he turned away.

CHAPTER XXIII

SEAMAN did not at once start on his mission to the Princess. He made his way instead to the servants' quarters and knocked at the door of the butler's sitting-room. There was no reply. He tried the handle in vain. The door was locked. A tall, grave-faced man in sombre black came out from an adjoining apartment.

"You are looking for the person who arrived this evening from abroad, sir?" he enquired.

"I am," Seaman replied. "Has he locked himself in?"

"He has left the Hall, sir!"

"Left!" Seaman repeated. "Do you mean gone away for good?"

"Apparently, sir. I do not understand his language myself, but I believe he considered his reception here, for some reason or other, unfavourable. He took advantage of the car which went down to the station for the evening papers and caught the last train."

Seaman was silent for a moment. The news was a shock to him.

"What is your position here?" he asked his informant.

"My name is Reynolds, sir," was the respectful reply. "I am Mr. Pelham's servant."

"Can you tell me why, if this man has left, the door here is locked?"

"Mr. Parkins locked it before he went out, sir. He accompanied—Mr. Miller, I think his name was—to the station."

Seaman had the air of a man not wholly satisfied.

"Is it usual to lock up a sitting-room in this fashion?" he asked.

"Mr. Parkins always does it, sir. The cabinets of cigars are kept there, also the wine-cellar key and the key of the plate chest. None of the other servants use the room except at Mr. Parkins' invitation."

"I understand," Seaman said, as he turned away. "Much obliged for your information, Reynolds. I will speak to Mr. Parkins later."

"I will let him know that you desire to see him, sir."

"Good night, Reynolds!"

"Good night, sir!"

Seaman passed back again to the crowded hall and billiard-room, exchanged a few remarks here and there, and made his way up the southern flight of stairs towards the west wing. Stephanie consented without hesitation to receive him. She was seated in front of the fire, reading a novel, in a boudoir opening out of her bedroom.

"Princess," Seaman declared, with a low bow, "we are in despair at your desertion."

She put down her book.

"I have been insulted in this house," she said. "To-morrow I leave it."

Seaman shook his head reproachfully.

"Your Highness," he continued, "believe me, I do not wish to presume upon my position. I am only a German tradesman, admitted to circles like these for reasons connected solely with the welfare of my country. Yet I know much, as it happens, of the truth of this matter, the matter which is causing you distress. I beg you to reconsider your decision. Our friend here is, I think, needlessly hard upon himself. So much the greater will be his reward when the end comes. So much the greater will be the rapture with which he will throw himself on his knees before you."

"Has he sent you to reason with me?"

"Not directly. I am to a certain extent, however, his major-domo in this enterprise. I brought him from Africa. I have watched over him from the start. Two brains are better than one. I try to show him where to avoid mistakes, I try to point out the paths of danger and of safety."

"I should imagine Sir Everard finds you useful," she remarked calmly.

"I hope he does."

"It has doubtless occurred to you," she continued, "that our friend has accommodated himself wonderfully to English life and customs?"

"You must remember that he was educated here. Nevertheless, his aptitude has been marvellous."

"One might almost call it supernatural," she agreed. "Tell me, Mr. Seaman, you seem to have been completely successful in the installation of our friend here as Sir Everard. What is going to be his real value to you? What work will he do?"

"We are keeping him for the big things. You have seen our gracious master lately?" he added hesitatingly.

"I know what is at the back of your mind," she replied. "Yes! Before the summer is over I am to pack up my trunks and fly. I understand."

"It is when that time comes," Seaman said impressively, "that we expect Sir Everard Dominey, the typical English country gentleman, of whose loyalty there has never been a word of doubt, to be of use to us. Most of our present helpers will be under suspicion. The authorised staff of our secret service can only work underneath. You can see for yourself the advantage we gain in having a confidential correspondent who can day by day reflect the changing psychology of the British mind in all its phases. We have quite enough of the other sort of help arranged for. Plans of ships, aerodromes and harbours, sailings of convoys, calling up of soldiers — all these are the A. B. C. of the secret service profession. We shall never ask our friend here for a single fact, but, from his town house in Berkeley Square, the host of Cabinet Ministers, of soldiers, of the best brains of the country, our fingers will never leave the pulse of Britain's day by day life."

Stephanie threw herself back in her easy-chair and clasped her hands behind her head.

"These things you are expecting from our present host?"

"We are, and we expect to get them. I have watched him day by day. My confidence in him has grown."

Stephanie was silent. She sat looking into the fire. Seaman, keenly observant as always, realised the change in her, yet found something of mystery in her new detachment of manner.

"Your Highness," he urged, "I am not here to speak on behalf of the man who at heart is, I know, your lover. He will plead his own cause when the time comes. But I am here to plead for patience, I am here to implore you to take no rash step, to do nothing which might imperil in any way his position here. I stand outside the gates of the world which your sex can make a paradise. I am no judge of the things that happen there. But in your heart I feel there is bitterness, because the man for whom you care has chosen to place his country first. I implore your patience, Princess. I implore you to believe what I know so well,—that it is the sternest sense of duty only which is the foundation of Leopold von Ragastein's obdurate attitude."

"What are you afraid that I shall do?" she asked curiously.

"I am afraid of nothing—directly."

"Indirectly, then? Answer me, please."

"I am afraid," he admitted frankly, "that in some corner of the world, if not in this country, you might whisper a word, a scoffing or an angry sentence, which would make people wonder what grudge you had against a simple Norfolk baronet. I would not like that word spoken in the presence of any one who knew your history and realised the rather amazing likeness between Sir Everard Dominey and Baron Leopold von Ragastein."

"I see," Stephanie murmured, a faint smile parting her lips. "Well, Mr. Seaman, I do not think that you need have many fears. What I shall carry away with me in my heart is not for you or any man to know. In a few days I shall leave this country."

"You are going back to Berlin—to Hungary?"

She shook her head, beckoned her maid to open the door, and held out her hand in token of dismissal.

"I am going to take a sea voyage," she announced. "I shall go to Africa."

The morrow was a day of mild surprises. Eddy Pelham's empty place was the first to attract notice, towards the end of breakfast time.

"Where's the pink and white immaculate?" the Right Honourable gentleman asked. "I miss my morning wonder as to how he tied his tie."

"Gone," Dominey replied, looking round from the sideboard.

"Gone?" every one repeated.

"I should think such a thing has never happened to him before," Dominey observed. "He was wanted in town."

"Fancy any one wanting Eddy for any serious purpose!" Caroline murmured.

"Fancy any one wanting him badly enough to drag him out of bed in the middle of the night with a telephone call and send him up to town by the breakfast train from Norwich!" their host continued. "I thought we had started a new ghost when he came into my room in a purple dressing-gown and broke the news."

"Who wanted him?" the Duke enquired. "His tailor?"

"Business of importance was his pretext," Dominey replied.

There was a little ripple of good-humoured laughter.

"Does Eddy do anything for a living?" Caroline asked, yawning.

"Mr. Pelham is a director of the Chelsea Motor Works," Mangan told them. "He received a small legacy last year, and his favourite taxicab man was the first to know about it."

"You're not suggesting," she exclaimed, "that it is business of that sort which has taken Eddy away!"

"I should think it most improbable," Mangan confessed. "As a matter of fact, he asked me the other day if I knew where their premises were."

"We shall miss him," she acknowledged. "It was quite one of the events of the day to see his costume after shooting."

"His bridge was reasonably good," the Duke commented.

"He shot rather well the last two days," Mangan remarked.

"And he had told me confidentially," Caroline concluded, "that he was going to wear brown to-day. Now I think Eddy would have looked nice in brown."

The missing young man's requiem was finished by the arrival of the local morning papers. A few moments later Dominey rose and left the room. Seaman, who had been unusually silent, followed him.

"My friend," he confided, "I do not know whether you have heard, but there was another curious disappearance from the Hall last night."

"Whose?" Dominey asked, pausing in the act of selecting a cigarette.

"Our friend Miller, or Wolff — Doctor Schmidt's emissary," Seaman announced, "has disappeared."

"Disappeared?" Dominey repeated. "I suppose he is having a prowl round somewhere."

"I have left it to you to make more careful enquiries," Seaman replied. "All I can tell you is that I made up my mind last night to interview him once more and try to fathom his very mysterious behaviour. I found the door of your butler's sitting-room locked, and a very civil fellow — Mr. Pelham's valet he turned out to be — told me that he had left in the car which went for the evening papers."

"I will go and make some enquiries," Dominey decided, after a moment's puzzled consideration.

"If you please," Seaman acquiesced. "The affair disconcerts me because I do not understand it. When there is a thing which I do not understand, I am uncomfortable."

Dominey vanished into the nether regions, spent half an hour with Rosamund, and saw nothing of his disturbed guest again until they were walking to the first wood. They had a moment together after Dominey had pointed out the stands.

"Well?" Seaman enquired.

"Our friend," Dominey announced, "apparently made up his mind to go quite suddenly. A bed was arranged for him — or rather it is always there — in a small apartment opening out of the butler's room, on the ground floor. He said nothing about leaving until he saw Parkins preparing to go down to the station with the chauffeur. Then he insisted upon accompanying him, and when he found there was a train to Norwich he simply bade them both good night. He left no message whatever for either you or me."

Seaman was thoughtful.

"There is no doubt," he said, "that his departure was indicative of a certain distrust in us. He came to find out something, and I suppose he found it out. I envy you your composure, my friend. We live on the brink of a volcano, and you shoot pheasants."

"We will try a partridge for a change," Dominey observed,

swinging round as a single Frenchman with a dull whiz crossed the hedge behind them and fell a little distance away, a crumpled heap of feathers. "Neat, I think?" he added, turning to his companion.

"Marvellous!" Seaman replied, with faint sarcasm. "I envy your nerve."

"I cannot take this matter very seriously," Dominey acknowledged. "The fellow seemed to me quite harmless."

"My anxieties have also been aroused in another direction," Seaman confided.

"Any other trouble looming?" Dominey asked.

"You will find yourself minus another guest when you return this afternoon."

"The Princess?"

"The Princess," Seaman assented. "I did my best with her last night, but I found her in a most peculiar frame of mind. We are to be relieved of any anxiety concerning her for some time, however. She has decided to take a sea voyage."

"Where to?"

"Africa!"

Dominey paused in the act of inserting a cartridge into his gun. He turned slowly around and looked into his companion's expressionless face.

"Why the mischief is she going out there?" he asked.

"I can no more tell you that," Seaman replied, "than why Johann Wolff was sent over here to spy upon our perfect work. I am most unhappy, my friend. The things which I understand, however threatening they are, I do not fear. Things which I do not understand oppress me."

Dominey laughed quietly.

"Come," he said, "there is nothing here which seriously threatens our position. The Princess is angry, but she is not likely to give us away. This man Wolff could make no adverse report about either of us. We are doing our job and doing it well. Let our clear consciences console us."

"That is well," Seaman replied, "but I feel uneasy. I must not stay here any longer. Too intimate an association between you and me is unwise."

"Well, I think I can be trusted," Dominey observed, "even if I am to be left alone."

"In every respect except as regards the Princess," Seaman admitted, "your deportment has been most discreet."

"Except as regards the Princess," Dominey repeated irritably. "Really, my friend, I cannot understand your point of view in this matter. You could not expect me to mix up a secret honeymoon with my present commitments!"

"There might surely have been some middle way?" Seaman persisted. "You show so much tact in other matters."

"You do not know the Princess," Dominey muttered.

Rosamund joined them for luncheon, bringing news of Stephanie's sudden departure, with notes and messages for everybody. Caroline made a little grimace at her host.

"You're in trouble!" she whispered in his ear. "All the same, I approve. I like Stephanie, but she is an exceedingly dangerous person."

"I wonder whether she is," Dominey mused.

"I think men have generally found her so," Caroline replied. "She had one wonderful love affair, which ended, as you know, in her husband being killed in a duel and her lover being banished from the country. Still, she's not quite the sort of woman to be content with a banished lover. I fancied I noticed distinct signs of her being willing to replace him whilst she has been down here!"

"I feel as though a blight had settled upon my house party," Dominey remarked with bland irrelevancy. "First Eddy, then Mr. Ludwig Miller, and now Stephanie."

"And who on earth was Mr. Ludwig Miller, after all?" Caroline enquired.

"He was a fat, flaxen-haired German who brought me messages from old friends in Africa. He had no luggage but a walking stick, and he seems to have upset the male part of my domestics last night by accepting a bed and then disappearing!"

"With the plate?"

"Not a thing missing. Parkins spent an agonised half hour, counting everything. Mr. Ludwig appears to be one of those unsolved mysteries which go to make up an imperfect world."

"Well, we've had a jolly time," Caroline said reminiscently. "To-morrow Henry and I are off, and I suppose the others. I must say on the whole I am delighted with our visit."

"You are very gracious," Dominey murmured.

"I came, perhaps, expecting to see a little more of you," she went on deliberately, "but there is a very great compensation for my disappointment. I think your wife, Everard, is worth taking trouble about. She is perfectly sweet, and her manners are most attractive."

"I am very glad you think that," he said warmly.

She looked away from him.

"Everard," she sighed, "I believe you are in love with your wife."

There was a strange, almost a terrible mixture of expressions in his face as he answered,—a certain fear, a certain fondness, a certain almost desperate resignation. Even his voice, as a rule so slow and measured, shook with an emotion which amazed his companion.

"I believe I am," he muttered. "I am afraid of my feelings for her. It may bring even another tragedy down upon us."

"Don't talk rubbish!" Caroline exclaimed. "What tragedy could come between you now? You've recovered your balance. You are a strong, steadfast person, just fitted to be the protector of anything so sweet and charming as Rosamund. Tragedy, indeed! Why don't you take her down to the South of France, Everard, and have your honeymoon all over again?"

"I can't do that just yet."

She studied him curiously. There were times when he seemed wholly incomprehensible to her.

"Are you still worried about that Unthank affair?" she asked.

He hesitated for a moment.

"There is still an aftermath to our troubles," he told her, "one cloud which leans over us. I shall clear it up in time—but other things may happen first."

"You take yourself very seriously, Everard," she observed, looking at him with a puzzled expression. "One would think that there was a side of your life, and a very important one, which you kept entirely to yourself. Why do you have that funny little man Seaman always round with you? You're not being blackmailed or anything, are you?"

"On the contrary," he told her, "Seaman was the first founder of my fortunes."

She shrugged her shoulders.

"I have made a little money once or twice on the Stock Exchange," she remarked, "but I didn't have to carry my broker about in my pocket afterwards."

"Seaman is a good-hearted little fellow, and he loves companionship. He will drift away presently, and one won't see anything of him for ages."

"Henry began to wonder," she concluded drily, "whether you were going to stand for Parliament on the Anglo-German alliance ticket."

Dominey laughed as he caught Middleton's reproachful eye in the doorway of the farmer's kitchen in which they were lunching. He gave the signal to rise.

"I have had some thoughts of Parliament," he admitted, "but — well, Henry need not worry."

CHAPTER XXIV

The next morning saw the breaking-up of Dominey's carefully arranged shooting party. The Prince took his host's arm and led him to one side for a few moments, as the cars were being loaded up. His first few words were of formal thanks. He spoke then more intimately.

"Von Ragastein," he said, "I desire to refer back for a moment to our conversation the other day."

Dominey shook his head and glanced behind.

"I know only one name here, Prince."

"Dominey, then. I will confess that you play and carry the part through perfectly. I have known English gentlemen all my life, and you have the trick of the thing. But listen. I have already told you of my disapproval of this scheme in which you are the central figure."

"It is understood," Dominey assented.

"That," the Prince continued, "is a personal matter. What I am now going to say to you is official. I had despatches from Berlin last night. They concern you."

Dominey seemed to stiffen a little.

"Well?"

"I am given to understand," the Ambassador continued, "that you practically exist only in the event of that catastrophe which I, for one, cannot foresee. I am assured that if your exposure should take place at any time, your personation will be regarded as a private enterprise, and there is nothing whatever to connect you with any political work."

"Up to the present that is absolutely so," Dominey agreed.

"I am further advised to look upon you as my unnamed and unsuspected successor here, in the event of war. For that reason I am begged to inaugurate terms of intimacy with you, to treat you with the utmost confidence, and, if the black end should come, to leave in your hands all such unfulfilled work as can be continued in secrecy and silence. I perhaps express myself in a somewhat confused manner."

"I understand perfectly," Dominey replied. "The authorities have changed their first ideas as to my presence here. They want to keep every shadow of suspicion away from me, so that in the event of war I shall have an absolutely unique position, an unsuspected yet fervently patriotic German, living hand in glove with the upper classes of English Society. One can well imagine that there would be work for me."

"Our understanding is mutual," Terniloff declared. "What I have to say to you, therefore, is that I hope you will soon follow us to London and give me the opportunity of offering you the constant hospitality of Carlton House Gardens."

"You are very kind, Prince," Dominey said. "My instructions are, as soon as I have consolidated my position here—an event which I fancy I may consider attained—to establish myself in London and to wait orders. I trust that amongst other things you will then permit me to examine the memoirs you spoke of the other day."

"Naturally, and with the utmost pleasure," the Ambassador assented. "They are a faithful record of my interviews and negotiations with certain Ministers here, and they reflect a desire and intention for peace which will, I think, amaze you— I venture now upon a somewhat delicate question," he continued, changing the subject of their conversation abruptly, as they turned back along the terrace. "Lady Dominey will accompany you?"

"Of that I am not sure," Dominey replied thoughtfully. "I have noticed, Prince, if I may be allowed to say so, your chivalrous regard for that lady. You will permit me to assure you that in the peculiar position in which I am placed I shall never forget that she is the wife of Everard Dominey."

Terniloff shook hands heartily.

"I wanted to hear that from you," he admitted. "You I felt instinctively were different, but there are many men of our race who are willing enough to sacrifice a woman without the slightest scruple, either for their passions or their policy. I find Lady Dominey charming."

"She will never lack a protector in me," Dominey declared.

There were more farewells and, soon after, the little procession of cars drove off. Rosamund herself was on the terrace, bidding all her guests farewell. She clung to Dominey's arm when at last they turned back into the empty hall.

"What dear people they were, Everard!" she exclaimed. "I only wish that I had seen more of them. The Duchess was perfectly charming to me, and I never knew any one with such delightful manners as Prince Terniloff. Are you going to miss them very much, dear?"

"Not a bit," he answered. "I think I shall take a gun now and stroll down the meadows and across the rough ground. Will you come with me, or will you put on one of your pretty gowns and entertain me downstairs at luncheon? It is a very long time since we had a meal alone together."

She shook her head a little sadly.

"We never have had," she answered. "You know that, Everard, and, alas! I know it. But we are going on pretending, aren't we?"

He raised her fingers to his lips and kissed them.

"You shall pretend all that you like, dear Rosamund," he promised, "and I will be the shadow of your desires. No! — No tears!" he added quickly, as she turned away. "Remember there is nothing but happiness for you now. Whoever I am or am not, that is my one aim in life."

She clutched at his hand passionately, and suddenly, as though finding it insufficient, twined her arms around his neck and kissed him.

"Let me come with you," she begged. "I can't bear to let you go. I'll be very quiet. Will you wait ten minutes for me?"

"Of course," he answered.

He strolled down towards the gun room, stood by the fire for a moment, and then wandered out into the courtyard, where Middleton and a couple of beaters were waiting for him with the dogs. He had scarcely taken a step towards them, however, when he stopped short. To his amazement Seaman was there, standing a little on one side, with his eyes fixed upon the windows of the servants' quarters.

"Hullo, my friend!" he exclaimed. "Why, I thought you went by the early train from Thursford Station?"

"Missed it by two minutes," Seaman replied with a glance towards the beaters. "I knew all the cars were full for the eleven o'clock, so I thought I'd wait till the afternoon."

"And where have you been to for the last few hours, then?"

Seaman had reached his side now and was out of earshot of the others.

"Trying to solve the mystery of Johann Wolff's sudden departure last night. Come and walk down the avenue with me a little way."

"A very short distance, then. I am expecting Lady Dominey."

They passed through the thin iron gates and paced along one of the back entrances to the Hall.

"Do not think me indiscreet," Seaman began. "I returned without the knowledge of any one, and I kept out of the way until they had all gone. It is what I told you before. Things which I do not understand depress me, and behold! I have found proof this morning of a further significance in Wolff's sudden departure."

"Proceed," Dominey begged.

"I learned this morning, entirely by accident, that Mr. Pelham's servant was either mistaken or wilfully deceived me. Wolff did not accompany your butler to the station."

"And how did you find that out?" Dominey demanded.

"It is immaterial! What is material is that there is a sort of conspiracy amongst the servants here to conceal the manner of his leaving. Do not interrupt me, I beg! Early this morning there was a fresh fall of snow which has now disappeared. Outside the window of the room which I found locked were the marks of footsteps and the tracks of a small car."

"And what do you gather from all this?" Dominey asked.

"I gather that Wolff must have had friends in the neighbourhood," Seaman replied, "or else —— "

"Well?"

"My last supposition sounds absurd," Seaman confessed, "but the whole matter is so incomprehensible that I was going to say — or else he was forcibly removed."

Dominey laughed softly.

"Wolff would scarcely have been an easy man to abduct, would he," he remarked, "even if we could hit upon any plausible reason for such a thing! As a matter of fact, Seaman," he concluded, turning on his heel a little abruptly as he saw Rosamund standing in the avenue, "I cannot bring myself to treat this Johann Wolff business seriously. Granted that the man was a spy, well, let him get on with it. We are doing our job here in the most perfect and praiseworthy fashion. We neither of us have the ghost of a secret to hide from his employers."

"In a sense that is true," Seaman admitted.

"Well, then, cheer up," Dominey enjoined. "Take a little walk with us, and we will see whether Parkins cannot find us a bottle of that old Burgundy for lunch. How does that sound, eh?"

"If you will excuse me from taking the walk," Seaman begged, "I would like to remain here until your return."

"You are more likely to do harm," Dominey reminded him, "and set the servants talking, if you show too much interest in this man's disappearance."

"I shall be careful," Seaman promised, "but there are certain things which I cannot help. I work always from instinct, and my instinct is never wrong. I will ask no more questions of your servants, but I know that there is something mysterious about the sudden departure of Johann Wolff."

Dominey and Rosamund returned about one o'clock to find only a note from Seaman, which the former tore open as his companion stood warming her feet in front of the fire. There were only a few lines:

"I am following an idea. It takes me to London. Let us meet there within a few days.

"S.'

"Has he really gone?" Rosamund asked.

"Back to London."

She laughed happily. "Then we shall lunch *à deux* after all! Delightful! I have my wish!"

There was a sudden glow in Dominey's face, a glow which was instantly suppressed.

"Shall I ever have mine?" he asked, with a queer little break in his voice.

CHAPTER XXV

TERNILOFF and Dominey, one morning about six months later, lounged underneath a great elm tree at Ranelagh, having iced drinks after a round of golf. Several millions of perspiring Englishmen were at the same moment studying with dazed wonder the headlines in the midday papers.

"I suppose," the Ambassador remarked, as he leaned back in his chair with an air of lazy content, "that I am being accused of fiddling while Rome burns."

"Every one has certainly not your confidence in the situation," Dominey rejoined calmly.

"There is no one else who knows quite so much," Terniloff reminded him.

Dominey sipped his drink for a moment or two in silence.

"Have you the latest news of the Russian mobilisation?" he asked "They had some startling figures in the city this morning."

The Prince waved his hand.

"My faith is not founded on these extraneous incidents," he replied. "If Russia mobilises, it is for defence. No nation in the world would dream of attacking Germany, nor has Germany the slightest intention of imperilling her coming supremacy amongst the nations by such crude methods as military enterprise. Servia must be punished, naturally, but to that, in principle, every nation in Europe is agreed. We shall not permit Austria to overstep the mark."

"You are at least consistent, Prince," Dominey remarked.

Terniloff smiled.

"That is because I have been taken behind the scenes," he said. "I have been shown, as is the privilege of ambassadors, the mind of our rulers. You, my friend," he went on, "spent your youth amongst the military faction. You think that you are the most important people in Germany. Well, you are not. The Kaiser has willed it otherwise.—By-the-by, I had yesterday a most extraordinary cable from Stephanie."

Dominey ceased swinging his putter carelessly over the head of a daisy and turned his head to listen.

"Is she on the way home?"

"She is due in Southampton at any moment now. She wants to know where she can see me immediately upon her arrival, as she has information of the utmost importance to give me."

"Did she ever tell you the reason for her journey to Africa?"

"She was most mysterious about it. If such an idea had had any logical outcome, I should have surmised that she was going there to seek information as to your past."

"She gave Seaman the same idea," Dominey observed. "I scarcely see what she has to gain. In Africa, as a matter of fact," he went on, "my life would bear the strictest investigation."

"The whole affair is singularly foolish," the Prince declared. "Still, I am not sure that you have been altogether wise. Even accepting your position, I see no reason why you should not have obeyed the Kaiser's behest. My experience of your Society here is that love affairs between men and women moving in the same circles are not uncommon."

"That," Dominey urged, "is when they are all tarred with the same brush. My behaviour towards Lady Dominey has been culpable enough as it is. To have placed her in the position of a neglected wife would have been indefensible. Further, it might have affected the position which it is in the interests of my work that I should maintain here."

"An old subject," the Ambassador sighed, "best not rediscussed. Behold, our womenkind!"

Rosamund and the Princess had issued from the house, and the two men hastened to meet them. The latter looked charming, exquisitely gowned, and stately in appearance. By her side Rosamund, dressed with the same success but in younger fashion, seemed almost like a child. They passed into the luncheon room, crowded with many little parties of distinguished and interesting people, brilliant with the red livery of the waiters, the profusion of flowers—all that nameless elegance which had made the place

Society's most popular rendezvous. The women, as they settled into their places, asked a question which was on the lips of a great many English people that day.

"Is there any news?"

Terniloff perhaps felt that he was the cynosure of many eager and anxious eyes. He smiled light-heartedly as he answered:

"None. If there were, I am convinced that it would be good. I have been allowed to play out my titanic struggle against Sir Everard without interruption."

"I suppose the next important question to whether it is to be peace or war is, how did you play?" the Princess asked.

"I surpassed myself," her husband replied, "but of course no ordinary human golfer is of any account against Dominey. He plays far too well for any self-respecting Ger——"

The Ambassador broke off and paused while he helped himself to mayonnaise.

"For any self-respecting German to play against," he concluded.

Luncheon was a very pleasant meal, and a good many people noticed the vivacity of the beautiful Lady Dominey whose picture was beginning to appear in the illustrated papers. Afterwards they drank coffee and sipped liqueurs under a great elm tree on the lawn, listening to the music and congratulating themselves upon having made their escape from London. In the ever-shifting panorama of gaily-dressed women and flannel-clad men, the monotony of which was varied here and there by the passing of a diplomatist or a Frenchman, scrupulously attired in morning clothes, were many familiar faces. Caroline and a little group of friends waved to them from the terrace. Eddy Pelham, in immaculate white, and a long tennis coat with dark blue edgings, paused to speak to them on his way to the courts.

"How is the motor business, Eddy?" Dominey asked, with a twinkle in his eyes.

"So, so! I'm not quite so keen as I was. To tell you the truth," the young man confided, glancing around and lowering his voice so that no one should share the momentous information, "I was lucky enough to pick up a small share in Jere Moore's racing stable at Newmarket, the other day. I fancy I know a little more about gee-gees than I do about the inside of motors, what?"

"I should think very possibly that you are right," Dominey assented, as the young man passed on with a farewell salute.

Terniloff looked after him curiously.

"It is the type of young man, that," he declared, "which we cannot understand. What would happen to him, in the event of a war? — In the event of his being called upon, say, either to fight or do some work of national importance for his country?"

"I expect he would do it," Dominey replied. "He would do it pluckily, whole-heartedly and badly. He is a type of the upper-class young Englishman, over-sanguine and entirely undisciplined. They expect, and their country expects for them, that in the case of emergency pluck would take the place of training."

The Right Honourable Gerald Watson stood upon the steps talking to the wife of the Italian Ambassador. She left him presently, and he came strolling down the lawn with his hands behind his back and his eyes seeming to see out past the golf links.

"There goes a man," Terniloff murmured, "whom lately I have found changed. When I first came here he met me quite openly. I believe, even now, he is sincerely desirous of peace and amicable relations between our two countries, and yet something has fallen between us. I cannot tell what it is. I cannot tell even of what nature it is, but I have an instinct for people's attitude towards me, and the English are the worst race in the world at hiding their feelings. Has Mr. Watson, I wonder, come under the spell of your connection, the Duke of Worcester? He seemed so friendly with both of us down in Norfolk."

Their womenkind left them at that moment to talk to some acquaintances seated a short distance away. Mr. Watson, passing within a few yards of them, was brought to a standstill by Dominey's greeting. They talked for a moment or two upon idle subjects.

"Your news, I trust, continues favourable?" the Ambassador remarked, observing the etiquette which required him to be the first to leave the realms of ordinary conversation.

"It is a little negative in quality," the other answered, after a moment's hesitation. "I am summoned to Downing Street again at six o'clock."

"I have already confided the result of my morning despatches to the Prime Minister," Terniloff observed.

"I went through them before I came down here," was the somewhat doubtful reply.

"You will have appreciated, I hope, their genuinely pacific tone?" Terniloff asked anxiously.

His interlocutor bowed and then drew himself up. It was obvious that the strain of the last few days was telling upon him. There were lines about his mouth, and his eyes spoke of sleepless nights.

"Words are idle things to deal with at a time like this," he said. "One thing, however, I will venture to say to you, Prince, here and under these circumstances. There will be no war unless it be the will of your country."

Terniloff was for a moment unusually pale. It was an episode of unrecorded history. He rose to his feet and raised his hat.

"There will be no war," he said solemnly.

The Cabinet Minister passed on with a lighter step. Dominey, more clearly than ever before, understood the subtle policy which had chosen for his great position a man as chivalrous and faithful and yet as simple-minded as Terniloff. He looked after the retreating figure of the Cabinet Minister with a slight smile at the corner of his lips.

"In a time like this," he remarked significantly, "one begins to understand why one of our great writers — was it Bernhardi, I wonder? — has written that no island could ever breed a race of diplomatists."

"The seas which engirdle this island," the Ambassador said thoughtfully, "have brought to England great weal, as they may bring to her much woe. The too-nimble brain of the diplomat has its parallel of insincerity in the people whose interests he seems to guard. I believe in the honesty of the English politicians. I have placed that belief on record in the small volume of memoirs which I shall presently entrust to you. But we talk too seriously for a summer afternoon. Let us illustrate to the world our opinion of the political situation and play another nine holes at golf."

Dominey rose willingly to his feet, and the two men strolled away towards the first tee.

"By the by," Terniloff asked, "what of our cheerful little friend Seaman? He ought to be busy just now."

"Curiously enough, he is returning from Germany to-night," Dominey announced. "I expect him at Berkeley Square. He is coming direct to me."

CHAPTER XXVI

THESE were days, to all dwellers in London, of vivid impressions, of poignant memories, reasserting themselves afterwards with a curious sense of unreality, as though belonging to another set of days and another world. Dominey long remembered his dinner that evening in the sombre, handsomely furnished dining-room of his town house in Berkeley Square. Although it lacked the splendid proportions of the banqueting hall at Dominey, it was still a fine apartment, furnished in the Georgian period, with some notable pictures upon the walls, and with a wonderful ceiling and fireplace. Dominey and Rosamund dined alone, and though the table had been reduced to its smallest proportions, the space between them was yet considerable. As soon as Parkins had gravely put the port upon the table, Rosamund rose to her feet and, instead of leaving the room, pointed for the servant to place a chair for her by Dominey's side.

"I shall be like your men friends, Everard," she declared, "when the ladies have left, and draw up to your side. Now what do we do? Tell stories? I promise you that I will be a wonderful listener."

"First of all you drink half a glass of this port," he declared, filling her glass, "then you peel me one of those peaches, and we divide it. After which we listen for a ring at the bell. To-night I expect a visitor."

"A visitor?"

"Not a social one," he assured her. "A matter of business which I fear will take me from you for the rest of the evening. So let us make the most of the time until he comes."

She commenced her task with the peach, talking to him all the time a little gravely, a sweet and picturesque picture of a graceful and very desirable woman, her delicate shape and artistic fragility more than ever accentuated by the sombreness of the background.

"Do you know, Everard," she said, "I am so happy in London here with you, and I feel all the time so strong and well. I can read and understand the books which were a maze of print to me before. I can see the things in the pictures, and feel the thrill of the music, which seemed to come to me, somehow, before, all dislocated and discordant. You understand, dear?"

"Of course," he answered gravely.

"I do not wonder," she went on, "that Doctor Harrison is proud of me for a patient, but there are many times when I feel a dull pain in my heart, because I know that, whatever he or anybody else might say, I am not quite cured."

"Rosamund dear," he protested.

"Ah, but don't interrupt," she insisted, depositing his share of the peach upon his plate. "How can I be cured when all the time there is the problem of you, the problem which I am just as far off solving as ever I was? Often I find myself comparing you with the Everard whom I married."

"Do I fail so often to come up to his standard?" he asked.

"You never fail," she answered, looking at him with brimming eyes. "Of course, he was very much more affectionate," she went on, after a moment's pause. "His kisses were not like yours. And he was far fonder of having me with him. Then, on the other hand, often when I wanted him he was not there, he did wild things, mad things; he seemed to forget me altogether. It was that," she went on, "that was so terrible. It was that which made me so nervous. I think that I should even have been able to stand those awful moments when he came back to me, covered with blood and reeling, if it had not been that I was already almost a wreck. You know, he killed Roger Unthank that night. That is why he was never able to come back."

"Why do you talk of these things to-night, Rosamund?" Dominey begged.

"I must, dear," she insisted, laying her fingers upon his hand and looking at him curiously. "I must, even though I see how they distress you. It is wonderful that you should mind so much, Everard, but you do, and I love you for it."

"Mind?" he groaned. "Mind!"

"You are so like him and yet so different," she went on meditatively. "You drink so little wine, you are always so self-controlled, so serious. You live as though you had a life around you of which others knew nothing. The Everard I remember would never have cared about being a magistrate or going into Parliament. He would never have had ambassadors for his friends. He would have spent his time racing or yachting, hunting or shooting, as the fancy took him. And yet——"

"And yet what?" Dominey asked, a little hoarsely.

"I think he loved me better than you," she said very sadly.

"Why?" he demanded.

"I cannot tell you," she answered, with her eyes upon her plate, "but I think that he did."

Dominey walked suddenly to the window and leaned out. There were drops of moisture upon his forehead, he felt the fierce need of air. When he came back she was still sitting there, still looking down.

"I have spoken to Doctor Harrison about it," she went on, her voice scarcely audible. "He told me that you probably loved more than you dared to show, because some day the real Everard might come back."

"That is quite true," he reminded her softly. "He may come back at any moment."

She gripped his hand, her voice shook with passion. She leaned towards him, her other arm stole around his neck.

"But I don't want him to come back!" she cried. "I want you!"

Dominey sat for a moment motionless, like a figure of stone. Through the wide-flung, blind-shielded windows came the raucous cry of a newsboy, breaking the stillness of the summer evening. And then another and sharper interruption,—the stopping of a taxicab outside, the firm, insistent ringing of the front doorbell. Recollection came to Dominey, and a great strength. The fire which had leaped up within him was thrust back. His response to her wave of passion was infinitely tender.

"Dear Rosamund," he said, "that front doorbell summons me to rather an important interview. Will you please trust in me a little while longer? Believe me, I am not in any way cold. I am not indifferent. There is something which you will have to be told,—something with which I never reckoned, something which is beginning to weigh upon me night and day. Trust me, Rosamund, and wait!"

She sank back into her chair with a piquant and yet pathetic little grimace.

"You tell me always to wait," she complained. "I will be patient, but you shall tell me this. You are so kind to me. You make or mar my life. You must care a little? Please?"

He was standing up now. He kissed her hands fondly. His voice had all the old ring in it.

"More than for any woman on earth, dear Rosamund!"

Seaman, in a light grey suit, a panama, and a white beflowered tie, had lost something of the placid urbanity of a few months ago. He was hot and tired with travel. There were new lines in his face and a queer expression of anxiety about his eyes, at the corners of which little wrinkles had begun to appear. He responded to Dominey's welcome with a fervour which was almost feverish, scrutinised him closely, as though expecting to find some change, and finally sank into an easy-chair with a little gesture of relief. He had been carrying a small, brown despatch case, which he laid on the carpet by his side.

"You have news?" Dominey asked.

"Yes," was the momentous reply, "I have news."

Dominey rang the bell. He had already surmised, from the dressing-case and coats in the hall, that his visitor had come direct from the station.

"What will you have?" he enquired.

"A bottle of hock with seltzer water, and ice if you have it," Seaman replied. "Also a plate of cold meat, but it must be served here. And afterwards the biggest cigar you have. I have indeed news, news disturbing, news magnificent, news astounding."

Dominey gave some orders to the servant who answered his summons. For a few moments they spoke trivialities of the journey. When everything was served, however, and the door closed, Seaman could wait no longer. His appetite, his thirst, his speech, seemed all stimulated to swift action.

"We are of the same temperament," he said. "That I know. We will speak first of what is more than disturbing—a little terrifying. The mystery of Johann Wolff has been solved."

"The man who came to us with messages from Schmidt in South Africa?" Dominey asked. "I had almost forgotten about him."

"The same. What was at the back of his visit to us that night I cannot even now imagine. Neither is it clear why he held aloof from me, who am his superior in practically the same service. There we are, from the commencement, confronted with a very singular happening, but scarcely so singular as the dénouement. Wolff vanished from your house that night into an English fortress."

"It seems incredible," Dominey declared bluntly.

"It is nevertheless true," Seaman insisted. "No member of our service is allowed to remain more than one month witnout communicating his existence and whereabouts to headquarters. No word has been received from Wolff since that night in January. On the other hand, indirect information has reached us that he is in durance over here."

"But such a thing is against the law, unheard of," Dominey protested. "No country can keep the citizen of another country in prison without formulating a definite charge or bringing him up for trial."

Seaman smiled grimly.

"That's all very well in any ordinary case," he said. "Wolff has been a marked man for years, though. Wilhelmstrasse would soon make fuss enough, if it were of any use, but it would not be. There are one or two Englishmen in German prisons at the present moment, concerning whose welfare the English Foreign Office has not even thought it worth while to enquire. What troubles me more than the actual fact of Wolff's disappearance is the mystery of his visit to you and his apprehension practically on the spot."

"They must have tracked him down there," Dominey remarked.

"Yes, but they couldn't thrust a pair of tongs into your butler's sitting-room, extract Johann Wolff, and set him down inside

Norwich Castle or whatever prison he may be in," Seaman objected. "However, the most disquieting feature about Wolff is that it introduces something we don't understand. For the rest, we have many men as good, and better, and the time for their utility is past. You are our great hope now, Dominey."

"It is to be, then?"

Seaman took a long and ecstatic draught of his hock and seltzer.

"It is to be," he declared solemnly. "There was never any doubt about it. If Russia ceases to mobilise to-morrow, if every statesman in Servia crawls to Vienna with a rope around his neck, the result would still be the same. The word has gone out. The whole of Germany is like a vast military camp. It comes exactly twelve months before the final day fixed by our great authorities, but the opportunity is too great, too wonderful for hesitation. By the end of August we shall be in Paris."

"You bring news indeed!" Dominey murmured, standing for a moment by the opened window.

"I have been received with favour in the very loftiest circles," Seaman continued. "You and I both stand high in the list of those to whom great rewards shall come. His Majesty approves altogether of your reluctance to avail yourself of his permission to wed the Princess Eiderstrom. 'Von Ragastein has decided well,' he declared. 'These are not the days for marriage or giving in marriage, these, the most momentous days the world has ever known, the days when an empire shall spring into being, the mightiest since the Continents fell into shape and the stars looked down upon this present world.' Those are the words of the All Highest. In his eyes the greatest of all attributes is singleness of purpose. You followed your own purpose, contrary to my advice, contrary to Terniloff's. You will gain by it."

Seaman finished his meal in due course, and the tray was removed. Soon the two men were alone again, Seaman puffing out dense volumes of smoke, gripping his cigar between his teeth, brandishing it sometimes in his hand to give effect to his words. A little of his marvellous caution seemed to have deserted him. For the first time he spoke directly to his companion.

"Von Ragastein," he said, "it is a great country, ours. It is a wonderful empire we shall build. To-night I am on fire with the mighty things. I have a list of instructions for you, many details. They can wait. We will talk of our future, our great and glorious destiny as the mightiest nation who has ever earned for herself the right to govern the world. You would think that in Germany there was excitement. There is none. The task of every one is allotted, their work made clear to them. Like a mighty piece of gigantic machinery, we move towards war. Every regiment knows its station, every battery commander knows his positions, every general knows his exact line of attack. Rations, clothing, hospitals, every unit of which you can think, has its movements calculated out for it to the last nicety."

"And the final result?" Dominey asked. "Is that also calculated?"

Seaman, with trembling fingers, unlocked the little despatch box which stood by his side and took from it jealously a sheet of linen-backed parchment.

"You, my friend," he said, "are one of the first to gaze upon this. This will show you the dream of our Kaiser. This will show you the framework of the empire that is to be."

He laid out a map upon the table. The two men bent over it. It was a map of Europe, in which England, a diminished France, Spain, Portugal and Italy, were painted in dark blue. For the rest, the whole of the space included between the two lines, one from Hamburg to Athens, the other from Finland to the Black Sea, was painted a deep scarlet, with here and there portions of it in slightly lighter colouring. Seaman laid his palm upon the map.

"There lies our future Empire," he said solemnly and impressively.

"Explain it to me," Dominey begged.

"Broadly speaking, everything between those two lines belongs to the new German Empire. Poland, Courland, Lithuania and the Ukraine will possess a certain degree of autonomous government, which will practically amount to nothing. Asia is there at our feet. No longer will Great Britain control the supplies of the world. Raw materials of every description will be ours. Leather, tallow, wheat, oil, fats, timber—they are all there for us to draw upon.

And for wealth — India and China! What more would you have, my friend?"

"You take my breath away. But what about Austria?"

Seaman's grin was almost sardonic.

"Austria," he said, "must already feel her doom creeping upon her. There is no room in middle Europe for two empires, and the House of Hapsburg must fall before the House of Hohenzollern. Austria, body and soul, must become part of the German Empire. Then further down, mark you. Roumania must become a vassal state or be conquered. Bulgaria is already ours. Turkey, with Constantinople, is pledged. Greece will either join us or be wiped out. Servia will be blotted from the map; probably also Montenegro. Those countries which are painted in fainter red, like Turkey, Bulgaria and Greece, become vassal states, to be absorbed one by one as opportunity presents itself."

Dominey's finger strayed northward.

"Belgium," he observed, "has disappeared."

"Belgium we shall occupy and enslave," Seaman replied. "Our line of advance into France lies that way, and we need her ports to dominate the Thames. Holland and the Scandinavian countries, as you observe, are left in the lighter shade of red. If an opportunity occurs, Holland and Denmark may be incited to take the field against us. If they do so, it means absorption. If they remain, as they probably will, scared neutrals, they will none the less be our vassal states when the last gun has been fired."

"And Norway and Sweden?"

Seaman looked down at the map and smiled.

"Look at them," he said. "They lie at our mercy. Norway has her western seaboard, and there might always be the question of British aid, so far as she is concerned. But Sweden is ours, body and soul. More than any other of these vassal states, it is our master's plan to bring her into complete subjection. We need her lusty manhood, the finest cannon food in the world, for later wars, if indeed such a thing should be. She has timber and minerals which we also need. — But there — it is enough. First of all men in this country, my friend, you, Von Ragastein, have gazed upon this picture of the future."

"This is marvellously conceived," Dominey muttered, "but

what of Russia with her millions? How is it that we propose, notwithstanding her countless millions of men, to help ourselves to her richest provinces, to drive a way through the heart of her empire?"

"This," Seaman replied, "is where genius steps in. Russia has been ripe for a revolution any time for the last fifteen years. We have secret agents now in every city and country place and throughout the army. We shall teach Russia how to make herself a free country."

Dominey shivered a little with an almost involuntary repulsion. For the second time that almost satyr-like grin on Seaman's face revolted him.

"And what of my own work?"

Seaman helped himself to a liqueur. He was, as a rule, a moderate man, but this was the third time he had replenished his glass since his hasty meal.

"My brain is weary, friend," he admitted, passing his hand over his forehead. "I have a great fatigue. The thoughts jump about. This last week has been one of fierce excitements. Everything, almost your daily life, has been planned. We shall go over it within a day or so. Meanwhile, remember this. It is our great aim to keep England out of the war."

"Terniloff is right, then, after all!" Dominey exclaimed.

Seaman laughed scornfully.

"If we want England out of the war," he pointed out, "it is not that we desire her friendship. It is that we may crush her the more easily when Calais, Boulogne and Havre are in our hands. That will be in three months' time. Then perhaps our attitude towards England may change a little! Now I go."

Dominey folded up the map with reluctance. His companion shook his head. It was curious that he, too, for the first time in his life upon the same day, addressed his host differently.

"Baron von Ragastein," he said, "there are six of those maps in existence. That one is for you. Lock it away and guard it as though it were your greatest treasure on earth, but when you are alone, bring it out and study it. It shall be your inspiration, it shall lighten your moments of depression, give you courage when you are in danger; it shall fill your mind with pride and wonder It is yours."

Dominey folded it carefully up, crossed the room, unlocked a little safe and deposited it therein.

"I shall guard it, according to your behest, as my greatest treasure," he assured his departing guest, with a fervour which surprised even himself.

CHAPTER XXVII

THERE was something dramatic, in the most lurid sense of the word, about the brief telephone message which Dominey received, not so many hours later, from Carlton House Terrace. In a few minutes he was moving through the streets, still familiar yet already curiously changed. Men and women were going about their business as usual, but an air of stupefaction was everywhere apparent. Practically every loiterer was studying a newspaper, every chance acquaintance had stopped to confer with his fellows. War, alternately the joke and bogey of the conversationalist, stretched its grey hands over the sunlit city. Even the lightest-hearted felt a thrill of apprehension at the thought of the horrors that were to come. In a day or two all this was to be changed. People went about then counting the Russian millions; the steamroller fetish was to be evolved. The most peaceful stockbroker or shopkeeper, who had never even been to a review in his life, could make calculations of man power with a stump of pencil on the back of an old envelope, which would convince the greatest pessimist that Germany and Austria were outnumbered by at least three to one. But on this particular morning, people were too stunned for calculations. The incredible had happened. The long-discussed war — the nightmare of the nervous, the derision of the optimist — had actually materialised. The happy-go-lucky years of peace and plenty had suddenly come to an end. Black tragedy leaned over the land.

Dominey, avoiding acquaintances as far as possible, his own mind in a curious turmoil, passed down St. James's Street and along Pall Mall and presented himself at Carlton House Terrace. Externally, the great white building, with its rows of flower boxes, showed no signs of undue perturbation. Inside, however, the anteroom was crowded with callers, and it was only by the intervention of Terniloff's private secretary, who was awaiting him, that Dominey was able to reach the inner sanctum where the Ambassador was busy dictating letters. He broke off immediately his visitor was announced and dismissed every one, including his secretaries. Then he locked the door.

"Von Ragastein," he groaned, "I am a broken man!"

Dominey grasped his hand sympathetically. Terniloff seemed to have aged years even in the last few hours.

"I sent for you," he continued, "to say farewell, to say farewell and to make a confession. You were right, and I was wrong. It would have been better if I had remained and played the country farmer on my estates. I was never shrewd enough to see until now that I have been made the cat's-paw of the very man whose policy I always condemned."

His visitor still remained silent. There was so little that he could say.

"I have worked for peace," Terniloff went on, "believing that my country wanted peace. I have worked for peace with honourable men who were just as anxious as I was to secure it. But all the time those for whom I laboured were making faces behind my back. I was nothing more nor less than their tool. I know now that nothing in this world could have hindered what is coming."

"Every one will at least realise," Dominey reminded him, "that you did your best for peace."

"That is one reason why I sent for you," was the agitated reply. "Not long ago I spoke of a little volume, a diary which I have been keeping of my work in this country. I promised to show it to you. You have asked me for it several times lately. I am going to show it to you now. It is written up to yesterday. It will tell you of all my efforts and how they were foiled. It is an absolutely faithful narrative of my work here and the English response to it."

The Prince crossed the room, unlocked one of the smaller safes, which stood against the side of the wall, withdrew a morocco-bound volume the size of a small portfolio, and returned to Dominey.

"I beg you," he said earnestly, "to read this with the utmost care and to await my instructions with regard to it. You can judge, no doubt," he went on a little bitterly, "why I give it into your keeping. Even the Embassy here is not free from our own spies, and the existence of these memoirs is known. The moment I reach Germany, their fate is assured. I am a German and a patriot, although my heart is bitter against those who are bringing this blot upon our country. For that reason, these memoirs must be kept in a safe place until I see a good use for them."

"You mean if the governing party in Germany should change?"

"Precisely! They would then form at once my justification, and place English diplomacy in such a light before the saner portion of my fellow countrymen that an honourable peace might be rendered possible. Study them carefully, Von Ragastein. Perhaps even your own allegiance to the Party you serve may waver for a moment as you read."

"I serve no Party," Dominey said quietly, "only my Country."

Terniloff sighed.

"Alas! there is no time for us to enter into one of our old arguments on the ethics of government. I must send you away, Von Ragastein. You have a terrible task before you. I am bound to wish you Godspeed. For myself I shall not raise my head again until I have left England."

"There is no other commission?" Dominey asked. "No other way in which I can serve you?"

"None," Terniloff answered sadly. "I am permitted to suffer no inconveniences. My departure is arranged for as though I were royalty. Yet believe me, my friend, every act of courtesy and generosity which I receive in these moments, bites into my heart. Farewell!"

Dominey found a taxicab in Pall Mall and drove back to Berkeley Square. He found Rosamund with a little troop of dogs, just entering the gardens, and crossed to her side.

"Dear," he asked, taking her arm, "would you mind very much coming down to Norfolk for a few days?"

"With you?" she asked quickly.

"Yes! I want to be in retreat for a short time. There are one or two things I must settle before I take up some fresh work."

"I should love it," she declared enthusiastically. "London is getting so hot, and every one is so excited."

"I shall order the touring car at three o'clock," Dominey told her. "We shall get home about nine. Parkins and your maid can go down by train. Does that suit you?"

"Delightfully!"

He took her arm and they paced slowly along the hot walk.

"Rosamund dear," he said, "the time has come which many people have been dreading. We are at war."

"I know," she murmured.

"You and I have had quite a happy time together, these last few months," he went on, "even though there is still that black cloud between us. I have tried to treat you as kindly and tenderly as though I were really your husband and you were indeed my wife."

"You're not going away?" she cried, startled. "I couldn't bear that! No one could ever be so sweet as you have been to me."

"Dear," he said, "I want you to think — of your husband — of Everard. He was a soldier once for a short time, was he not? What do you think he would have done now that this terrible war has come?"

"He would have done what you will do," she answered, with the slightest possible tremor in her tone. "He would have become a soldier again, he would have fought for his country."

"And so must I — fight for my country," he declared. "That is why I must leave you for an hour now while I make some calls. I shall be back to luncheon. Directly afterwards we must start. I have many things to arrange first, though. Life is not going to be very easy for the next few days."

She held on to his arm. She seemed curiously reluctant to let him go.

"Everard," she said, "when we are at Dominey shall I be able to see Doctor Harrison?"

"Of course," he assured her.

"There is something I want to say to him," she confided, "something I want to ask you, too. Are you the same person, Everard, when you are in town as when you are in the country?"

He was a little taken aback at her question — asked, too, with such almost plaintive seriousness. The very aberration it suggested seemed altogether denied by her appearance. She was wearing a dress of black and white muslin, a large black hat, Paris shoes. Her stockings, her gloves, all the trifling details of her toilette, were carefully chosen, and her clothes themselves gracefully and naturally worn. Socially, too, she had been amazingly successful. Only the week before, Caroline had come to him with a little shrug of the shoulders.

"I have been trying to be kind to Rosamund," she said, "and finding out instead how unnecessary it is. She is quite the most popular of the younger married women in our set. You don't deserve such luck, Everard."

"You know the proverb about the old roué," he had replied.

His mind had wandered for a moment. He realised Rosamund's question with a little start.

"The same person, dear?" he repeated. "I think so. Don't I seem so to you?"

She shook her head.

"I am not sure," she answered, a little mysteriously. "You see, in the country I still remember sometimes that awful night when I so nearly lost my reason. I have never seen you look as you looked that night."

"You would rather not go back, perhaps?"

"That is the strange part of it," she replied. "There is nothing in the world I want so much to do. There's an empty taxi, dear," she added, as they reached the gate. "I shall go in and tell Justine about the packing."

CHAPTER XXVIII

WITHIN the course of the next few days, a strange rumour spread through Dominey and the district,—from the farm labourer to the farmer, from the school children to their homes, from the village post-office to the neighbouring hamlets. A gang of woodmen from a neighbouring county, with an engine and all the machinery of their craft, had started to work razing to the ground everything in the shape of tree or shrub at the north end of the Black Wood. The matter of the war was promptly forgotten. Before the second day, every man, woman and child in the place had paid an awed visit to the outskirts of the wood, had listened to the whirr of machinery, had gazed upon the great bridge of planks leading into the wood, had peered, in the hope of some strange discovery, into the tents of the men who were camping out. The men themselves were not communicative, and the first time the foreman had been known to open his mouth was when Dominey walked down to discuss progress, on the morning after his arrival.

"It's a dirty bit of work, sir," he confided. "I don't know as I ever came across a bit of woodland as was so utterly, hopelessly rotten. Why, the wood crumbles when you touch it, and the men have to be within reach of one another the whole of the time, though we've a matter of five hundred planks down there."

"Come across anything unusual yet?"

"We ain't come across anything that isn't unusual so far, sir. My men are all wearing extra leggings to keep them from being bitten by them adders—as long as my arm, some on 'em. And there's a fungus there which, when you touch it, sends out a smell enough to make a strong man faint. We killed a cat the first day, as big and as fierce as a young tigress. It's a queer job, sir."

"How long will it take?"

"Matter of three weeks, sir, and when we've got the timber out you'll be well advised to burn it. It's not worth a snap of the fingers.—Begging your pardon, sir," the man went on, "the old lady in the distance there hangs about the whole of the time. Some of my men are half scared of her."

Dominey swung around. On a mound a little distance away in the park, Rachael Unthank was standing. In her rusty black clothes, unrelieved by any trace of colour, her white cheeks and strange eyes, even in the morning light she was a repellent figure. Dominey strolled across to her.

"You see, Mrs. Unthank," he began——

She interrupted him. Her skinny hand was stretched out towards the wood.

"What are those men doing, Sir Everard Dominey?" she demanded. "What is your will with the wood?"

"I am carrying out a determination I came to in the winter," Dominey replied. "Those men are going to cut and hew their way from one end of the Black Wood to the other, until not a tree or a bush remains upright. As they cut, they burn. Afterwards, I shall have it drained. We may live to see a field of corn there, Mrs. Unthank."

"You will dare to do this?" she asked hoarsely.

"Will you dare to tell me why I should not, Mrs. Unthank?"

She relapsed into silence, and Dominey passed on. But that night, as Rosamund and he were lingering over their dessert, enjoying the strange quiet and the wonderful breeze which crept in at the open window, Parkins announced a visitor.

"Mrs. Unthank is in the library, sir," he announced. "She would be glad if you could spare her five minutes."

Rosamund shivered slightly but nodded as Dominey glanced towards her enquiringly.

"Don't let me see her, please," she begged. "You must go, of course.—Everard!"

"Yes, dear?"

"I know what you are doing out there, although you have never said a word to me about it," she continued, with an odd little note of passion in her tone. "Don't let her persuade you to stop. Let them cut and burn and hew till there isn't room for a mouse to hide. You promise?"

"I promise," he answered.

Mrs. Unthank was making every effort to keep under control her fierce discomposure. She rose as Dominey entered the room and dropped an old-fashioned curtsey.

"Well, Mrs. Unthank," he enquired, "what can I do for you?"

"It's about the wood again, sir," she confessed. "I can't bear it. All night long I seem to hear those axes, and the calling of the men."

"What is your objection, Mrs. Unthank, to the destruction of the Black Wood?" Dominey asked bluntly. "It is nothing more nor less than a noisome pest-hole. Its very presence there, after all that she has suffered, is a menace to Lady Dominey's nerves. I am determined to sweep it from the face of the earth."

The forced respect was already beginning to disappear from her manner.

"There's evil will come to you if you do, Sir Everard," she declared doggedly.

"Plenty of evil has come to me from that wood as it is," he reminded her.

"You mean to disturb the spirit of him whose body you threw there?" she persisted.

Dominey looked at her calmly. Some sort of evil seemed to have lit in her face. Her lips had shrunk apart, showing her yellow teeth. The fire in her narrowed eyes was the fire of hatred.

"I am no murderer, Mrs. Unthank," he said. "Your son stole out from the shadow of that wood, attacked me in a cowardly manner, and we fought. He was mad when he attacked me, he fought like a madman, and, notwithstanding my superior strength, I was glad to get away alive. I never touched his body. It lay where he fell. If he crept into the wood and died there, then his death was not at my door. He sought for my life as I never sought for his."

"You'd done him wrong," the woman muttered.

"That again is false. His passion for Lady Dominey was uninvited and unreciprocated. Her only feeling concerning him was one of fear; that the whole countryside knows. Your son was a lonely, a morose and an ill-living man, Mrs. Unthank. If either of us had murder in our hearts, it was he, not I. And as for you," Dominey went on, after a moment's pause, "I think that you have had your revenge, Mrs. Unthank. It was you who nursed my wife into insanity. It was you who fed her with the horror of your son's so-called spirit. I think that if I had stayed away another two years, Lady Dominey would have been in a mad-house to-day."

"I would to Heaven," the woman cried, "that you'd rotted to death in Africa!"

"You carry your evil feelings far, Mrs. Unthank," he replied. "Take my advice. Give up this foolish idea that the Black Wood is still the home of your son's spirit. Go and live on your annuity in another part of the country and forget."

He moved across the room to throw open a window. Her eyes followed him wonderingly.

"I have heard a rumour," she said slowly; "there has been a word spoken here and there about you. I've had my doubts sometimes. I have them again every time you speak. Are you really Everard Dominey?"

He swung around and faced her.

"Who else?"

"There's one," she went on, "has never believed it, and that's her ladyship. I've heard strange talk from the people who've come under your masterful ways. You're a harder man than the Everard Dominey I remember. What if you should be an impostor?"

"You have only to prove that, Mrs. Unthank," Dominey replied, "and a portion, at any rate, of the Black Wood may remain standing. You will find it a little difficult, though.—You must excuse my ringing the bell. I see no object in asking you to remain longer."

She rose unwillingly to her feet. Her manner was sullen and unyielding.

"You are asking for the evil things," she warned him.

"Be assured," Dominey answered, "that if they come I shall know how to deal with them."

Dominey found Rosamund and Doctor Harrison, who had

walked over from the village, lingering on the terrace. He welcomed the latter warmly.

"You are a godsend, Doctor," he declared. "I have been obliged to leave my port untasted for want of a companion. You will excuse us for a moment, Rosamund?"

She nodded pleasantly, and the doctor followed his host into the dining-room and took his seat at the table where the dessert still remained.

"Old woman threatening mischief, eh?" the latter asked, with a keen glance from under his shaggy grey eyebrows.

"I think she means it," Dominey replied, as he filled his guest's glass. "Personally," he went on, after a moment's pause, "the present situation is beginning to confirm an old suspicion of mine. I am a hard and fast materialist, you know, Doctor, in certain matters, and I have not the slightest faith in the vindictive mother, terrified to death lest the razing of a wood of unwholesome character should turn out into the cold world the spirit of her angel son."

"What do you believe?" the doctor asked bluntly.

"I would rather not tell you at the present moment," Dominey answered. "It would sound too fantastic."

"Your note this afternoon spoke of urgency," the doctor observed.

"The matter is urgent. I want you to do me a great favour — to remain here all night."

"You are expecting something to happen?"

"I wish, at any rate, to be prepared."

"I'll stay, with pleasure," the doctor promised. "You can lend me some paraphernalia, I suppose? And give me a shake-down somewhere near Lady Dominey's. By-the-by," he began, and hesitated.

"I have followed your advice, or rather your orders," Dominey interrupted, a little harshly. "It has not always been easy, especially in London, where Rosamund is away from these associations. I am hoping great things from what may happen to-night, or very soon."

The doctor nodded sympathetically.

"I shouldn't wonder if you weren't on the right track," he declared.

Rosamund came in through the window to them and seated herself by Dominey's side.

"Why are you two whispering like conspirators?" she demanded.

"Because we are conspirators," he replied lightly. "I have persuaded Doctor Harrison to stay the night. He would like a room in our wing. Will you let the maids know, dear?"

She nodded thoughtfully.

"Of course! There are several rooms quite ready. Mrs. Midgeley thought that we might be bringing down some guests. I am quite sure that we can make Doctor Harrison comfortable."

"No doubt about that, Lady Dominey," the doctor declared. "Let me be as near to your apartment as possible."

There was a shade of anxiety in her face.

"You think that to-night something will happen?" she asked.

"To-night, or one night very soon," Dominey assented. "It is just as well for you to be prepared. You will not be afraid, dear? You will have the doctor on one side of you and me on the other."

"I am only afraid of one thing," she answered a little enigmatically. "I have been so happy lately."

Dominey, changed into ordinary morning clothes, with a thick cord tied round his body, a revolver in his pocket, and a loaded stick in his hand, spent the remainder of that night and part of the early morning concealed behind a great clump of rhododendrons, his eyes fixed upon the shadowy stretch of park which lay between the house and the Black Wood. The night was moonless but clear, and when his eyes were once accustomed to the pale but sombre twilight, the whole landscape and the moving objects upon it were dimly visible. The habits of his years of bush life seemed instinctively, in those few hours of waiting, to have reëstablished themselves. Every sense was strained and active; every night sound—of which the hooting of some owls, disturbed from their lurking place in the Black Wood, was predominant—heard and accounted for. And then, just as he had glanced at his watch and found that it was close upon two o'clock, came the first real intimation that something was likely to happen. Moving across the park towards him he heard the sound of a faint patter, curious and irregular in rhythm, which came from behind a range of low hillocks. He raised himself on his hands and knees to watch. His eyes were fastened upon a certain spot,—a stretch of the open park between himself and the hillocks. The patter ceased and began again. Into the open there came a dark shape, the irregularity of its movements swiftly explained. It moved at first upon all fours, then on two legs, then on all fours again. It crept nearer and nearer, and Dominey, as he watched, laid aside his stick. It reached the terrace, paused underneath Rosamund's window, now barely half a dozen yards from where he was crouching. Deliberately he waited, waited for what he knew must soon come. Then the deep silence of the breathless night was broken by that familiar, unearthly scream. Dominey waited till even its echoes had died away. Then he ran a few steps, bent double, and stretched out his hands. Once more, for the last time, that devil's cry broke the deep stillness of the August morning, throbbing a little as though with a new fear, dying away as though the fingers which crushed it back down the straining throat had indeed crushed with it the last flicker of some unholy life.

When Doctor Harrison made his hurried appearance, a few moments later, he found Dominey seated upon the terrace, furiously smoking a cigarette. On the ground, a few yards away, lay something black and motionless.

"What is it?" the doctor gasped.

For the first time Dominey showed some signs of a lack of self-control. His voice was choked and uneven.

"Go and look at it, Doctor," he said. "It's tied up, hand and foot. You can see where the spirit of Roger Unthank has hidden itself."

"Bosh!" the doctor answered, with grim contempt. "It's Roger Unthank himself. The beast!"

A little stream of servants came running out. Dominey gave a few orders quickly.

"Ring up the garage," he directed, "and I shall want one of the men to go into Norwich to the hospital. Doctor, will you go up and see Lady Dominey?"

The habits of a lifetime broke down: Parkins, the immaculate, the silent, the perfect automaton, asked an eager question.

"What is it, sir?"

There was the sound of a window opening overhead. At that moment Parkins would not have asked in vain for an annuity. Dominey glanced at the little semicircle of servants and raised his voice.

"It is the end, I trust, of these foolish superstitions about Roger Unthank's ghost. There lies Roger Unthank, half beast, half man. For some reason or other — some lunatic's reason, of course — he has chosen to hide himself in the Black Wood all these years. His mother, I presume, has been his accomplice and taken him food. He is still alive but in a disgusting state."

There was a little awed murmur. Dominey's voice had become quite matter of fact.

"I suppose," he continued, "his first idea was to revenge himself upon us and this household, by whom he imagined himself badly treated. The man, however, was half a madman when he came to the neighbourhood and has behaved like one ever since. — Johnson," Dominey continued, singling out a sturdy footman with sound common sense, "get ready to take this creature into Norwich Hospital. Say that if I do not come in during the day, a letter of explanation will follow from me. The rest of you, with the exception of Parkins, please go to bed."

With little exclamations of wonder they began to disperse. Then one of them paused and pointed across the park. Moving with incredible swiftness came the gaunt, black figure of Rachael Unthank, swaying sometimes on her feet, yet in their midst before they could realise it. She staggered to the prostrate body and threw herself upon her knees. Her hands rested upon the unseen face, her eyes glared across at Dominey.

"So you've got him at last!" she gasped.

"Mrs. Unthank," Dominey said sternly, "you are in time to accompany your son to the hospital at Norwich. The car will be here in two minutes. I have nothing to say to you. Your own conscience should be sufficient punishment for keeping that poor creature alive in such a fashion and ministering during my absence to his accursed desires for vengeance."

"He would have died if I hadn't brought him food," she muttered. "I have wept all the tears a woman's broken heart could wring out, beseeching him to come back to me."

"Yet," Dominey insisted, "you shared his foul plot for vengeance against a harmless woman. You let him come and make his ghoulish noises, night by night, under these windows, without a word of remonstrance. You knew very well what their accursed object was — you, with a delicate woman in your charge who trusted you. You are an evil pair, but of the two you are worse than your half-witted son."

The woman made no reply. She was still on her knees, bending over the prostrate figure, from whose lips now came a faint moaning. Then the lights of the car flashed out as it left the garage, passed through the iron gates and drew up a few yards away.

"Help him in," Dominey ordered. "You can loosen his cords, Johnson, as soon as you have started. He has very little strength. Tell them at the hospital I shall probably be there during the day, or tomorrow."

With a little shiver the two men stooped to their task. Their prisoner muttered to himself all the time, but made no resistance. Rachael Unthank, as she stepped in to take her place by his side, turned once more to Dominey. She was a broken woman.

"You're rid of us," she sobbed, "perhaps forever. — You've said harsh things of both of us. Roger isn't always — so bad. Sometimes he's more gentle than at others. You'd have thought then that he was just a baby, living there for love of the wind and the trees and the birds. If he comes ——"

Her voice broke. Dominey's reply was swift and not unkind. He pointed to the window above.

"If Lady Dominey recovers, you and your son are forgiven. If she never recovers, I wish you both the blackest corner of hell."

The car drove off. Doctor Harrison met Dominey on the threshold as he turned towards the house.

"Her ladyship is unconscious now," he announced. "Perhaps that is a good sign. I never liked that unnatural calm. She'll be unconscious, I think, for a great many hours. For God's sake, come and get a whisky and soda and give me one!"

The early morning sunshine lay upon the park when the two men at last separated. They stood for a moment looking out. From the Black Wood came the whirr of a saw. The little troop of men had left their tents. The crash of a fallen tree heralded their morning's work.

"You are still going on with that?" the doctor asked.

"To the very last stump of a tree, to the last bush, to the last cluster of weeds," Dominey replied, with a sudden passion in his tone. "I will have that place razed to the bare level of the earth, and I will have its poisonous swamps sucked dry. I have hated that foul spot," he went on, "ever since I realised what suffering it meant to her. My reign here may not be long, Doctor—I have my own tragedy to deal with—but those who come after me will never feel the blight of that accursed place."

The doctor grunted. His inner thoughts he kept to himself.

"Maybe you're right," he conceded.

CHAPTER XXIX

THE heat of a sulphurous afternoon—a curious parallel in its presage of coming storm to the fast-approaching crisis in Dominey's own affairs—had driven Dominey from his study out on to the terrace. In a chair by his side lounged Eddy Pelham, immaculate in a suit of white flannels. It was the fifth day since the mystery of the Black Wood had been solved.

"Ripping, old chap, of you to have me down here," the young man remarked amiably, his hand stretching out to a tumbler which stood by his side. "The country, when you can get ice, is a paradise this weather, especially when London's so full of ghastly rumours and all that sort of thing, eh? What's the latest news of her ladyship?"

"Still unconscious," Dominey replied. "The doctors, however, seem perfectly satisfied. Everything depends on her waking moments."

The young man abandoned the subject with a murmur of hopeful sympathy. His eyes were fixed upon a little cloud of dust in the distance.

"Expecting visitors to-day?" he asked.

"Should not be surprised," was the somewhat laconic answer.

The young man stood up, yawned and stretched himself.

"I'll make myself scarce," he said. "Jove!" he added approvingly, lingering for a moment. "Jolly well cut, the tunic of your uniform, Dominey! If a country in peril ever decides to waive the matter of my indifferent physique and send me out to the rescue, I shall go to your man."

Dominey smiled.

"Mine is only the local Yeomanry rig-out," he replied. "They will nab you for the Guards!"

Dominey stepped back through the open windows into his

study as Pelham strolled off. He was seated at his desk, poring over some letters, when a few minutes later Seaman was ushered into the room. For a single moment his muscles tightened, his frame became tense. Then he realised his visitor's outstretched hands of welcome and he relaxed. Seaman was perspiring, vociferous and excited.

"At last!" he exclaimed. "Donner und! — My God, Dominey, what is this?"

"Thirteen years ago," Dominey explained, "I resigned a commission in the Norfolk Yeomanry. That little matter, however, has been adjusted. At a crisis like this —— "

"My friend, you are wonderful!" Seaman interrupted solemnly. "You are a man after my own heart, you are thorough, you leave nothing undone. That is why," he added, lowering his voice a little, "we are the greatest race in the world. Drink before everything, my friend," he went on, "drink I must have. What a day! The very clouds that hide the sun are full of sulphurous heat."

Dominey rang the bell, ordered hock and seltzer and ice. Seaman drank and threw himself into an easy-chair.

"There is no fear of your being called out of the country because of that, I hope?" he asked a little anxiously, nodding his head towards his companion's uniform.

"Not at present," Dominey answered. "I am a trifle over age to go with the first batch or two. Where have you been?"

Seaman hitched his chair a little nearer.

"In Ireland," he confided. "Sorry to desert you as I did, but you do not begin to count for us just yet. There was just a faint doubt as to what they were going to do about internment. That is why I had to get the Irish trip off my mind."

"What has been decided?"

"The Government has the matter under consideration," Seaman replied, with a chuckle. "I can certainly give myself six months before I need to slip off. Now tell me, why do I find you down here?"

"After Terniloff left," Dominey explained, "I felt I wanted to get away. I have been asked to start some recruiting work down here."

"Terniloff—left his little volume with you?"

"Yes!"

"Where is it?"

"Safe," Dominey replied.

Seaman mopped his forehead.

"It needs to be," he muttered. "I have orders to see it destroyed. We can talk of that presently. Sometimes, when I am away from you, I tremble. It may sound foolish, but you have in your possession just the two things — that map and Von Terniloff's memoirs — which would wreck our propaganda in every country of the world."

"Both are safe," Dominey assured him. "By the by, my friend," he went on, "do you know that you yourself are forgetting your usual caution?"

"In what respect?" Seaman demanded quickly.

"As you stooped to sit down just now, I distinctly saw the shape of your revolver in your hip pocket. You know as well as I do that with your name and the fact that you are only a naturalised Englishman, it is inexcusably foolish to be carrying firearms about just now."

Seaman thrust his hand into his pocket and threw the revolver upon the table.

"You are quite right," he acknowledged. "Take care of it for me. I took it with me to Ireland, because one never knows what may happen in that amazing country."

Dominey swept it carelessly into the drawer of the desk at which he was sitting.

"Our weapons, from now on," Seaman continued, "must be weapons of guile and craft. You and I will have, alas! to see less of one another, Dominey. In many ways it is unfortunate that we have not been able to keep England out of this for a few more months. However, the situation must be dealt with as it exists. So far as you are concerned, you have practically secured yourself against suspicion. You will hold a brilliant and isolated place amongst those who are serving the great War Lord. When I do approach you, it will be for sympathy and assistance against the suspicions of these far-seeing Englishmen!"

Dominey nodded.

"You will stay the night?" he asked.

"If I may," Seaman assented. "It is the last time for many months when it will be wise for us to meet on such intimate terms. Perhaps our dear friend Parkins will take vinous note of the occasion."

"In other words," Dominey said, "you propose that we shall drink the Dominey cabinet hock and the Dominey port to the glory of our country."

"To the glory of our country," Seaman echoed. "So be it, my friend. — Listen."

A car had passed along the avenue in front of the house. There was the sound of voices in the hall, a knock at the door, the rustle of a woman's clothes. Parkins, a little disturbed, announced the arrivals.

"The Princess of Eiderstrom and — a gentleman. The Princess said that her errand with you was urgent, sir," he added, turning apologetically towards his master.

The Princess was already in the room, and following her a short man in a suit of sombre black, wearing a white tie, and carrying a black bowler hat. He blinked across the room through his thick glasses, and Dominey knew that the end had come. The door was closed behind them. The Princess came a little farther into the room. Her hand was extended towards Dominey, but not in greeting. Her white finger pointed straight at him. She turned to her companion.

"Which is that, Doctor Schmidt?" she demanded.

"The Englishman, by God!" Schmidt answered.

The silence which reigned for several seconds was intense and profound. The coolest of all four was perhaps Dominey. The Princess was pale with a passion which seemed to sob behind her words.

"Everard Dominey," she cried, "what have you done with my lover? What have you done with Leopold von Ragastein?"

"He met with the fate," Dominey replied, "which he had prepared for me. We fought and I conquered."

"You killed him?"

"I killed him," Dominey echoed. "It was a matter of necessity. His body sleeps on the bed of the Blue River."

"And your life here has been a lie!"

"On the contrary, it has been the truth," Dominey objected. "I assured you at the Carlton, when you first spoke to me, and I have assured you a dozen times since, that I was Everard Dominey. That is my name. That is who I am."

Seaman's voice seemed to come from a long way off. For the moment the man had neither courage nor initiative. He seemed as though he had received some sort of stroke. His mind was travelling backwards.

"You came to me at Capetown," he muttered; "you had all Von Ragastein's letters, you knew his history, you had the Imperial mandate."

"Von Ragastein and I exchanged the most intimate confidences in his camp," Dominey said, "as Doctor Schmidt there knows. I told him my history, and he told me his. The letters and papers I took from him."

Schmidt had covered his face with his hands for a moment. His shoulders were heaving.

"My beloved chief!" he sobbed. "My dear devoted master! Killed by that drunken Englishman!"

"Not so drunk as you fancied him," Dominey said coolly, "not so far gone in his course of dissipation but that he was able to pull himself up when the great incentive came."

The Princess looked from one to the other of the two men. Seaman had still the appearance of a man struggling to extricate himself from some sort of nightmare.

"My first and only suspicion," he faltered, "was that night when Wolff disappeared!"

"Wolff's coming was rather a tragedy," Dominey admitted. "Fortunately, I had a secret service man in the house who was able to dispose of him."

"It was you who planned his disappearance?" Seaman gasped.

"Naturally," Dominey replied. "He knew the truth and was trying all the time to communicate with you."

"And the money?" Seaman continued, blinking rapidly. "One hundred thousand pounds, and more?"

"I understood that was a gift," Dominey replied. "If the German Secret Service, however, cares to formulate a claim and sue me——"

The Princess suddenly interrupted. Her eyes seemed on fire.

"What are you, you two?" she cried, stretching out her hands toward Schmidt and Seaman. "Are you lumps of earth — clods — creatures without courage and intelligence? You can let him stand there — the Englishman who has murdered my lover, who has befooled you? You let him stand there and mock you, and you do and say nothing! Is his life a sacred thing? Has he none of your secrets in his charge?"

"The great God above us!" Seaman groaned, with a sudden white horror in his face. "He has the Prince's memoirs! He has the Kaiser's map!"

"On the contrary," Dominey replied, "both are deposited at the Foreign Office. We hope to find them very useful a little later on."

Seaman sprang forward like a tiger and went down in a heap as he almost threw himself upon Dominey's out-flung fist. Schmidt came stealing across the room, and from underneath his cuff something gleamed.

"You are two to one!" the Princess cried passionately, as both assailants hesitated. "I would to God that I had a weapon, or that I were a man!"

"My dear Princess," a good-humoured voice remarked from the window, "four to two the other way, I think, what?"

Eddy Pelham, his hands in his pockets, but a very alert gleam in his usually vacuous face, stood in the windowed doorway. From behind him, two exceedingly formidable-looking men slipped into the room. There was no fight, not even a struggle. Seaman, who had never recovered from the shock of his surprise, and was now completely unnerved, was handcuffed in a moment, and Schmidt disarmed. The latter was the first to break the curious silence.

"What have I done?" he demanded. "Why am I treated like this?"

"Doctor Schmidt?" Eddy asked pleasantly.

"That is my name, sir," was the fierce reply. "I have just landed from East Africa. We knew nothing of the war when we started. I came to expose that man. He is an impostor — a murderer! He has killed a German nobleman."

"He has committed *lèse majesté!*" Seaman gasped. "He has

deceived the Kaiser! He has dared to sit in his presence as the Baron von Ragastein!"

The young man in flannels glanced across at Dominey and smiled.

"I say, you two don't mean to be funny but you are," he declared. "First of all, there's Doctor Schmidt accuses Sir Everard here of being an impostor because he assumed his own name; accuses him of murdering a man who had planned in cold blood — you were in that, by the by, Schmidt — to kill him; and then there's our friend here, the secretary of the society for propagating better relations between the business men of England and Germany, complaining because Sir Everard carried through in Germany, for England, exactly what he believed the Baron von Ragastein was carrying out here — for Germany. You're a curious, thick-headed race, you Germans."

"I demand again," Schmidt shouted, "to know by what right I am treated as a criminal?"

"Because you are one," Eddy answered coolly. "You and Von Ragastein together planned the murder of Sir Everard Dominey in East Africa, and I caught you creeping across the floor just now with a knife in your hand. That'll do for you. Any questions to ask, Seaman?"

"None," was the surly reply.

"You are well-advised," the young man remarked coolly. "Within the last two days, your house in Forest Hill and your offices in London Wall have been searched."

"You have said enough," Seaman declared. "Fate has gone against me. I thank God that our master has abler servants than I and the strength to crush this island of popinjays and fools!"

"Popinjays seems severe," Eddy murmured, in a hurt tone. "However, to get on with this little matter," he added, turning to one of his two subordinates. "You will find a military car outside. Take these men over to the guardroom at the Norwich Barracks. I have arranged for an escort to see them to town. Tell the colonel I'll be over later in the day."

The Princess rose from the chair into which she had subsided a few moments before. Dominey turned towards her.

"Princess," he said, "there can be little conversation between us. Yet I shall ask you to remember this. Von Ragastein planned my death in cold blood. I could have slain him as an assassin, without the slightest risk, but I preferred to meet him face to face with the truth upon my lips. It was his life or mine. I fought for my country's sake, as he did for his."

The Princess looked at him with glittering eyes.

"I shall hate you to the end of my days," she declared, "because you have killed the thing I love, but although I am a woman, I know justice. You were chivalrous towards me. You treated Leopold perhaps better than he would have treated you. I pray that I shall never see your face again. Be so good as to suffer me to leave this house at once, and unattended."

Dominey threw open the windows which led on to the terrace and stood on one side. She passed by without a glance at him and disappeared. Eddy came strolling along the terrace a few moments later.

"Nice old ducks, those two, dear heart," he confided. "Seaman has just offered Forsyth, my burly ruffian in the blue serge suit, a hundred pounds to shoot him on the pretence that he was escaping."

"And what about Schmidt?"

"Insisted on his rights as an officer and demanded the front seat and a cigar before the car started! A pretty job, Dominey, and neatly cleaned up."

Dominey was watching the dust from the two cars which were disappearing down the avenue.

"Tell me, Eddy," he asked, "there's one thing I have always been curious about. How did you manage to keep that fellow Wolff when there wasn't a war on, and he wasn't breaking the law?"

The young man grinned.

"We had to stretch a point there, old dear," he admitted. "Plans of a fortress, eh?"

"Do you mean to say that he had plans of a fortress upon him?" Dominey asked.

"Picture post-card of Norwich Castle," the young man confided, "but keep it dark. Can I have a drink before I get the little car going?"

The turmoil of the day was over, and Dominey, after one silent but passionate outburst of thankfulness at the passing from his life of this unnatural restraint, found all his thoughts absorbed by the struggle which was being fought out in the bedchamber above. The old doctor came down and joined him at dinner time. He met Dominey's eager glance with a little nod.

"She's doing all right," he declared.

"No fever or anything?"

"Bless you, no! She's as near as possible in perfect health physically. A different woman from what she was this time last year, I can tell you. When she wakes up, she'll either be herself again, without a single illusion of any sort, or —— "

The doctor paused, sipped his wine, emptied his glass and set it down approvingly.

"Or?" Dominey persisted.

"Or that part of her brain will be more or less permanently affected. However, I am hoping for the best. Thank heavens you're on the spot!"

They finished their dinner almost in silence. Afterwards, they smoked for a few minutes upon the terrace. Then they made their way softly upstairs. The doctor parted with Dominey at the door of the latter's room.

"I shall remain with her for an hour or so," he said. "After that I shall leave her entirely to herself. You'll be here in case there's a change?"

"I shall be here," Dominey promised.

The minutes passed into hours, uncounted, unnoticed. Dominey sat in his easy-chair, stirred by a tumultuous wave of passionate emotion. The memory of those earlier days of his return came back to him with all their poignant longings. He felt again the same tearing at his heart-strings, the same strange, unnerving tenderness. The great world's drama, in which he knew that he, too, would surely continue to play his part, seemed like a thing far off, the concern of another race of men. Every fibre of his being seemed attuned to the magic and the music of one wild hope. Yet when there came what he had listened for so long, the hope seemed frozen into fear. He sat a little forward in his easy-chair, his hands gripping its sides, his eyes fixed upon the slowly widening crack in the panel. It was as it had been before. She stooped low, stood up again and came towards him. From behind an unseen hand closed the panel. She came to him with her arms outstretched and all the wonderful things of life and love in her shining eyes. That faint touch of the somnambulist had passed. She came to him as she had never come before. She was a very real and a very live woman.

"Everard!" she cried.

He took her into his arms. At their first kiss she thrilled from head to foot. For a moment she laid her head upon his shoulder.

"Oh, I have been so silly!" she confessed. "There were times when I couldn't believe that you were my Everard—mine! And now I know."

Her lips sought his again, his parched with the desire of years. Along the corridor, the old doctor tiptoed his way to his room, with a pleased smile upon his face.